INTRODUCTION TO GUY MANNERING.

The Novel or Romance of WAVERLEY made its way to the public slowly, of course, at first, but afterwards with such accumulating popularity as to encourage the author to a second attempt. He looked about for a name and a subject; and the manner in which the novels were composed cannot be better illustrated than by reciting the simple narrative on which Guy Mannering was originally founded; but to which, in the progress of the work, the production ceased to bear any, even the most distant resemblance. The tale was originally told me by an old servant of my father's, an excellent old Highlander, without a fault, unless a preference to mountain-dew over less potent liquors be accounted one. He believed as firmly in the story, as in any part of his creed.

A grave and elderly person, according to old John MacKinlay's account, while travelling in the wilder parts of Galloway, was benighted. With difficulty he found his way to a country-seat, where, with the hospitality of the time and country, he was readily admitted. The owner of the house, a gentleman of good fortune, was much struck by the reverend appearance of his guest, and apologised to him for a certain degree of confusion which must unavoidably ,attend his reception, and could not escape his eye. she lady of the house was, he said, confined to her apartment, and on the point of making her husband a father for the first time, though they had been ten years married. At such an emergency, the Laird said, he feared his guest might meet with some apparent neglect.

"Not so, sir," said the stranger, "my wants are few, and easily supplied, and I trust the present circumstances may even afford an opportunity of showing my gratitude for your hospitality. Let me only request that I may be informed of the exact minute of the birth; and I hope to be able to put you in possession of some particulars, which may influence, in an important manner, the future prospects of the child now about to come into this busy and changeful world. I will not conceal from you that I am skilful in understanding and interpreting the movements of those planetary bodies which exert their influences on the destiny of mortals. It is a science which I do not practise, like others who call themselves astrologers, for hire or reward; for I have a competent estate, and only use the knowledge I possess for the benefit of those in whom I feel an interest." The Laird bowed in respect and gratitude, and the stranger was accommodated with an apartment which commanded an ample view of the astral regions.

The guest spent a part of the night in ascertaining the position of the heavenly bodies, and calculating their probable influence; until at length the result of his observations induced him to send for the father, and conjure him, in the most solemn manner, to cause the assistants to retard the birth, if practicable, were it but for five minutes. The answer declared this to be impossible; and almost in the instant that the message was returned, the father and his guest were made acquainted with the birth of a boy.

The Astrologer on the morrow met the party who gathered around the breakfast-table, with looks so grave and ominous, as to alarm the fears of the father, who had hitherto exulted in the prospects held out by the birth of an heir to his ancient property, failing which event it must have passed to a distant branch of the family. He hastened to draw the stranger into a private room.

"I fear from your looks," said the father, "that you have bad tidings to tell me of my young stranger; perhaps God will resume the blessing He has bestowed ere he attains the age of manhood, or perhaps he is destined to be unworthy of the affection which we are naturally disposed to devote to our offspring."

"Neither the one nor the other," answered the stranger;" unless my judgment greatly err, the infant will survive the years of minority, and in temper and disposition will prove all that his parents can wish. But with much in his horoscope which promises many blessings, there is one evil influence strongly predominant, which threatens to subject him to an unhallowed and unhappy temptation about the time when he shall attain the age of twenty-one, which period, the constellations intimate, will he the crisis of his fate. In what shape, or with what peculiar urgency, this temptation may beset him, my art cannot discover."

"Your knowledge, then, can afford us no defence," said the anxious father, "against the threatened evil?"

"Pardon me," answered the stranger, "it can. The influence of the constellations is powerful, but He, who made the heavens, is more powerful than all, if His aid be invoked in sincerity and truth. You ought to dedicate this boy to the immediate service of his Maker, with as much sincerity as Samuel was devoted to the worship in the Temple by his parents. You must regard him as a being separated from the rest of the world. In childhood, in boyhood, you must surround him with the pious and virtuous, and protect him, to the utmost of your power, from the sight or hearing of any crime, in word or action. He must be educated in religious and moral principles of the strictest description. Let him not enter the world, lest he learn to partake of its follies, or perhaps of its vices. In short, preserve him as far as possible from all sin, save that of which too great a portion belongs to all the fallen race of Adam. With the approach of his twenty-first birthday comes the crisis of his fate. If he survive it, he will be happy and prosperous on earth, and a chosen vessel among those elected for heaven. But if it be otherwise—"The Astrologer stopped, and sighed deeply.

"Sir," replied the parent, still more alarmed than before, "your words are so kind, your advice so serious, that I will pay the deepest attention to your behests; but can you not aid me further in this most important concern? Believe me, I will not be ungrateful."

"I require and deserve no gratitude for doing a good action," said the stranger, "in especial for contributing all that lies in my power to save from an abhorred fate the harmless infant to whom, under a singular conjunction of planets, last night gave life. There is my address; you may write to me from time to time concerning the progress of the boy in religious knowledge. If he be bred up as I advise, I think it will be best that he come to my house at the time when the fatal and decisive period approaches, that is, before he has attained his twenty-first year complete. If you send him such as I desire, I humbly trust that God will protect His own, through whatever strong temptation his

3

fate may subject him to." He then gave his host his address, which was a country-seat near a post-town in the south of England, and bid him an affectionate farewell.

The mysterious stranger departed, but his words remained impressed upon the mind of the anxious parent. He lost his lady while his boy was still in infancy. This calamity, I think, had been predicted by the Astrologer; and thus his confidence, which, like most people of the period, he had freely given to the science, was riveted and confirmed. The utmost care, therefore, was taken to carry into effect the severe and almost ascetic plan of education which the sage had enjoined. A tutor of the strictest principles was employed to superintend the youth's education; he was surrounded by domestics of the most established character, and closely watched and looked after by the anxious father himself.

The years of infancy, childhood, and boyhood, passed as the father could have wished. A young Nazarene could not have been bred up with more rigour. All that was evil was withheld from his observation—he only heard what was pure in precept—he only witnessed what was worthy in practice.

But when the boy began to be lost in the youth, the attentive father saw cause for alarm. Shades of sadness, which gradually assumed a darker character, began to overcloud the young man's temper. Tears, which seemed involuntary, broken sleep, moonlight wanderings, and a melancholy for which he could assign no reason, seemed to threaten at once his bodily health, and the stability of his mind. The Astrologer was consulted by letter, and returned for answer, that this fitful state of mind was but the commencement of his trial, and that the poor youth must undergo more and more desperate struggles with the evil that assailed him. There was no hope of remedy, save that he showed steadiness of mind in the study of the Scriptures. "He suffers," continued the letter of the sage," from the awakening of those harpies, the passions, which have slept with him as with others, till the period of life which he has now attained. Better, far better, that they torment him by ungrateful cravings, than that he should have to repent having satiated them by criminal indulgence."

The dispositions of the young man were so excellent, that he combated, by reason and religion, the fits of gloom which at times overcast his mind, and it was not till he attained the commencement of his twenty-first year, that they assumed a character which made his father tremble for the consequences. It seemed as if the gloomiest and most hideous of mental maladies was taking the form of religious despair. Still the youth was gentle, courteous, affectionate, and submissive to his father's will, and resisted with all his power the dark suggestions which were breathed into his mind, as it seemed, by some emanation of the Evil Principle, exhorting him, like the wicked wife of Job, to curse God and die.

The time at length arrived when he was to perform what was then thought a long and somewhat perilous journey, to the mansion of the early friend who had calculated his nativity. His road lay through several places of interest, and he enjoyed the amusement of travelling, more than he himself thought would have been possible. Thus he did not reach the place of his destination till noon, on the day preceding his birthday. It seemed as if he had been carried away with an unwonted tide of pleasurable sensation, so as to forget, in some degree, what his father had communicated concerning the purpose of his journey. He halted at length before a respectable but solitary old mansion, to which he was directed as the abode of his father's friend.

The servants who came to take his horse told him he had been expected for two days. He was led into a study, where the stranger, now a venerable old man, who had been his father's guest, met him with a shade of displeasure, as well as gravity, on his brow. "Young man," he said, "wherefore so slow on a journey of such importance?"—"I thought," replied the guest, blushing and looking downward, "that there was no harm in travelling slowly, and satisfying my curiosity, providing I could reach your residence by this day; for such was my father's charge."—"You were to blame," replied the sage, "in lingering, considering that the avenger of blood was pressing on your footsteps. But you are come at last, and we will hope for the best, though the conflict in which you are to be engaged will be found more dreadful, the longer it is postponed. But first, accept of such refreshments as nature requires, to satisfy, but not to pamper, the appetite."

The old man led the way into a summer parlour, where a frugal meal was placed on the table. As they sat down to the board, they were joined by a young lady about eighteen years of age, and so lovely, that the sight of her carried off the feelings of the young stranger from the peculiarity and mystery of his own lot, and riveted his attention to everything she did or said. She spoke little, and it was on the most serious subjects. She played on the harpsichord at her father's command, but it was hymns with which she accompanied the instrument. At length, on a sign from the sage, she left the room, turning on the young stranger, as she departed, a look of inexpressible anxiety and interest.

The old man then conducted the youth to his study, and conversed with him upon the most important points of religion, to satisfy himself that he could render a reason for the faith that was in him. During the examination, the youth, in spite of himself, felt his mind occasionally wander, and his recollections go in quest of the beautiful vision who had shared their meal at noon. On such occasions, the Astrologer looked grave, and shook his head at this relaxation of attention; yet, upon the whole, he was pleased with the youth's replies.

At sunset the young man was made to take the bath; and, having done so, he was directed to attire himself in a robe, somewhat like that worn by Armenians, having his long hair combed down on his shoulders, and his neck, hands, and feet bare. In this guise, he was conducted into a remote chamber totally devoid of furniture, excepting a lamp, a chair, and a table, on which lay a Bible. "Here," said the Astrologer, "I must leave you alone, to pass the most critical period of your life. If you can, by recollection of the great truths of which we have spoken, repel the attacks which will be made on your courage and your principles, you have nothing to apprehend. But the trial will be severe and arduous." His features then assumed a pathetic solemnity, the tears stood in his eyes and his voice faltered with emotion as he said, "Dear child, at whose coming into the world I foresaw this fatal trial, may God give thee grace to support it with firmness!"

The young man was left alone; and hardly did he find himself so, when, like a swarm of demons, the recollection of all his sins of omission and commission, rendered even more terrible by the scrupulousness with which he had been educated, rushed on his mind, and, like furies armed with fiery scourges, seemed determined to drive him to despair. As he combated these horrible recollections with distracted feelings, but with a resolved mind, he became aware that his arguments were answered by the sophistry of another, and that the dispute was no longer confined to his own thoughts. The Author of Evil was present in the room with him in bodily shape, and, potent with spirits of a melancholy cast, was impressing upon him the desperation of his state, and urging suicide as the readiest mode to put an end to his sinful career. Amid his errors, the pleasure he had taken in prolonging his journey unnecessarily, and the attention which he had bestowed on the beauty of the fair female, when his thoughts ought to have been dedicated to the religious discourse of her father, were set before him in the darkest colours; and he was treated as one who, having sinned against light, was, therefore, deservedly left a prey to the Prince of Darkness.

As the fated and influential hour rolled on, the terrors of the hateful Presence grew more confounding to the mortal senses of the victim, and the knot of the accursed sophistry became more inextricable in appearance, at least to the prey whom its meshes surrounded. He had not power to explain the assurance of pardon which he continued to assert, or to name the victorious name in which he, trusted. But his faith did not abandon him, though he lacked for a time the power of expressing it. "Say what you will," was his answer to the Tempter; "I know there is as much betwixt the two boards of this Book as can insure me forgiveness for my transgressions, and safety for my soul." As he spoke, the clock, which announced the lapse of the fatal hour, was heard to strike. The speech and intellectual powers of the youth were instantly and fully restored; he burst forth into prayer, and expressed, in the most glowing terms, his reliance on the truth, and on the Author, of the gospel. The demon retired, yelling and discomfited, and the old man, entering the apartment, with tears congratulated his guest on his victory in the fated struggle.

The young man was afterwards married to the beautiful maiden, the first sight of whom had made such an impression on him, and they were consigned over at the close of the story to domestic happiness.—So ended John MacKinlay's legend.

The author of Waverley had imagined a possibility of framing an interesting, and perhaps not an unedifying, tale, out of the incidents of the life of a doomed individual, whose efforts at good and virtuous conduct were to be for ever disappointed by the intervention, as it were, of some malevolent being, and who was at last to come off victorious from the fearful struggle. In short, something was meditated upon a plan resembling the imaginative tale of Sintram and his Companions, by Mons. Le Baron de la Motte Fouque, although, if it then existed, the author had not seen it.

The scheme projected may be traced in the three or four first chapters of the work, but further consideration induced the author to lay his purpose aside. It appeared, on mature consideration, that Astrology, though its influence was once received and admitted by Bacon himself, does not now retain influence over the general mind sufficient even to constitute the mainspring of a romance. Besides, it occurred, that to do justice to such a subject would have required not only more talent than the author could be conscious of possessing, but also involved doctrines and discussions of a nature too serious for his purpose, and for the character of the narrative. In changing his plan, however, which wets done in the course of printing, the early sheets retained the vestiges of the original tenor of the story, although they now hang upon it as an unnecessary and unnatural encumbrance. The cause of such vestiges is now explained, and apologised for.

It is here worthy of observation, that while the astrological doctrines have fallen into general contempt, and been supplanted by superstitions of a more gross and far less beautiful character, they have, even in modern days, retained some votaries.

One of the most remarkable believers in that forgotten and despised science, was a late eminent professor of the art of legerdemain. One would have thought that a person of this description ought, from his knowledge of the thousand ways in which human eyes could be deceived, to have been less than others subject to the fantasies of superstition. Perhaps the habitual use of those abstruse calculations, by which, in a manner surprising to the artist himself, many tricks upon cards, etc., are performed, induced this gentleman to study the combination of the stars and planets, with the expectation of obtaining prophetic communications.

He constructed a scheme of his own nativity, calculated according to such rules of art as he could collect from the best astrological authors. The result of the past he found agreeable to what had hitherto befallen him, but in the important prospect of the future a singular difficulty occurred. There were two years, during the course of which he could by no means obtain any exact knowledge, whether the subject of the scheme would be dead or alive. Anxious concerning so remarkable a circumstance, he gave the scheme to a brother Astrologer, who was also baffled in the same manner. At one period he found the native, or subject, was certainly alive; at another, that he was unquestionably dead; but a space of two years extended between these two terms, during which he could find no certainty as to his death or existence.

The Astrologer marked the remarkable circumstance in his Diary, and continued his exhibitions in various parts of the empire until the period was about to expire, during which his existence had been warranted as actually ascertained. At last, while he was exhibiting to a numerous audience his usual tricks of legerdemain, the hands, whose activity had so often baffled the closest observer, suddenly lost their power, the cards dropped from them, and he sunk down a disabled paralytic. In this state the artist languished for two years, when he was at length removed by death. It is said that the Diary of this modern Astrologer will soon be given to the public.

The fact, if truly reported, is one of those singular coincidences which occasionally appear, differing so widely from ordinary calculation, yet without which irregularities, human life would not present to mortals, looking into futurity, the abyss of impenetrable darkness, which it is the pleasure of the Creator it should offer to them. Were everything to happen in the ordinary train of events, the future would be subject to the rules of arithmetic, like the chances of gaming. But extraordinary events, and wonderful runs of luck, defy the calculations ox mankind, and throw impenetrable darkness on future contingencies.

To the above anecdote, another, still more recent, may be here added. The author was lately honoured with a letter from a gentleman deeply skilled in these mysteries, who kindly undertook to calculate the nativity of the writer of Guy Mannering, who might be supposed to be friendly to the divine art which he professed. But it was impossible to supply data for the construction of a horoscope, had the native been otherwise desirous of it, since all those who could supply the minutiae of day, hour, and minute have been long removed from the mortal sphere.

Having thus given some account of the first idea, or rude sketch, of the story, which was soon departed from, the author, in following out the plan of the present edition, has to mention the prototypes of the principal characters in Guy Mannering.

Some circumstances of local situation gave the author, in his youth, an opportunity of seeing a little, and hearing a great deal, about that degraded class who are called gipsies; who are in most cases a mixed race, between the ancient Egyptians who arrived in Europe about the beginning of the fifteenth century, and vagrants of European descent.

The individual gipsy, upon whom the character of Meg Merrilies was. founded, was well known about the middle of the last century, by the name of Jean Gordon, an inhabitant of the village of Kirk Yetholm, in the Cheviot hills, adjoining to the English Border. The author gave the public some account of this remarkable person, in one of the early numbers of. Blackwood's Magazine, to the following purpose :-

"My father remembered old Jean Gordon of Yetholm, who had great sway among her tribe. She was quite a Meg Merrilies, and possessed the savage virtue of fidelity in the same perfection. Having been often hospitably received at the farm-house of Lochside, near

Yetholm, she had carefully abstained from committing any depredations an the farmer's property. But her sons (nine in number) had not, it seems, the same delicacy, and stole a brood-sow from their kind entertainer. Jean was mortified at this ungrateful conduct, and so much ashamed of it, that she absented herself from Lochside for several years.

"It happened, in course of time, that in consequence Of some temporary pecuniary necessity, the Goodman of Lochside was obliged to go to Newcastle to raise some money to pay his rent. He succeeded in his purpose, but returning through the mountains of Cheviot, he was benighted and lost his way.

"A light, glimmering through the window of a large waste barn, which had survived the farm-house to which it had once belonged, guided him to a place of shelter; and when he knocked at the door, it was opened by Jean Gordon. Her very remarkable figure, for she was nearly six feet high, and her equally remarkable features and dress, rendered it impossible to mistake her for a moment, though he had not seen her for years; and to meet with such a character in so solitary a place, and probably at no great distance from her clan, was a grievous surprise to the poor man, whose rent (to lose which would have been ruin) was about his person.

"Jean set up a loud shout of joyful recognition—'Eh, sirs! the winsome Gudeman of Lochside! Light down, light down; for ye maunna gang farther the night, and a friend's house sae near.' The farmer was obliged to dismount, and accept of the gipsy's offer of supper and a bed. There was plenty of meat in the barn, however it might be come by, and preparations were going on for a plentiful repast, which the farmer, to the great increase of his anxiety, observed, was calculated for ten or twelve guests, of the same description, probably, with his landlady.

"Jean left him in no doubt on the subject. She brought to his recollection the story of the stolen sow, and mentioned how much pain and vexation it had given her. Like other philosophers, she remarked that the world grew worse daily; and, like other parents, that the bairns got out of her guiding, and neglected the old gipsy regulations, which commanded them to respect, in their depredations, the property of their benefactors. The end of all this was, an inquiry what money the farmer had about him; and an urgent request, or command, that he would make her his purse-keeper, since the bairns, as she called her sons, would be soon home. The poor farmer made a virtue of necessity, told his story, and surrendered his gold to Jean's custody. She made him put a few shillings in his pocket, observing it would excite— suspicion should he be found travelling altogether penniless.

"This arrangement being made, the farmer lay down on a sort of shake-down, as the Scotch call it, or bed-clothes disposed upon some straw, but, as will easily be believed, slept not.

"About midnight the gang returned, with various articles of plunder, and talked over their exploits in language which made the farmer tremble. They were not long in discovering they had a guest, and demanded of Jean whom she had got there.

"'E'en the winsome Gudeman of Lochside, poor body,' replied Jean; 'he's been at Newcastle seeking siller to pay his rent, honest man, but deil-be-lickit he's been able to gather in, and sae he's gaun e'en hame wi' a toom purse and a sair heart.'

"'That may be, Jean,' replied one of the banditti, 'but we maun ripe his pouches a bit, and see if the tale be true or no.' Jean set up her throat in exclamations against this breach of hospitality, but without producing any change in their determination. The farmer soon heard their stifled whispers and light steps by his bedside, and understood they were rummaging his clothes. When they found the money which the providence of Jean Gordon had made him retain, they held a consultation if they should take it or no; but the smallness of. the booty, and the vehemence of Jean's remonstrances, determined them in the negative. They caroused and went to rest. As soon as day dawned, Jean roused her guest, produced his horse, which she had accommodated behind the hallan, and guided him for some miles, till he was on the high-road to Lochside. She then restored his whole property; nor could his earnest entreaties prevail on her to accept so much as a single guinea.

"I have heard the old people at Jedburgh say, that all Jean's sons were condemned to die there on the same day. It is said the jury were equally divided, but that a friend to justice, who had slept during the whole discussion, waked suddenly, and gave his vote for condemnation, in the emphatic words, 'Hang them a'!' Unanimity is not required in a Scottish jury, so the verdict of guilty was returned. Jean was present, and only said, 'The Lord help the innocent in a day like this!' Her own death was accompanied with circumstances of brutal outrage, of which poor Jean was in many respects wholly undeserving. She had, among other demerits, or merits, as the reader may choose to rank it, that of being a staunch Jacobite. She chanced to be at Carlisle upon a fair or market-day, soon after the year 1746, where she gave vent to her political partiality, to the great offence of the rabble of that city. Being zealous in their loyalty, when there was no danger, in proportion to the tameness with which they had surrendered to the Highlanders in 1745, the mob inflicted upon poor Jean Gordon no slighter penalty than that of ducking her to death in the Eden. It was an operation of some time, for Jean was a stout woman, and, struggling with her murderers, often got her head above water; and, while she had voice left, continued to exclaim at such intervals, 'Charlie yet! Charlie yet!' When a child, and among the scenes which she frequented, I have often heard these stories, and cried piteously for poor Jean Gordon.

"Before quitting the Border gipsies, I may mention, that my grandfather, while riding over Charterhouse moor, then a very extensive common, fell suddenly among a large band of them, who were carousing in a hollow of the moor, surrounded by bushes. They instantly seized on his horse's bridle with many shouts of welcome, exclaiming—(for he was well known to most of them) that they had often dined at his expense, and he must now stay and share their good cheer. My ancestor was a little alarmed, for, like the Goodman of Lochside, he had more money about his person than he cared to risk in such society. However, being naturally a bold lively-spirited man, he entered into the humour of the thing, and sat down to the feast, which consisted of all the varieties of game, poultry, pigs, and so forth, that—could be collected by a wide and indiscriminate system of plunder. The dinner was a very merry one; but my relative got a hint from some of the older gipsies to retire just when—

The mirth and fun grew fast and furious,

and, mounting his horse accordingly, he took a French leave of his entertainers, but without experiencing the least breach of hospitality. I believe Jean Gordon was at this festival"— (Blackwood's Magazine, vol. i. p. 54.)

Notwithstanding the failure of Jean's issue, for which,

Weary fa' the waefu' wuddie,

a granddaughter survived her whom I remember to have seen. That is, as Dr. Johnson had a shadowy recollection of Queen Anne, as a stately lady in black, adorned with diamonds, so my memory is haunted by a solemn remembrance of a woman of more than female height, dressed in a long red cloak, who commenced acquaintance by giving me an apple, but whom, nevertheless, I looked on with as much awe as the future Doctor, High Church and Tory as he was doomed to be, could look upon the Queen. I conceive this woman to have been Madge Gordon, of whom an impressive account is given in the same article in which her mother Jean is mentioned, but not by the present writer.—

"The late Madge Gordon was at this time accounted the Queen of the Yetholm clans. She was, we believe, a granddaughter of the celebrated Jean Gordon, and was said to have much resembled her in appearance. The following account of her is extracted from the letter of a friend, who for many years enjoyed frequent and favourable opportunities of observing the characteristic peculiarities of the Yetholm tribes.—'Madge Gordon was descended from the Faas by the mother's side, and was married to a Young. She was a remarkable personage of a very commanding presence, and high stature, being nearly six feet high. She had a large aquiline nose-penetrating eyes, even in her old age-bushy hair, that hung around her shoulders from beneath a gipsy bonnet of straw-a short cloak of a peculiar fashion, and a long staff nearly as tall as herself. I remember her well;—every week she paid my father a visit for her awmous, when I was a little boy, and I looked upon Madge with no common degree of awe, and terror. When she spoke vehemently (for she made loud complaints), she used to strike her staff upon the floor, and throw herself into an attitude which it was impossible to regard with indifference. She used to say that she could bring from the remotest parts of the island, friends to revenge her quarrel, while she sat motionless in her cottage; and she frequently boasted that there was a time when she was of still more considerable importance, for there were at her wedding fifty saddled asses, and unsaddled asses with. out number. If Jean Gordon was the prototype of the character of Meg Merrilies, I imagine Madge must have sat to the unknown author as the representative of her person.' "—(Blackwood's Magazine, vol. i. p. 56.)

How far Blackwood's ingenious correspondent was right, how far mistaken in his conjecture, the reader has been informed.

To pass to a character of a very different description, Dominie Sampson, the reader may easily suppose that a poor, modest, humble scholar, who has won his way through the classics, yet has fallen to leeward in the voyage of life, is no uncommon personage in a country, where a certain portion of learning is easily attained by those who are willing to suffer hunger and thirst in exchange for acquiring Greek and Latin. But there is a far more exact prototype of the worthy Dominie, upon which is founded the part which he performs in the romance, and which, for certain particular reasons, must be expressed very generally.

Such a preceptor as Mr. Sampson is supposed to have been, was actually tutor in the family of a gentleman of considerable property. The young lads, his pupils, grew up and went out in the world, but the tutor continued to reside in the family, no uncommon circumstance in Scotland (in former days), where food and shelter were readily afforded to humble friends and dependants. The Laird's predecessors had been imprudent, he himself was passive and unfortunate. Death swept away his sons, whose success in life might have balanced his own bad luck and incapacity. Debts increased and funds diminished, until ruin came. The estate was sold; and the old man was about to remove from the house of his fathers, to go he knew not whither, when, like an old piece of furniture, which, left alone in its wonted corner, may hold together for a long while, but breaks to pieces on an attempt to move it, he fell down on his own threshold under a paralytic affection.

The tutor awakened as from a dream. He saw his patron dead, and that his patron's only remaining child, an elderly woman, now neither graceful nor beautiful, if she had ever been either the one or the other, had by this calamity become a homeless and penniless orphan. He addressed her nearly in the words which Dominie Sampson uses to Miss Bertram, and professed his determination not to leave her. Accordingly, roused to the exercise of talents which had long slumbered, he opened a little school, and supported his patron's child for the rest of her life, treating her with the same humble observance and devoted attention which he had used towards her in the days of her prosperity.

Such is the outline of Dominie Sampson's real story, in which there is neither romantic incident nor sentimental passion; but which, perhaps, from the rectitude and simplicity of character which it displays, may interest the heart and fill the eye of the reader as irresistibly as if it respected distresses of a more dignified or refined character.

These preliminary notices concerning the tale of Guy Mannering, and some of the characters introduced, may save the author and reader, in the present instance, the trouble of writing and perusing a long string of detached notes.

CHAPTER I.

He could not deny, that looking round upon the dreary region, and seeing nothing but bleak fields, and naked trees, hills obscured
by fogs, and flats covered with inundations, he did for some time suffer melancholy to prevail on him, and wished himself again safe
at home—Travels of Will Marvel, Idler, No. 49.

It was in the beginning of the month of November, 17—, when a young English gentleman, who had just left the university of Oxford, made use of the liberty afforded him, to visit some parts of the north of England; and curiosity extended his tour into the adjacent frontier of the sister country. He had visited, on the day that opens our history, some monastic ruins in the county of Dumfries, and spent much of the day in making drawings of them from different points; so that, on mounting his horse to resume his journey, the brief and gloomy twilight of the season had already commenced. His way lay through a wide tract of black moss, extending for miles on each side and before him. Little eminences arose like islands on its surface, bearing here and there patches of corn, which even at this season was green, and sometimes a but, or farm-house, shaded by a willow or two, and surrounded by large elder bushes. These insulated dwellings communicated with each other by winding passages through the moss, impassable by any but the natives themselves. The public road, however, was tolerably well made and safe, so that the prospect of being benighted brought with it no real danger. Still it is uncomfortable to travel, alone and in the dark, through an unknown country; and there are few ordinary occasions upon which Fancy frets herself so much as in a situation like that of Mannering.

As the light grew faint and more faint, and the morass appeared blacker and blacker, our traveller questioned more closely each chance passenger on his distance from the village of Kippletringan, where he proposed to quarter for the night. His queries were usually answered by a counter-challenge respecting the place from whence he came. While sufficient daylight remained to show the dress and appearance of a gentleman, these cross interrogatories were usually put in the form of a case supposed, as, "Ye'll hae been at the auld abbey o' Halycross, sir? there's mony English gentlemen, gang to see that."—Or, "Your honour will be come frae the house o' Pouderloupat?" But when the voice of the querist alone was distinguishable, the response usually was, "Where are ye coming frae at sic a time o' night as the like o' this?"—or, "Ye'll no be o' this country, freend?" The answers, when obtained, were neither very reconcilable to each other, nor accurate in the information which they afforded. Kippletringan was distant at first "a gey bit"; [* Considerable distance] then the "gey bit" was more accurately described as "ablins [* Perhaps] three mile"; then the "three mile" diminished into "like a mile and a bittock "; then extended themselves into "four mile or thereawa"; and, lastly, a female voice, having hushed a waiting infant which the spokeswoman carried in her arms, assured Guy Mannering, "It was a weary lang gate yet to Kippletringan, and unco heavy road for foot passengers." The poor hack upon which Mannering was mounted was probably of opinion that it suited him as ill as the female respondent; for he began to flag very much, answered each application of the spur with a groan, and stumbled at every stone (and they were not few) which lay in his road.

Mannering now grew impatient. He was occasionally betrayed into a deceitful hope that the end of his journey was near, by the apparition of a twinkling light or two; but, as he came up, he was disappointed to find that the gleams proceeded from some of those farm-houses which occasionally ornamented the surface of the extensive bog. At length, to complete his perplexity, he arrived at a place where the road divided into two. If there had been light to consult the relics of a finger-post which stood there, it would have been of little avail, as, according to the good custom of North Britain, the inscription had been defaced shortly after its erection. Our adventurer was therefore compelled, like a knight-errant of old, to trust to the sagacity of his horse, which, without any demur, chose the left-hand path, and seemed to proceed at a somewhat livelier pace than before, affording thereby a hope that he knew he was drawing near to his quarters for the evening. This hope, however, was not speedily accomplished, and Mannering, whose impatience made every furlong seem three, began to think that Kippletringan was actually retreating before him in proportion to his advance.

It was now very cloudy, although the stars, from time to time, shed a twinkling and uncertain light. Hitherto nothing had broken the silence around him, but the deep cry of the bog-blitter, or bull-of-the-bog, a large species of bittern; and the sighs of the wind as it passed along the dreary morass. To these was now joined the distant roar of the ocean, towards which the traveller seemed to be fast approaching. This was no circumstance to make his mind easy. Many of the roads in that country lay along the sea-beach, and were liable to be flooded by the tides, which rise with great height,—and advance with extreme rapidity. Others were intersected with creeks and small inlets, which it was only safe to pass at particular times of the tide. Neither circumstance would have suited a dark night, a fatigued horse, and a traveller ignorant of his road. Mannering resolved, therefore, definitely to halt for the night at the first inhabited place, however poor, he might chance to reach, unless he could procure a guide to this unlucky village of Kippletringan.—

A miserable hut gave him an opportunity to execute his purpose. He found out the door with no small difficulty, and for some time knocked without producing any other answer than a duet between a female and a cur-dog, the latter yelping as if he would have barked his heart out, the other screaming in chorus. By degrees the human tones predominated; but the angry bark of the cur being at the instant changed into a howl, it is probable something more than fair strength of lungs had contributed to the ascendency.

"Sorrow be in your thrapple [*Throat] then these were the first articulate words,—"will ye no let me hear what the man wants, wi' your yaffing?" [* Barking]

"Am I far from Kippletringan, good dame?"

"Frae Kippletringan!!!" in an exalted tone of wonder, which we can but faintly express by three points of admiration; "Ow, man! ye should hae hadden eassel to Kippletringan—ye maun gae back as far as the Whaap, and haud the Whaap [*The Hope, often pronounced Whaap, is the sheltered part or hollow of the hill Hoff, howff, haaf, and haven, are all modifications of the same word.] till ye come to Ballenloan, and then—"

"This will never do, good dame! my horse is almost quite knocked up —can you not give me a night's lodgings?"

"Troth can I no—I am a lone woman, for James he's awa to Drumshourloch fair with the year-aulds, and I daurna for my life open the door to ony o' your gang-there-out sort o' bodies."

"But what must I do then, good dame? for I can't sleep here upon the road all night."

"Troth, I kenna, unless ye like to gae down and speer [*Ask] for quarters at the Place. I'se warrant they'll tak ye in, whether ye be gentle or semple."

"Simple enough, to be wandering here at such a time of night," thought Mannering, who was ignorant of the meaning of the phrase; "but how shall I get to the place, as you call it?"

"Ye maun haud wessel by the end o' the loan, and take tent o' the jaw-hole."

"Oh, if ye get to eassel and wessel [*Eastward and Westward] again, I am undone!—Is there nobody that could guide me to this place? I will pay him handsomely."

The ward pay operated like magic. "Jock, ye villain," exclaimed the voice from the interior, "are ye lying routing there, and a. young gentleman seeking the way to the Place? Get up, ye fause loon, [*Young fellow] and show him the way down the muckle loaning. —He'll show you the way, sir, and I'se warrant ye'll be weel put up; for they never turn awa naebody frae the door; and ye'll be come in the canny moment, I'm thinking, for the Laird's servant— that's no to say his body-servant, but the helper like—rade express by this e'en to fetch the houdie, [*Midwife] and he just staid the drinking o' twa pints o' tippenny, to tell us how my leddy was ta'en wi' her pains."

"Perhaps," said Mannering, "at such a time a stranger's arrival might be inconvenient?"

"Hout, na, ye needna be blate about that; their house is muckle eneugh, and clecking [*Hatching time] time's aye canty time."

By this time Jock had found his way into all the intricacies of a tattered doublet, and more tattered pair of breeches, and sallied forth, a great white-headed, bare-legged, lubberly boy of twelve years old, so exhibited by the glimpse of a rush-light, which his half-naked mother held in such a manner as to get a peep at the stranger, without greatly exposing herself to view in return. Jock moved on westward, by the end of the house, leading Mannering's horse by the bridle, and piloting, with some dexterity, along the little path which bordered the formidable jaw-hole, whose vicinity the stranger was made sensible of by means of more organs than one. His guide then dragged the weary hack along a broken and stony cart-track, next over a ploughed field, then broke down a slap, [*A gap] as he called it, in a dry-stone fence, and lugged the unresisting animal through the breach, about a rood of the simple masonry giving way in the splutter with which he passed. Finally, he led the way, through a wicket, into something which had still the air of an avenue, though many of the trees were felled. The roar of the ocean was now near and full, and the moon, which began to make her appearance, gleamed on a turreted and apparently a ruined mansion, of considerable extent. Mannering fixed his eyes upon it with a disconsolate sensation.

"Why, my little fellow," he said, "this is a ruin, not a house?"

"Ah, but the lairds lived there langsyne—that's Ellangowan Auld
Place; there's a hantle bogles [*Ghosts] about it—but ye needna be

feared—I never saw ony mysell, and we're just at the door o' the
New Place."

Accordingly, leaving the ruins on the right, a few steps brought the traveller in front of a modern house of moderate size, at which his guide rapped with great importance. Mannering told his circumstances to the servant; and the gentleman of the house, who heard his tale from the parlour, stepped forward, and welcomed the stranger hospitably to Ellangowan. The boy, made happy with half a crown, was dismissed to his cottage, the weary horse was conducted to a stall, and Mannering found himself in a few minutes seated by a comfortable supper, for which his cold ride gave him a hearty appetite.

CHAPTER II.

—Comes me cranking in, And cuts me from the best of all my land,
A huge half-moon, a monstrous cantle out.

Henry IV. Part I

The company in the parlour at Ellangowan consisted of the Laird, and a sort of person who might be the village schoolmaster, or perhaps the minister's assistant; his appearance was too shabby to indicate the minister, considering he was on a visit to the Laird.

The Laird himself was one of those second-rate sort of persons, that are to be found frequently in rural situations. Fielding has described one class as feras consumere nati; but the love of field-sports indicates a certain activity of mind, which had forsaken Mr. Bertram, if ever he possessed it. A good-humoured listlessness of countenance formed the only remarkable expression of his features, although they were rather handsome than otherwise. In fact, his physiognomy indicated the inanity of character which pervaded his life. I will give the reader some insight into his state and conversation, before he has finished a long lecture to Mannering, upon the propriety and comfort of wrapping his stirrup-irons round with a wisp of straw when he had occasion to ride in a chill evening.

Godfrey Bertram, of Ellangowan, succeeded to a long pedigree, and a short rent-roll, like many lairds of that period. His list of forefathers ascended so high, that they were lost in the barbarous ages of Galwegian independence; so that his genealogical tree, besides the Christian and crusading names of Godfreys, and Gilberts, and Dennises, and Rolands, without end, bore heathen fruit of yet darker ages,— Arths, and Knarths, and Donagilds, and Hanlons. In truth, they had been formerly the stormy chiefs of a desert, but extensive domain, and the heads of a numerous tribe, called Mac-Dingawaie, though they afterwards adopted the Norman surname of Bertram. They had made war, raised rebellions, been defeated, beheaded, and hanged, as became a family of importance, for many centuries. But they had gradually lost ground in the world, and, from being themselves the heads of treason and traitorous conspiracies, the Bertrams, or Mac-Dingawaies, of Ellangowan, had sunk into subordinate accomplices. Their most fatal exhibitions in this capacity took place in the seventeenth century, when the foul fiend possessed them with a spirit of contradiction, which uniformly involved them in controversy with the ruling powers. They reversed the conduct of the celebrated Vicar of Bray, and adhered as tenaciously to the weaker side, as that worthy divine to the stronger. And truly, like him, they had their reward.

Allan Bertram of Ellangowan, who flourished tempore Caroli primi was, says my authority, Sir Robert Douglas, in his Scottish Baronage (see the title Ellangowan), "a steady loyalist, and full of zeal for the cause of his sacred majesty, in which he united with the great Marquis of Montrose, and other truly zealous and honourable patriots, and sustained great losses in that behalf. He had the honour of knighthood conferred upon him by his most sacred majesty, and was sequestrated as a malignant by the parliament, 1642, and afterwards as a resolutioner, in the year 1648."—These two cross-grained epithets of malignant and resolutioner cost poor Sir Allan one half of the family estate. His son Dennis Bertram married a daughter of an eminent fanatic, who had a seat in the council of state, and saved by that union the remainder of the family property. But, as ill chance would have it, he became enamoured of the lady's principles as well as of her charms, and my author gives him this character: "He was a man of eminent parts and resolution, for which reason he was chosen by the western counties one of the committee of noblemen and gentlemen, to report their griefs to the privy council of Charles II, anent the coming in of the Highland host in 1678." For undertaking this patriotic task he underwent a fine, to pay which he was obliged to mortgage half of the remaining moiety of his paternal property. This loss he might have recovered by dint of severe economy, but on the breaking out of Argyle's rebellion, Dennis Bertram was again suspected by government, apprehended, sent to Dunnottar Castle on the coast of the Mearns, and there broke his neck in an attempt to escape from a subterranean habitation, called the Whigs' Vault, in which he was confined with some eighty of the same persuasion. The apprizer, therefore (as the holder of a mortgage was then called), entered upon possession, and, in the language of Hotspur, "came me cranking in," and cut the family out of another monstrous cantle of their remaining property.

Donohoe Bertram, with somewhat of an Irish name, and somewhat of an Irish temper, succeeded to the diminished property of Ellangowan. He turned out of doors the Rev. Aaron Macbriar, his mother's chaplain (it is said they quarrelled about the good graces of a milkmaid), drank himself daily drunk with brimming healths to the king, council, and bishops; held orgies with the Laird of Lagg, Theophilus Oglethorpe, and Sir James Turner; and lastly, took his gray gelding, and joined Clavers at Killiecrankie. At the skirmish of Dunkeld, 1689, he was shot dead by a Cameronian with a silver button (being supposed to have proof from the Evil One against lead and steel), and his grave is still called, the Wicked Laird's Lair.

His son, Lewis, had more prudence than seems usually to have belonged to the family. He nursed what property was yet left to him; for Donohoe's excesses, as well as fines and forfeitures, had made another inroad upon the estate. And although even he did not escape the fatality which induced the Lairds of Ellangowan to interfere with politics, he had yet the prudence, ere he went out with Lord Kenmore In 1715, to convey his estate to trustees, in order to parry pains and penalties, in case the Earl of Mar could not put down the Protestant succession. But Scylla and Charybdis —a word to the wise—he only saved his estate at expense of a lawsuit, which again subdivided the family property. He was, however, a man of resolution. He sold part of the lands, evacuated the old castle, where the family lived in their decadence, as a mouse (said an old farmer) lives under a firlot. Pulling down part of these venerable ruins, he built with the stones a narrow house of three stories high, with a front like a grenadier's cap, having in the very centre a round window, like the single eye of a Cyclops, two windows on each side, and a door in the middle, leading to a parlour and withdrawing room, full of all manner of cross lights.

This was the New Place of Ellangowan, in which we left our hero, better amused perhaps than our readers, and to this Lewis Bertram retreated, full of projects for re-establishing the prosperity of his family. He took some land into his own hand, rented some from neighbouring proprietors, bought and sold Highland cattle and Cheviot sheep, rode to fairs and trysts, fought hard bargains, and held necessity at the stairs end as well as he might. But what he gained in purse, he lost in honour, for such agricultural and commercial negotiations were very ill looked upon by his brother lairds, who minded nothing but cock-fighting, hunting, coursing, and horse-racing, with now and then the alternation of a desperate duel. The occupations which he followed encroached, in their opinion, upon the article of Ellangowan's gentry, and he found it necessary gradually to estrange himself from their society, and sink into what was then a very ambiguous character, a gentleman farmer. In the midst of his schemes death claimed his tribute, and the scanty remains of a large property descended upon Godfrey Bertram, the present possessor, his only son.

The danger of the father's speculations was soon seen. Deprived of Laird Lewis's personal and active superintendence, all his undertakings miscarried, and became either abortive or perilous. Without a single spark of energy to meet or repel these misfortunes, Godfrey put his faith in the activity of another. He kept neither hunters, nor hounds, nor any other southern preliminaries to ruin; but, as has been observed of his countrymen, he kept a man of business, who answered the purpose equally well. Under this gentleman's supervision small debts grew into large, interests were accumulated upon capitals, movable bonds became heritable, and law charges were heaped upon all; though Ellangowan possessed so little the spirit of a litigant, that he was on two occasions charged to make payment of the expenses of a long lawsuit, although he had never before heard that he had such cases in court. Meanwhile his neighbours predicted his final ruin. Those of the higher rank, with some malignity, accounted him already a degraded brother. The lower classes, seeing nothing enviable in his situation, marked his embarrassments with more compassion. He was even a kind of favourite with them, and upon the division of a common, or the holding of a black-fishing, or poaching court, or any similar occasion, when they conceived themselves, oppressed by the gentry, they were in the habit of saying to each other, "Ah, if Ellangowan, honest man, had his ain that his forebears had afore him, he wadna see the puir folk trodden down this gait." Meanwhile, this general good opinion never prevented their taking the advantage of him on all possible occasions, turning their cattle into his parks, stealing his wood, shooting his game, and so forth, "for the laird, honest man, he'll never find it,—he never minds what a puir body does."—Pedlars, gipsies, tinkers, vagrants of all descriptions, roosted about his outhouses, or harboured in his kitchen; and the laird, who was "nae nice body," but a thorough gossip, like most weak men, found recompense for his hospitality in the pleasure of questioning them on the news of the country-side.

A circumstance arrested Ellangowan's progress on the high-road to ruin. This was his marriage with a lady who had a portion of about four thousand pounds. Nobody in the neighbourhood could conceive why she married him, and endowed him with her wealth, unless because he had a tall, handsome figure, a good set of features, a genteel address, and the most perfect good-humour. It might be some additional consideration, that she was herself at the reflecting age of twenty-eight, and had no near relations to control her actions or choice.

It was in this lady's behalf (confined for the first time after her marriage) that the speedy and active express, mentioned by the old dame of the cottage, had been despatched to Kippletringan on the night of Mannering's arrival.

Though we have said so much of the Laird himself, it still remains that we make the reader in some degree acquainted with his companion. This was Abel Sampson, commonly called, from his occupation as a pedagogue, Dominie Sampson. He was of low birth, but having evinced, even from his cradle, an uncommon seriousness of disposition, the poor parents were encouraged to hope that their bairn, as they expressed it, "might wag his pow [* Head] in a pulpit yet."

With an ambitious view to such consummation, they pinched and pared, rose early and lay down late, ate dry bread and drank cold water, to secure to Abel the means of learning. Meantime, his tall, ungainly, figure, his taciturn and grave manners, and some grotesque habits of swinging his limbs, and screwing his visage, while reciting his task, made poor Sampson the ridicule of all his school-companions. The same qualities secured him at Glasgow college a plentiful share of the same sort of notice. Half the youthful mob "of the yards" used to assemble regularly to see Dominie Sampson (for he had already attained that honourable title) descend the stairs from the Greek class, with his Lexicon under his arm, his long misshapen legs sprawling abroad, and keeping awkward time to the play of his immense shoulder-blades, as they raised and depressed the loose and threadbare black coat which was his constant and only wear. When he spoke, the efforts of the professor (professor of divinity, though he was) were totally inadequate to restrain the inextinguishable laughter of the students, and sometimes even to repress his own. The long, sallow visage, the goggle eyes, the huge under-jaw, which appeared not to open and shut by an act of volition, but to be dropped and hoisted up again by some complicated machinery within the inner man,—the harsh and dissonant voice. and the screech-owl notes to which it was exalted when he was exhorted to pronounce more distinctly,— all added fresh subject for mirth to the torn cloak and shattered shoe, which have afforded legitimate subjects of raillery against the poor scholar, from Juvenal's time downward. It was never known that Sampson either exhibited irritability at this ill usage, or made the least attempt to retort upon his tormentors. He slunk from college by the most secret paths he could discover, and plunged himself into his miserable lodgings, where, for eighteenpence a week, he was allowed the benefit of a straw mattress, and, if his landlady was in good humour, permission to study his task by her fire. Under all these disadvantages, he obtained a competent knowledge of Greek and Latin, and some acquaintance with the sciences.

In progress of time, Abel Sampson, probationer of divinity, was admitted to the privileges of a preacher. But, alas! partly from his own bashfulness, partly owing to a strong and obvious disposition to risibility which pervaded the congregation upon his first attempt, he became totally incapable of proceeding in his intended discourse, gasped, grinned, hideously rolled his eyes till the congregation thought them flying out of his head, shut the Bible, stumbled down the pulpit-stairs, trampling upon the old women who generally take their station there, and was ever after designated as a "stickit minister." And thus he wandered back to his own country, with blighted hopes and prospects, to share the poverty of his parents. As he had neither friend nor confidant, hardly even an acquaintance, no one had the means of observing closely how Dominie Sampson bore a disappointment which supplied the whole town with a week's sport. It would be endless even to mention the numerous jokes to which it gave birth, from a ballad, called "Sampson's Riddle," written upon the subject by a smart young student of humanity, to the sly hope of the Principal, that the fugitive had not, in imitation of his mighty namesake, taken the college gates along with him in his retreat.

To all appearance, the equanimity of Sampson was unshaken. He sought to assist his parents by teaching a school, and soon had plenty of scholars, but very few fees. In fact, he taught the sons of farmers for what they chose to give him, and the poor for nothing; and, to the shame of the former be it spoken, the pedagogue's gains never equalled those of a skilful ploughman. He wrote, however, a good hand, and added something to his pittance by copying accounts and writing letters for Ellangowan. By degrees, the Laird, who was much estranged from general society, became partial to that of Dominie Sampson. Conversation, it is true, was out of the question, but the Dominie was a good listener, and stirred the fire with some address. He attempted even to snuff the candies, but was unsuccessful, and relinquished that ambitious post of courtesy after having twice reduced the parlour to total darkness. So his civilities, thereafter, were confined to taking off his glass of ale in exactly the same time and measure with the Laird, and in uttering certain indistinct murmurs of acquiescence at the conclusion of the long and winding stories of Ellangowan.

On one of these occasions, he presented for the first tine to Mannering his tall, gaunt, awkward, bony figure, attired in a threadbare suit of blacks with a coloured handkerchief, not over clean, about his sinewy, scraggy neck, and his nether person arrayed in gray breeches, dark-blue stockings, clouted shoes, and small copper buckles.

Such is a brief outline of the lives and fortunes of those two persons, in whose society Mannering now found himself comfortably seated.

CHAPTER III.

Do not the hist'ries of all ages Relate miraculous presages, Of strange turns in the world's affairs, Foreseen by Astrologers, Sooth-sayers, Chaldeans learned Genethliacs, And some that have writ almanacks?

Hudibras.

The circumstances of the landlady were pleaded to Mannering, first, as an apology for her not appearing to welcome her guest, and for those deficiencies in his entertainment which her attention might have supplied, and then as an excuse for pressing an extra bottle of good wine.

"I cannot weel sleep," said the Laird, with the anxious feelings of a father in such a predicament, "till I hear she's gatten ower with it—and if you, sir, are not very sleepry, and would do me and the Dominie the honour to sit up wi' us, I am sure we shall not detain you very late. Luckie Howatson is very expeditious;—there was ance a lass that was in that way—she did not live far from hereabouts—ye needna shake your head and groan, Dominie—I am sure the kirk dues were a' weel paid, and what can man do mair?—it was laid till her ere she had a sark ower her head; and the man that she since wadded does not think her a pin the waur for the misfortune.—They live, Mr. Mannering, by the shore-side, at Annan, and a mair decent, orderly couple, with six as fine bairns as ye would wish to see plash in a salt-water dub; and little curlie Godfrey—that's the eldest, the come o' will, as I may say —he's on board an excise yacht—I hae a cousin at the board of excise—that's 'Commissioner Bertram; he got his commissionership in the great contest for the county, that ye must have heard of, for it was appealed to the House of Commons—now I should have voted there for the Laird of Balruddery; but ye see my father was a Jacobite, and out with Kenmore, so he never took the oaths; and I ken not weel how it was, but all that I could do and say, they keepit me off the roll, though my agent, that had a vote upon my estate, ranked as a good vote for auld Sir Thomas Kittlecourt. But, to return to what I was saying, Luckie Howatson is very. expeditious, for this lass—"

Here the—desultory and long-winded narrative of the Laird was interrupted by the voice of someone ascending the stairs from the kitchen story, and singing at full pitch of voice. The high notes were too shrill for a man, the low seemed too deep for a woman. The words, as far as Mannering could distinguish them, seemed to run thus:—

Canny moment, lucky fit; Is the lady lighter yet? Be it lad, or be it lass, Sign wi' cross, and sain wi' mass.

"It's Meg Merrilies, the gipsy, as sure as I am a sinner," said Mr. Bertram. The Dominie groaned deeply, uncrossed his legs, drew in the huge splay foot which his former posture had extended, placed it perpendicularly, and stretched the other limb over it instead, puffing out between whiles huge volumes of tobacco smoke. "What needs ye groan, Dominie? I am sure Meg's sangs do nae ill."

"Nor good neither," answered Dominie Sampson, in a voice whose untuneable harshness corresponded with the awkwardness of his figure. They were the first words which Mannering had heard him speak; and as he had been watching with some curiosity, when this eating, drinking, moving, and smoking automaton would perform the part of speaking, he was a good deal diverted with the harsh timber tones which issued from him. But at this moment the door opened, and Meg Merrilies entered.

Her appearance made Mannering start. She was full six feet high, wore a man's greatcoat over the rest of her dress, had in her hand a goodly sloe-thorn cudgel, and in all points of equipment, except her petticoats, seemed rather masculine than feminine. Her dark elf-locks shot out like the snakes of the gorgon, between an old-fashioned bonnet called a bongrace, heightening the singular effect of her strong and weather-beaten features, which they partly shadowed, while her eye had a wild roll that indicated something like real or affected insanity.

"Aweel, Ellangowan," she said, "wad it no hae been a bonnie thing, an the leddy had been brought-to-bed, and me at the fair o' Drumshourloch, no kenning, nor dreaming a word about it? Wha was to hae keepit awa the worriecows, [* goblins] I trow? Ay, and the elves and gyre-carlings [* Witches] frae the bonny bairn, grace be wi' it? Ay, or 'said Saint Colme's charm for its sake, the dear?" And without waiting an answer she began to sing.

Trefoil, vervain, John's-wort, dill, Hinders witches of their will; Weel is them, that weel may Fast upon St. Andrew's day.

Saint Bride and her brat, Saint Colme and his cat, Saint Michael and his spear, Keep the house frae reif and wear.

This charm she sung to a wild tune, in a high and shrill voice, and, cutting three capers with such strength and agility, as almost to touch the roof of the room, concluded, "And now, Laird, will ye no order me a tass o' brandy?"

"That you shall have, Meg—Sit down yont there at the door, and tell us what news ye have heard at the fair o' Drumshourloch."

"Troth, Laird, and there was muckle want o' you, and the like b' you; for there was a whin bonnie lasses there, forbye mysell, and deil ane to gie them hansels."

"Weel, Meg, and how mony gipsies were sent to the tolbooth?"

"Troth, but three, Laird, for there were nae mair in the fair, bye mysell, as I said before, and I e'en gae them leg-bail, for there's nae case in dealing wi' quarrelsome fowk. And there's Dunbog has warned the Red Rotten and John Young aff his grunds—black be his cast! [*Fate] he's nae gentleman, nor drap's bluid o' gentleman, wad grudge twa gangrel [*Vagrant] pair bodies the shelter o' a waste house, and the thistles by the roadside for a bit cuddy,. [*Donkey] and the bits o' rotten birk [*Birch] to boil their drap parritch wi'. Weel, there's ane abune a'—but we'll see if the red cock craw not in his bonnie barn-yard ae morning before day-dawing."

"Hush! Meg, hush! hush that's not safe talk."

"What does she mean?" said Mannering to Sampson, in an undertone.

"Fire-raising," answered the laconic Dominie.

11

"Who, or what is she, in the name of wonder?"

"Harlot, thief, witch, and gipsy." Answered Sampson again.

"Oh, troth, Laird," continued Meg, during this by-talk, "it's but to the like o' you ane can open their heart; ye see, they say Dunbog is nae mair a gentleman than the blunker that's biggit [*Built] the bonnie house down in the howm. But the like o' you, Laird, that's a real gentleman for sae mony hundred years, and never hunds puir fowk aff your grund as if they were mad tykes, [*Dogs] nane o' our fowk wad stir your gear [*Property] if ye had as mony capons as there's leaves on the trysting-tree.—And now some o' ye maun lay down your watch, and tell me the very minute o' the hour the wean's born, and I'll spae its fortune."

"Ay, but, Meg, we shall not want your assistance, for here's a student from Oxford that kens much better than you how to spae its fortune—he does it by the stars."

"Certainly, sir," said Mannering, entering into the simple humour of his landlord, "I will calculate his nativity according to the rule of the Triplicities, as recommended by Pythagoras, Hippocrates, Diocles, and Avicenna. Or I will begin ab hora questionis, as Haly, Messahala, Ganwehis, and Guido Bonatus, have recommended."

One of Sampson's great recommendations to the favour of Mr. Bertram was, that he never detected the most gross attempt at imposition, so that the Laird, whose humble efforts at jocularity were chiefly confined to what were then called-bites and bams, since denominated hoaxes and quizzes, had the fairest possible subject of wit in the unsuspecting Dominie. It is true, he never laughed, or joined in the laugh which his own simplicity afforded —nay, it is said, he never laughed but once in his life and on that memorable occasion his landlady miscarried, partly through surprise at the event itself, and partly from terror at the-hideous grimaces which attended this unusual cachinnation. The only effect which the discovery of such impositions produced upon this saturnine personage was, to extort an ejaculation of "Prodigious!" or "Very facetious!" pronounced syllabically, but without moving a muscle of his own countenance.

On the present occasion, he turned a gaunt and ghastly stare upon the youthful astrologer, and seemed to doubt if he had rightly understood his answer to his patron.

"I am afraid, sir," said Mannering, turning towards him, "you may be one of those unhappy persons, who, their dim eyes being unable to penetrate the starry spheres, and to discern therein the decrees of heaven at a distance, have their hearts barred against conviction by prejudice and misprision."

"Truly," said Sampson, "I opine with Sir Isaac Newton, Knight, and umwhile [*Late] master of his Majesty's mint, that the (pretended) science of astrology is altogether vain, frivolous, and unsatisfactory." And here he reposed his oracular jaws.

"Really," resumed the traveller, "I am sorry to see a gentleman of your learning and gravity labouring under such strange blindness and delusion. Will you place the brief, the modern, and, as I may say, the vernacular name of Isaac Newton, in opposition to the grave and sonorous authorities of Dariot, Bonatus, Ptolemy, Haly, Eztler, Dieterick, Naibob, Harfurt, Zael, Taustettor, Agrippa, Duretus, Maginus, Origen, and Argol? Do not Christians and Heathens, and Jews and Gentiles, and poets and philosophers, unite in allowing the starry influences?"

"Communis error—it is a general mistake," answered the inflexible
Dominie Sampson.

"Not so," replied the young Englishman; it is a general and well-grounded belief."

"It is the resource of cheaters, knaves, and cozeners," said
Sampson.

"Abusus non tollit usum. The abuse of anything doth not abrogate the lawful use thereof."

During this discussion, Ellangowan was somewhat like a woodcock caught in his own springe. He turned his face alternately from the one spokesman to the other, and began, from the gravity with which Mannering plied his adversary, and the learning which he displayed in the controversy, to give him credit for. being half serious. As for Meg, she fixed her bewildered eyes upon the astrologer, overpowered by a jargon more mysterious than her own.

Mannering pressed his advantage, and ran over all the hard terms of art which a tenacious memory supplied, and which, from circumstances hereafter to be noticed, had been familiar to him in early youth.

Signs and planets, in aspects sextuple, quartile, trine, conjoined or opposite; houses of heaven, with their cusps, hours, and minutes; Almuten, Alinochoden, Anabibazon, Catahibazon, a thousand terms of equal sound and significance, poured thick and threefold upon the unshrinking Dominie, whose stubborn incredulity bore him out against the pelting of this pitiless storm.

At length, the joyful annunciation that the lady had presented her husband with a fine boy, and was (of course) as well as could be expected, broke off this intercourse. Mr. Bertram hastened to the lady's apartment, Meg Merrilies descended to the kitchen to secure her share of the groaning malt, [*The groaning malt mentioned in the text was the ale brewed for the purpose of being drunk after the lady or goodwife's safe delivery. The ken-no has a more ancient source, and perhaps the custom may he derived from the secret rites of the Bona Dea. A large and rich cheese was made by the women of the family, with great affectation of secrecy, for the refreshment of the gossips who were to attend at the canny minute This was the ken-no, so called because its existence was secret (that is, presumed to be so) from all the males of the family, but especially from the husband and master. He was, accordingly, expected to conduct himself as if he knew of no such preparation, to act as if desirous to press the female guests to refreshments, and to seem surprised at their obstinate refusal. But the instant his back was turned ken-no was produced, and after all had eaten their fill, with a proper accompaniment of the groaning malt, the remainder was divided among the gossips, each carrying a large portion home with the same affectation of great secrecy.] and the "ken-no," and Mannering, after looking at his watch, and noting, with great exactness, the hour and minute of the birth, requested, with becoming gravity, that the Dominie would conduct him to some place where he might have a view of the heavenly bodies.

The schoolmaster, without further answer, rose and threw open a door half sashed with glass, which led to an old-fashioned terrace-walk, behind the modern house, communicating with the platform on which the ruins of the ancient castle were situated The wind had arisen, and swept before it the clouds which had formerly obscured the sky. The moon was high, and at the full, and all the lesser satellites of heaven shone forth in cloudless effulgence. The scene which their light presented to Mannering was in the highest degree unexpected and striking.

We have observed, that in the latter part of his journey our traveller approached the seashore, without being aware how nearly. He now perceived that the ruins of Ellangowan castle were situated upon a promontory, or projection of rock, which formed one side of a small and placid bay on the seashore. The modern mansion was placed lower, though closely adjoining, and the ground behind it descended to the sea by a small swelling green bank, divided into levels by natural terraces, on which grew some old trees, and terminating upon the white sand. The other side of the bay, opposite to the old castle, was a sloping and varied promontory, covered chiefly with copsewood, which on that favoured coast grows almost within water-mark. A fisherman's cottage peeped from among the trees. Even at this dead hour of night there were lights moving upon the shore, probably occasioned by the unloading a smuggling lugger from the Isle of Man, which was lying in the bay. On the light from the sashed door of the house being observed, a halloo from the vessel, of "Ware hawk! Douse the glim!" [*Put out the light] alarmed those who were on shore, and the lights instantly disappeared.

It was one hour after midnight, and the prospect around was lovely. The gray old towers of the ruin, partly entire, partly broken, here bearing the, rusty weather-stains of ages, and there partially mantled with ivy, stretched along the verge of the dark rock which rose on Mannering's right hand. In his front was the quiet bay, whose little waves, crisping and sparkling to the moonbeams, rolled successively along its surface, and dashed with a soft and murmuring ripple against the silvery beach. To the left the woods advanced far into the ocean, waving in the moonlight along ground of an undulating and varied form, and presenting those varieties of light and shade, and that interesting combination of glade and thicket, upon which the eye delights to rest, charmed with what it sees, yet curious to pierce still deeper into the intricacies of the woodland scenery. Above rolled the planets, each, by its own liquid orbit of light, distinguished from the inferior or more distant stars. So strangely can imagination deceive even those :by whose volition it has been excited, that Mannering, while gazing upon these brilliant bodies, was half inclined to believe in the influence ascribed to them by, superstition over human events. But Mannering was a youthful lover, and might perhaps be influenced by the feelings so exquisitely expressed by a modern poet

For fable is Love's world, his home, his birth-place—Delightedly dwells he 'mong fays, and talismans, And spirits, and delightedly believes Divinities, being himself divine. The intelligible forms of ancient poets, The fair humanities of old religion, The power, the beauty, and the majesty, That had their haunts in dale, or piny mountains, Or forest, by slow stream, or pebbly spring Or chasms of wat'ry depths—all these have vanish'd; They live no longer in the faith of reason! But still the heart doth need a language, still Doth the old instinct bring back the old names. And to yon starry world they now are gone, Spirits or gods, that used to shave this earth With man as with their friend, and to the lover Yonder they move, from yonder visible sky Shoot influence down; and even at this day 'Tis Jupiter who brings whate'er is great, And Venus who brings everything that's fair.

Such musings soon gave way to others. "Alas!" he muttered, "my good old tutor, who used to enter so deep into the controversy between Heydon and Chambers on the subject of astrology, he would have looked upon the scene with other eyes, and would have seriously endeavoured to discover from the respective positions of these luminaries their probable effects on the destiny of the new-born infant, as if the courses or emanations of the stars superseded, or, at least, were co-ordinate with, Divine Providence. Well, rest be with him! he instilled into me enough of knowledge for erecting a scheme of nativity, and therefore will I presently go about it." So saying, and having noted the position of the principal planetary bodies, Guy Mannering returned to the house. The Laird met him in the parlour, and acquainting him, with great glee, that the boy was a fine healthy little fellow, seemed rather disposed to press further conviviality. He admitted, however, Mannering's plea of weariness, and, conducting him to his sleeping apartment, left him to repose for the evening.

CHAPTER IV.

—Come and see! trust thine own eyes, A fearful sign stands
in the house of life, An enemy; a fiend lurks close behind …
The radiance of thy planet—O be warned!
Coleridge, from Schiller.

The belief in astrology was almost universal in the middle of the seventeenth century; it began to waver and become doubtful towards the close of that period, and in the beginning of the eighteenth the art fell into general disrepute, and even under general ridicule. Yet it still retained many partisans even in the seats of learning. Grave and studious men were loath to relinquish the calculations which had early become the principal objects of their studies, and felt reluctant to descend from the predominating height to which a supposed insight into futurity, by the power of consulting abstract influences and conjunctions, had exalted them over the rest of mankind.

Among those who cherished this imaginary privilege with undoubting faith, was an old clergyman, with whom Mannering was placed during his youth. He wasted his eves in observing the stars, and his brains in calculations upon their various combinations. His pupil, in early youth, naturally caught some portion of his enthusiasm, and laboured for a time to make himself master of the technical process of astrological research; so that, before he became convinced of its absurdity, William Lilly himself would have allowed him "a curious fancy and piercing judgment in resolving a question of nativity."

On the present occasion, he arose as early in the morning as the shortness of the day permitted, and proceeded to calculate the nativity of the young heir of Ellangowan. He undertook the task secundum artem, as well to keep up appearances, as from a sort of curiosity to know whether he yet remembered, and could practise, the imaginary science. He accordingly erected his scheme, or figure of heaven, divided into its twelve houses, placed the planets therein according to the Ephemeris, and rectified their position to the hour and moment of the nativity. Without troubling our readers with the general prognostications which judicial astrology would have inferred from these circumstances, in this diagram there was one significator, which pressed remarkably upon our astrologers attention. Mars having dignity in the cusp of the twelfth house, threatened captivity, or sudden and violent death, to the native; and Mannering having recourse to those further rules by which diviners pretend to ascertain the vehemency of this evil direction, observed from the result, that three periods would be particularly hazardous—his fifth—his tenth—his twenty-first year.

It was somewhat remarkable, that Mannering had once before tried a similar piece of foolery, at the instance of Sophia Wellwood, the young lady to whom he was attached, and that a similar conjunction of planetary influence threatened her with death, or imprisonment, in her thirty-ninth year. She was at this time eighteen; so that, according to the result of the scheme in both cases, the same year threatened her with the same misfortune that was presaged to the native or infant, whom that night had introduced into the world. Struck with this coincidence, Mannering repeated his calculations; and the result approximated the events predicted, until, at length, the same month, and day of the month, seemed assigned as the period of peril to both.

It will be readily believed, that, in mentioning this circumstance, we lay no weight whatever upon the pretended information thus conveyed. But it often happens, such is our natural love for the marvellous, that we willingly contribute our own efforts to beguile our

13

better judgments. Whether the coincidence which I have mentioned was really one of those singular chances, which sometimes happen against all ordinary calculations; or whether Mannering, bewildered amid the arithmetical labyrinth and technical jargon of astrology, had insensibly twice followed the same clew to guide him out of the maze; or whether his imagination, seduced by some point of apparent resemblance, lent its aid to make the similitude between the two operations more exactly accurate than it might otherwise have been, it is impossible to guess; but the impression upon his mind, that the results exactly corresponded, was vividly and undelibly strong.

He could not help feeling surprise at a coincidence so singular and unexpected. "Does the devil mingle in the dance, to avenge himself for our trifling with an art said to be of magical origin? Or is it possible, as Bacon and Sir Thomas Browne admit, that there is some truth in a sober and regulated astrology, and that the influence of the stars is not to be denied, though the due application of it, by the knaves—who pretend to practise the art, is greatly to be suspected?"—A moment's consideration of the subject induced him to dismiss this opinion as fantastical, and only sanctioned by those learned men. Either because they durst not at once shock the universal prejudices of their age, or because they themselves were not altogether freed from the contagious influence of a prevailing superstition. Yet the result of his calculations in these two instances left so unpleasing an impression on his mind, that, like Prospero, he mentally relinquished his art, and resolved, neither in jest nor earnest, ever again to practise judicial astrology.

He hesitated a good deal what he should say to the Laird of Ellangowan, concerning the horoscope of his first-born; and, at length, resolved plainly to tell him the judgment which he had formed, at the same time acquainting him—with the futility of the rules of art on which he had proceeded. With this resolution he walked out upon the terrace.

If the view of the scene around Ellangowan had been pleasing by moonlight, it lost none of its beauty by the light of the morning sun. The land, even in the month of November, smiled under its influence. A steep, but regular ascent, led from the terrace to the neighbouring eminence, and conducted Mannering to the front of the old castle. It consisted of two massive round towers, projecting, deeply and darkly, at the extreme angles of a curtain, or flat wall, which united them, and thus protecting the main entrance, that opened through a lofty arch in the centre of the curtain into the inner court of the castle. The arms of the family, carved in freestone, frowned over the gateway, and the portal showed the spaces arranged by the architect for lowering the portcullis, and raising the drawbridge. A rude farm-gate, made of young fir-trees nailed together, now formed the only safeguard of this once formidable entrance. The esplanade in front of the castle commanded a noble prospect.

The dreary scene of desolation, through which Mannering's road had lain on the preceding evening, was excluded from the view by some rising ground, and the landscape showed a pleasing alternation of hill and dale, intersected by a river, which was in some places visible, and hidden in others, where it rolled betwixt deep and wooded banks. The spire of a church, and the appearance of some houses, indicated the situation of a village at the place where the stream had its junction with the ocean. The vales seemed well cultivated, the little enclosures into which they were divided skirting the bottom of the hills, and sometimes carrying their lines of straggling hedge-rows a little way up the ascent. Above these were green pastures, tenanted chiefly by herds of black cattle, then the staple commodity of the country—, whose distant low gave no unpleasing animation to the landscape. The remoter hills were of a sterner character, and, at still greater distance, swelled into mountains of dark heath, bordering the horizon with a screen which gave a defined and limited boundary to the cultivated country, and added, at the same time, the pleasing idea, that it was sequestered and solitary. The sea-coast, which Mannering now saw in its extent, corresponded in variety and beauty with the inland view. In some places it rose into tall rocks, frequently crowned with the ruins of old buildings, towers, or beacons, which, according to tradition, were placed within sight of each other, that, in times of invasion or civil war, they might. communicate by signal for mutual defence and protection. Ellangowan castle was by far the most extensive and important of these ruins, and asserted, from size and situation, the superiority which its founders were said once to have possessed among the chiefs and nobles of the district. In other places, the shore was of a more gentle description, indented with small bays, where the land sloped smoothly down, or sent into the sea promontories covered with wood.

A scene so different from what last night's journey had presaged, produced a proportional effect upon Mannering. Beneath his eye lay the modern house; an awkward mansion, indeed, in point of architecture, but well situated, and with a warm, pleasant exposure.—How happily, thought our hero, would life glide on in such a retirement! On the one hand, the striking remnants of ancient grandeur, with the secret consciousness of family pride which they inspire; on the other, enough of modern elegance and comfort to satisfy every moderate wish. Here then, and with thee Sophia!—

We shall not pursue a lover's day-dream any farther. Mannering stood a minute with his arms folded, and then turned to the ruined castle.

On entering the gateway, he found that the rude magnificence of the inner court amply corresponded with the grandeur of the exterior. On the one side ran a range of windows lofty and large, divided by carved mullions of stone, which had once lighted the great hall of the castle; on the other, were various buildings of different heights and dates, yet so united as to present to the eye a certain general effect of uniformity of front. The doors and windows were ornamented with projections exhibiting rude specimens of sculpture and tracery, partly entire and partly broken down, partly covered by ivy and trailing plants, which grew luxuriantly among the ruins. That end of the court which faced the entrance had also been formerly closed by a range of buildings; but owing, it was said, to its having been battered by the ships of the Parliament under Deane, during the long civil war, this part of the castle was much more ruinous than the rest, and exhibited a great chasm, through which Mannering could observe the sea, and the little vessel (an armed lugger) which retained her station in the centre of the bay. [*The outline of the above description, as far as the supposed ruins are concerned, will be found somewhat to resemble the noble remains of Carlaverock castle, six or seven miles from Dumfries, and near to Lochar-moss.]

While Mannering was gazing round the ruins, he heard from the interior of an apartment on the left hand the voice of the gipsy he had seen on the preceding evening. He soon found an aperture, through which he could observe her without being himself visible; and could not help feeling, that her figure, her employment, and her situation, conveyed the exact impression of an ancient sibyl.

She sat upon a broken corner-stone in the angle of a paved apartment, part of which she had swept clean to afford a smooth space for the evolutions of her spindle. A strong sunbeam, through a lofty and narrow window, fell upon her wild dress and features, and afforded her light for her occupation; the rest of the apartment was very gloomy. Equipt in a habit which mingled the national dress of the Scottish common people with something of an Eastern costume, she spun a thread, drawn from wool of three different colours, black, white, and gray, by assistance of those ancient implements of house-wifely, now almost banished from the land, the distaff and spindle. As she spun, she sung what seemed to be a charm. Mannering, after in vain attempting to make himself master of the exact words of her song, afterwards attempted the following paraphrase of what, from a few intelligible phrases, he concluded to be its purport.

Twist ye, twine ye! even so Mingle shades of joy and woe, Hope, and fear, and peace, and strife, In the thread of human life.

While the mystic twist is spinning, And the infant's life beginning, Dimly seen through twilight bending, Lo, what varied shapes attending!

Passions wild, and Follies vain, Pleasures soon exchanged for pain
Doubt, and Jealousy and Fear, In the magic dance appear.

Now they wax, and now they dwindle, Whirling with the whirling spindle. Twist ye, twine ye! even so Mingle human bliss and woe.

Ere our translator, or rather our free imitator, had arranged these stanzas in his head, and while he was yet hammering out a rhyme for dwindle, the task of the sibyl was accomplished, or her wool was expended. She took the spindle, now charged with her labours, and, undoing the thread gradually, measured it, by casting it over her elbow, and bringing each loop round between her forefinger and thumb. When she had measured it out, she muttered to herself—"A hank, but not a haill ane—the full years o' three scare and ten, but thrice broken, and thrice to oop (ie. to unite); he'll be a lucky lad an he win through wi't."

Our hero was about to speak to the prophetess, when a voice, hoarse as the waves with which it mingled, halloo'd twice, and with increasing impatience—"Meg, Meg Merrilies!—Gipsy—hag—tousand deyvils!"

"I am coming, I am coming, Captain," answered Meg; and in a moment or two the impatient commander whom she addressed made his appearance from the broken part of the ruins.

He was apparently a seafaring man, rather under the middle size, and with a countenance bronzed by a thousand conflicts with the north-east wind. His frame was prodigiously muscular, strong, and thick-set; so that it seemed as if a man of much greater height would have been an inadequate match in any close personal conflict. He was hard-favoured, and, which was worse, his face bore nothing of the insouciance, the careless frolicsome jollity and vacant curiosity of a sailor on shore. These qualities, perhaps, as much as any others, contribute to the high popularity of our seamen, and the general good inclination which our society expresses towards them. Their gallantry, courage, and hardihood, are qualities which excite reverence, and perhaps rather humble pacific landsmen in their presence; and neither respect, nor a sense of humiliation, are feelings easily combined with a familiar fondness towards those who inspire. them. But the boyish frolics, the exulting high spirits, the unreflecting mirth of a sailor, when enjoying himself on shore, temper the more formidable points of his character. There was nothing like these in this man's face; on the contrary, a surly and even savage scowl appeared to darken features which would have been harsh and unpleasant under any expression or modification. "Where are you, Mother Deyvilson?" he said, with somewhat of a foreign accent, though speaking perfectly good English. "Donner and blitzen! we have been staying this half-hour. — Come, bless the good ship and the voyage, and be cursed to ye for a hag of Satan!"

At this moment he noticed Mannering, who, from the position which he had taken to watch Meg Merrilies's incantations, had the appearance of some one who was concealing himself, being half hidden by the buttress behind which he stood. The Captain, for such he styled himself, made a sudden and startled pause, and thrust his right hand into his bosom, between his jacket and waistcoat, as if to draw some weapon. "What cheer, brother?—you seem on the outlook—eh?"

Ere Mannering, somewhat struck by the man's gesture and insolent tone of voice, had made any answer, the gipsy emerged from her vault and joined the stranger. He questioned her in an undertone, looking at Mannering—"A shark alongside; eh?"

She answered in the same tone of under-dialogue, using the cant language of her tribe—"Cut ben Whids, and stow them—a gentry cove of the ken." [* Meaning a Stop your uncivil tongue—that is a gentleman from the house below.]

The fellow's cloudy visage cleared up. "The top of the morning to you, sir; I find you are a visitor of my friend Mr. Bertram—I beg pardon, but I took you for another sort of a person."

Mannering replied, "And you, sir, I presume, are the master of that vessel in the bay?"

"Ay, ay, sir; I am Captain Dirk Hatteraick, of the Yungfrauw Hagenslaapen, well known on this coast; I am not ashamed of my name, nor of my vessel,—no, nor of my cargo neither, for that matter."

"I dare say you have no reason, sir."

"Tousand donner—no; I'm all in the way of fair trade—just loaded yonder at Douglas, in the Isle of Man—neat cogniac—real hyson and souchong—Mechlin lace, if you want any—Right cogniac—We bumped ashore a hundred kegs last night."

"Really, sir, I am only a traveller, and have no sort of occasion for anything of the kind at present."

"Why, then, good-morning to you, for business must be minded— unless ye'll go aboard and take schnaps? [*A dram of liquor.]—you shall have a pouch-full of tea ashore.—Dirk Hatteraick knows how to be civil."

There was a mixture of impudence, hardihood, and suspicious fear about this man, which was inexpressibly disgusting. His manners were those of a ruffian, conscious of the suspicion attending his character, yet aiming to bear it down by the affectation of a careless and hardy familiarity. Mannering briefly rejected his proffered civilities; and after a surly good-morning, Hatteraick retired with the gipsy to that part of the ruins from which he had first made his appearance. A very narrow staircase here went down to the beach, intended probably for the convenience of the garrison during a siege. By this stair, the couple, equally amiable in appearance, and respectable by profession, descended to the seaside. The soi-disant captain embarked in a small boat with two men who appeared to wait for him, and the gipsy remained on the shore, reciting or singing, and gesticulating with great vehemence.

CHAPTER V.

—You have fed upon my seignories, Dispark'd my parks, and fell'd my forest woods, From mine own windows torn my household coat, Razed out my impress, leaving me no sign, Save men's opinions and my living blood, To show the world I am a gentleman.
Richard II.

WHEN the boat which carried the worthy captain on board his vessel had accomplished that task, the sails began to ascend, and the ship was got under way. She fired three guns as a salute to the house of Ellangowan, and then shot away rapidly before the wind, which blew off shore, under all the sail she could crowd.

"Ay, ay," said the Laird, who had sought Mannering for some time, and now joined him, "there they go—there go the free-traders—there go Captain Dirk Hatteraick, and the Yungfrauw Hagenslaapen, half Manks, half Dutchman, half devil! run out the bowsprit, up mainsail, top and top-gallant sails, royals, and sky-scrapers, and away,—follow who can! That fellow, Mr. Mannering, is the terror of all the excise and custom-house cruisers; they can make nothing of him; he drubs them, or he distances them;—and, speaking of excise, I come to bring you to breakfast; and you shall have some tea, that—"

Mannering, by this time, was aware that one thought linked strangely on to another in the concatenation of worthy Mr. Bertram's ideas,
    Like orient pearls at random strung;

and, therefore, before the current of his associations had drifted farther from the point he had left, he brought him back by some inquiry about Dirk Hatteraick.

"Oh, he's a—a—gude sort of blackguard fellow eneugh—naebody cares to trouble him—smuggler, when his guns are in ballast—privateer, or pirate faith, when he gets them mounted. He has done more mischief to the revenue folk than ony rogue that ever came out of Ramsay."

"But, my good sir, such being his character, I wonder he has any protection and encouragement on this coast." "Why, Mr. Mannering, people must have brandy and tea, and there's none in the country but what comes this way—and then there's short accounts, and maybe a keg or two, or a dozen pounds left at your stable door, instead of a d-d lang account at Christmas from Duncan Robb, the grocer at Kippletringan, who has aye a sum to—make up, and either wants ready money, or a short-dated bill. Now, Hatteraick will take wood, or he'll take bark, or he'll take barley, or he'll take just what's convenient at the time. I'll tell you a gude story about that. There was ance a laird—that's Macfie of Gudgeonford,—he had a great number of kain hens—that's hens that the tenant pays to the landlord—like a sort of rent in kind—they aye feed mine very ill; Luckie Finniston sent up three that were a shame to be seen only last week, and yet she has twelve bows [* Bolls (a large measure of grain)] sowing of victual; indeed her goodman, Duncan Finniston—that's him that's gone—(we must all die, Mr. Mannering; that's ower true)—and speaking of that, let us live in the meanwhile, for here's breakfast on the table, and the Dominie ready to say the grace."

The Dominie did accordingly pronounce a benediction, that exceeded in length any speech which Mannering had yet heard him utter. The tea, which of course belonged to the noble Captain Hatteraick's trade, was pronounced excellent. Still Mannering hinted, though with due delicacy, at the risk of encouraging such desperate characters: "Were it but in justice to the revenue, I should have supposed—"

"Ah, the revenue-lads"—for Mr. Bertram never embraced a general or abstract idea, and his notion of the revenue was personified in the commissioners, surveyors, comptrollers, and riding officers, whom he happened to know—"the revenue-lads can look sharp enough out for themselves—no one needs to help them—and they have a' the soldiers to assist them besides—and as to justice—you'll be surprised to hear it, Mr. Mannering—but I am not a justice of peace."

Mannering assumed the expected look of surprise, but thought within himself that the worshipful bench suffered no great deprivation from wanting the assistance of his good-humoured landlord. Mr. Bertram had now hit upon one of the few subjects on which he felt sore, and went on with some energy. "No, sir,—the name of Godfrey Bertram of Ellangowan is not in the last commission, though there's scarce a carle in the country that has a plough-gate of land, but what he must ride to quarter-sessions, and write J.P. after his name. I ken fu' weel whom I am obliged to—Sir Thomas Kittlecourt as good as tell'd me he would sit in my skirts, if he had not my interest at the last election; and because I chose to go with my own blood and third cousin, the Laird of Balruddery, they keepit me off the roll of freeholders; and now there comes a new nomination of justices, and I am left out! And whereas they pretend it was because I let David Mac-Guffog, the constable, draw the warrants, and manage the business his ain gate, [*Own way] as if I had been a nose a' wax, it's a main untruth; for I granted but seven warrants in my life, and the Dominie wrote every one of them—and if it had not been that unlucky business of Sandy Mac-Gruthar's, that the constables should have keepit twa or three days up yonder at the auld castle, just till they could get conveniency to send him to the county jail—and that cost me eneugh o' siller—But I ken what Sir Thomas wants very weel—it was just sic and siclike about the seat in the kirk o' Kilmagirdle—was I not entitled to have the front gallery facing the minister, rather than Mac-Crosskie of Creochstone, the son of Deacon Mac-Crosskie, the Dumfries weaver?"

Mannering expressed his acquiescence in the justice of these various complaints.

"And then, Mr. Mannering, there was the story about the road, and the fauld-dike—I ken Sir Thomas was behind there, and I said plainly to the clerk to the trustees that I saw the cloven foot, let them take that as they like.—Would any gentleman, or set of gentlemen, go and drive a road right through the corner of a fauld-dike, and take away, as my agent observed to them, like twa roods of gude moorland pasture?—And there was the story about choosing the collector of the cess—"

"Certainly, sir, it is hard you should meet with any neglect in a country, where, to judge from the extent of their residence, your ancestors must have made a very important figure."

"Very true, Mr. Mannering—I am a plain man, and do not dwell on these things; and I must needs say, I have little memory for them; but I wish ye could have heard my father's stories about the auld fights of the Mac-Dingawaies—that's the Bertrams that now is—wi' the Irish, and wi' the Highlanders, that came here in their berlings from Islay and Cantire—and how they went to the Holy Land-that is, to Jerusalem and Jericho, wi' a' their clan at their heels—they had better have gaen to Jamaica, like Sir Thomas Kittlecourt's uncle—and how they brought hame relics, like those that Catholics have, and a flag that's up yonder in the garret—if they had been casks of Muscavado, and puncheons of rum, it would have been better for the estate at this day—but there's little comparison between the auld keep at Kittlecourt and the castle o' Ellangowan—I doubt if the keep's forty feet of front—But ye make no breakfast, Mr. Mannering; ye're no eating your meat; allow me to recommend some of the kipper—It was John Hay that catcht it, Saturday was three weeks, down at the stream below Hempseed ford," etc., etc., etc.

The Laird, whose indignation had for some time kept him pretty steady to one topic, now launched forth into his usual roving style of conversation, which gave Mannering ample time to reflect upon the disadvantages attending the situation, which, an hour before, he had thought worthy of so much envy. Here was a country gentleman, whose most estimable quality seemed his perfect good nature, secretly fretting himself and murmuring against others, for causes which, compared with any real evil in life, must weigh like dust in the balance. But such is the equal distribution of Providence. To those who lie out of the road of great afflictions, are assigned petty vexations, which answer all the purpose of disturbing their serenity; and every reader must have observed, that neither natural apathy nor acquired philosophy can render country gentlemen insensible to the grievances which occur at elections, quarter-sessions, and meetings of trustees.

Curious to investigate the manners of the country Mannering took the advantage of a pause in good Mr. Bertram's string of stories, to inquire what Captain Hatteraick so earnestly wanted with the gipsy woman.

"Oh, to bless his ship, I suppose. You must know, Mr. Mannering, that these free-traders, whom the law calls smugglers, having no religion, make it all up in superstition; and they have as many spells, and charms, and nonsense—"

"Vanity and waur!" said the Dominie—"it is a trafficking with the Evil One. Spells, periapts, and charms, are of his device—choice arrows out of Apollyon's quiver."

"Hold your peace, Dominie—ye're speaking for ever" (by the way they were the first words the poor man had uttered that morning, excepting that he had said grace, and returned thanks)—"Mr. Mannering cannot get in a word for ye!—and so, Mr. Mannering, talking of astronomy, and spells, and these matters, have ye been so kind as to consider what we were speaking about last night?"

"I begin to think, Mr. Bertram, with your worthy friend here, that I have been rather jesting with edge-tools; and although neither you nor I, nor any sensible man, can put faith in the predictions of astrology, yet as it has sometimes happened that inquiries into futurity, undertaken in jest, have in their results produced serious and unpleasant effects both upon actions and characters, I really wish you would dispense with my replying to your question."

It was easy to see that this evasive answer only rendered the Laird's curiosity more uncontrollable. Mannering however, was determined in his own mind, not to expose the infant to the inconveniences which might have arisen from his being supposed the object of evil prediction. He therefore delivered the paper into Mr. Bertram's hand, and requested him to keep it for five years with the seal unbroken, until the month of November was expired. After that date had intervened, he left him at liberty to examine the writing, trusting that the first fatal period being then safely overpassed, no credit would be paid to its further contents. This Mr. Bertram was content to promise, and Mannering, to ensure his fidelity, hinted at misfortunes which would certainly take place if his injunctions were neglected. The rest of the day, which Mannering, by Mr. Bertram's invitation, spent at Ellangowan, passed over without anything remarkable; and on the morning of that which followed, the traveller mounted his palfrey, bade a courteous adieu to his hospitable landlord, and to his clerical attendant, repeated his good wishes for the prosperity of the family, and then, turning his horse's head towards England, disappeared from the sight of the inmates of Ellangowan. He must also disappear from that of our readers, for it is to another and later period of his life that the present narrative relates.

CHAPTER VI.

—Next, the justice, In fair round belly, with good capon
lined, With eyes severe, and beard of formal cut, Full of
wise saws, and modern instances: And so he plays his part.
—As You Like It.

When Mrs. Bertram of Ellangowan was able to hear the news of what had passed during her confinement, her apartment rung with all manner of gossiping respecting the handsome young student from Oxford, who had told such a fortune by the stars to the young Laird, "blessings on his dainty face." The form, accent, and manners, of the stranger, were expatiated upon. His horse, bridle, saddle, and stirrups, did not remain unnoticed. All this made a great impression upon the mind of Mrs. Bertram, for the good lady had no small store of superstition.

Her first employment, when she became capable of a little work, was to make a small velvet bag for the scheme of nativity which she had obtained from her husband. Her fingers itched to break the seal, but credulity proved stronger than curiosity; and she had the firmness to enclose it, in all its integrity, within two slips of parchment, which she sewed round it, to prevent its being chafed. The whole was then put into the velvet bag aforesaid, and hung as a charm round the neck of the infant, where his mother resolved it should remain until the period for the legitimate satisfaction of her curiosity should arrive.

The father also resolved to do his part by the child, in securing him a good education; and with the view that it should commence with the first dawnings of reason, Dominie Sampson was easily induced to renounce his public profession of parish schoolmaster, make his constant residence at the Place, and, in consideration of a sum not quite equal to the wages of a footman even at that time, to undertake to communicate to the future Laird of Ellangowan all the erudition which he had, and all the graces and accomplishments which—he had not indeed, but which he had never discovered that he wanted. In this arrangement, the Laird found also his private advantage; securing the constant benefit of a patient auditor, to whom he told his stories when they were alone, and at whose expense he could break a sly jest when he had company.

About four years after this time, a great commotion took place in the district where Ellangowan is situated.

Those who watched the signs of the times, had long been of opinion that a change of ministry was about to take place; and, at length, after a due proportion of hopes, fears, and delays, rumours from good authority, and bad authority, and no authority at all; after some clubs had drunk Up with this statesman, and others Down with him; after riding, and running, and posting and addressing, and counter-addressing, and proffers of lives and fortunes, the blow was at length struck, the administration of the day was dissolved, and parliament, as a natural consequence, was dissolved also.

Sir Thomas Kittlecourt, like other members in the same situation, posted down to his county, and met but an indifferent reception. He was a partisan of the old administration and the friends of the new had already set about an active canvass in behalf of John Featherhead, Esq., who kept the best hounds and hunters in the shire. Among others who joined the standard of revolt was Gilbert Glossin, writer in—, agent for the Laird of Ellangowan. This honest gentleman had either been refused some favour by the old member, or, what is as probable, he had got all that he had the most distant pretension to ask, and could only look to the other side for fresh advancement. Mr. Glossin had a vote upon Ellangowan's property; and he was now determined that his patron should have one also, there being no doubt which side Mr. Bertram would embrace in the contest. He easily persuaded Ellangowan, that it would be creditable to him to take the field at the head of as strong a party as possible; and immediately went to work, making votes, as every Scotch lawyer knows how, by splitting and subdividing the superiorities upon this ancient and once powerful barony. These were so extensive, that by dint of clipping and paring here, adding and eking there, and creating over-lords upon all the estate which Bertram held of the crown, they advanced, at the day of contest, at the head of ten as good men of parchment as ever took the oath of trust and possession. This strong reinforcement turned the dubious day of battle. The principal and his agent divided the honour; the reward fell to the latter exclusively. Mr. Gilbert Glossin was made clerk of the peace, and Godfrey Bertram had his name inserted in a new commission of justices, issued immediately upon the sitting of the parliament.

This had been the summit of Mr. Bertram's ambition; not that he liked either the trouble or the responsibility of the office, but he thought it was a dignity to which he was well entitled, and that it had been withheld from him by malice prepense. But there is an old and true Scotch proverb, "Fools should not have chapping sticks"; that is, weapons of offence. Mr. Bertram was no sooner possessed of the judicial authority which he had so much longed for, than he began to exercise it with more severity than mercy, and totally belied all the opinions which had hitherto been formed of his inert good nature. We have read somewhere of a justice of peace, who, on being nominated in the commission, wrote a letter to a bookseller for the statutes respecting his official duty, in the following orthography,—"Please send the ax relating to a gustus pease." No doubt, when this learned gentleman had possessed himself of the axe, he hewed the laws with it to some purpose. Mr. Bertram was not quite so ignorant of English grammar as his worshipful predecessor: but Augustus Pease himself could not have used more indiscriminately the weapon unwarily put into his hand.

In good earnest, he considered the commission with which he had been intrusted as a personal mark of favour from his sovereign, forgetting that he had formerly thought his being deprived of a privilege, or honour, common to those of his rank, was the result of mere party cabal. He commanded his trusty aide-de-camp, Dominie Sampson, to read aloud the commission; and at the first words, "The king has been pleased to appoint"—"Pleased!" he exclaimed, in a transport of gratitude; "honest gentleman! I'm sure he cannot be better pleased than I am."

Accordingly, unwilling to confine his gratitude to mere feelings, or verbal expressions, he gave full current to the new-born zeal of office, and endeavoured to express his sense of the honour conferred upon him, by an unmitigated activity in the discharge of his duty. New brooms, it is said, sweep clean; and I myself can bear witness, that, on the arrival of a new housemaid, the ancient, hereditary, and domestic spiders, who have spun their webs over the lower division of my book-shelves (consisting chiefly of law and divinity) during the peaceful reign of her predecessor, fly at full speed before the probationary inroads of the new mercenary. Even so the Laird of Ellangowan ruthlessly commenced his magisterial reform, at the expense of various established and superannuated pickers and stealers, who had been his neighbours for half a century. He wrought his miracles like a second Duke Humphrey; and by the influence of the beadle's rod, caused the lame to walk, the blind to see, and the palsied to labour. He detected poachers, black-fishers, orchard-breakers, and pigeon-shooters; had the applause of the bench for his reward, and the public credit of an active magistrate.

All this good had its rateable proportion of evil. Even an admitted nuisance, of ancient standing, should not be abated without some caution. The zeal of our worthy friend now involved in great distress sundry personages whose idle and mendicant habits his own lochesse had contributed to foster, until these habits had become irreclaimable, or whose real incapacity for exertion rendered them fit objects, in their own phrase, for the charity of all well-disposed Christians. The "long-remembered beggar," who for twenty years had made his regular rounds within the neighbourhood, received rather as an humble friend than as an object of charity, was sent to the neighbouring workhouse. The decrepit dame, who travelled round the parish upon a hand-barrow, circulating from house to house like a bad shilling, which every one is in haste to pass to his neighbour; she, who used to call for her bearers as loud, or louder, than a traveller demands post-horses, even she shared the same disastrous fate. The "daft Jock," who, half knave, half idiot, had been the sport of each succeeding race of village children for a good part of a century, was remitted to the county bridewell, where, secluded from free air and sunshine, the only advantages he was capable of enjoying, he pined and died in the course of six months. The old sailor, who had so long rejoiced the smoky rafters of every kitchen in the country, by singing Captain Ward, and Bold Admiral Benbow, was banished from the district for no better reason, than that he was supposed to speak with a strong Irish accent. Even the annual rounds of the pedlar were abolished by the justice, in his hasty zeal for the administration of rural police.

These things did not pass without notice and censure. We are not made of wood or stone, and the things which connect themselves with our hearts and habits cannot, like bark or lichen, be rent away without our missing them. The farmer's dame lacked her usual share of intelligence, perhaps also the self-applause which she had felt while distributing the awmous (alms), in shape of a gowpen (handful) of oatmeal, to the mendicant who brought the news. The cottage felt inconvenience from interruption of the petty trade carried on by the itinerant dealers. The children lacked their supply of sugar-plums and toys; the young women wanted pins, ribbons, combs, and ballads; and the old could no longer barter their eggs for salt, snuff, and tobacco. All these circumstances brought the busy Laird of Ellangowan into discredit, which was the more general on account of his former popularity. Even his lineage was brought up in judgment against him. They thought "naething of what the like of Greenside, or Burnville, or Viewforth, might do, that were strangers in the country; but Ellangowan! that had been a name amang them since the mirk Monanday, and lang before—him to be grinding the puir at that rate!—They ca'd his grandfather the Wicked Laird; but, though he was whiles fractious aneuch, when he got into roving company" and had ta'en the drap drink, he would have scorned to gang on at this gate. Na, na, the muckle chumlay in the Auld Place reeked like a killogie [*Lime-kiln] in his time, and there were as mony puir folk riving at the banes in the court, and about the door, as there were gentles in the ha'. And the leddy, on ilka Christmas night as it came round, gae twelve siller pennies to ilka puir body about, in honour of the twelve apostles like. They were fond to ca' it papistrie; but I think our great folk might take a lesson frae the papists whiles. They gie another sort o' help to puir folk than just dinging down a saxpence in the brod [*Collection-plate] on the Sabbath, and kilting, and scourging, and drumming them a' the sax days o' the week besides."

Such was the gossip over the good twopenny in every alehouse within three or four miles of Ellangowan, that being about the diameter of the orbit in which our friend Godfrey Bertram, Esq., J.P., must be considered as the principal luminary. Still greater scope was given to evil tongues by the removal of a colony of gipsies, with one of whom our reader is somewhat acquainted, and who had for a great many years enjoyed their chief settlement upon the estate of Ellangowan.

CHAPTER VII.

Come, princes of the ragged regiment, You of the blood!
Prigg, my most upright lord, And these, what name or title
e'er they bear, Jarkman, or Patrico, Cranke or
Clapper-dudgeon, Frater or Abram-man—I speak of all.—
Beggar's Bush.

ALTHOUGH the character of those gipsy tribes which formerly inundated most of the nations of Europe, and which in some degree still subsist among them as a distinct people, is generally understood, the reader will pardon my saying a few words respecting their situation in Scotland.

It is well known that the gipsies were, at an early period, acknowledged as a separate and independent race by one of the Scottish monarchs, and that they were less favourably distinguished by a subsequent law, which rendered the character of gipsy equal, in the judicial balance, to that of common and habitual thief, and prescribed his punishment accordingly. Notwithstanding the severity of this and other statutes, the fraternity prospered amid the distresses of the country, and received large accessions from among those whom famine, oppression, or the sword of war, had deprived of the ordinary means of subsistence. They lost, in a great measure, by this intermixture, the national character of Egyptians, and became a mingled race, having all the idleness and predatory habits of their Eastern ancestors, with a ferocity which they probably borrowed from the men of the north who joined their society. They travelled in different bands, and had rules among themselves, by which each tribe was confined to its own district. The slightest invasion of the precincts which had been assigned to another tribe produced desperate skirmishes, in which there was often much blood shed.

The patriotic Fletcher of Saltoun drew a picture of these banditti about a century ago, which my readers will peruse with astonishment.

"There are at this day in Scotland (besides a great many poor families very meanly provided for by the church boxes, with others, who, by living on bad food, fall into various diseases) two hundred thousand people begging from door to door. These are not only no way advantageous, but a very grievous burden to so poor a country. And though the number of them be perhaps double to what it was formerly, by reason of this present great distress, yet in all times there have been about one hundred thousand of those vagabonds, who have lived without any regard or subjection either to the laws of the land, or even those of God and nature; . . . No magistrate could ever discover or be informed, which way one in a hundred of these wretches died, or that ever they were baptized. Many murders have been discovered among them; and they are not only a most unspeakable oppression to poor tenants (who, if they give not bread, or some kind of provision to perhaps forty such villains in one day, are sure to be insulted. by them), but they rob many poor people who live in houses distant from any neighbourhood. In years of plenty many thousands of them meet together in the mountains, where they feast and riot for many days; and at country weddings, markets, burials, and other the like public occasions, they are to be seen, both man and woman, perpetually drunk, cursing, blaspheming, and fighting together."

Notwithstanding the deplorable picture presented in this extract, and which Fletcher himself, though the energetic and eloquent friend of freedom, saw no better mode of correcting than by introducing a system of domestic slavery, the progress of time, and increase both of the means of life and of the power of the laws, gradually reduced this dreadful evil within more narrow bounds. The tribes of gipsies, jockies, or cairds,—for by all these denominations such banditti were known,—became few in number, and many were entirely rooted out. Still, however, a sufficient number remained to give occasional alarm and constant vexation. Some rude handicrafts were entirely resigned to these itinerants, particularly the art of trencher-making, of manufacturing horn-spoons, and the whole mystery of the tinker. To these they added a petty trade in the coarse sorts of earthenware. Such were their ostensible means of livelihood. Each tribe had usually some fixed place of rendezvous, which they occasionally occupied. and considered as their standing camp, and in the vicinity of which they generally abstained from depredation. They had even talents and accomplishments, which made them occasionally useful and entertaining. Many cultivated music with success; and the favourite fiddler or piper of a district was often to be found in a gipsy town. They understood all out-of-door sports, especially otter-hunting, fishing, or finding game. They bred the best and boldest terriers, and sometimes had good pointers for sale. In winter, the women told fortunes, the men showed tricks of legerdemain; and these accomplishments often helped to while away a weary or stormy evening in the circle of the "farmer's ha'." The wildness of their character, and the indomitable pride with which they despised all regular labour, commanded a certain awe, which was not diminished by the consideration, that these strollers were a vindictive race, and were restrained by no check, either of fear or conscience, from taking desperate vengeance upon those who had offended them. These tribes were, in short, the Parias of Scotland, living like wild Indians among European settlers, and, like them, judged of rather by their own customs, habits, and opinions, than as if they had been members of the civilised part of the community. Some hordes of them yet remain, chiefly in such situations as afford a ready escape either into a waste country, or into another jurisdiction. Nor are the features of their character much softened. Their numbers, however, are so greatly diminished, that, instead of one hundred thousand, as calculated by Fletcher, it would now perhaps be impossible to collect above five hundred throughout all Scotland.

A tribe of these itinerants, to whom Meg Merrilies appertained, had long been as stationary as their habits permitted, in a glen upon the estate of Ellangowan. They had there erected a few huts, which they denominated their "city of refuge," and where, when not absent on excursions, they harboured unmolested, as the crows that roosted in the old ash-trees around them. They had been such long occupants, that they were considered in some degree as proprietors of the wretched shealings which they inhabited. This protection they were said anciently to have repaid, by service to the laird in war, or, more frequently, by infesting or plundering the lands of those neighbouring barons with whom he chanced to be at feud. Latterly, their services were of a more pacific nature. The women spun mittens for the lady, and knitted boot-hose for the laird, which were annually presented at Christmas with great form. The aged sibyls blessed the bridal bed of the laird when he married, and the cradle of the heir when born. The men repaired her ladyship's cracked china, and assisted the laird in his sporting parties, wormed his dogs, and cut the ears of his terrier puppies. The children gathered nuts in the woods, and cranberries in the moss, and mushrooms on the pastures, for tribute to the Place. These acts of voluntary service, and acknowledgments of dependence, were rewarded by protection on some occasions, connivance on others, and broken victuals, ale, and brandy, when circumstances called for a display of generosity; and this mutual intercourse of good offices, which had been carried on for at least two centuries, rendered the inhabitants of Derncleugh a kind of privileged retainers upon the estate of Ellangowan. "The knaves" were the Laird's "exceeding good friends"; and he would have deemed himself very ill used, if his countenance could not now and then have borne them out against the law of the country and the local magistrate. But this friendly union was soon to be dissolved.

The community of Derncleugh, who cared for no rogues but their own, were wholly without alarm at the severity of the justice's proceedings towards other itinerants. They had no doubt that he determined to suffer no mendicants or strollers in the country, but what resided on his own property, and practised their trade by his immediate permission, implied or expressed. Nor was Mr. Bertram in a hurry to exert his newly-acquired authority at the expense of these old settlers. But he was driven on by circumstances.

19

At the quarter-sessions, our new justice was publicly upbraided by a gentleman of the opposite party in county politics, that, while he affected a great zeal for the public police, and seemed ambitious of the fame of an active magistrate, he fostered a tribe of the greatest rogues in the country, and permitted them to harbour within a mile of the house of Ellangowan. To this there was no reply, for the fact was too evident and well known. The Laird digested the taunt as he best could, and in his way home amused himself with speculations on the easiest method of ridding himself of these vagrants, who brought a stain upon his fair fame as a magistrate. Just as he had resolved to take the first opportunity of quarrelling with the Parias of Derncleugh, a cause of provocation presented itself.

Since our friend's advancement to be a conservator of the peace, he had caused the gate at the head of his avenue, which formerly, having only one hinge remained at all times hospitably open—he had caused this gate, I say, to be newly hung and handsomely painted. He had also shut up with paling, curiously twisted with furze, certain holes in tie fences adjoining, through which the gipsy boys used to scramble into the plantations to gather birds' nests, the seniors of the village to make a short cut from one point to another, and the lads and lasses for evening rendezvous—all without offence taken, or leave asked. But these halcyon days were now to have an end, and a minatory inscription on one side of the gate intimated "prosecution according to law" (the painter had spelt it persecution—l'un vaut bien l'autre) to all who should be found trespassing on these enclosures. On the other side, for uniformity's sake, was a precautionary annunciation of spring-guns and man-traps of such formidable powers, that, said the rubrick, with an emphatic nota bene—"if a man goes in, they will break a horse's leg."

In defiance of these threats, six well-grown gipsy boys and girls were riding cock-horse upon the new gate, and plaiting May-flowers, which it was but too evident had been gathered within the forbidden precincts. With as much anger as he was capable of feeling, or perhaps of assuming, the Laird commanded them to descend;—they paid no attention to his mandate: he then began to pull them down one after another;—they resisted, passively at least, each sturdy bronzed varlet making himself as heavy as he could, or climbing up as fast as he was dismounted.

The Laird then called in the assistance of his servant, a surly fellow, who had immediate recourse to his horse-whip. A few lashes sent the party a-scampering; and thus commenced the first breach of the peace between the house of Ellangowan and the Gipsies of Derncleugh.

The latter could not for some time imagine that the war was real; until they found that their children were horse-whipped by the grieve when found trespassing; that their asses were poinded by the ground-officer when left in the plantations, or even when turned to graze by the roadside, against the provision of the turnpike acts; that the constable began to make curious inquiries into their made of gaining a livelihood, and expressed his surprise that the men should sleep in the hovels all day, and be abroad the greater part of the night.

When matters came to this point, the gipsies, without scruple, entered upon measures of retaliation. Ellangowan's hen-roosts were plundered, his linen stolen from the lines or bleaching ground, his fishings poached, his dogs kidnapped, his growing trees cut or barked. Much petty mischief was done, and some evidently for the mischief's sake. On the other hand, warrants went forth, without mercy, to pursue, search for, take, and apprehend; and, notwithstanding their dexterity, one or two of the depredators were unable to avoid conviction. One, a stout young fellow, who sometimes had gone to sea a-fishing, was handed over to the Captain of the impress service at D—; two children were soundly flogged, and one Egyptian matron sent to the house of correction.

Still, however, the gipsies made no motion to leave the spot which they had so long inhabited, and Mr. Bertram felt an unwillingness to deprive them of their ancient "city of refuge"; so that the petty warfare we have noticed continued for several months, without increase or abatement of hostilities on either side.

CHAPTER VIII.

So the red Indian, by Ontario's side, Nursed hardy on the
brindled panther's hide, As fades his swarthy race, with
anguish sees The white man's cottage rise beneath the trees
He leaves the shelter of his native wood, He leaves the
murmur of Ohio's flood, And forward rushing in indignant
grief, Where never foot has trod the fallen leaf, He bends
his course where twilight reigns sublime, O'er forests
silent since the birth of
time,
Scenes of Infancy.

In tracing the rise and progress of the Scottish Maroon war, we must not omit to mention that years had rolled on, and that little Harry Bertram, one of the hardiest and most lively children that ever made a sword and grenadier's cap of rushes, now approached his fifth revolving birthday. A hardihood of disposition, which early developed itself, made him already a little wanderer; he was well acquainted with every patch of lea ground and dingle around Ellangowan, and could tell in his broken language upon what baulks [* Uncultivated places] grew the bonniest flowers, and what copse had the ripest nuts. He repeatedly terrified his attendants by clambering about the ruins of the old castle, and had more than once made a stolen excursion as far as the gipsy hamlet.

On these occasions he was generally brought back by Meg Merrilies, who, though she could not be prevailed upon to enter the Place of Ellangowan after her nephew had been given up to the pressgang, did not apparently extend her resentment to the child. On the contrary, she often contrived to waylay him in his walks, sing him a gipsy song, give him a ride upon her jackass, and thrust into his pocket a piece of gingerbread or red-cheeked apple. This woman's ancient attachment to the family, repelled and checked in every other direction, seemed to rejoice in having some object on which it could yet repose and expand itself. She prophesied a hundred times, "that young Mr. Harry would be the pride o' the family, and that there hadna been sic a sprout frae the auld aik since the death of Arthur Mac-Dingawaie, that was killed in the battle o' the Bloody Bay; as for the present stick, it was good for naething but firewood." On one occasion, when the child was ill, she lay all night below the window, chanting a rhyme which she believed sovereign as a febrifuge, and could neither be prevailed upon to enter the house, nor to leave the station she had chosen, till she was informed that the crisis was over.

The affection of this woman became matter of suspicion, not indeed to the Laird, who was never hasty in suspecting evil, but to his wife, who had indifferent health and poor spirits. She was now far advanced in a second pregnancy, and, as she could not walk abroad herself, and the woman who attended upon Harry was young and thoughtless, she prayed Dominie Sampson to undertake the task of watching the boy in his rambles, when he should not be otherwise accompanied. The Dominie loved his young charge, and was enraptured with his own success, in having already brought him so far in his learning as to spell words of three syllables. The idea of this early prodigy of erudition being carried off by the gipsies, like a second Adam Smith, [* The father of Economical Philosophy was, when a child, carried off by gipsies, and remained some hours in their possession.] was not to be tolerated; and accordingly, though the charge was contrary to all his habits of life, he readily undertook it, and might be seen stalling about with a mathematical problem in his head, and his eye upon a child of five years old, whose rambles led him into a hundred awkward situations. Twice was the Dominie chased by a cross-grained cow, once he fell into the brook crossing at the stepping-stones, and another time was bogged up to the middle in the slough of Lochend, in attempting to gather a water-lily for the young Laird. It was the opinion of the village matrons who relieved Sampson on the latter occasion, "that the Laird might as weel trust the care o' his bairn to a potato bogle"; but the good Dominie bore all his disasters with gravity and serenity equally imperturbable. "Pro-di-gi-ous!" was the only ejaculation they ever extorted from the much-enduring man.

The Laird had, by this time, determined to make root-and-branch work with the Maroons of Derncleugh. The old servants shook their heads at his proposal, and even Dominie Sampson ventured upon an indirect remonstrance. As, however, it was couched in the oracular phrase, "Ne moveas Camerinam," neither the allusion, nor the language in which it was expressed, were calculated for Mr. Bertram's edification, and matters proceeded against the gipsies in form of law. Every door in the hamlet was chalked by the ground-officer, in token of a formal warning to remove at next term. Still, however, they showed no symptoms either of submission or of compliance. At length the term-day, the fatal Martinmas, arrived, and violent measures of ejection were resorted to. A strong posse of peace-officers, sufficient to render all resistance vain, charged the inhabitants to depart by noon; and, as they did not obey, the officers, in terms of the warrant, proceeded to unroof the cottages, and pull down the wretched doors and windows, —a summary and effectual mode of ejection still practised in some remote parts of Scotland, when a tenant proves refractory. The gipsies, for a time, beheld the work of destruction in sullen silence and inactivity; then set about saddling and loading their asses, and making preparations for their departure. These were soon accomplished, where all had the habits of wandering Tartars; and they set forth on their journey to seek new settlements, where their patrons should neither be of the quorum, nor custos rotulorum.

Certain qualms of feeling had deterred Ellangowan from attending in person to see his tenants expelled. He left the executive part of the business to the officers of the law, under the immediate direction of Frank Kennedy, a supervisor, or riding-officer, belonging to the excise, who had of late become intimate at the Place, and of whom we shall have more to say in the next chapter. Mr. Bertram himself chose that day to make a visit to a friend at some distance. But it so happened, notwithstanding his precautions, that he could not avoid meeting his late tenants during their retreat from his property.

It was in a hollow way, near the top of a steep ascent, upon the verge of the Ellangowan estate, that Mr. Bertram met the gipsy procession. Four or five men formed the advanced guard, wrapped in long loose greatcoats that hid their tall slender figures, as the large slouched hats, drawn over their brows, concealed their wild features, dark eyes, and swarthy faces. Two of them carried long fowling-pieces, one wore a broadsword without a sheath, and all had the Highland dirk, though they did not wear that weapon openly or ostentatiously. Behind them followed the train of laden asses, and small carts or tumblers, as they were called in that country, on which were laid the decrepit and the helpless, the aged and infant part of the exiled community. The women in their red cloaks and straw hats, the elder children with bare heads and bare feet, and almost naked bodies, had the immediate care of the little caravan. The road was narrow, running between two broken banks of sand, and Mr. Bertram's servant rode forward, smacking his whip with an air of authority, and motioning to the drivers to allow free passage to their betters. His signal was unattended to. He then called to the men who lounged idly on before, "Stand to your beasts' heads, and make room for the Laird to pass."

"He shall have his share of the road," answered a male gipsy from under his slouched and large-brimmed hat, and without raising his face, "and he shall have nae mair; the highway is as free to our cuddies as to his gelding."

The tone of the man being sulky, and even menacing, Mr. Bertram thought it best to put his dignity in his pocket, and pass by the procession quietly, on such space as they chose to leave for his accommodation, which was narrow enough. To cover with an appearance of indifference his feeling of the want of respect with which he was treated, he addressed one of the men, as he passed him without any show of greeting, salute, or recognition,—"Giles Baillie," he said, "have you heard that your son Gabriel is well?" (The question respected the young man who had been pressed.)

"If I had heard otherwise," said the old man, looking up with a stern and menacing countenance, "you should have heard of it too." And he plodded on his way, tarrying no further question. [*This anecdote is a literal fact.] When the Laird had pressed on with difficulty among a crowd of familiar faces, which had on all former occasions marked his approach with the reverence due to that of a superior being, but in which he now only read hatred and contempt, and had got clear of the throng, he could not help turning his horse, and looking back to mark the progress of their march. The group would have been an excellent subject for the pencil of Calotte. The van had already reached a small and stunted thicket, which was at the bottom of the hill, and which gradually hid the line of march until the last stragglers disappeared.

His sensations were bitter enough. The race, it is true, which he had thus summarily dismissed from their ancient place of refuge, was idle and vicious; but had he endeavoured to render them otherwise? They were not more irregular characters now, than they had been while they were admitted to consider themselves as a sort of subordinate dependants of his family; and ought the mere circumstance of his becoming a magistrate to have made at once such a change in his conduct towards them? Some means of reformation ought at least to have been tried, before sending seven families at once upon the wide world, and depriving them of a degree of countenance, which withheld them at least from atrocious guilt. There was also a natural yearning of heart on parting with so many known and familiar faces; and to this feeling Godfrey Bertram was peculiarly accessible, from the limited qualities of his mind, which sought its principal amusements among the petty objects around him. As he was about to turn his horse's head to pursue his journey, Meg Merrilies, who lagged behind the troop, unexpectedly presented herself.

She was standing upon one of those high precipitous banks, which, as we before noticed, overhung the road; so that she was placed considerably higher than Ellangowan, even though he was on horseback; and her tall figure, relieved against the clear blue sky, seemed almost of supernatural stature. We have noticed, that there was in her general attire, or rather in her mode of adjusting it, somewhat of a foreign costume, artfully, adopted perhaps for the purpose of adding to the effect of her spells and predictions, or perhaps from some traditional notions respecting the dress of her ancestors. On this occasion, she had a large piece of red cotton cloth rolled about her head in the form of a turban, from beneath which her dark eyes flashed with uncommon lustre. Her long and tangled black hair fell in elf-locks from the folds of this singular head-gear. Her attitude was that of a sibyl in frenzy, and she stretched out, in her right hand, a sapling bough which seemed just pulled.

"I'll be d-d," said the groom, "if she has not been cutting the young ashes in the Dukit park!"—The Laird made no answer, but continued to look at the figure which was thus perched above his path.

"Ride your ways," said the gipsy, "ride your ways, Laird of Ellangowan—ride your ways, Godfrey Bertram!—This day have ye quenched seven smoking hearths—see if the fire in your ain parlour burn the blyther for that. Ye have riven the back off seven cottar houses—look if your ain roof-tree stand the faster. Ye may stable your stirks in the shealings at Derncleugh—see that the hare does not couch on the hearth-stone at Ellangowan.—Ride your ways, Godfrey Bertram—what do ye glower after our folk for?—There's thirty hearts there, that wad hae wanted bread ere ye had wanted sunkets, [*Delicacies] and spent their lifeblood ere ye had scratched your finger. Yes—there's thirty yonder, from the auld wife of a hundred to the babe that was born last week, that ye have turned out o' their bits o' bields, to sleep with the tod and the black-cock in the muirs!—Ride your ways, Ellangowan.—Our bairns are hinging at our weary backs—look that your braw cradle at hame be the fairer spread up—not that I am wishing ill to little Harry, or to the babe that's yet to be born—God forbid—and make them kind to the poor, and better folk than their father! And now, ride e'en your ways; for these are the last words ye'll ever hear Meg Merrilies speak, and this is the last reise that I'll ever cut in the bonnie woods of Ellangowan."

So saying, she broke the sapling she held in her hand, and flung it into the road Margaret of Anjou, bestowing on her triumphant foes her keen-edged malediction, could not have turned from them with a gesture more proudly contemptuous. The Laird was clearing his voice to speak, and thrusting his hand in his pocket to find a half-crown; the gipsy waited neither for his reply nor his donation, but strode down the hill to overtake the caravan.

Ellangowan rode pensively home; and it was remarkable that he did not mention this interview to any of his family. The groom was not so reserved. He told the story at great length to a full audience in the kitchen, and concluded by swearing, that if ever the devil spoke by the mouth of a woman, he had spoken by that of Meg Merrilies that blessed day.

CHAPTER IX.

Paint Scotland greeting ower her thrissle,
Her mutchkin stoup as toom's a whistle,
And d-n'd excisemen in a bustle,
   Seizing a stell;
Triumphant crushin't like a mussell,
   Or lampit shell.
   Burns.

During the period of Mr. Bertram's active magistracy, he did not forget the affairs of the revenue. Smuggling, for which the Isle of Man then afforded peculiar facilities, was general, or rather universal, all along the south-western coast of Scotland. Almost all the common people were engaged in these practices; the gentry connived at them, and the officers of the revenue were frequently discountenanced in the exercise of their duty, by those who should have protected them.

There was, at this period, employed as a riding-officer, or supervisor, in that part of the country, a certain Francis Kennedy, already named in our narrative; a stout, resolute, and active man, who had made seizures to a great amount, and was proportionally hated by those who had an interest in the fair Trade, as they called the pursuit of these contraband adventurers. This person was natural son to a gentleman of good family, owing to which circumstance, and to his being of a jolly convivial disposition, and singing a good song, he was admitted to the occasional society of the gentlemen of the country, and was a member of several of their clubs for practising athletic games, at which he was particularly expert.

At Ellangowan, Kennedy was a frequent and always an acceptable guest. His vivacity relieved Mr. Bertram of the trouble of thought, and the labour which it cost him to support a detailed communication of ideas; while the daring and dangerous exploits which he had undertaken in the discharge of his office, formed excellent conversation. To all these revenue adventures did the Laird of Ellangowan seriously incline, and the amusement which he derived from Kennedy's society, formed an excellent reason for countenancing and assisting the narrator in the execution of his invidious and hazardous duty.

"Frank Kennedy," he said, "was a gentleman, though on the wrang side of the blanket—he was connected with the family of Ellangowan through the house of Glengubble. The last Laird of Glengubble would have brought the estate into the Ellangowan line; but happening to go to Harrigate, he there met with Miss Jean Hadaway—by the bye, the Green Dragon at Harrigate is the best house of the twa—but for Frank Kennedy, he's in one sense a gentleman born, and it's a shame not to support him against these blackguard smugglers."

After this league had taken place between judgment and execution, it chanced that Captain Dirk Hatteraick had landed a cargo of spirits, and other contraband goods, upon the beach not far from Ellangowan, and, confiding in the indifference with which the Laird had formerly regarded similar infractions of the law, he was neither very anxious to conceal nor to expedite the transaction. The consequence was, that Mr. Frank Kennedy, armed with a warrant from Ellangowan, and supported by some of the Laird's people who knew the country, and by a party of military, poured down upon the kegs, bates, and bags, and after a desperate affray, in which severe wounds were given and received, succeeded in clapping the broad arrow upon the articles, and bearing them off in triumph to the next custom-house. Dirk Hatteraick vowed, in Dutch, German, and English, a deep and full revenge, both against the gauger and his abettors; and all who knew him thought it likely he would keep his word.

A few days after the departure of the gipsy tribe, Mr. Bertram asked his lady one morning at breakfast, whether this was not little Harry's birthday?

"Five years auld exactly, this blessed day," answered the lady; "so we may look into the English gentleman's paper."

Mr. Bertram liked to show his authority in trifles. "No, my dear, not till to-morrow. The last time I was at quarter-sessions, the sheriff told us, that dies—that dies inceptus—in short, you don't understand Latin, but it means that a term-day is not begun till it's ended."

"That sounds like nonsense, my dear."

"May be so, my dear; but it may be very good law for all that. I am sure, speaking of term-days, I wish, as Frank Kennedy says, that Whitsunday would kill Martinmas and be hanged for the murder—for there I have got a letter about that interest of Jenny Gairns's, and deil a tenant's been at the Place yet wi' a boddle [*A small copper coin] of rent,—nor will not till Candlemas—but, speaking of Frank Kennedy, I dare say he'll be here the day, for he was away round to Wigton to warn a king's ship that's lying in the bay about Dirk Hatteraick's lugger being on the coast again, and he'll be back this day; so we'll have a bottle of claret, and drink little Harry's health."

"I wish," replied the lady, "Frank Kennedy would let Dirk Hatteraick alane. What needs he make himself mair busy than other folk? Cannot he sing his sang, and take his drink, and draw his salary, like Collector Snail, honest man, that never fashes [*Troubles] onybody? And I wonder at you, Laird, for meddling and making—Did we ever want to send for tea or brandy frae the Borough-town, when Dirk Hatteraick used to come quietly into the bay?"

"Mrs. Bertram, you know nothing of these matters. Do you think it becomes a magistrate to let his own house be made a receptacle for smuggled goods? Frank Kennedy will show you the penalties in the Act, and ye ken yourself they used to put their run goods into the Auld Place of Ellangowan up by there."

"Oh, dear, Mr. Bertram, and what the waur were the wa's and the vault o' the old castle for having a whin kegs o' brandy in them at an orra time? I am sure ye were not obliged to ken onything about it; and what the waur was the King that the lairds here got a soup o' drink, and the ladies their drap o' tea, at a reasonable rate?—it's a shame to them to pit such taxes on them!—and was na I much the better of these Flanders head and pinners, [*A head-dress with lappets] that Dirk Hatteraick sent me a' the way from Antwerp? It will be lang or the King sends me onything, or Frank Kennedy either. And then ye would quarrel with these gipsies too! I expect every day to hear the barn-yard's in a low." [*A flame]

"I tell you once more, my dear, you don't understand these things—and there's Frank Kennedy, coming galloping up the avenue."

"Aweel! aweel! Ellangowan," said the lady, raising her voice as the Laird left the room, "I wish ye may understand them yourself, that's a'!"

From this nuptial dialogue the Laird joyfully escaped to meet his faithful friend, Mr. Kennedy who arrived in high spirits. "For the love of life, Ellangowan," he said, "get up to the castle! you'll see that old fox Dirk Hatteraick, and his Majesty's hounds in full cry after him." "So saying, he flung his horse's bridle to a boy, and ran up the ascent to the old castle, followed by the Laird, and indeed by several others of the family, alarmed by the sound of guns from the sea, now distinctly heard.

On gaining that part of the ruins which commanded the most extensive outlook, they saw a lugger, with all her canvas crowded, standing across the bay, closely pursued by a sloop of war, that kept firing upon the chase from her bows, which the lugger returned with her stern-chasers. "They're but at long bowls yet," cried Kennedy, in great exultation, "but they will be closer by and by.—D-n him, he's starting his cargo! I see the good Nantz pitching overboard, keg after keg!—that's a d-d ungenteel thing of Mr. Hatteraick, as I shall let him know by and by.—Now, now! they've got the wind of him!—that's it, that's it!—Hark to him, hark to him! Now, my dogs! now, my dogs!—hark to Ranger, hark!"

"I think," said the old gardener to one of the maids, "the gauger's fie;" by which word the common people express those violent spirits which they think a presage of death.

Meantime the chase continued. The lugger, being piloted with great ability, and using every nautical shift to make her escape, had now reached, and was about to double, the headland which formed the extreme point of land on the left side of the bay, when a ball having hit the yard in the slings, the main-sail fell upon the deck. The consequence of this accident appeared inevitable, but could not be seen by the spectators; for the vessel, which had just doubled the headland, lost steerage, and fell out of their sight behind the promontory. The sloop of war crowded all sail to pursue, but she had stood too close upon the cape, so that they were obliged to wear the vessel for fear of going ashore, and to make a large tack back into the bay, in order to recover sea-room enough to double the headland.

"They'll lose her, by—, cargo and lugger, one or both," said Kennedy; "I must gallop away to the Point of Warroch (this was the headland so often mentioned), and make them a signal where she has drifted to on the other side. Good-bye for an hour, Ellangowan—get out the gallon punchbowl and plenty of lemons. I'll stand for the French article by the time I come back, and we'll drink the young Laird's health in a bowl that would swim the Collector's yawl." So saying, he mounted his horse, and galloped off.

About a mile from the house, and upon the verge of the woods, which, as we have said, covered a promontory terminating in the cape called the Point of Warroch, Kennedy met young Harry Bertram, attended by his tutor, Dominie Sampson. He had often promised the child a ride upon his galloway; and, from singing, dancing, and playing Punch for his amusement, was a particular favourite. He no sooner came scampering up the path, than the boy loudly claimed his promise; and Kennedy, who saw no risk in indulging him, and wished to tease the Dominie, in whose visage he read a remonstrance, caught up Harry from the ground, placed him before him, and continued his route; Sampson's "Peradventure, Master Kennedy—" being lost in the clatter of his horse's feet. The pedagogue hesitated a moment whether he should go after them; but Kennedy being a person in full confidence of the family, and with whom he himself had no delight in associating, "being that he was addicted unto profane and scurrilous jests," he continued his own walk at his own pace, till he reached the Place of Ellangowan.

The spectators from the ruined walls of the castle were still watching the sloop of war, which at length, but not without the loss of considerable time, recovered sea-room enough to weather the Point of Warroch, and was lost to their sight behind that wooded promontory. Some time afterwards the discharges of several cannon were heard at a distance, and, after an interval, a still louder explosion, as of a vessel blown up, and a cloud of smoke rose above the trees, and mingled with the blue sky. All then separated on their different occasions, auguring variously upon the fate of the smuggler, but the majority insisting that her capture was inevitable, if she had not already gone to the bottom.

"It is near our dinner-time, my dear," said Mrs. Bertram to her husband; "will it be lang before Mr. Kennedy comes back?"

"I expect him every moment, my dear," said the Laird; "perhaps he is bringing some of the officers of the sloop with him."

"My stars, Mr. Bertram! why did not ye tell me this before, that we might have had the large round table?—and then, they're a' tired o' saut meat, and, to tell you the plain truth, a rump o' beef is the best part of your dinner—and then I wad have put on another gown, and ye wadna have been the waur o' a clean neckcloth yourself—But ye delight in surprising and hurrying one—I am sure I am no to haud out for ever against this sort of going on—But when folk's missed, then they are moaned."

23

"Pshaw, pshaw! deuce take the beef, and the gown, and table, and the neckcloth!—we shall doall very well.—Where's the Dominie, John?—(to a servant who was busy about the table)—where's the Dominie and little Harry?"

"Mr. Sampson's been at hame these twa hours and mair, but I dinna think Mr. Harry cam hame wi' him."

"Not come hame wi' him?" said the lady; "desire Mr. Sampson to step this way directly."

"Mr. Sampson," said she, upon his entrance, "is it not the most extraordinary tiring in this world wide, that you, that have free up-putting—bed, board, and washing—and twelve pounds sterling a year, just to look after that boy, should let him out of your sight for twa or three hours?"

Sampson made a bow of humble acknowledgment at each pause which the angry lady made in her enumeration of the advantages of his situation, in order to give more weight to her remonstrance, and then, in words which we will not do him the injustice to imitate, told how Mr. Francis Kennedy "had assumed spontaneously the charge of Master Harry, in despite of his remonstrances in the contrary."

"I am very little obliged to Mr. Francis Kennedy for his pains," said the lady peevishly; "suppose he lets the boy drop from his horse, and lames him? or suppose one of the cannons comes ashore and kills him?—or suppose—"

"Or suppose, my dear," said Ellangowan, "what is much more likely than anything else, that they have gone aboard the sloop or the prize, and are to come round the Point with the tide?"

"And then they may be drowned," said the lady.

"Verily," said Sampson, "I thought M r. Kennedy had returned an hour since—Of a surety I deemed I heard his horse's feet."

"That," said John, with a broad grin, "was Grizzel chasing the humble-cow [A cow without horns] out of the close."

Sampson coloured up to the eyes—not at the implied taunt, which he would never have discovered, or resented if he had, but at some idea which crossed his own mind. "I have been in an error," he said; "of a surety I should have tarried for the babe." So saying, he snatched his bone-headed cane and hat, and hurried away towards Warroch wood, faster than he was ever known to walk before, or after.

The Laird lingered some time, debating the point with the lady. At length, he saw the sloop of war again make her appearance; but, without approaching the shore, she stood away to the westward with all her sails set, and was soon out of sight. The lady's state of timorous and fretful apprehension was so habitual, that her fears went for nothing with her lord and master; but an appearance of disturbance and anxiety among the servants now excited his alarm, especially, when he was called out of the room, and told in private that Mr. Kennedy's horse had come to the stable door alone, with the saddle turned round below its belly, and the reins of the bridle broken; and that a farmer had informed them in passing, that there was a smuggling lugger burning like a furnace on the other side of the Point of Warroch, and that, though he had come through the wood, he had seen or heard nothing of Kennedy or the young Laird, "only there was Dominie Sampson, gaun rumpaugin about, like mad, seeking for them."

All was now bustle at Ellangowan. The Laird and his servants, male and female, hastened to the wood of Warroch. The tenants and cottagers in the neighbourhood lent their assistance, partly out of zeal, partly from curiosity. Boats were manned to search the seashore, which, on the other side of the Point, rose into high and indented rocks. A vague suspicion was entertained, though too horrible to be expressed, that the child might have fallen from one of these cliffs.

The evening had begun to close when the parties entered the wood, and dispersed different ways in quest of the boy and his companion. The darkening of the atmosphere, and the hoarse sighs of the November wind through the naked trees, the rustling of the withered leaves which strewed the glades, the repeated halloos of the different parties, which often drew them together in expectation of meeting the objects of their search, gave a cast of dismal sublimity to the scene.

At length, after a minute and fruitless investigation through the wood, the searchers began to draw together into one body, and to compare notes. The agony of the father grew beyond concealment, yet it scarcely equalled the anguish of the tutor. "Would to God I had died for him!" the affectionate creature repeated, in notes of the deepest distress. Those who were less interested, rushed into a tumultuary discussion of chances and possibilities. Each gave his opinion, and each was alternately swayed by that of the others. Some thought the objects of their search had gone aboard the sloop; some that they had gone to a village at three miles' distance; some whispered they might have been on board the lugger, a few planks and beams of which the tide now drifted ashore.

At this instant a shout was heard from the beach, so loud, so shrill, so piercing, so different from every sound which the woods that day had rung to, that nobody hesitated a moment to believe that it conveyed tidings, and tidings of dreadful import. All hurried to the place, and, venturing without scruple upon paths, which, at another time, they would have shuddered to lock at, descended towards a cleft of the rock, where one boat's crew was already landed. "Here, sirs!—here!—this way, for God's sake!—this way! this way!" was the reiterated cry. Ellangowan broke through the throng which had already assembled at the fatal spot, and beheld the object of their terror. It was the dead body of Kennedy. At first sight he seemed to have perished by a fall from the rocks, which rose above the spot on which he lay, in a perpendicular precipice of a hundred feet above the beach. The corpse was lying half in, half out of the water; the advancing tide, raising the arm and stirring the clothes, had given it at some distance the appearance of motion, so that those who first discovered the body thought that life remained. But every spark had been long extinguished.

"My bairn! my bairn!" cried the distracted father, "where can he be?"—A dozen mouths were opened to communicate hopes which no one felt. Some one at length mentioned—the gipsies! In a moment Ellangowan had reascended the cliffs, flung himself upon the first horse he met, and rode furiously to the huts at Derncleugh. All was there dark and desolate; and, as he dismounted to make more minute search, he stumbled over fragments of furniture which had been thrown out of the cottages, and the broken wood and thatch which had been pulled down by his orders. At that moment the prophecy, or anathema, of Meg Merrilies fell heavy on his mind. "You have stripped the thatch from seven cottages, see that the roof-tree of your own house stand the surer!"

"Restore," he cried, "restore my bairn! bring me back my son, and all shall be forgot and forgiven!" As he uttered these words in a sort of frenzy, his eye caught a glimmering of light in one of the dismantled cottages—it was that in which Meg Merrilies formerly resided. 'The light, which seemed to proceed from fire, glimmered not only through the window, but also through the rafters of the hut where the roofing had been torn off.

24

He flew to the place; the entrance was bolted despair gave the miserable father the strength of ten men; he rushed against the door with such violence, that it gave way before the momentum of his weight and force. The cottage was empty, but bore marks of recent habitation He flew to the place; the entrance was bolted there was fire on the hearth, a kettle, and some preparation for food. As he eagerly gazed around for something that might confirm his hope that his child yet lived, although in the power of those strange people, a man entered the hut.

It was his old gardener. "O sir!" said the old man, "such a night as this I trusted never to live to see!—ye maun come to the Place directly!"

"Is my boy found? is he alive? have ye found Harry Bertram? Andrew, have ye found Harry Bertram?"

"No, sir; but—"

"Then he is kidnapped!. I am sure of it, Andrew as sure as that I tread upon earth! She has stolen him—and I will never stir from this place till I have tidings of my bairn!"

"Oh, but ye maun come hame, sir! ye maun come hame!-We have sent for the Sheriff, and we'll set a watch here a' night, in case the gipsies return; but you—ye maun come hame, sir,—for my lady's in the dead-thraw." [*Death-agony.]

Bertram turned a stupefied and unmeaning eye on the messenger who uttered this calamitous news; and, repeating the words, "in the dead-thraw!" as if he could not comprehend their meaning, suffered the old man to drag him towards his horse. During the ride home, he only said, "Wife and bairn, baith—mother and son, baith—Sair, sair to abide!"

It is needless to dwell upon the new scene of agony which awaited him. The news of Kennedy's fate had been eagerly and incautiously communicated at Ellangowan, with the gratuitous addition, that, doubtless, "he had drawn the Young Laird over the craig with him, though the tide had swept away the child's body—he was light, puir thing, and would flee farther into the surf."

Mrs. Bertram heard the tidings; she was far advanced in her pregnancy; she fell into the pains of premature labour, and, ere Ellangowan had recovered his agitated faculties, so as to comprehend the full distress of his situation, he was the father of a female infant, and a widower.

CHAPTER X.

But see, his face is black, and full of blood; His eye-balls farther out than when he lived, Staring full ghastly like a strangled man; His hair uprear'd, his nostrils stretch'd with struggling, His hands abroad display'd, as one that gasp'd And tugg'd for life, and was by strength subdued.

Henry IV. Part I

THE Sheriff-depute of the county arrived at Ellangowan next morning by daybreak. To this provincial magistrate the law of Scotland assigns judicial powers of considerable extent, and the task of inquiring into all crimes committed within his jurisdiction, the apprehension and commitment of suspected persons, and so forth. [* The Scottish Sheriff discharges, on such occasions as that now mentioned, pretty much the same duty as a Coroner.]

The gentleman who held the office in the shire of—at the time of this catastrophe, was well born and well educated; and, though somewhat pedantic and professional in his habits, he enjoyed general respect as an active and intelligent magistrate. His first employment was to examine all witnesses whose evidence could throw light upon this mysterious event, and make up the written report, proces verbal or precognition, as it is technically called, which the practice of Scotland has substituted for a coroner's inquest. Under the Sheriffs minute and skilful inquiry, many circumstances appeared, which seemed incompatible with the original opinion, that Kennedy had accidentally fallen from the cliffs. We shall briefly detail some of these.

The body had been deposited in a neighbouring fisher-hut, but without altering the condition in which it was found. This was the first object of the Sheriff's examination. Though fearfully crushed and mangled by the fall from such a height, the corpse was found to exhibit a deep cut in the head, which, in the opinion of a skilful surgeon, must have been inflicted by a broadsword, or cutlass. The experience of this gentleman discovered other suspicious indications. The face was much blackened, the eyes distorted, and the veins of the neck swelled. A coloured handkerchief, which the unfortunate man had worn round his neck, did not present the usual appearance, but was much loosened, and the knot displaced and dragged extremely tight: the folds were also compressed, as if it had been used as a means of grappling the deceased, and dragging him perhaps to the precipice.

On the other hand, poor Kennedy's purse was found untouched; and, what seemed yet more extraordinary, the pistols which he usually carried when about to encounter any hazardous adventure, were found in his pockets loaded. This appeared particularly strange, for he was known and dreaded by the contraband traders as a man equally fearless and dexterous in the use of his weapons, of which he had given many signal proofs. The Sheriff inquired, whether Kennedy was not in the practice of carrying any other arms? Most of Mr. Bertram's servants recollected that he generally had a couteau de chasse, or short hanger, but none such was found upon the dead body; nor could those who had seen him on the morning of the fatal day, take it upon them to assert whether he then carried that weapon or not.

The corpse afforded no other indicia respecting the, fate of Kennedy; for, though the clothes were much displaced, and the limbs dreadfully fractured, the one seemed the probable, the other the certain, consequences of such a fall. The hands of the deceased were clenched fast, and full of turf and earth; but this also seemed equivocal.

The magistrate then proceeded to the place where the corpse was first discovered, and made those who had found it give, upon the spot, a particular and detailed account of the manner in which it was lying. A large fragment of the rock appeared to have accompanied, or followed, the fall of the victim from the cliff above. It was of so solid and compact a substance, that it had fallen without any great diminution by splintering, so that the Sheriff was enabled. first, to estimate the weight by measurement, and then to calculate, from the appearance of the fragment, what portion of it had been bedded into the cliff from which it had descended. This was easily detected, by the raw appearance of the stone where it had not been exposed to the atmosphere. They then ascended the cliff, and surveyed the place from whence the stony fragment had fallen. It seemed plain, from the appearance of the bed, that the mere weight of one man standing upon the projecting part of the fragment, supposing it in its original situation, could not have destroyed its balance, and precipitated it, with himself, from the cliff. At the same time, it appeared to have lain so loose, that the use of a lever, or the combined strength of three or four men, might easily have hurled it from its position. The short turf about the brink of the precipice was much trampled, as if stamped by the heels of men in a mortal struggle, or in the act of some violent exertion. Traces of the same kind, less visibly marked, guided the sagacious investigator to the verge of the copsewood, which, in that place, crept high up the bank towards the top of the precipice.

With patience and perseverance, they traced these marks into the thickest part of the copse, a route which no person would have voluntarily adopted, unless for the purpose of concealment. Here they found plain vestiges of violence and struggling, from space to space. Small boughs were torn down, as if grasped by some resisting wretch who was dragged forcibly along; the ground, where in the least degree soft or marshy, showed the print of many feet; there were vestiges also, which might be those of human blood. At any rate, it was certain that several persons must have forced their passage among the oaks, hazels, and underwood, with which they were mingled; and in some places appeared traces, as if a sack full of grain, a dead body, or something of that heavy and solid description, had been dragged along the ground. In one part of the thicket there was a small swamp, the clay of which was whitish, being probably mixed with marl. The back of Kennedy's coat appeared besmeared with stains of the same colour.

At length, about a quarter of a mile from the brink of the fatal precipice, the traces conducted them to a small open space of ground, very much trampled, and plainly stained with blood, although withered leaves had been strewed upon the spot, and other means hastily taken to efface the marks, which seemed obviously to have been derived from a desperate affray. On one side of this patch of open ground, was found the sufferer's naked hanger, . which seemed to have been thrown into the thicket; on the other, the belt and sheath, which appeared to have been hidden with more leisurely care and precaution.

The magistrate caused the footprints which marked this spot to be carefully measured and examined. Some corresponded to the foot of the unhappy victim; some were larger, some less; indicating, that at least four or five men had been busy around him. Above all, here, and here only, were observed the vestiges of a child's foot; and as it could be seen nowhere else, and the hard horse-track which traversed the wood at Warroch was contiguous to the spot, it was natural to think that the boy might have escaped in that direction during the confusion. But as he was never heard of, the Sheriff, who made a careful entry of all these memoranda, did not suppress his opinion, that the deceased had met with foul play, and that the murderers, whoever they were, had possessed themselves of the person of the child Harry Bertram.

Every exertion was now made to discover the criminals. Suspicion hesitated between the smugglers and the gipsies. The fate of Dirk Hatteraick's vessel was certain. Two men from the opposite side of Warroch Bay (so the inlet on the southern side of the Point of Warroch is called) had seen, though it a great distance, the lugger drive eastward, after doubling the headland, and, as they judged from her manoeuvres, in a disabled state. Shortly after, they perceived that she grounded, smoked, and, finally, took fire. She was, as one of them expressed himself, in a light low (bright flame) when they observed a king's ship, with her colours up, heave in sight from behind the cape. The guns of the burning vessel discharged themselves as the fire reached them; and they saw her, at length, blow up with a great explosion. The sloop of war kept aloof for her own safety; and, after hovering till the other exploded, stood away southward under a press of sail. The Sheriff anxiously interrogated these men whether any boats had left the vessel. They could not say—they had seen none—but they might have put off in such a direction as placed the burning vessel, and the thick smoke which floated landward from it, between their course and the witnesses' observation.

That the ship destroyed was Dirk Hatteraick's, no one doubted. His lugger was well known on the coast, and had been expected just at this time. A letter from the commander of the king's sloop, to whom the Sheriff made application, put the matter beyond doubt; he sent also an extract from his log-book of the transactions of the day, which intimated their being on the outlook for a smuggling lugger, Dirk Hatteraick master, upon the information and requisition of Francis Kennedy, of his Majesty's excise service; and that Kennedy was to be upon the outlook on the shore, in case Hatteraick, who was known to be a desperate fellow, and had been repeatedly outlawed, should attempt to run his sloop aground. About nine o'clock A.M. they discovered a sail, which answered the description of Hatteraick's vessel, chased her, and after repeated signals to her to show colours and bring-to, fired upon her. The chase then showed Hamburgh colours, and returned the fire; and a running fight was maintained for three hours, when, just as the lugger was doubling the Point of Warroch, they observed that the main-yard was shot in the slings, and that the vessel was disabled. It was not in the power of the man-of-war's men for some time to profit by this circumstance, owing to their having kept too much in-shore for doubling the headland. After two tacks, they accomplished this, and observed the chase on fire, and apparently deserted. The fire having reached some casks of spirits, which were placed on the deck, with other combustibles, probably on purpose, burnt with such fury, that no boats durst approach the vessel, especially as her shotted guns were discharging, one after another, by the heat. The captain had no doubt whatever that the crew had set the vessel on fire, and escaped in their boats. After watching the conflagration till the ship blew up, his Majesty's sloop, the Shark, stood towards the Isle of Man, with the purpose of intercepting the retreat of the smugglers, who, though they might conceal themselves in the woods for a day or two, would probably take the first opportunity of endeavouring to make for this asylum. But they never saw more of them than is above narrated.

Such was the account given by William Pritchard, master and commander of his Majesty's sloop of war, Shark, who concluded by regretting deeply that he had not had the happiness to fall in with the scoundrels who had had the impudence to fire on his Majesty's flag, and with an assurance, that, should he meet Mr. Dirk Hatteraick in any future cruise, he would not fall to bring him into port under his stern, to answer whatever might be alleged against him.

As, therefore, it seemed tolerably certain that the men on board the lugger had escaped, the death of Kennedy, if he fell in with them in the woods, when irritated by the loss of their vessel, and by the share he had in it, was easily to be accounted for. And it was not improbable, that to such brutal tempers, rendered desperate by their own circumstances, even the murder of the child, against whose father, as having become suddenly active in the prosecution of smugglers, Hatteraick was known to have uttered deep threats, would not appear a very heinous crime.

Against this hypothesis it was urged, that a crew of fifteen or twenty men could not have lain hidden upon the coast, when so close a search took place immediately after the destruction of their vessel; or, at least, that if they had hid themselves in the woods, their boats must have been seen on the beach;—that in such precarious circumstances, and when a retreat must have seemed difficult, if not impossible, it was not to be thought that they would have all united to commit a useless murder, for the mere sake of revenge. Those who held this opinion, supposed, either that the boats of the lugger had stood out to sea without being observed by those who were intent upon gazing at the burning vessel, and so gained safe distance before the sloop got round the headland; or else, that, the boats being stayed or destroyed by the fire of the Shark during the chase, the crew had obstinately determined to perish with the vessel. What gave some countenance to this supposed act of desperation was, that neither Dirk Hatteraick nor any of his sailors, all well-known men in the fair-trade, were again seen upon that coast, or heard of in the Isle of Man, where strict inquiry was made. On the other hand, only one dead body, apparently that of a seaman killed by a cannon-shot, drifted ashore. So, all that could be done was to register the names, description, and appearance of the individuals belonging to the ship's company, and offer a reward for the apprehension of them, or any one of them; extending also to any person, not the actual murderer, who should give evidence tending to convict those who had murdered Francis Kennedy.

Another opinion, which was also plausibly supported, went to charge this horrid crime upon the late tenants of Derncleugh. They were known to have resented highly the conduct of the Laird of Ellangowan towards them, and to have used threatening expressions, which every one supposed them capable of carrying into effect. The kidnapping the child was a crime much more consistent with their habits than with those of smugglers, and his temporary guardian might have fallen in an attempt to protect him. Besides it was remembered that Kennedy had been an active agent, two or three days before,—in the forcible expulsion of these people from Derncleugh, and that harsh and menacing language had been exchanged between him and some of the Egyptian patriarchs on that memorable occasion.

The Sheriff received also the depositions of the unfortunate father and his servant, concerning what had passed at their meeting the caravan of gipsies as they left the estate of Ellangowan. The speech of Meg Merrilies seemed particularly suspicious. There was, as the magistrate observed in his law language, damnum minatum—a damage, or evil turn, threatened, and malum secutum—an evil of the very kind predicted shortly afterwards following. A young woman, who had been gathering nuts in Warroch wood upon the fatal day, was also strongly of opinion, though she declined to make positive oath, that she had seen Meg Merrilies, at least a woman of her remarkable size and appearance, start suddenly out of a thicket—she said she had called to her by name, but, as the figure turned from her, and made no answer, she was uncertain if it were the gipsy, or her wraith, and was afraid to go nearer to one who was always reckoned, in the vulgar phrase, no canny. This vague story received some corroboration from the circumstance of a fire being that evening found in the gipsy's deserted cottage. To this fact Ellangowan and his gardener bore evidence. Yet it seemed extravagant to suppose, that, had this woman been accessory to such a dreadful crime, she would have returned that very evening on which it was committed, to the place, of all others, where she was most likely to be sought after.

Meg Merrilies was, however, apprehended and examined. She denied strongly having been either at Derncleugh or in the wood of Warroch upon the day of Kennedy's death; and several of her tribe made oath in her behalf, that she had never quitted their encampment, which was in a glen about ten miles distant from Ellangowan. Their oaths were indeed little to be trusted to; but what other evidence could be had in the circumstances? There was one remarkable fact, and only one, which arose from her examination. Her arm appeared to be slightly wounded by the cut of a sharp weapon, and was tied up with a handkerchief of Harry Bertram's. But the chief of the horde acknowledged he had "corrected her" that day with his whinger—she herself, and others, gave the same account of her hurt; and, for the handkerchief, the quantity of linen stolen from Ellangowan during the last months of their residence on the estate, easily accounted for it, without charging Meg with a more heinous crime.

It was observed upon her examination, that she treated the questions respecting the death of Kennedy, or "the gauger," as she called him, with indifference; but expressed great and emphatic scorn and indignation at being supposed capable of injuring little Harry Bertram. She was long confined in jail, under the hope that something might yet be discovered to throw light upon this dark and bloody transaction. Nothing, however, occurred; and Meg was at length liberated, but under sentence of banishment from the county, as a vagrant, common thief, and disorderly person. No traces of the boy could ever be discovered; and, at length, the story, after making much noise, was gradually given up as altogether inexplicable, and only perpetuated by the name of "The Gauger's Loup," which was generally bestowed on the cliff from which the unfortunate man had fallen, or been precipitated.

CHAPTER XI.

Enter Time, as Chorus.
> I—that please some, try all; both joy and terror Of good and had; that make and unfold error—Now take upon me, in the name of
> Time, To use my wings. Impute it not a crime To me, or my swift passage, that I slide O'er sixteen years, and leave the growth
> untried Of that wide gap.

Winter's Tale.

Our narration is now about to make a large stride, and omit a space of nearly seventeen years; during which nothing occurred of any particular consequence with respect to the story we have undertaken to tell. The gap is a wide one; yet if the reader's experience in life enables him to look back on so many years, the space will scarce appear longer in his recollection, than the time consumed in turning these pages.

It was, then, in the month of November, about seventeen years after the catastrophe related in the fast chapter, that, during a cold and stormy night, a social group had closed around the kitchen fire of the Gordon Arms at Kippletringan, a small but comfortable inn, kept by Mrs. Mac-Candlish in that village. The conversation which passed among them will save me the trouble of telling the few events occurring during this chasm in our history, with which it is necessary that the reader should be acquainted.

Mrs. Mac-Candlish, throned in a comfortable easy-chair lined with black leather, was regaling herself, and a neighbouring gossip or two, with a cup of genuine tea, and at the same time keeping a sharp eye upon her domestics, as they went and came in prosecution of their various duties and commissions. The clerk and precentor of the parish enjoyed at a little distance his Saturday night's pipe, and aided its bland fumigation by an occasional sip of brandy-and-water. Deacon Bearcliff, a man of great importance in the village, combined the indulgence of both parties—he had his pipe and his teacup, the latter being laced with a little spirits. One or two clowns sat at some distance, drinking their twopenny ale.

"Are ye sure the parlour's ready for them, and the fire burning clear, and the chimney no smoking?" said the hostess to a chambermaid.

She was answered in the affirmative.—"Ane wadna be uncivil to them, especially in their distress," said she, turning to the Deacon.

"Assuredly not, Mrs. Mac-Candlish; assuredly not. I am sure ony sma' thing they might want frae my shop, under seven, or eight, or ten pounds, I would book them as readily for it as the first in the country.—Do they come in the auld chaise?"

"I dare say no," said the precentor; "for Miss Bertram comes on the white powny ilka day to the kirk—and a constant kirk-keeper she is—and it's a pleasure to hear her singing the psalms, winsome young thing."

"Ay, and the young Laird of Hazlewood rides hame half the road wi' her after sermon," said one of the gossips in company; "I wonder how auld Hazlewood likes that."

"I kenna how he may like it now," answered another of the tea-drinkers; "but the day has been when Ellangowan wad hae liked as little to see his daughter taking up with their son."

"Ay, has been," answered the first, with somewhat of emphasis.

"I am sure, neighbour Ovens," said the hostess, "the Hazlewoods of Hazlewood, though they are a very gude auld family in the county, never thought, till within these twa score o' years, of evening themselves till the Ellangowans—Wow, woman, the Bertrams of Ellangowan are the auld Dingawaies lang syne—there is a sang about ane o' them marrying a daughter of the King of Man; it begins—

"Blythe Bertram's ta'en him ower the faem,
To wed a wife, and bring her hame—
I daur say Mr. Skreigh can sing us the ballant."

"Gudewife," said Skreigh, gathering up his mouth, and sipping his tiff of brandy punch with great solemnity, "our talents were gien us to other use than to sing daft auld sangs sae near the Sabbath day."

"Hout fie, Mr. Skreigh; I'se warrant I hae heard you sing a blythe sang on Saturday at e'en before now.—But as for the chaise, Deacon, it hasna been out of the coachhouse since Mrs. Bertram died, that's sixteen or seventeen years sin syne—. Jock Jabos is away wi' a chaise of mine for them;—I wonder he's no come back. It's pit mirk [*Pitch dark]—but there's no an ill turn on the road but twa, and the brigg ower Warroch burn is safe eneugh, if he baud to the right side. But then there's Heavieside-brae, that's just a murder for post-cattle—but Jock kens the road brawly." [*Very well]

A loud rapping was heard at the door. "That's no them. I dinna hear the wheels.—Grizzel, ye limmer, gang to the door."

"It's a single gentleman," whined out Grizzel; "maun I take him into the parlour?"

"Foul be in your feet, then; it'll be some English rider. Coming without a servant at this time o' night!—Has the ostler ta'en the horse?—Ye may light a spunk o' fire in the red room."

"I wish, ma'am," said the traveller, entering the kitchen, "you would give me leave to warm myself here, for the night is very cold."

His appearance, voice, and manner, produced an instantaneous effect in his favour. He was a handsome, tall, thin figure, dressed in black, as appeared when he laid aside his riding-coat; his age might be between forty and fifty; his cast of features grave and interesting, and his air somewhat military. Every point of his appearance and address bespoke the gentleman. Long habit had given Mrs. Mac-Candlish an acute tact in ascertaining the quality of her visitors, and proportioning her reception accordingly To every guest the appropriate speech was made, And every duty with distinction paid; Respectful, easy, pleasant, or polite—"Your honour's servant!—Mister Smith, good-night."

On the present occasion, she was low in her curtsey, and profuse in her apologies. The stranger begged his horse might be attended to—she went out herself to school the hostler.

"There was never a prettier bit o' horse-flesh in the stable o' the Gordon Arms," said the man; which information increased the landlady's respect for the rider. Finding, on her return, that the stranger declined to go into another apartment (which, indeed, she allowed, would be but cold and smoky till the fire bleezed up), she installed her guest hospitably by the fireside, and offered what refreshment her house afforded.

"A cup of your tea, ma'am, if you will favour me." Mrs. Mac-Candlish bustled about, reinforced her teapot with hyson, and proceeded in her duties with her best grace. "We have a very nice parlour, sir, and everything very agreeable for gentlefolks; but it's bespoke the night for a gentleman and his daughter, that are going to leave this part of the country—ane of my chaises is gane for them, and will be back forthwith—they're no sae weel in the warld as they have been; but we're a' subject to ups and downs in this life, as your honour must needs ken—but is not the tobacco-reek disagreeable to your honour?"

"By no means, ma'am; I am an old campaigner, and perfectly used to it.—Will you permit me to make some inquiries about a family in this neighbourhood?"

The sound of wheels was now heard, and the landlady hurried to the door to receive her expected guests; but returned in an instant, followed by the postilion—

"No, they canna come at no rate, the Laird's sae ill."

"But God help them," said the landlady, "the morn's the term—the very last day they can bide in the house—a' thing's to be roupit." [*Sold by auction]

"Weel, but they can come at no rate, I tell ye—Mr. Bertram canna be moved."

"What Mr. Bertram?" said the stranger; "not Mr. Bertram of Ellangowan, I hope?"

"Just e'en that same, sir; and if ye be a friend o' his, ye have come at a time when he's sair bested."

"I have been abroad for many years—is his health so much deranged?"

"Ay, and his affairs an' a'," said the Deacon "the creditors have entered into possession o' the estate, and it's for sale; and some that made the maist by him—I name nae names, but Mrs. Mac-Candlish kens wha I mean—(the landlady shook her head significantly) they're sairest on him e'en now. I have a sma' matter due mysell, but I would rather have lost it than gane to turn the auld man out of his house, and him just dying."

"Ay, but," said the parish-clerk, "Factor Glossin wants to get rid of the auld Laird, and drive on the sale, for fear the heir-male should cast up upon them; for I have heard say, if there was an heir-male, they couldna sell the estate for auld Ellangowan's debt."

"He had a son born a good many years ago," said the stranger; "he is dead, I suppose?"

"Nae man can say for that," answered the clerk mysteriously.

"Dead!" said the Deacon, "I'se warrant him dead lang syne; he hasna been heard o' these twenty years or thereby."

"I wot weel it's no twenty years," said the landlady; "it's no abune seventeen at the outside in this very month; it made an unco noise ower a' this country—the bairn disappeared the very day that Supervisor Kennedy cam by his end.—If ye kenn'd this country lang syne, your honour wad maybe ken Frank Kennedy the Supervisor. He was a heartsome pleasant man, and company for the best gentlemen in the county, and muckle mirth he's made in this house. I was young then, sir, and newly married to Bailie Mac-Candlish, that's dead and gone—

(a sigh)—and muckle fun I've had wi' the Supervisor. He was a daft dog—Oh, an he could hae hauden aff the smugglers a bit! but he was aye venturesome.—And so ye see, sir, there was a king's sloop down in Wigton Bay, and Frank Kennedy, he behoved to have her up to chase Dirk Hatteraick's lugger—ye'll mind Dirk Hatteraick, Deacon? I dare say ye may have dealt wi' him—(the Deacon gave a sort of acquiescent nod and humph). He was a daring chield, and he fought his ship till she blew up like peelings of ingans; and Frank Kennedy he had been the first man to board, and he was flung like a quarter of a mile off, and fell into the water below the rock at Warroch Point, that they ca' the Gauger's Loup to this day."

"And Mr. Bertram's child," said the stranger, "what is all this to him?"

"Ou, sir, the bairn aye held an unca wark wi' the Supervisor; and it was generally thought he went on board the vessel alang wi' him, as bairns are aye forward to be in mischief."

"No, no," said the Deacon, "ye're clean out there, Luckie—for the young Laird was stown away by a randy gipsy woman they ca'd Meg Merrilies,—I mind her looks weel,—in revenge for Ellangowan having gar'd her be drumm'd through Kippletringan for stealing a silver spoon."

"If ye'll forgie me, Deacon," said the precentor, "ye're e'en as far wrang as the gudewife."

"And what is your edition of the story, sir?" said the stranger, turning to him with interest.

"That's maybe no sae canny to tell," said the precentor, with solemnity.

Upon being urged, however, to speak out, he preluded with, two or three large puffs of tobacco-smoke, and out of the cloudy sanctuary which these whiffs formed around him, delivered the following legend, having cleared his voice with one or two hems, and imitating, as near as he could, the eloquence which weekly thundered over his head from the pulpit.

"What we are now to deliver, my brethren,—hem—hem,—I mean, my good friends,—was not done in a corner, and may serve as an answer to witch-advocates, atheists, and misbelievers of all kinds.—Ye must know that the worshipful Laird of Ellangowan was not so preceese as he might have been in clearing his land of witches (concerning whom it is said, 'Thou shalt not suffer a witch to live'), nor of those who had familiar spirits, and consulted with divination, and sorcery, and lots, which is the fashion with the Egyptians, as they ca' themsells, and other unhappy bodies, in this our country. And the Laird was three years married without having a family-and he was sae left to himself, that it was thought he held ower muckle troking [*Trafficking] and communing wi' that Meg Merrilies, wha was the maist notorious, witch in a' Galloway and Dumfriesshire baith."

"Aweel I wot there's something in that," said Mrs. Mac-Candlish; "I've kenn'd him order her twa' glasses o' brandy in this very house."

"Aweel, gudewife, then the less I lee.—Sae the lady was wi' bairn at last, and in the night when she should have been delivered, there comes to the door of the ha' house—the Place of Ellangowan as they ca'd—an ancient man, strangely habited, and asked for quarters. His head, and his legs, and his arms were bare, although it was winter time o' the year, and he had a gray beard three quarters lang. Weel, he was admitted; and when the lady was delivered, he craved to know the very moment of the hour of the birth, and he went out and consulted the stars. And when he came back, he tell'd the Laird, that the Evil One wad have power over the knave-bairn, that was that night born, and he charged him that the babe should be bred up in the ways of piety, and that he should aye hae a godly minister at his elbow, to pray wi' the bairn and for him. And the aged man vanished away, and no man of this country saw mair o' him."

"Now, that will not pass," said the postilion, who, at a respectful distance, was listening to the conversation, "begging Mr. Skreigh's and the company's pardon,—there was no sae mony hairs on the warlock's face as there's on Letter-Gae's [*The precentor is called by Allan Ramsay,—"The Letter-Gae of haly rhyme."] ain at this moment; and he had as gude a pair o' boots as a man need streik on his legs, and gloves too;—and I should understand boots by this time, I think."

"Whisht, Jock," said the landlady.

"Ay? and what do ye ken o' the matter, friend Jabos?" said the precentor contemptuously.

"No muckle, to be sure, Mr. Skreigh—only that I lived within a penny-stane cast o' the head o' the avenue at Ellangowan, when a man cam jingling to our door that night the young Laird was born, and my mother sent me, that was a hafflin callant, [*Half-grown lad] to show the stranger the gate to the Place, which, if he had been sic a warlock, he might hae kenn'd himself, ane wad think—and he was a young, weel-faured, weel-dressed lad, like an Englishman. And I tell ye he had as gude a hat, and boots, and gloves, as ony gentleman need to have. To be sure he did gie an awesome glance up at the auld castle—and there was some spae-work gaed on—I aye heard that; but as for his vanishing, I held the stirrup mysell when he gaed away, and he gied me a round half-crown—he was riding on a haick they ca'd Souple Sam—it belanged to the George at Dumfries—it was a blood-bay beast, very ill o' the spavin—I hae seen the beast baith before and since."

"Aweel, aweel, Jock," answered Mr. Skreigh, with a tone of mild solemnity, "our accounts differ in no material particulars; but I had no knowledge that ye had seen the man.—So ye see, my friends, that this soothsayer having prognosticated evil to the boy, his father engaged a godly minister to be with him morn and night."

"Ay, that was him they ca'd Dominie Sampson," said the postilion.

"He's but a dumb dog that," observed the Deacon; "I have heard that he never could preach five words of a sermon endlang, for as lang as he has been licensed."

"Weel, but," said the precentor, waving his hand, as if eager to retrieve the command of the discourse, he waited on the young Laird by night and day. Now, it chanced, when the bairn was near five years auld, that the Laird had a sight of his errors, and determined to put these Egyptians aff his ground; and he caused them to remove; and that Frank Kennedy, that was a rough swearing fellow, he was sent to turn them off. And he cursed and damned at them, and they swure at him; and that Meg Merrilies, that was the maist powerfu' with the Enemy of Mankind, she as gude as said she would have him, body and soul, before three days were ower his head. And I have it from a sure hand, and that's ane wha saw it, and that's John Wilson, that was the laird's groom, that Meg appeared to the Laird as he was riding hame from Singleside, over Gibbie's-know, and threatened him wi' what she wad do to his family; but whether it was Meg, or something waur in her likeness, for it seemed bigger than ony mortal creature, John could not say."

"Aweel," said the postilion, "it might be sae—I canna say against it, for I was not in the country at the time; but John Wilson was a blustering kind of chield, without the heart of a sprug." [*Sparrow]

"And what was the end of all this?" said the stranger, with some impatience.

"Ou, the event and upshot of it was, sir," said the precentor, "that while they were all looking on, beholding a king's ship chase a smuggler, this Kennedy suddenly brake away frae them without ony reason that could be descried—ropes nor tows wad not hae held him—and made for the wood of Warroch as fast as his beast could carry him; and by the way he met the young Laird and his governor, and he snatched up the bairn, and swure, if he was bewitched, the bairn should have the same luck as him; and the minister followed as fast as he could, and almaist as fast as them, for he was wonderfully swift of foot—and he saw Meg the witch, or her master in her similitude, rise suddenly out of the ground, and claught the bairn suddenly out of the gauger's arms—and then he rampauged and drew his sword—for ye ken a fie man and a cusser fearsna the deil."

"I believe that's very true," said the postilion.

"So, sir, she grippit him, and clodded [*Hurled] him like a stane from the sling ower the craigs of Warroch Head, where he was found that evening—but what became of the babe, frankly I cannot say. But he that was minister here then, that's now in a better place, had an opinion that the bairn was only conveyed to Fairyland for a season."

The stranger had smiled slightly at some parts of this recital, but ere he could answer, the clatter of a horse's hoofs was heard, and a smart servant, handsomely dressed, with a cockade in his hat, bustled into the kitchen, with "Make a little room, good people"; when, observing the stranger, he descended at once into the modest and civil domestic, his hat sunk down by his side, and he put a letter into his master's hands. "The family at Ellangowan, sir, are in great distress, and unable to receive any visits."

"I know it," replied his master.—"And now, madam, if you will have the goodness to allow me to occupy the parlour you mentioned, as you are disappointed of your guests—"

"Certainly, sir," said Mrs. Mac-Candlish, and hastened to light the way with all the imperative bustle which an active landlady loves to display on such occasions.

"Young man," said the Deacon to the servant, filling a glass, "ye'll no be the waur o' this, after your ride."

"Not a feather, sir,—thank ye—your very good health, sir."

"And wha may your master be, friend?"

"What, the gentleman that was here?—that's the famous Colonel
Mannering, sir, from the East Indies."

"What, him we read of in the newspapers?"

"Ay, ay, just the same. It was he relieved Cuddieburn, and defended Chingalore, and defeated the great Mahratta chief, Ram Jolli Bundleman—I was with him in most of his campaigns."

"Lord safe us," said the landlady, "I must go see what he would have for supper—that I should set him down here!"

"Oh, he likes that all the better, mother;—you never saw a plainer creature in your life than our old Colonel; and yet he has a spice of the devil in him too."

The rest of the evening's conversation below stairs tending little to edification, we shall, with the reader's leave, step up to the parlour.

CHAPTER XII.

—Reputation?—that's man's idol set up against God, the Maker of all laws, Who hath commanded us we should not kill, And yet we say we must, for Reputation! What honest man can either fear his own, Or else will hurt another's reputation? Fear to do base unworthy things is valour; If they be done to us, to suffer them Is valour too.— BEN JONSON,

The Colonel was walking pensively up and down the parlour, when the officious landlady re-entered to take his commands. Having given them in the manner he thought would be most acceptable "for the good of the house," he begged to detain her a moment.

"I think," he said, "madam, if I understood the good people right,
Mr. Bertram lost his son in his fifth year?"

"Oh ay, sir, there's nae doubt o' that, though there are mony idle clashes [* Tittle-tattle], about the way and manner, for it's an auld story now, and everybody tells it, as we were doing, their ain way by the ingleside. But lost the bairn was in his fifth year, as your honour says, Colonel; and the news being rashly tell'd to the leddy, then great with child, cost her her life that samyn night—and the Laird never throve after that day, but was just careless of everything—though, when his daughter Miss Lucy grew up, she tried to keep order within doors—but what could she do, poor thing so now they're out of house and hauld."

"Can you recollect, madam, about what time of the year the child was lost?" The landlady, after a pause, and some recollection, answered, "she was positive it was about this season and added some local recollections that fixed the date in her memory, as occurring about the beginning of November, 17-."

The stranger took two or three turns round the room in silence, but signed to Mrs. Mac-Candlish not to leave it.

Did I rightly apprehend," he said, "that the estate of Ellangowan is in the market?"

"In the market?—it will be sell'd the morn to the highest bidder—that's no the morn, Lord help me! which is the Sabbath, but on Monday, the first free day; and the furniture and stocking is to be roupit [*Auctioned] at the same time on the ground—it's the opinion of the haill country, that the sale has been shamefully forced on at this time, when there's sae little money stirring in Scotland wi' this weary American war, that somebody may get the land a bargain—Deil be in them, that I should say sae!"—the good lady's wrath rising at the supposed injustice.

"And where will the sale take place?"

"On the, premises, as the advertisement says—that's at the house of Ellangowan, your honour, as I understand it."

"And who exhibits the title-deeds, rent-roll, and plan?"

"A very decent man, sir; the Sheriff-substitute of the county, who has authority from the Court of Session. He's in the town just now, if your honour would like to see hint; and he can tell you mair about the loss of the bairn than onybody, for the Sheriff-depute (that's his principal, like) took much pains to come at the truth o' that matter, as I have heard."

"And this gentleman's name is—"

"Mac-Morlan, sir,—he's a man o' character, and weel spoken o'."

"Send my compliments—Colonel Mannering's compliments to him, and I would be glad he would do me the pleasure of supping with me, and bring these papers with him—and I beg, good madam, you will say nothing of this to any one else."

"Me, sir? ne'er a word shall I say—I wish your honour (a curtsey), or ony honourable gentleman that's fought for his country (another curtsey), had the land, since the auld family maun quit (a sigh), rather than that wily scoundrel, Glossin, that's risen on the ruin of the best friend he ever had—and now I think on't, I'll slip on my hood and pattens, and gang to Mr. Mac-Morlan mysell—he's at hame e'en now-it's hardly a step."

"Do so, my good landlady, and many thanks—and bid my servant step here with my portfolio in the meantime."

In a minute or two, Colonel Mannering was quietly seated with his writing materials before him. We have the privilege of looking over his shoulder as he writes, and we willingly communicate its substance to our readers. The letter was addressed to Arthur Mervyn, Esq., of Mervyn Hall, Llanbraithwaite, Westmoreland. It contained some account of the writer's previous journey since parting with him, and then proceeded as follows:-

"And now, why will you still upbraid me with my melancholy, Mervyn?—Do you think, after the lapse of twenty-five years, battles, wounds, imprisonment, you, who have remained in the bosom of domestic happiness, experience little change, that your step is as light, and your fancy as full of sunshine, is a blessed effect of health and temperament, co-operating with content and a smooth current down the course of life. But my career has been one of difficulties, and doubts, and errors. From my infancy I have been the sport of accident, and though the wind has often borne me into harbour, it has seldom been into that which the pilot destined. Let me recall to you—but the task must be brief—the odd and wayward fates of my youth, and the misfortunes or my manhood.

"The former, you will say, had nothing very appalling. All was not for the best; but all was tolerable. My father, the eldest son of an ancient but reduced family, left me with little, save the name of the head of the house, to the protection of his more fortunate brothers. They were so fond of me that they almost quarrelled about me. My uncle, the bishop, would have had me in orders, and offered me a living—my uncle, the merchant, would have put me into a counting-house, and proposed to give me a share in the thriving concern of Mannering and Marshall, in Lombard' Street—So, between these two stools, or rather these two soft, easy, well-stuffed chairs of divinity and commerce, my unfortunate person slipped down, and pitched upon a dragoon saddle. Again, the bishop wished me to marry the niece and heiress of the Dean of Lincoln; and my uncle, the alderman, proposed to me the only daughter of old Sloethorn, the great wine-merchant, rich enough to play at span-counters with moidores, and make thread-papers of bank notes—and somehow I slipped my neck out of both nooses, and married—poor—poor Sophia Wellwood.

"You will say, my military career in India, when I followed my regiment there, should have given me some satisfaction; and so it assuredly has. You will remind me also, that if I disappointed the hopes of my guardians, I did not incur their displeaslure—that the bishop, at his death, bequeathed me his blessing, his manuscript sermons, and a curious portfolio, containing the heads of eminent divines of the Church of England; and that my uncle, Sir Paul Mannering, left me sole heir and executor to his large fortune.

"Yet this availeth me nothing—I told you I had that upon my mind which I should carry to my grave with me, a perpetual aloes in the draught of existence. I will tell you the cause more in detail than I had the heart to do while under your hospitable roof. You will often hear it mentioned, and perhaps with different and unfounded circumstances. I will, therefore, speak it out; and then let the event itself, and the sentiments of melancholy with which it has impressed me, never again be subject of discussion between us.

"Sophia, as you well know, followed me to India. She was as innocent as gay; but, unfortunately for us both, as gay as innocent. My own manners were partly formed by studies I had forsaken, and habits of seclusion, not quite consistent with my situation as commandant of a regiment in a country, where universal hospitality is offered and expected by every settler claiming the rank of a gentleman. In a moment of peculiar pressure (you know how hard we were sometimes run to obtain white faces to countenance our line-of-battle), a young man, named Brown, joined our regiment as a volunteer, and finding the military duty more to his fancy than commerce, in which he had been engaged, remained with us as a cadet. Let me do my unhappy victim justice—he behaved with such gallantry on every occasion that offered, that the first vacant commission was considered as his due. I was absent for some weeks upon a distant expedition; when I returned, I found this young fellow established quite as the friend of the house, and habitual attendant of my wife and daughter. It was an arrangement which displeased me in many particulars, though no objection could be made to his manners or character—Yet I might have been reconciled to his familiarity in my family, but for the suggestions of another. If you read over—what I never dare open—the play of Othello, you will have some idea of what followed—I mean of my motives—my actions, thank God! were less reprehensible. There was another cadet ambitious of the vacant situation. He called my attention to what he led me to term coquetry between my wife and this young man. Sophia was virtuous, but proud of her virtue; and, irritated by my jealousy, she was so imprudent as to press and encourage an intimacy which she saw I disapproved and regarded with suspicion. Between Brown and me there existed a sort of internal dislike. He made an effort or two to overcome my prejudice; but, prepossessed as I was, I placed them to a wrong motive. Feeling himself repulsed, and with scorn, he desisted; and as he was without family and friends, he was naturally more watchful of the deportment of one who had both.

"It is odd with what torture I write this letter, I feel inclined, nevertheless, to protract the operation, just as if my doing so could put off the catastrophe which has so long embittered my life. But—it must he told, and it shall be told briefly.

"My wife, though no longer young, was still eminently handsome, and—let me say thus far in my own justification—she was fond of being thought so—I am repeating what I said before—In a word, of her virtue I never entertained a doubt; but, pushed by the artful suggestions of Archer, I thought she cared little for my peace of mind, and that the young fellow, Brown, paid his attentions in my despite, and in defiance of me. He perhaps considered me, on his part, as an oppressive aristocratic man, who made my rank in society, and in the army, the means of galling those whom circumstances placed beneath me. And if he discovered my silly jealousy, he probably considered the fretting me in that sore point of my character, as one means of avenging the petty indignities to which I had it in my power to subject him. Yet an acute friend of mine gave a more harmless, or at least a less offensive, construction to his attentions, which he conceived to be meant for my daughter Julia, though immediately addressed to propitiate the influence of her mother. This could have been no very flattering or pleasing enterprise on the part of an obscure and nameless young man; but I should not have been offended at this folly, as I was at the higher degree of presumption I suspected. Offended, however, I was, and in a mortal degree.

"A very slight spark will kindle a flame where everything lies open to catch it. I have absolutely forgot the proximate cause of quarrel, but it was some trifle which occurred at the card-table, which occasioned high words and a challenge. We met in the morning beyond the walls and esplanade of the fortress which I then commanded, on the frontiers of the settlement. This was arranged for Brown's safety, had he escaped. I almost wish he had, though at my own expense but he fell by the first fire. We strove to assist him but some of these Loolies, a species of native banditti who were always on the watch for prey, poured in upon us. Archer and I gained our horses with difficulty, and cut our way through them after a hard conflict, in the course of which he received some desperate wounds. To complete the misfortunes of this miserable day, my wife, who suspected the design with which I left the fortress, had ordered her palanquin to follow me, and was alarmed and almost made prisoner by another troop of these plunderers. She was quickly released by a party of our cavalry; but I cannot disguise from myself, that the incidents of this fatal morning gave a severe shock to health already delicate. The confession of Archer, who thought himself dying, that he had invented some circumstances, and, for his purposes, put the worst construction upon others, and the full explanation and exchange of forgiveness with me which this produced, could not check the progress of her disorder. She died within about eight months after this incident, bequeathing me only the girl, of whom Mrs. Mervyn is so good as to undertake the temporary charge. Julia was also extremely ill; so much so, that I was induced to throw up my command and return to Europe, where her native air, time, and the novelty of the scenes around her, have contributed to dissipate her dejection, and restore her health.

"Now that you know my story, you will no longer ask me the reason of my melancholy, but permit me to brood upon it as I may. There is, surely, in the above narrative, enough to embitter, though not to poison, the chalice, which the fortune and fame you so often mention had prepared to regale my years of retirement.

"I could add circumstances which our old tutor would have quoted as instances of day fatality,—you would laugh were I to mention such particulars, especially as you know I put no faith in them. Yet, since I have come to the very house from which I now write, I have learned a singular coincidence, which, if I find it truly established by tolerable evidence, will serve us hereafter for subject of curious discussion. But I will spare you at present, as I expect a person to speak about a purchase of property now open in this part of the country. It is a place to which I have a foolish partiality, and I hope my purchasing may be convenient to those who are parting with it, as there is a plan for buying it under the value. My respectful compliments to Mrs. Mervyn, and I will trust you, though you boast to be so lively a young gentleman, to kiss Julia for me.—

"Adieu, dear Mervyn.—

Mr. Mac-Morlan now entered the room. The well-known character of Colonel Mannering at once disposed this gentleman, who was a man of intelligence and probity, to be open and confidential. He explained the advantages and disadvantages of the property. "It was settled," he said, "the greater part of it at least, upon heirs-male, and the purchaser would have the privilege of retaining in his hands a large proportion of the price, in case of the reappearance, within a certain limited term, of the child who had disappeared."

"To what purpose, then, force forward a sale?" said Mannering.

Mac-Morlan smiled. "Ostensibly," he answered, "to substitute the interest of money, instead of the ill-paid and precarious rents of an unimproved estate; but chiefly, it was believed, to suit the wishes and views of a certain intended purchaser, who had become a principal creditor, and forced himself into the management of the affairs by means best known to himself, and who, it was thought, would find it very convenient to purchase the estate without paying down the price."

Mannering consulted with Mr. Mac-Morlan upon the steps for thwarting this unprincipled attempt. They then conversed long on the singular disappearance of Harry Bertram upon his fifth birthday, verifying thus the random prediction of Mannering, of which, however, it will readily be supposed he made no beast. Mr. Mac-Morlan was not himself in office when that incident took place; but he was well acquainted with all the circumstances, and promised that our hero should have them detailed by the Sheriff-depute himself, if, as he proposed, he should become a settler in that part of Scotland. With this assurance they parted, well satisfied with each other, and with the evening's conference.

On the Sunday following, Colonel Mannering attended the parish church with great decorum. None of the Ellangowan family were present; and it was understood that the old Laird was rather worse than better. Jock Jabos, once more despatched for him, returned once more without his errand; but, on the following day, Miss Bertram hoped he might be removed.

CHAPTER XIII.

They told me, by the sentence of the law, They had commission to seize all thy fortune.— Here stood a ruffian with a horrid face,
Lording it o'er a pile of massy plate, Tumbled into a heap for public sale;—There was another, making villainous jests At thy
undoing; but had tacit possession Of all thy ancient most domestic ornaments. —OTWAY.

Early next morning, Mannering mounted his horse, and, accompanied by his servant, took the road to Ellangowan. He had no need to inquire the way. A sale in the country is a place of public resort and amusement, and people of various descriptions streamed to it from all quarters.

After a pleasant ride of about an hour, the old towers of the ruin presented themselves in the landscape. The thoughts, with what different feelings he had lost sight of them so many years before, thronged upon the mind of the traveller. The landscape was the same; but how changed the feelings, hopes, and views, of the spectator! Then, life and love were new, and all the prospect was gilded by their rays. And now, disappointed in affection, sated with fame, and what the world calls success, his mind goaded by bitter and repentant recollection, his best hope was to find a retirement in which he might nurse the melancholy that was to accompany him to his grave. "Yet why should an individual mourn over the instability of his hopes, and the vanity of his prospects? The ancient chiefs, who erected these enormous and massive towers 'to be the fortress of their race and the seat of their power', could they have dreamed the day was to come, when the last of their descendants should be expelled, a ruined wanderer, from his possessions! But Nature's bounties are unaltered. The sun will shine as fair on these ruins, whether the property of a stranger, or of a sordid and obscure trickster of the abused law, as when the banners of the founder first waved upon their battlements."

These reflections brought Mannering to the door of the house, which was that day open to all. He entered among others, who traversed the apartments, some to select articles for purchase, others to gratify their curiosity. There is something melancholy in such a scene, even under the most favourable circumstances. The confused state of the furniture, displaced for the convenience of being easily viewed and carried off by the purchasers, is disagreeable to the eye. Those articles which, properly and decently arranged, look creditable and handsome, have then a paltry and wretched appearance; and the apartments, stripped of all that render them commodious and comfortable, have an aspect of ruin and dilapidation. It is disgusting also, to see the scenes of domestic society and seclusion thrown open to the gaze of the curious and the vulgar; to hear their coarse speculations and brutal jests upon the fashions and furniture to which they are unaccustomed,—a frolicsome humour much cherished by, the whisky which in Scotland is always put in circulation on such occasions. All these are ordinary effects of such a scene as Ellangowan now presented; but the moral feeling, that, in this case, they indicated the total ruin of an ancient and honourable family, gave them treble weight and poignancy.

It was some time before Colonel Mannering could find any one disposed to answer his reiterated questions concerning Ellangowan himself. At length, an old maid-servant, who held her apron to her eyes as she spoke, told him, "the Laird was something better, and they hoped he would be able to leave the house that day. Miss Lucy expected the chaise every moment, and, as the day was fine for the time o' year, they had carried him in his easy-chair up to the green before the auld castle, to be out of the way of this unco spectacle." Hither Colonel Mannering went in quest of him, and soon came in sight of the little group, which consisted of four persons. The ascent was steep, so that he had time to reconnoitre them as he advanced, and to consider in what mode he should make his address.

Mr. Bertram, paralytic, and almost incapable of moving, occupied his easy-chair, attired in his night-cap, and a loose camlet coat, his feet wrapped in blankets. Behind him, with his hands crossed on the cane upon which he rested, stood Dominie Sampson, whom Mannering recognised at once. Time had made no change upon him, unless that his black coat seemed more brown, and his gaunt cheeks more lank, than when Mannering last saw him. On one side of the old man was a sylph-like form—a young woman of about seventeen, whom the Colonel accounted to be his daughter. She was looking, from time to time, anxiously towards the avenue, as if expecting the post-chaise; and between whiles busied herself in adjusting the blankets, so as to protect her father from the cold, and in answering inquiries, which he seemed to make with a captious and querulous manner. She did not trust herself to look towards the Place, although the hum of the assembled crowd must have drawn her attention in that direction. The fourth person of the group was a handsome and genteel young man, who seemed to share Miss Bertram's anxiety, and her solicitude to soothe and accommodate her parent.

This young man was the first who observed Colonel Mannering, and immediately stepped forward to meet him, as if politely to prevent his drawing nearer to the distressed group. Mannering instantly paused and explained. "He was," he said, "a stranger, to whom Mr. Bertram had formerly shown kindness and hospitality; he would not have intruded himself upon him at a period of distress, did it not seem to be in some degree a moment also of desertion; he wished merely to offer such services as might be in his power to Mr. Bertram and the young lady."

He then paused at a little distance from the chair. His old acquaintance gazed at him with lack-lustre eye, that intimated no tokens of recognition—the Dominie seemed too deeply sunk in distress even to observe his presence. The young man spoke aside with Miss Bertram, who advanced timidly, and thanked Colonel Mannering for his goodness; "but," she said, the tears gushing fast into her eyes—"her father, she feared, was not so much himself as to be able to remember him."

She then retreated towards the chair, accompanied by the Colonel.—"Father," she said, "this is Mr. Mannering, an old friend, come to inquire after you."

"He's very heartily welcome," said the old man, raising himself in his chair, and attempting a gesture of courtesy, while a gleam of hospitable satisfaction seemed to pass over his faded features; "but, Lucy, my dear, let us go down to the house; you should not keep the gentleman here in the cold.—Dominie, take the key of the wine-cooler. Mr. a—a—the gentleman will surely take something after his ride."

Mannering was unspeakably affected by the contrast which his recollection made between this reception and that with which he had been greeted by the same individual when they last met. He could not restrain his tears, and his evident emotion at once attained him the confidence of the friendless young lady.

"Alas!" she said, "this is distressing even to a stranger; but it may be better for my poor father to be in this way, than if he knew and could feel all."

A servant in livery now came up the path, and spoke in an undertone to the young gentleman—"Mr. Charles, my lady's wanting you yonder sadly, to bid for her for the black ebony cabinet; and Lady Jean Devorgoil is wi' her an' a'—ye maun come away directly."

"Tell them ye could not find me, Tom; or, stay,—say I am looking at the horses."

"No, no, no," said Lucy Bertram earnestly; "if you would not add to the misery of this miserable moment, go to the company directly.—This gentleman, I am sure, will see us to the carriage."

"Unquestionably, madam," said Mannering; "your young friend may rely on my attention."

"Farewell, then," said young Hazlewood, and whispered a word in her ear—then ran down the steep hastily, as if not trusting his resolution at a slower pace.

"Where's Charles Hazlewood running?" said the invalid, who apparently was accustomed to his presence and attentions; "where's Charles Hazlewood running?—what takes him away now?"

"He'll return in a little while," said Lucy gently.

The sound of voices was now heard from the ruins. The reader may remember there was a communication between the castle and the beach, up which the speakers had ascended.

"Yes, there's plenty of shells and sea-ware for manure, as you observe—and if one inclined to build a new house, which might indeed be necessary, there's a great deal of good hewn stone about this old dungeon for the devil here—"

"Good God!" said Miss Bertram hastily to Sampson, "'tis that wretch Glossin's voice!—if my father sees him, it will kill him outright!"

Sampson wheeled perpendicularly round, and moved with long strides to confront the attorney, as he issued from beneath the portal arch of the ruin. "Avoid ye!" he said—"I avoid ye! wouldst thou kill and take possession?"

"Come, come, Master Dominie Sampson," answered Glossin insolently, "if ye cannot preach in the pulpit, we'll have no preaching here. We go by the law, my good friend; we leave the gospel to you."

The very mention of this man's name had been of late a subject of the most violent irritation to the unfortunate patient. The sound of his voice now produced an instantaneous effect. Mr. Bertram started up without assistance, and turned round towards him; the ghastliness of his features forming a strange contrast with the violence of his exclamations.—"Out of my sight, ye viper!—ye frozen viper, that I warmed till ye stung me!—Art thou not afraid that the walls of my father's dwelling should fall and crush thee limb and bone?—Are ye not afraid the very lintels of the door of Ellangowan castle should break open and swallow you up?—Were ye not friendless,—houseless,—penniless,—when I took ye by the hand—and are Ye not expelling me—me, and that innocent girl— friendless, houseless, and penniless, from the house that has sheltered us and ours for a thousand years?"

33

Had Glossin been alone, he would probably have slunk off; but the consciousness that a stranger was present, besides the person who came with him (a sort of land-surveyor), determined him to resort to impudence. The task, however, was almost too hard, even for his effrontery—"Sir—Sir—Mr. Bertram—Sir, you should not blame me, but your own imprudence, Sir—"

The indignation of Mannering was mounting very high. "Sir," he said to Glossin, "without entering into the merits of this controversy, I must inform you, that you have chosen a very improper place, time, and presence for it. And you will oblige me by withdrawing without more words."

Glossin, being a tall, strong, muscular man, was not unwilling rather to turn upon a stranger whom he hoped to bully, than maintain his wretched cause against his injured patron:—"I do not know who you are, sir," he said, "and I shall permit no man to use such d-d freedom with me."

Mannering was naturally hot-tempered—his eyes flashed a dark light—he compressed his nether lip so closely that the blood sprung, and approaching Glossin—"Look you, sir," he said, "that you do not know me is of little consequence. I know you; and, if you do not instantly descend that bank, without uttering a single syllable, by the Heaven that is above us, you shall make but one step from the top to the bottom!"

The commanding tone of rightful anger silenced at once the ferocity of the bully. He hesitated, turned on his heel, and, muttering something between his teeth about unwillingness to alarm the lady, relieved them of his hateful company.

Mrs. Mac-Candlish's postilion, who had come up in time to hear what passed, said aloud, "If he had stuck by the way, I would have lent him a heezie, [* Kick] the dirty scoundrel, as willingly as ever I pitched a boddle." [* A small copper coin]

He then stepped forward to announce that his horses were in readiness for the invalid and his daughter.

But they were no longer necessary. The debilitated frame of Mr. Bertram was exhausted by this last effort of indignant anger, and when he sunk again upon his chair, he expired almost without a struggle or groan. So little alteration did the extinction of the vital spark make upon his external appearance, that the screams of his daughter, when she saw his eye fix and felt his pulse stop, first announced his death to the spectators.

CHAPTER XIV.

The bell strikes one.—We take no note of time But from its loss. To give it then a tongue Is wise in man. As if an angel spoke, I feel the solemn sound.— YOUNG.

The moral which the poet has rather quaintly deduced from the necessary mode of measuring time, may he well applied to our feelings respecting that portion of it which constitutes human life. We observe the aged, the infirm, and those engaged in occupations of immediate hazard, trembling as it were upon the very brink of non-existence, but we derive no lesson from the precariousness of their tenure until it has altogether failed. Then, for a moment at least,

Our hopes and fears
Start up alarm'd, and o'er life's narrow verge
Look down—On what? —a fathomless abyss,
A dark eternity,—how surely ours!—

The crowd of assembled gazers and idlers at Ellangowan had followed the views of amusement, or what they called business, which brought them there, with little regard to the feelings of those who were suffering—upon that occasion. Few, indeed, knew anything of the family. The father, betwixt seclusion, misfortune, and imbecility, had drifted, as it were, for many years out of the notice of his contemporaries-the daughter had never been known to them. But when the general murmur announced that the unfortunate Mr. Bertram had broken his heart in the effort to leave the mansion of his forefathers, there poured forth a torrent of sympathy, like the waters from the rock when stricken by the wand of the, prophet. The ancient descent and unblemished integrity of the family were respectfully remembered; above all, the sacred veneration due to misfortune, which in Scotland seldom demands its tribute in vain, then claimed and received it.

Mr. Mac-Morlan hastily announced, that he would suspend all further proceedings in the sale of the estate and other property, and relinquish the possession of the premises to the young lady, until she could consult with her friends, and provide for the burial of her father.

Glossin had cowered for a few minutes under the general expression of sympathy, till, hardened by observing that no appearance of popular indignation was directed his way, he had the audacity to require that the sale should proceed.

"I will take it upon my own authority to adjourn it," said the Sheriff-substitute," and will be responsible for the consequences. I will also give due notice when it is again to go forward. It is for the benefit of all concerned that the lands should bring the highest price the state of the market will admit, and this is surely no time to expect it—I will take the responsibility upon myself."

Glossin left the room, and the house too, with secrecy and despatch; and it was probably well for him he did so, since our friend Jock Jabos was already haranguing a numerous tribe of barelegged boys on the propriety of pelting him off the estate.

Some of the rooms were hastily put in order for the reception of the young lady, and of her father's dead body. Mannering now found his further interference would be unnecessary, and might be misconstrued. He observed, too, that several families connected with that of Ellangowan, and who indeed derived their principal claim of gentility from the alliance, were now disposed to pay to their trees of genealogy a tribute, which the adversity of their supposed relatives had been inadequate to call forth; and that the honour of superintending the funeral rites of the dead Godfrey Bertram (as in the memorable case of Homer's birthplace) was likely to be debated by seven gentlemen of rank and fortune, none of whom had offered him an asylum while living. He therefore resolved, as his presence was altogether useless, to make a short tour of a fortnight, at the end of which period the adjourned sale of the estate of Ellangowan was to proceed.

But before he departed, he solicited an interview with the Dominie. The poor man appeared, on being informed a gentleman wanted to speak to him, with some expression of surprise in his gaunt features, to which recent sorrow had given an expression yet more grisly. He made two or three profound reverences to Mannering, and then, standing erect, patiently waited an explanation of his commands.

"You are probably at a loss to guess, Mr. Sampson," said Mannering, "what a stranger may have to say to you?"

"Unless it were to request, that I would undertake to train up some youth in polite letters, and humane learning—but I cannot—I cannot—I have yet a task to perform."

"No, Mr. Sampson, my wishes are not so ambitious. I have no son, and my only daughter, I presume, you would not consider as a fit pupil."

"Of a surety, no," replied the simple-minded Sampson. "Nathless, it was I who did educate Miss Lucy in all useful learning,—albeit it was the housekeeper who did teach her those unprofitable exercises of hemming and shaping."

"Well, sir," replied Mannering, "it is of Miss Lucy I meant to speak—you have, I presume, no recollection of me?"

Sampson, always sufficiently absent in mind, neither remembered the astrologer of past years, nor even the stranger who had taken his patron's part against Glossin, so much had his friend's sudden death embroiled his ideas.

"Well, that does not signify," pursued the Colonel; "I am an old acquaintance of the late Mr. Bertram, able and willing to assist his daughter in her present circumstances. Besides, I have thoughts of making this purchase, and I should wish things kept in order about the place; will you have the goodness to apply this small sum in the usual family expenses?"—He put into the Dominie's hand a purse containing some gold.

"Pro-di-gi-ous!" exclaimed Dominie Sampson. "But if your honour would tarry—"

"Impossible, sir—impossible," said Mannering, making his escape from him.

"Pro-di-gi-ous!" again exclaimed Sampson, following to the head of the, stairs, still holding out the purse. "But as touching this coined money—" Mannering escaped downstairs as fast as possible.

"Pro-di-gi-ous!" exclaimed Dominie Sampson, yet the third time, now standing at the front door. "But as touching this specie—"

But Mannering was now on horseback, and out of hearing. The Dominie, who had never, either in his own right, or as trustee for another, been possessed of a quarter part of this sum, though it was not above twenty guineas, "took counsel," as he expressed himself, "how he should demean himself with respect unto the fine gold thus left in his charge." Fortunately he found a disinterested adviser in Mac-Morlan, who pointed out the most proper means of disposing of it for contributing to Miss Bertram's convenience, being no doubt the purpose to which it was destined by the bestower.

Many of the neighbouring gentry were now sincerely eager in pressing offers of hospitality and kindness upon Miss Bertram. But she felt a natural reluctance to enter any family, for the first time, as an object rather of benevolence than hospitality, and determined to wait the opinion and advice of her father's nearest female relation, Mrs. Margaret Bertram of Singleside, an old unmarried lady, to whom she wrote an account of her present distressful Situation.

The funeral of the late Mr. Bertram was performed with decent privacy, and the unfortunate young lady was now to consider herself as but the temporary tenant of the house in which she had been born, and where her patience and soothing attentions had so long "rocked the cradle of declining age." Her communication with Mr. Mac-Morlan encouraged her to hope that she would not be suddenly or unkindly deprived of this asylum; but fortune had ordered otherwise.

For two days before the appointed day for the sale of the lands and estate of Ellangowan, Mac-Morlan daily expected the appearance of Colonel Mannering, or at least a letter containing powers to act for him. But none such arrived. Mr. Mac-Morlan waked early in the morning,—walked over to the Post-office,—there were no letters for him. He endeavoured to persuade himself that he should see Colonel Mannering to breakfast, and ordered his wife to place her best china, and prepare herself accordingly. But the preparations were in vain. "Could I have foreseen this," he said, "I would have travelled Scotland over, but I would have found some one to bid against Glossin."—Alas! such reflections were all too late. The appointed hour arrived; and the parties met in the Masons' Lodge at Kippletringan, being the place fixed for the adjourned sale. Mac-Morlan spent as much time in preliminaries as decency would permit, and read over the articles of sale as slowly as if he—had been reading his own death-warrant. He turned his eye every time the door of the room opened, with hopes which grew fainter and fainter. He listened to every noise in the street of the village, and endeavoured to distinguish in it the sound of hoofs or wheels. It was all in vain. A bright idea then occurred, that Colonel Mannering might have employed some other person in the transaction—he would not have wasted a moment's thought upon the want of confidence in himself, which such a manoeuvre would have evinced. But this hope also was groundless. After a solemn pause, Mr. Glossin offered the upset price for the lands and barony of Ellangowan. No reply was made, and no competitor appeared; so, after a lapse of the usual interval by the running of a sand-glass, upon the intended purchaser entering the proper sureties, Mr. Mac-Morlan was obliged, in technical terms, to "find and declare the sale lawfully completed, and to prefer the said Gilbert Glossin as the purchaser of the said lands and estate." The honest writer refused to partake of a splendid entertainment with which Gilbert Glossin, Esquire, now of Ellangowan, treated the rest of the company, and returned home in huge bitterness of spirit, which he vented in complaints against the fickleness and caprice of these Indian nabobs, who never knew what they would be at for ten days together. Fortune generously determined to take the blame upon herself, and cut off even this vent of Mac-Morlan's resentment.

An express arrived about six o'clock at night, "very particularly drunk," the maidservant said, with a packet from Colonel Mannering, dated four days back, at a town about a hundred miles' distance from Kippletringan, containing full powers to Mr. Mac-Morlan, or any one whom he might employ, to make the intended purchase, and stating, that some family business of consequence called the Colonel himself to Westmoreland, where a letter would find him, addressed to the care of Arthur Mervyn, Esq., of Mervyn Hall.

Mac-Morlan, in the transports of his wrath, flung the power of attorney at the head of the innocent maid-servant, and was only forcibly withheld from horsewhipping the rascally messenger, by whose sloth and drunkenness the disappointment had taken place.

CHAPTER XV.

My gold is gone, my money is spent, My land now take it
unto thee. Give me thy gold, good John o' Scales, And
thine for aye my land shall be. Then John he did him to
record draw, And John he caste him a gods-pennie; But for
every pounde that John agreed, The land, I wis, was well
worth three.

Heir of Linne.

The Galwegian John o' the Scales was a more clever fellow than his prototype. He contrived to make himself heir of Lione without the disagreeable ceremony of "telling down the good red gold." Miss Bertram no sooner heard this painful, and of late unexpected intelligence, than she proceeded in the preparations she had already made for leaving the mansion-house immediately. Mr. Mac-Morlan assisted her in these arrangements, and pressed upon her so kindly the hospitality and protection of his roof, until she should receive an answer from her cousin' or be enabled to adopt some settled plan of life, that she felt there would be unkindness in refusing an invitation urged with such earnestness. Mrs. Mac-Morlan was a lady-like person, and well qualified by birth and manners to receive the visit, and to make her house agreeable to Miss Bertram. A home, therefore, and an hospitable reception, were secured to her, and she went on, with better heart, to pay the wages and receive the adieus of the few domestics of her father's family.

Where there are estimable qualities or, either side, this task is always affecting—the present circumstances rendered it doubly so. All received their due, and even a trifle more, and with thanks and good wishes, to which some added tears, took farewell of their young mistress. There remained in the parlour only Mr. Mac-Morlan, who came to attend his guest to his house, Dominie Sampson, and Miss Bertram. "And now," said the poor girl, "I must bid farewell to one of my oldest and kindest friends.—God bless you, Mr. Sampson, and requite to you all the kindness of your instructions to your poor pupil, and your friendship to him that is gone—I hope I shall often hear from you." She slid into his hand a paper containing some pieces of gold, and rose, as if to leave the room.

Dominie Sampson also rose; but it was to stand aghast with utter astonishment. The idea of parting from Miss Lucy, go where she might, had never once occurred to the simplicity of his understanding.—He laid the money on the table. "It is certainly inadequate," said Mac-Morlan, mistaking his meaning, "but the circumstances—"

Mr. Sampson waved his hand impatiently.—"It is not the lucre—it is not the lucre—but that I, that have ate of her father's loaf, and drank of his cup, for twenty years and more—to think that I am going to leave her—and to leave her in distress and dolour—No, Miss Lucy, you need never think it! You would not consent to put forth your father's poor dog, and would you use me waur than a messan? No, Miss Lucy Bertram, while I live I will not separate from you. I'll be no burden—I have thought how to prevent that. But, as Ruth said unto Naomi, 'Entreat me not to leave thee, nor to depart from thee; for whither thou goest I will go, and where thou dwellest I will dwell; thy people shall be my people, and thy God shall be my God. Where thou diest will I die, and there will I be buried. The Lord do so to me, and more also, if aught but death do part thee and me.' "

During this speech, the longest ever Dominie Sampson was known to utter, the affectionate creature's eyes streamed with tears, and neither Lucy nor Mac-Morlan could refrain from sympathising with this unexpected burst of feeling and attachment. "Mr. Sampson," said Mac-Morlan, after having had recourse to his snuff-box and handkerchief alternately, "my house is large enough, and if you will accept of a bed there, while Miss Bertram honours us with her residence, I shall think myself very happy, and my roof much favoured by receiving a man of your worth and fidelity." And then, with a delicacy which was meant to remove any objection on Miss Bertram's part to bringing with her this unexpected satellite, he added, "My business requires my frequently having occasion for a better accountant than any of my present clerks, and I should be glad to have recourse to your assistance in that way now and then."

"Of a surety, of a surety," said Sampson eagerly; "I understand book-keeping by double entry and the Italian method."

Our postilion had thrust himself into the room to announce his chaise and horses; he tarried, unobserved, during this extraordinary scene, and assured Mrs. Mac-Candlish it was the most moving thing he ever saw; "the death of the gray mare, puir hizzie, was naething till't." This trifling circumstance afterwards had consequences of greater moment to the Dominie.

The visitors were hospitably welcomed by Mrs. Mac-Morlan, to whom, as well as to others, her Husband intimated that he had engaged . Dominie Sampson's assistance to disentangle some perplexed accounts; during which occupation he would, for convenience' sake, reside with the family. Mr. MacMorlan's knowledge of the world induced him to put this colour upon the matter, aware, that however honourable the fidelity of the Dominie's attachment might be, both to his own heart and to the family of Ellangowan, his exterior ill qualified him to be a "squire of dames," and rendered him, upon the whole, rather a ridiculous appendage to a beautiful young woman of seventeen.

Dominie Sampson achieved with great zeal such tasks as Mr. Mac-Morlan chose to intrust him with; but it was speedily observed that at a certain hour after breakfast he regularly disappeared, and returned again about dinner-time. The evening he occupied in the labour of the office. On Saturday, he appeared before Mac-Morlan with a look of great triumph, and laid on the table two pieces of gold. "What is this for, Dominie?" said Mac-Morlan.

"First to indemnify you of your charges in my behalf, worthy sir—and the balance for the use of Miss Lucy Bertram."

"But, Mr. Sampson, your labour in the office much more than recompenses me—I am your debtor, my good friend."

"Then be it all," said the Dominie, waving his hand, "for Miss Lucy Bertram's behoof."

"Well, but, Dominie, this money—"

"It is honestly come by, Mr. Mac-Morlan; it is the bountiful reward of a young gentleman, to whom I am teaching the tongues; reading with him three hours daily—"

A few more questions extracted from the Dominie that this liberal pupil was young Hazlewood, and that he met his preceptor daily at the house of Mrs. Mac-Candlish, whose proclamation of Sampson's disinterested attachment to the young lady had procured him this indefatigable and bounteous scholar.

Mac-Morlan was much struck with what he heard.

Dominie Sampson was doubtless a very good scholar, and an excellent man, and the classics were unquestionably very well worth reading; yet that a young man of twenty should ride seven miles and back again each day in the week, to hold this sort of tete-a-tete of three hours, was a zeal for literature to which he was not prepared to give entire credit. Little art was necessary to sift the Dominie, for the honest man's head never admitted any but the most direct and simple ideas. "Does Miss Bertram know how your time is engaged, my good friend?"

"Surely not as yet—Mr. Charles recommended it should be concealed from her, lest she should scruple to accept of the small assistance arising from it; but," he added, "it would not be possible to conceal it long, since Mr. Charles proposed taking his lessons occasionally in this house."

"Oh, he does!" said Mac-Morlan Yes, yes, I can understand that better.—And pray, Mr. Sampson, are these three hours entirely spent in construing and translating?"

"Doubtless, no—we have also colloquial intercourse to sweeten study—neque semper arcum tendit Apollo."

The querist proceeded to elicit from this Galloway Phoebus what their discourse chiefly turned upon.

"Upon our past meetings at Ellangowan—and, truly, I think very often we discourse concerning Miss Lucy—for Mr. Charles Hazlewood, in that particular, resembleth me, Mr. Mac-Morlan. When I begin to speak of her I never know when to stop—and, as I say (jocularly), she cheats us out of half our lessons."

"Oh ho!" thought Mr. Mac-Morlan, "sits the wind in that quarter?
I've heard something like this before."

He then began to consider what conduct was safest for his protege, and even for himself; for the senior Mr. Hazlewood was powerful, wealthy, ambitious, and vindictive, and looked for both fortune and title in any connection which his son might form. At length, having the highest opinion of his guest's good sense and penetration, he determined to take an opportunity, when they should happen to be alone, to communicate the matter to her as a simple piece of intelligence. He did so in as natural a manner as he could;—"I wish you joy of your friend Mr. Sampson's good fortune, Miss Bertram; he has got a pupil who pays him two guineas for twelve lessons of Greek and Latin."

"Indeed!—I am equally happy and surprised—who can be so liberal?—is Colonel Mannering returned?"

"No, no, not Colonel Mannering; but what do you think of your acquaintance, Mr. Charles Hazlewood?—He talks of taking his lessons here—I wish we may have accommodation for him."

Lucy blushed deeply. "For Heaven's sake, no, Mr. Mac-Morlan—do not let that be—Charles Hazlewood has had enough of mischief about that already."

"About the classics, my dear young lady?" wilfully seeming to misunderstand her;—"most young gentlemen have so at one period or another, sure enough, but his present studies are voluntary."

Miss Bertram let the conversation drop, and her host made no effort to renew it, as she seemed to pause upon the intelligence in order to form some internal resolution.

The next day Miss Bertram took an opportunity of conversing with Mr. Sampson. Expressing in the kindest manner her grateful thanks for his disinterested attachment, and her joy that he had get such a provision, she hinted to him that his present mode of superintending Charles Hazlewood's studios must be so inconvenient to his pupil, that, while that engagement lasted, he had better consent to a temporary separation, and reside either with his scholar, or as near him as might be. Sampson refused, as indeed she had expected, to listen a moment to this proposition—he would not quit her to be made preceptor to the Prince of Wales. "But I see," he added, "you are too proud to share my pittance; and, peradventure, I grow wearisome unto you."

"No, indeed—you were my father's ancient, almost his only friend—I am not proud—God knows, I have no reason to be so—you shall do what you judge best in other matters; but oblige me by telling Mr. Charles Hazlewood, that you had some conversation with me concerning his studies, and that I was of opinion that his carrying them on in this house was altogether impracticable, and not to be thought of."

Dominie Sampson left her presence altogether crestfallen, and, as he shut the door, could not help muttering the "varium et mutabile" of Virgil. Next day he appeared with a very rueful visage, and tendered Miss Bertram a letter.—"Mr. Hazlewood," he said, "was to discontinue his lessons, though he had generously made up the pecuniary loss.—But how will he make up the loss to himself of the knowledge he might have acquired under my instruction? Even in that one article of writing, he was an hour before he could write that brief note, and destroyed many scrolls, four quills, and some good white paper—I would have taught him in three weeks a firm, current, clear, and legible hand—he should have been a calligrapher—but God's will be done."—

The letter contained but a few lines, deeply regretting and murmuring against Miss Bertram's cruelty, who not only refused to see him, but to permit him in the most indirect manner to hear of her health and contribute to her service. But it concluded with assurances that her severity was vain, and that nothing could shake the attachment of Charles Hazlewood.

Under the active patronage of Mrs. Mac-Candlish, Sampson picked up some other scholars—very different indeed from Charles Hazlewood in rank—and whose lessons were proportionally unproductive. Still, however, he gained something, and it was the glory of his heart to carry it to Mr. Mac-Morlan weekly, a slight peculium only subtracted, to supply his snuff-box and tobacco-pouch.

And here we must leave Kippletringan to look after our hero, lest our readers should fear they are to lose sight of him for another quarter of a century.

CHAPTER XVI.

Our Polly is a sad slut, nor heeds what we have taught her;
I wonder any man alive will ever rear a daughter;
For when she's drest with care and cost, all tempting, fine and gay,
As men should serve a cucumber, she flings herself away.

Beggar's Opera.

After the death of Mr. Bertram, Mannering had set out upon a short tour, proposing to return to the neighbourhood of Ellangowan before the sale of that property should take place. He went, accordingly,' to Edinburgh and elsewhere, and it was ill his return towards the south-western district of Scotland,—in which our scene lies, that, at a post-town about a hundred miles from Kippletringan, to which he had requested his friend, Mr. Mervyn, to address his letters, he received one from that gentleman, which contained rather unpleasing intelligence. We have assumed already the privilege of acting a secretis to this gentleman, and therefore shall present,—the reader with an extract from this epistle.

"I beg your pardon, my dearest friend, for the pain I have given you, in, forcing you to open wounds so festering as those your letter referred to. I have always heard, though erroneously perhaps, that the attentions of Mr. Brown were intended for Miss Mannering. But, however that were, it could not be supposed that in your situation his boldness should escape notice and chastisement. Wise men say, that we resign to civil society our natural rights of self-defence, only on condition that the ordinances of law should protect us. Where the price cannot be paid, the resignation becomes void. For instance, no one supposes that I am not entitled to defend my purse and person against a highwayman, as much as if I were a wild Indian, who owns neither law nor magistracy. The question of resistance, or submission, must be determined by my means and situation. But, if, armed and equal in force, I submit to injustice and violence from any man, high or low, I presume it will hardly be attributed to religious or moral feeling in me, or in any one but a Quaker. An aggression on my honour seems to me much the same. The insult, however trifling in itself, is one of much deeper consequence to all views in life than any wrong which can be inflicted by a depredator or the highway, and to redress the injured party is much less in the power of public jurisprudence, or rather it is entirely beyond its reach. If any man chooses to rob Arthur Mervyn of the contents of his purse, supposing the said Arthur has not means of defence, or the skill and courage to use them, the assizes at Lancaster or Carlisle will do him justice by tucking up the robber:-Yet who will say I am bound to wait for this justice, and submit to being plundered in the first instance, if I have myself the means and spirit to protect my own property? But if an affront is offered to me, submission under which is to tarnish my character for ever with men of honour, ant for which the twelve judges of England, with the Chancellor to boot, can afford me no redress, by what rule of law or reason am I to be deterred from protecting what ought to be, and is, so infinitely dearer to every man of honour than his whole fortune? Of the religious views of the matter I shall say nothing, until I end a reverend divine who shall condemn self-defence in the article of life and property. If its propriety in that case be generally admitted, I suppose little distinction can be drawn between defence of person and goods, and protection of reputation. That the latter is liable to be assailed by persons of a different rank in life, untainted perhaps in morals, and fair in character, cannot affect my legal right of self-defence. I may be sorry that circumstances have engaged me in personal strife with such an individual; but I should feel the same sorrow for a generous enemy who fell under my sword in a national quarrel. I shall leave the question with the casuists, however; only observing, that what I have written will not avail either the professed duellist, or him who is the aggressor in a dispute of honour. I only presume to exculpate him who is dragged into the field by such an offence, as, submitted to in patience, would forfeit for ever his rank and estimation in society.

"I am sorry you have thoughts of settling in Scotland, and yet glad that you will still be at no immeasurable distance, and that the latitude is all in our favour. To move to Westmoreland from Devonshire might make an East Indian shudder; but to come to us from Galloway or Dumfriesshire, is a step, though a short one, nearer the sun. Besides, if, as I suspect, the estate in view be connected with the old haunted castle in which you played the astrologer in your northern tour some twenty years since, I have heard you too often describe the scene with comic unction, to hope you will be deterred from making the purchase. I trust, however, the hospitable gossiping Laird has not run himself upon the shallows, and that his chaplain, whom you so often made us laugh at, is still in rerum natura.

"And here, dear Mannering, I wish I could stop, for I have incredible pain in felling the rest of my story; although I am sure I can warn you against any intentional impropriety on the part of my temporary ward, Julia Mannering. But I must still earn my college nickname of Downright Dunstable. In one word, then, here is the matter.

"Your daughter has much of the romantic turn of your disposition, with a little of that love of admiration which all pretty women share less or more. She will besides, apparently, be your heiress; a trifling circumstance to those who view Julia with my eyes, but a prevailing bait to the specious, artful, and worthless. You know how I have jested with her about her soft melancholy, and lonely walks at morning before any one is up, and in the moonlight when all should be gone to bed, or set down to cards, which is the same thing. The incident which follows may not be beyond the bounds of a joke, but I had rather the jest upon it came from you than me.

"Two or three times during the last fortnight, I heard, at a late hour in the night, or very early in the morning, a flageolet play the little Hindu tune to which your daughter is so partial. I thought for some time that some tuneful domestic, whose taste for music was laid under constraint during the day, chose that silent hour to imitate the strains which he had caught up by the ear during his attendance in the drawing-room. But last night I sat late in. my study, which is immediately under Miss Mannering's apartment, and to my surprise, I not only heard the flageolet distinctly, but satisfied myself that it came from the lake under the window. Curious to know who serenaded us at that unusual hour, I stole softly to the window of my apartment. But there were other watchers than me. You may remember, Miss Mannering preferred that apartment on account of a balcony which opened from her window upon the lake. Well, sir, I heard the sash of her window thrown up, the shutters opened, and her own voice in conversation with some person who answered from below. This is not 'Much ado about nothing'; I could not be mistaken in her voice, and such tones, so soft, so insinuating—and, to say the truth, the accents from below were in passion's tenderise cadence too—but of the sense I can say nothing. I raised the sash of my own window that I might hear something more than the mere murmur of this Spanish rendezvous, but, though I used every precaution, the noise alarmed the speakers; down slid the young lady's casement, and the shutters were barred in an instant. The dash of a pair or oars in the water announced the retreat of the male person of the dialogue. Indeed, I saw his boat, which he rowed with great swiftness and dexterity, fly across the lake like a twelve-oared barge. Next morning I examined some of my domestics, as if by accident. and I found the gamekeeper, when making his rounds, had twice seen that boat beneath the house, with a single person, and had heard the flageolet. I did not care to press any further questions, for fear of implicating Julia in the opinions of those of whom they might be asked. Next morning, at breakfast, I dropped a casual hint about the serenade of the evening before, and I promise you Miss Mannering looked red and pale alternately. I immediately gave the circumstance such a turn as might lead her to suppose that my observation was merely casual. I have since caused a watch-light to be burnt in my library, and have left the shutters open, to deter the approach of our nocturnal guest; and I have stated the severity of approaching winter, and the rawness of the fogs, as an objection to solitary walks. Miss Mannering acquiesced with a passiveness which is no part of her character, and which, to tell you the plain truth, is a feature about the business which I like least of all. Julia has too much of her own dear papa's disposition to be curbed in any of her humours, were there not some little lurking consciousness that it may be as prudent to avoid debate.

"Now my story is told, and you will judge what you ought to do. I have not mentioned the matter to my good woman, who, a faithful secretary to her sex's foibles, would certainly remonstrate against your being made acquainted with these particulars, and might, instead, take it into her head to exercise her own eloquence on Miss Mannering; a faculty, which, however powerful when directed against me, its legitimate object, might, I fear, do more harm than good in the case supposed. Perhaps even you yourself will find it most prudent to act without remonstrating, or appearing to be aware of this little anecdote. Julia is very like a certain friend of mine; she has a quick and lively imagination, and keen feelings, which are apt to exaggerate both the good and evil they find in life. She is a charming girl, however, as generous and spirited as she is lovely. I paid her the kiss you sent her with all my heart, and she rapped my fingers for my reward with all hers. Pray return as soon as you can. Meantime, rely upon the care of, yours faithfully,

"Arthur Mervyn.

"P.S.—You will naturally wish to know if I have the least guess concerning the person of the serenader. In truth, I have none. There is no young gentleman of these parts, who might be in rank or fortune a match for Miss Julia, that I think at all likely to play such a character. . .

But on the other side of the lake, nearly opposite to Mervyn Hall, is a d-d cake-house, the resort of walking gentlemen of all descriptions, poets, players, painters, musicians, who come to rave, and recite, and madden, about this picturesque land of ours. It is paying some penalty for its beauties, that they are the means of drawing this swarm of coxcombs together. But were Julia my daughter, it is one of those sort of fellows that I should fear on her account. She is generous and romantic, and writes six sheets a week to a female correspondent; and it's a sad thing to lack a subject in such a case, either for exercise of the feelings or of the pen. Adieu, once more. Were I to treat this matter more seriously than I have done, I should do injustice to your feelings; were I altogether to overlook it, I should discredit my own."

The consequence of this letter was, that, having first despatched the faithless messenger with the necessary powers to Mr. Mac-Morlan for purchasing the estate of Ellangowan, Colonel Mannering turned his horse's head in a more southerly direction, and neither "stinted nor staid" until he arrived at the mansion of his friend Mr. Mervyn, upon the banks of one of the lakes of Westmoreland.

CHAPTER XVII.

Heaven first, in its mercy, taught mortals their letters,
For ladies in limbo, and lovers in fetters,
Or some author, who, placing his persons before ye,
Ungallantly leaves them to write their own story.

Pope, imitated.

When Mannering returned to England, his first object had been to place his daughter in a seminary for female education, of established character. Not, however, finding her progress in the accomplishments which he wished her to acquire so rapid as his impatience expected, he had withdrawn Miss Mannering from the school at the end of the first quarter. So she had only time to form an eternal friendship with Miss Matilda Marchmont, a young lady about her own age, which was nearly eighteen. To her faithful eye were addressed those formidable quires which issued forth from Mervyn Hall, on the wings of the post, while Miss Mannering was a guest there. The perusal of a few short extracts from these may be necessary to render our story intelligible.

First Extract

"Alas! my dearest Matilda, what a tale is mine to tell! Misfortune from the cradle has set her seal upon your unhappy friend. That we should be severed for so slight a cause—an ungrammatical phrase in my Italian exercise, and three false notes in one of Paesiello's sonatas! But it is a part of my father's character, of whom it is impossible to say, whether I love, admire, or fear him the most. His success in life and in war-his habit of making every obstacle yield before the energy of his exertions, even where they seemed insurmountable-all these have given a hasty and peremptory cast to his character, which can neither endure contradiction, nor make allowance for deficiencies. Then he is himself so very accomplished. Do you know there was a murmur half confirmed too by some mysterious words which, dropped from my poor mother, that he possesses other sciences, now lost to the world, which enable the possessor to summon up before him the dark and shadowy forms of future events! Does not the very idea of such a power, or even of the high talent and commanding intellect which the world may mistake for it,—does it not, dear Matilda, throw a mysterious grandeur about its possessor? You will call this romantic: but consider I was born in the land of talisman and spell, and my childhood lulled by tales which you can only enjoy through the gauzy frippery of a French translation. O Matilda, I wish you could have seen the dusky visages of my Indian attendants, bending in earnest devotion round the magic narrative, that flowed, half poetry, half prose, from the lips of the tale-teller! No wonder that European fiction sounds cold and meagre, after the wonderful effects which I have seen the romances of the East produce upon their hearers."

Second Extract.

"You are possessed, my dear Matilda, of my bosom-secret, in those sentiments with which I regard Brown. I will not say his memory. I am convinced he lives, and is faithful. His addresses to me were countenanced by my deceased parent; imprudently countenanced perhaps, considering the prejudices of my father, in favour of birth and rank. But I, then almost a girl, could not be expected surely to be wiser than her, under whose charge nature had placed me. My father, constantly engaged in military duty, I saw but at rare intervals, and was taught to look up to him with more awe than confidence. Would to Heaven it had been otherwise! It might have been better for us all at this day!"

Third Extract.

"You ask me why I do not make known to my father that Brown yet lives, at least that he survived the wound he received in that unhappy duel; and had written to my mother, expressing his entire convalescence, and his hope of speedily escaping from captivity. A soldier, that 'in the trade of war has oft slain men,' feels probably no uneasiness at reflecting upon the supposed catastrophe, which almost turned me into stone. And should I show him that letter, does it not follow, that Brown, alive and maintaining with pertinacity the pretensions to the affections of your poor friend, for which my father formerly sought his life would be a more formidable disturber of Colonel Mannering's peace of mind than in his supposed grave? If he escapes from the hands of these marauders, I am convinced he will soon be in England, and it will be then time to consider how his existence is to be disclosed to my father—But if, alas! my earnest and confident hope should betray me, what would it avail to tear open a mystery fraught with so many painful recollections?—My dear mother had such dread of its being known, that I think she even suffered my father to suspect that Brown's attentions were directed towards herself, rather than permit him to discover their real object; and, oh, Matilda, whatever respect I owe to the memory of a deceased parent, let me do justice to a living one. I cannot but condemn the dubious policy which she adopted, as unjust to my father, and highly perilous to herself and me.—But peace be with her ashes! her actions were guided by the heart rather than the head; and shall her daughter, who inherits all her weakness, be the first to withdraw the veil from her defects?"

Fourth Extract

"Mervyn Hall.

"If India be the land of magic, this my dearest Matilda, is the country of romance. The scenery is such as nature brings together in her sublimest moods;—sounding cataracts-hills which rear their scathed heads to the sky-lakes, that, winding up the shadowy valleys, lead at every turn to yet more romantic recesses-rocks which catch the clouds of heaven. All the wildness of Salvator here, and there the fairy scenes of Claude. I am happy too, in finding at least one object upon which my father can share my enthusiasm. An admirer of nature, both as an artist and a poet, I have experienced the utmost pleasure from the observations by which he explains the character and the effect of these brilliant specimens of her power. I wish he would settle in this enchanting land' But his views lie still farther north, and he is at present absent on a tour in Scotland, looking, I believe, for some purchase of land which may suit him as a residence. He is partial, from early recollections, to that country. So, my dearest Matilda, I must be yet farther removed from you before I am established in a home—And oh how delighted shall I be when I can say, Come, Matilda, and be the guest of your faithful Julia!

"I am at present the inmate of Mr. and Mrs. Mervyn, old friends of my father. The latter is precisely a good sort of woman;—ladylike and housewifely, but, for accomplishments or fancy—good lack, my dearest Matilda, your friend might as well seek sympathy from Mrs. Teach'em,—you see I have not forgot school nicknames. Mervyn is a different—quite a different being from my father; yet he amuses and endures me. He is fat and good-natured, gifted with strong shrewd sense, and some powers of humour; but having been handsome, I suppose, in his youth, has still some pretension to be a beau garcon, as well as an enthusiastic agriculturist. I delight to make him scramble to the tops of eminences and to the foot of waterfalls, and am obliged in turn to admire his turnips, his lucerne, and his timothy grass.—He thinks me, I fancy, a simple romantic Miss, with some—(the word will he out) beauty, and some good nature; and I hold that the gentleman has good taste for the female outside, and do not expect he should comprehend my sentiments further. So he rallies, hands, and hobbles (for the dear creature has got the gout too), and tells old stories of high life of which he has seen a great deal; and I listen, and smile, and look as pretty, as pleasant, and as simple as I can, and we do very well. But, alas! my dearest Matilda, how would time pass away, even in this paradise of romance, tenanted as it is by a pair assorting so ill with the scenes around them, were it not for your fidelity in replying to my uninteresting details? Pray do not fail to write three times a week at least—you can be at no loss what to say."

Fifth Extract.

"How shall I communicate what I have now to tell!—My hand and Heart still flutter so much, that the task of writing is almost impossible!—Did I not say that he lived? did I not say I would not despair? How could you suggest, my dear Matilda, that my feelings, considering I had parted from him so young, rather arose from the warmth of my imagination than of my heart?—Oh! I was sure that they were genuine, deceitful as the dictates of our bosom so frequently are.—But to my tale—let it be, my friend, the most sacred, as it is the most sincere, pledge of our friendship.

"Our hours here are early—earlier than my heart, with its load of care, can compose itself to rest. I, therefore, usually take a book for an hour or two after retiring to my own room, which I think I have told you opens to a small balcony, looking down upon that beautiful lake, of which I attempted to give you a slight sketch. Mervyn Hall, being partly an ancient building—, and constructed with a view to defence, is situated an the verge of the lake. A stone dropped from the projecting balcony plunges into water deep enough to float a skiff. I had left my window partly unbarred, that, before I went to bed, I might, according to my custom, look out and see the moonlight shining upon the lake. I was deeply engaged with that beautiful scene in the Merchant of Venice, where two lovers, describing the stillness of a summer night, enhance on each other its charms, and was lost in the associations of story and of feeling which it awakens, when I heard upon the lake the sound of a flageolet. I have told you it was Brown's favourite instrument. Who could touch it in a night which, though still and serene, was too cold, and too late in the year, to invite forth any wanderer for more pleasure? I drew yet nearer the window, and hearkened with breathless attention—the sounds paused a space, were then resumed—paused again—and again reached my ear, ever coming nearer and nearer. At length, I distinguished plainly that little Hindu air which you called my favourite—I have told you by whom it was taught me—the instrument, the tones, were his own!—was it earthly music, or notes passing on the wind, to warn me of his death?

"It was some time ere I could summon courage to step on the balcony—nothing could have emboldened me to do so but the strong conviction of my mind, that he was still alive, and that we should again meet—but that conviction did embolden me, and I ventured, though with a throbbing heart. There was a small skiff with a single person—O Matilda, it was himself!—I knew his appearance after so long an absence, and through the shadow of the night, as perfectly as if we had parted yesterday, and met again in the broad sunshine! He guided his boat under the balcony, and spoke to me; I hardly knew what he said, or what I replied. Indeed, I could scarcely speak for weeping, but they were joyful tears. We were disturbed by the barking of a dog at some distance, and parted, but not before he had conjured me to prepare to. meet him at the same place and hour this evening.

"But where and to what is all this tending?—Can I answer this question? I cannot.—Heaven, that saved him from death, and delivered him from captivity; that saved my father too, from shedding the blood of one who would not have blemished a hair of his head, that Heaven must guide me out of this labyrinth. Enough for lane the firm resolution, that Matilda shall not blush for her friend, my father for his daughter, nor my lover for her on whom he has fixed his affection."

CHAPTER XVIII.

Talk with a man out of a window!—a proper saying.—

Much Ado About Nothing.

WE must proceed with our extracts from Miss Mannering's letters, which throw light upon natural good sense, principle, and feelings, blemished by an imperfect education, and the folly of a misjudging mother, who called her husband in her heart a tyrant until she feared him as such, and read romances until she became so enamoured of the complicated intrigues which they contain, as to assume the management of a little family novel of her own, and constitute her daughter, a girl of sixteen, the principal heroine. She delighted in petty mystery, and intrigue, and secrets, and yet trembled at the indignation which these paltry manoeuvres excited in her husband's mind. Thus she frequently entered upon a scheme merely for pleasure, or perhaps for the love of contradiction, plunged deeper into it than she was aware, endeavoured to extricate herself by new arts, or to cover her error by dissimulation, became involved in meshes of her own weaving, and was forced to carry on, for fear of discovery, machinations which she had at first resorted to in mere wantonness.

Fortunately the young man whom she so imprudently introduced into her intimate society, and encouraged to look up to her daughter, had a fund of principle and honest pride, which rendered him a safer intimate than Mrs. Mannering ought to have dared to hope or expect. The obscurity of his birth could alone he objected to him; in every other respect,

With prospects bright upon the world he came,
Pure love of virtue, strong desire of fame;
Men watched the way his lofty mind would take,
And all foretold the progress he would make.

But it could not be expected that he should resist the snare which Mrs. Mannering's imprudence threw in his way, or avoid becoming attached to a young lady, whose beauty and manners might have justified his passion, even in scenes where these are more generally met with, than in a remote fortress in our Indian settlements. The scenes which followed have been partly detailed in Mannering's letter to Mr.

Mervyn; and to expand what is there stated into further explanation, would be to abuse the patience of our readers. We shall, therefore, proceed with our promised extracts from Miss Mannering's letters to her friend.

Sixth Extract.

I have seen him again, Matilda—seen him twice. I have used every argument to convince him that this secret intercourse is dangerous to us both—I even pressed him to pursue his views of fortune without further regard to me, and to consider my peace of mind as sufficiently secured by the knowledge that he had not fallen under my father's sword. He answers—but how can I detail all he has to answer? he claims those hopes as his due which my mother permitted him to entertain, and would persuade me to the madness of a union without my father's sanction. But to this, Matilda, I will not be persuaded. I have resisted, I have subdued, the rebellious feelings which arose to aid his plea; yet how to extricate myself from this unhappy labyrinth, in which fate and folly have entangled us both!

"I have thought, upon it, Matilda, till my head is almost giddy—nor can I conceive a better plan than to make a full confession to my father. He deserves it, for his kindness is unceasing; and I think I have observed in his character, since I have studied it more nearly, that his harsher feelings are chiefly excited where he suspects deceit or imposition; and in that respect, perhaps, his character was formerly misunderstood by one who was dear to him. He has, too, a tinge of romance in his disposition; and I have seen the narrative of a generous action, a trait of heroism, or virtuous self-denial, extract tears from him, which refused to flow at a tale of mere distress. But then, Brown urges, that he is personally hostile to him—And the obscurity of his birth—that would be indeed a stumbling-block. O Matilda, I hope none of your ancestors ever fought at Poictiers or Agincourt! If it were not for the veneration which my father attaches to the memory of old Sir Miles Mannering, I should make out my explanation with half the tremor which must now attend it."

Seventh Extract.

"I have this instant received your letter—your most welcome letter!—Thanks, my dearest friend, for your sympathy and your counsels—I can only repay them with unbounded confidence.

"You ask me, what Brown is by origin, that his descent should be so displeasing to my father. His story is shortly told. He is of Scottish extraction, but, being left an orphan, his education was undertaken by a family of relations, settled in Holland. He was bred to commerce, and sent very early to one of our settlements in the East, where his guardian had a correspondent. But this correspondent was dead when he arrived in India, and he had no other resource than to offer himself as a clerk to a counting-house. The breaking out of the war, and the straits to which we were at first reduced, threw the army open to all young men who were disposed to embrace that mode of life; and Brown, whose genius had a strong military tendency, was the first to leave what might have been the road to wealth, and to choose that of fame. The rest of his history is well known to you; but conceive the irritation of my father, who despises commerce (though, by the way, the best part of his property was made in that honourable profession by my great-uncle), and has a particular antipathy to the Dutch; think with what ear he would be likely to receive proposals for his only child from Vanbeest Brown, educated for charity by the house of Vanbeest and Vanbruggen! O Matilda, it will never do—nay, so childish am I, I hardly can help sympathising with his aristocratic feelings. Mrs. Vanbeest Brown! The name has little to recommend it, to be sure.—What children we are!"

EIGHTH EXTRACT.

"It is all over now, Matilda!—I shall never have courage to tell my father—nay, most deeply do I fear he has already learned my secret from another quarter, which will entirely remove the grace of my communication, and ruin whatever gleam of hope I had ventured to connect with it. Yesternight, Brown came as usual, and his flageolet on the lake announced his approach. We had agreed, that he should continue to use this signal. These romantic lakes attract numerous visitors, who indulge their enthusiasm in visiting the scenery at all hours, and we hoped, that—if Brown were noticed from the house, he might pass for one of those admirers of nature, who was giving vent to his feelings through the medium of music. The sounds might also be my apology, should I be observed on the balcony. But last night, while I was eagerly enforcing my plan of a full confession to my father, which he as earnestly deprecated, we heard the window of Mr. Mervyn's library, which is under my room, open softly. I signed to Brown to make his retreat, and immediately re-entered, with some faint hopes that our interview had not been observed.

"But, alas! Matilda, these hopes vanished the instant I beheld Mr. Mervyn's countenance at breakfast the next morning. He looked so provokingly intelligent and confidential, that, had I dared, I could have been more angry than ever I was in my life; but I must be on good behaviour, and my walks are now limited within his farm precincts, where the good gentleman can amble along by my side without inconvenience. I have detected him once or twice attempting to sound my thoughts, and watch the expression of my countenance. He has talked of the flageolet more than once; and has, at different times, made eulogiums upon the watchfulness and ferocity of his dogs, and the regularity with which the keeper makes his rounds with a loaded fowling-piece. He mentioned even man-traps and spring-guns. I should be loath to affront my father's old friend in his own house; but I do long to show him that I am my father's daughter, a fact of which Mr. Mervyn will certainly be convinced, if ever I trust my voice and temper with a reply to these indirect hints. Of one thing I am certain—I am grateful to him on that account—he has not told Mrs. Mervyn. Lord help me, I should have had such lectures about the dangers of love and the night air on the lake, the risk arising from colds and fortune-hunters, the comfort and convenience of sack-whey and closed windows!— I cannot help trifling, Matilda, though my heart is sad enough What Brown will do I cannot guess. I presume however, the fear of detection prevents his resuming his nocturnal visits. He lodges at an inn on the opposite shore of the lake, under the name, he tells me, of Dawson— he has a bad choice in names, that be allowed. He has not left the army, I believe, but he says nothing of his present views.

"To complete my anxiety, my father is returned suddenly, and in high displeasure. Our good hostess, as I learned from a bustling conversation between her housekeeper and her, had no expectation of seeing him for a week; but I rather suspect his arrival was no surprise to his friend Mr. Mervyn. His manner to me was singularly cold and constrained—sufficiently so to have damped all the courage with which I once resolved to throw myself on his generosity. He lays the blame of his being discomposed and out of humour to the loss of a purchase in the south-west of Scotland, on which he had set his heart; but I do not suspect his equanimity of being so easily thrown off its balance. His first excursion was with Mr. Mervyn's barge across the lake, to the inn I have mentioned. You may imagine the agony with which I waited his return—Had he recognised Brown, who can guess the consequence! He returned, however, apparently without having made any discovery. I understand, that in consequence of his late disappointment, he means now to hire a house in the neighbourhood of this same Ellangowan, of which I am doomed to hear so much—he seems to think it probable that the estate for which he wishes may soon be again in the market. I will not send away this letter until I hear more distinctly what are his intentions."

41

"I have now had an interview with my father, as confidential as, I presume, he means to allow me. He requested me today, after breakfast, to walk with him into the library; my knees, Matilda, shook under me, and it is no exaggeration to say, I could scarce follow him into the room. I feared I knew not what—From my childhood I had seen all around him tremble at his frown. He motioned me to seat myself, and I never obeyed a command so readily, for, in truth, I could hardly stand. He himself continued to walk up and down the room. You have seen my father, and noticed, I recollect, the remarkably expressive cast of his features. His eyes are naturally rather light in colour, but agitation or anger gives them a darker and more fiery glance; he has a custom also of drawing in his lips, when much moved, which implies a combat between native ardour of temper and the habitual power of self-command. This was the first time we had been alone since his return from Scotland, and, as he betrayed these tokens of agitation, I had little doubt that he was about to enter upon the subject I most dreaded.

"To my unutterable relief, I found I was mistaken, and that whatever he knew of Mr. Mervyn's suspicions or discoveries, he did not intend to converse with me on the topic. Coward as I was, I was inexpressibly relieved, though if he had really investigated the reports which may have come to his ear, the reality could have been nothing to what his suspicions might have conceived. But, though my spirits rose high at my unexpected escape, I had not courage myself to provoke the discussion, and remained silent to receive his commands.

"'Julia,' he said, 'my agent writes me from Scotland, that he has been able to hire a house for me, decently furnished, and with the necessary accommodation for my family—it is within three miles of that I had designed to purchase—' Then he made a pause, and seemed to expect an answer.

"'Whatever place of residence suits you, sir, must be perfectly agreeable to me.'

"'Umph!—I do not propose, however, Julia, that you shall reside quite alone in this house during the winter.'

"Mr. and Mrs. Mervyn, thought I to myself.—'Whatever company is agreeable to you, sir,' I answered aloud.

"'Oh, there is a little too much of this universal spirit of submission; an excellent disposition in action, but your constantly repeating the jargon of it, puts me in mind of the eternal salaams of our black dependants in the East. In short, Julia, I know you have a relish for society, and I intend to invite a young person, the daughter of a deceased friend, to spend a few months with us. '

"'Not a governess, for the love of Heaven, papa!' exclaimed poor I, my fears at that moment totally getting the better of my prudence.

"'No, not a governess, Miss Mannering,' replied the Colonel, somewhat sternly, 'but a young lady from whose excellent example, bred as she has been in the school of adversity, I trust you may learn the art to govern yourself. '

"To answer this was trenching upon too dangerous ground, so there was a pause.

"'Is the young lady a Scotchwoman, papa?'

"'Yes'—dryly enough.

"'Has she much of the accent, sir?'

"'Much of the devil!' answered my father hastily; 'do you think I care about a's and aa's, and i's and ee's?—I tell you, Julia, I am serious in the matter. You have a genius for friendship, that is, for running up intimacies which you call such'—(was not this very harshly said, Matilda?)—'Now I wish to give you an opportunity at least to make one deserving friend, and therefore I have resolved that this young lady shall be a member of my family for some months, and I expect you will pay to her that attention which is due to misfortune and virtue.'

"'Certainly, sir.—Is my future friend red-haired?'

"He gave me one of his stern glances; you will say, perhaps, I deserved it; but I think the deuce prompts me with teasing questions on some occasions.

"'She is as superior to you, my love, in personal appearance, as in prudence and affection for her friends.'

"'Lord, papa, do you think that superiority a recommendation ?—Well, sir, but I see you are going to take all this too seriously; whatever the young lady may be, I am sure, being recommended by you, she shall have no reason to complain of my want of attention.—(After a pause)—Has she any attendant? because you know I must provide for her proper accommodation, if she is without one.'

"'N-no-no-not properly an attendant—the chaplain who lived with her father is a very good sort of man, and I believe I shall make room for him in the house.'

"'Chaplain, papa? Lord bless us!'

"'Yes, Miss Mannering, chaplain; is there anything very new in that word ? Had we not a chaplain at the Residence, when we were in India?'

"'Yes, papa, but you were a commandant then.'

"'So I will be now, Miss Mannering—in my own family at least.'

"'Certainly, sir—but will he read us the Church of England service?'

"The apparent simplicity with which I asked this question got the better of his gravity. 'Come, Julia,' he said, 'you are a sad girl, but I gain nothing by scolding you.—Of these two strangers, the young lady is one whom you cannot fail, I think, to love—the person whom, for want of a better term, I called chaplain, is a very worthy, and somewhat ridiculous personage, who will never find out you laugh at him, if you don't laugh very loud indeed.'

"'Dear papa, I am delighted with that part of his character. — But pray, is the house we are going to as pleasantly situated as this?'

"'Not perhaps as much to your taste—there is no lake under the windows, and you will be under the necessity of having all your music within doors.'

"This last coup de main ended the keen encounter of our wits, for you may believe, Matilda, it quelled all my courage to reply.

"Yet my spirits, as perhaps will appear too manifest from this dialogue, have risen insensibly, and, as it were, in spite of myself. Brown alive, and free, and in England! Embarrassment and anxiety I can and must endure. We leave this in two days for our new residence. I shall not fail to let you know what I think of these Scotch inmates, whom I have but too much reason to believe my father means to quarter in his house as a brace of honourable spies; a sort of female Rozencrantz and reverend Guildenstern, one in tartan petticoats, the other in a cassock. What a contrast to the society I would willingly have secured to myself! I shall write instantly on my arriving at our new place of abode, and acquaint my dearest Matilda with the further fates of—her

"Julia Mannering."

CHAPTER XIX.

Which sloping hills around enclose, Where many a beech and brown oak grows, Beneath whose dark and branching bowers, Its tides a far-fam'd river pours, By nature's beauties taught to please, Sweet Tusculan of rural ease!— Warton.

Woodbourne, the habitation which Mannering, by Mr. Mac-Morlan's mediation, had hired for a season, was a large comfortable mansion, snugly situated beneath a hill covered with wood, which shrouded the house upon the north and east; the front looked upon a little lawn bordered by a grove of old trees; beyond were some arable fields, extending down to the river, which was seen from the windows of the house. A tolerable, though old-fashioned garden, a well-stocked dovecot, and the possession of any quantity of ground which the convenience of the family might require, rendered the place in every respect suitable, as the advertisements have it, "for the accommodation of a genteel family."

Here, then, Mannering resolved, for some time at least, to set up the staff of his rest. Though an East-Indian, he was not partial to an ostentatious display of wealth. In fact, he was too proud a man to be a vain one. He resolved, therefore, to place himself upon the footing of a country gentleman of easy fortune, without assuming, or permitting, his household to assume, any of the faste which then was considered as characteristic of a nabob.

He had still his eye upon the purchase of Ellangowan, which Mac-Morlan conceived Mr. Glossin would be compelled to part with, as some of the creditors disputed his title to retain so large a part of the purchase-money in his own hands, and his power to pay it was much questioned. In that case MacMorlan was assured he would readily give up his bargain, if 'tempted with something above the price which he had stipulated to pay. It may seem strange,—that Mannering was so much attached to a spot which he had only seen once, and that for a short time, in early life. But the circumstances which passed there had laid a strong hold on his imagination. There seemed to be a fate which conjoined the remarkable passages of his own family history with those of the inhabitants of Ellangowan, and he felt a mysterious desire to call the terrace his own, from which he had read in the book of heaven a fortune strangely accomplished in the person of the infant Heir of that family, and corresponding so closely with one which had been strikingly fulfilled in his own. Besides, when once this thought had got possession of his imagination, he could not, without great reluctance, brook the, idea of his plan being defeated, and by a fellow like Glossin. So pride came to the aid of fancy, and both combined to fortify his resolution to buy the estate if possible.

Let us do Mannering justice. A desire to serve the distressed had also its share in determining him. He had considered the advantage which Julia might receive from the company of Lucy Bertram, whose genuine prudence and good sense could so surely be relied upon. This idea had become much stronger since Mac-Morlan had confided to him, under the solemn seal of secrecy, the whole of her conduct towards young Hazlewood. To propose to her to become an inmate in his family, if distant from the scenes of her youth and the few whom she called friends, would have been less delicate; but at Woodbourne she might without difficulty be induced to become the visitor of a season, without being depressed into the situation of an humble companion. Lucy Bertram, with some hesitation, accepted the invitation to reside a few weeks with Miss Mannering. She felt too well, that however the Colonel's delicacy might disguise the truth, his principal motive was a generous desire to afford her his countenance and protection, which his high connections, and higher character, were likely to render influential in the neighbourhood.

About the same time the orphan girl received a letter from Mrs. Bertram, the relation to whom she had written, as cold and comfortless as could well be imagined. It enclosed, indeed, a small sum of money, but strongly recommended economy, and that Miss Bertram should board herself in some quiet family, either at Kippletringan or in the neighbourhood, assuring her, that though her own income was very scanty, she would not see her kinswoman want.

Miss Bertram shed some natural tears over this cold-hearted epistle; for in her mother's time, this good lady. had been a guest at Ellangowan for nearly three years, and it was only upon succeeding to a property of about 400L a-year that she had, taken farewell of that hospitable mansion, which, otherwise, might have had the honour of sheltering her until the death of its owner. Lucy was strongly inclined to return the paltry donation, which, after some struggles with avarice, pride had extorted from the old lady. But on consideration, she contented herself with writing, that she accepted it as a loan, which she hoped in a short time to repay, and consulted her relative upon the invitation she had received from Colonel and Miss Mannering. This time the answer came in course of post, so fearful was Mrs. Bertram, that some frivolous delicacy, or nonsense, as she termed it, might induce her cousin to reject such a promising offer, and thereby at the same time to leave herself still a burden upon her relations. Lucy, therefore, had no alternative, unless she preferred continuing a burden upon the worthy Mac-Morlans, who were too liberal to be rich. Those kinsfolk who formerly requested the favour of her company, had of late either silently, or with expressions of resentment that she should have preferred Mac-Morlan's invitation to theirs, gradually withdrawn their notice.

The fate of Dominie Sampson would have been deplorable had it depended upon any one except Mannering, who was an admirer of originality, for a separation from Lucy Bertram would have certainly broken his heart. Mac-Morlan had given a full account of his proceedings towards the daughter of his patron. The answer was a request from Mannering to know, whether the Dominie still possessed that admirable virtue of taciturnity by which he was so notably distinguished at Ellangowan. Mac-Morlan replied in the affirmative. "Let Mr. Sampson know," said the Colonel's next letter, "that I shall want his assistance to catalogue and put in order the library of my uncle, the bishop, which I have ordered to be sent down by sea. I shall also want him to copy and arrange some papers. Fix his salary at what you think befitting. Let the poor man be properly dressed, and accompany his young lady to Woodbourne."

Honest Mac-Morlan received this mandate with great joy, but pondered much upon executing that part of it which related to newly attiring the worthy Dominie. He looked at him with a scrutinising eye, and it was but too plain that his present garments were daily waxing more deplorable. To give him money, and bid him go and furnish himself, would be only giving him the means of making himself ridiculous; for when such a rare event arrived to Mr. Sampson as the purchase of new garments, the additions which he made to his wardrobe, by the guidance of his own taste, usually brought all the boys of the village after him for many days. On the other hand, to bring a tailor to measure him, and send home his clothes, as for a schoolboy, would probably give offence. At length Mac-Morlan resolved to consult Miss Bertram, and request her interference. She assured him, that though she could not pretend to superintend a gentleman's wardrobe, nothing was more easy than to arrange the Dominie's.

"At Ellangowan," she said, "whenever my poor father thought any part of the Dominie's dress wanted renewal, a servant was directed to enter his room by night, for he sleeps as fast as a dormouse, carry off the old vestment, and leave the new one; nor could anyone observe that the Dominie exhibited the least consciousness of the change put upon him on such occasions."

Mac-Morlan, in conformity with Miss Bertram's advice, procured a skilful artist, who, on looking at the Dominie attentively, undertook to make for him two suits of clothes, one black, and one raven-gray, and even engaged that they should fit him—as well at least (so the tailor qualified his enterprise), as a man of such an out-of-the-way build could be fitted by merely human needles and shears. When this fashioner had accomplished his task, and the dresses were brought home, Mac-Morlan, judiciously resolving to accomplish his purpose by degrees, withdrew that evening an important part of his dress, and substituted the new article of raiment in its stead. Perceiving that this passed totally without notice, he next ventured on the waistcoat, and lastly on the coat. When fully metamorphosed, and arrayed for the first time in his life in a decent dress, they did observe, that the Dominie seemed to have some indistinct and embarrassing consciousness that a change had taken place on his outward man. Whenever they observed this dubious expression gather upon his countenance, accompanied with a glance, that fixed now upon the sleeve of his coat, now upon the knees of his breeches, where he probably missed some antique patching and darning, which, being executed with blue thread upon a black ground, had somewhat the effect of embroidery, they always took care to turn his attention into some other channel, until his garments, "by the aid of use, cleaved to their mould." The only remark he was ever known to make on the subject was, that "the air of a town like Kippletringan, seemed favourable unto wearing apparel, for he thought his coat looked almost as new as the first day he put it on, which was when he went to stand trial for his licence as a preacher."

When the Dominie first heard the liberal proposal of Colonel Mannering, he turned a jealous and doubtful glance towards Miss Bertram, as if he suspected that the project involved their separation, but when Mr Mac-Morlan hastened to explain that she would be a guest at Woodbourne for some time, he rubbed his huge hands together, and burst into a portentous sort of chuckle, like that of the Afrite in the tale of the Caliph Vathek. After this unusual explosion of satisfaction, he remained quite passive in all the rest of the transaction.

It had been settled that Mr. and Mrs. Mac-Morlan should take possession of the house a few days before Mannering's arrival, both to put everything in perfect order, and to make the transference of Miss Bertram's residence from their family to his as easy and delicate as possible. Accordingly, in the beginning of the month of December, the party were settled at Woodbourne.

CHAPTER XX.

A gigantic genius, fit to grapple with whole libraries.

BOSWELL's Life of Johnson.

THE appointed day arrived, when the Colonel and Miss Mannering were expected at Woodbourne. The hour was fast approaching, and the little circle within doors had each their separate subjects of anxiety. Mac-Morlan naturally desired to attach to himself the patronage and countenance of a person of Mannering's wealth and consequence. He was aware, from his knowledge of mankind, that Mannering, though generous and benevolent, had the foible of expecting and exacting a minute compliance with his directions. He was therefore racking his recollection to discover if everything had been arranged to meet the Colonel's wishes and instructional and, under this uncertainty of mind, he traversed the house more than once from the garret to the stables. Mrs. Mac-Morlan revolved in a lesser orbit, comprehending the dining-parlour, housekeeper's room, and kitchen. She was only afraid that the dinner might be spoiled, to the . discredit of her housewifely accomplishments. Even the usual passiveness of the Dominie was so far disturbed, that he twice went to the window, which looked out upon the avenue, and twice exclaimed, "Why tarry the wheels of their chariot?" Lucy, the most quiet of the expectants, had her own melancholy thoughts. She was now about to be consigned to the charge, almost to the benevolence, of strangers, with whose character, though hitherto very amiably displayed, she was but imperfectly acquainted. The moments, therefore, of suspense passed anxiously and heavily.

At length the trampling of horses and the sound of wheels were heard. The servants, who had already arrived, drew up in the hall to receive their master and mistress, with an importance and empressement, which, to Lucy, who had never been accustomed to society, or witnessed what is called the manners of the great, had something alarming. Mac-Morlan went to she door to receive the master and mistress of the family, and in a few moments they were in the drawing-room.

Mannering, who had travelled as usual on horseback, entered with his daughter hanging upon his arm. She was of the middle size, or rather less, but formed with much elegance; piercing dark eyes, and jet-black hair of great length, corresponded with the vivacity and intelligence of features, in which were blended a little haughtiness, and a little bashfulness, a great deal of shrewdness, and some power of humorous sarcasm. "I shall not like her," was the result of Lucy Bertram's first glance; "and yet I rather think I shall," was the thought excited by the second.

Miss Mannering was furred and mantled up to the throat against the severity of the weather; the Colonel in his military greatcoat. He bowed to Mrs. Mac-Morlan, whom his daughter also acknowledged with a fashionable curtsey, not dropped so low as at all to incommode her person. The Colonel then led his daughter up to Miss Bertram, and, taking the hand of the latter, with an air of great kindness, and almost paternal affection, he said, "Julia, this is the young lady whom I hope our good friends have prevailed on to honour our house with a long visit. I shall be much gratified indeed if you can render Woodbourne as pleasant to Miss Bertram, as Ellangowan was to me when I first came as a wanderer into this country."

The young lady curtsied acquiescence, and took her new friend's hand. Mannering now turned his eye upon the Dominie, who had made bows since his entrance into the room, sprawling out his leg, and bending his back like an automaton, which continues to repeat the same movement until the motion is stopt by the artist. "My good friend, Mr. Sampson,"—said Mannering, introducing him to his daughter, and darting at the same time a reproving glance at the damsel, notwithstanding he had himself some disposition to join her too obvious inclination to risibility—"This gentleman, Julia, is to put my books in order when they arrive, and I expect to derive great advantage from his extensive learning."

"I am sure we are obliged to the gentleman, papa; and, to borrow a ministerial mode of giving thanks, I shall never forget the extraordinary countenance he has been pleased to show us.—But, Miss Bertram," continued she hastily, for her father's brows began to darken, "we have travelled a good way,—will you permit me to retire before dinner?"

This intimation dispersed all the company, save the Dominie, who, having no idea of dressing but when he was to rise, or of undressing but when he meant to go to bed, remained by himself, chewing the cud of a mathematical demonstration, until the company again assembled in the drawing-room, and from thence adjourned to the dining-parlour.

When the day was concluded, Mannering took an opportunity, to hold a minute's conversation with his daughter in private.

"How do you like your guests, Julia?"

"Oh, Miss Bertram of all things—but this is a most original parson—why, dear sir, no human being will be able to look at him without laughing."

"While he is under my roof, Julia, every one must learn to do so."

"Lord, papa, the very footmen could not keep their gravity!"

"Then let them strip off my livery," said the Colonel,—"and oath at their leisure. Mr. Sampson is a man whom I esteem for his simplicity and benevolence of character."

"Oh, I am convinced of his generosity too," said this lively lady; "he cannot lift a spoonful of soup to his mouth without bestowing a share on everything round."

"Julia, you are incorrigible;—but remember, I expect your mirth on this subject to be under such restraint, that it shall neither offend this worthy man's feelings nor those of Miss Bertram, who may be more apt to feel upon his account than he on his own. And so good-night, my dear; and recollect, that though Mr. Sampson has certainly not sacrificed to the graces, there are many things in this world more truly deserving of ridicule than either awkwardness of manners or simplicity of character."

In a day or two Mr. and Mrs. Mac-Morlan left Woodbourne, after taking an affectionate farewell of their late guest. The household were now settled in their new quarters. The young ladies followed their studies and amusements together. Colonel Mannering was agreeably surprised to find that Miss Bertram was well skilled in French and Italian, thanks to the assiduity of Dominie Sampson, whose labour had silently made him acquainted with most modern as well as ancient languages. Of music she knew little or nothing, but her new friend undertook to give her lessons; in exchange for which, she was to learn from Lucy the habit of walking, and the art of riding, and the courage necessary to defy the season. Mannering was careful to substitute for their amusement in the evening such. books as might convey some solid instruction with entertainment, and as he read aloud with great skill and taste, the winter nights passed pleasantly away.

Society was quickly formed where there were so many inducements. Most of the families of the neighbourhood visited Colonel Mannering, and he was soon able to select from among them such as best suited his taste and habits. Charles Hazlewood held a distinguished place in his favour, and was a frequent visitor, not without the consent and approbation of his parents; for there was no knowing, they thought, what assiduous attention might product, and the beautiful Miss Mannering, of high family, with an Indian fortune, was a prize worth looking after. Dazzled with such a prospect, they never considered the risk which had once been some object of their apprehension, that his boyish and inconsiderate fancy might form an attachment to the penniless Lucy Bertram, who had nothing on earth to recommend her, but a pretty face, good birth, and a most amiable disposition. Mannering was more prudent. He considered himself acting as Miss Bertram's guardian, and, while he did not think it incumbent upon him altogether to check her intercourse with a young gentleman for whom, excepting in wealth, she was a match in every respect, he laid it under such insensible restraints as might prevent any engagement or eclaircissement taking place until the young man should have seen a little more of life and of the world, and have attained that age when he might be considered as entitled to judge for himself in the matter in which his happiness was chiefly interested.

While these matters engaged the attention of the other members of the Woodbourne family, Dominie Sampson was occupied, body and soul, in the arrangement of the late bishop's library, which had been sent from Liverpool by sea, and conveyed by thirty or forty carts from the seaport at which it was landed. Sampson's joy at beholding the ponderous contents of these chests arranged upon the floor of the large apartment, from whence he was to transfer them to the shelves, baffles all description. He grinned like an ogre, swung his arms like the sails of a windmill, shouted "Prodigious" till the roof rung to his raptures. "He had never," he said, "seen so many books together, except in the College Library; "and now his dignity and delight in being superintendent of the collection, raised him, in his own opinion, almost to the rank of the academical librarian, whom he had always regarded as the greatest and happiest man on earth. Neither were his transports diminished upon a hasty examination of the contents of these volumes. Some, indeed, of belles lettres, poems, plays, or memoirs, he tossed indignantly aside, with the implied censure of "psha," or "frivolous"; but the greater and bulkier part of the collection bore a very different character. The deceased prelate, a divine of the old and deeply-learned cast, had loaded his shelves with volumes which displayed the antique and venerable attributes so happily described by a modern poet.

That weight of wood, with leathern coat o'erlaid, Those ample clasps of solid metal made, The close-press'd leaves unoped for many an age, The dull red edging of the well-filled page, On the broad back the stubborn ridges roll'd, Where yet the title stands in tarnish'd gold.

Books of theology and controversial divinity, commentaries, and polyglots, sets of the fathers, and sermons, which might each furnish forth ten brief discourses of modern date, books of science, ancient and modern, classical authors in their best and rarest forms; such formed the late bishop's venerable library, and over such the eye of Dominie Sampson gloated with rapture. He entered them in the catalogue in his best running hand, forming each letter with the accuracy of a lover writing a valentine, and placed each individually on the destined shelf with all the reverence which I have seen a lady pay to a jar of old china. With all this zeal his labours advanced slowly. He often opened a volume when halfway up the library steps, fell upon some interesting passage, and, without shifting his inconvenient posture, continued immersed in the fascinating perusal until the servant pulled him by the skirts to assure him that dinner waited.

> How happily the days
> Of Thalaba went by!

And, having thus left the principal characters of our ,tale in a situation which, being sufficiently comfortable to themselves, is, of course, utterly uninteresting to the reader, we take up the history of a person who has as yet only been named, and who has all the interest that uncertainty and misfortune can give.

CHAPTER XXI.

What say'st thou, Wise One?—that all-powerful Love
Can fortune's strong impediments remove;
Nor is it strange that worth should wed to worth,
The pride of genius with the pride of birth.
  Crabbe.

V. Brown,—I will not give at full length his thrice unhappy name—had been from infancy a ball for fortune to spurn at; but nature had given him that elasticity of mind which rises higher from the rebound. His form was tall, manly, and active, and his features corresponded with his person; for, although far from regular, they had an expression of intelligence and good humour, and when he spoke, or was particularly animated, might be decidedly pronounced interesting. His manner indicated the military profession, which had been his choice, and in which he had now attained the rank of captain, the person who succeeded Colonel Mannering in his command having laboured to repair the injustice which Brown had sustained by that gentleman's prejudice against him. But this, as well as his liberation from captivity, had taken place after Mannering left India. Brown followed at no distant period, his regiment being recalled home. His first inquiry was after the family of Mannering, and, easily learning their route northward, he followed it with the purpose of, resuming his addresses to Julia. With her father he deemed he had no measures to keep; for, ignorant of the more venomous belief which had been instilled into the Colonel's mind, he regarded him as an oppressive aristocrat, who had used his power as a commanding officer to deprive him of the preferment due to his behaviour, and who had forced upon him a personal quarrel without any better reason than his attentions to a pretty young woman, agreeable to herself, and permitted and countenanced by her mother. He was determined, therefore, to take no rejection unless from the young lady herself, believing that the heavy misfortunes of his painful wound and imprisonment were direct injuries received from the father, which might dispense with his using much ceremony towards him. How far his scheme had succeeded when his nocturnal visit was discovered by Mr. Mervyn, our readers are already informed.

Upon this unpleasant occurrence, Captain Brown absented himself from the inn in which he had resided under the name of Dawson, so that Colonel Mannering's attempts to discover and trace him were unavailing. He resolved, however, that no difficulties should prevent his continuing his enterprise, while Julia left him a ray of hope. The interest he had secured in her bosom was such as she had been unable to conceal from him, and with all the courage of romantic gallantry he determined upon perseverance. But we believe the reader will be as well pleased to learn his mode of thinking and intentions from his own communication to his special friend and confidant, Captain Delaserre, a Swiss gentleman, who had a company in his regiment.

"Let me hear from you soon, dear Delaserre.—Remember, I can learn nothing about regimental affairs but through your friendly medium, and I long to know what has become of Ayre's court-martial, and whether Elliot gets the majority; also how recruiting comes on, and how the young officers like the mess. Of our kind friend, the Lieutenant-Colonel, I need ask nothing; I saw him as I passed through Nottingham, happy in the bosom of his family. What a happiness it is, Philip, for us poor devils, that we have a little resting-place between the camp and the grave, if we can manage to escape disease, and steel, and lead, and the effects of hard living. A retires old soldier is always a graceful and respected character. He grumbles a little now and then, but then his is licensed murmuring-were a lawyer, or a physician, or a clergyman, to breathe a complaint of hard luck or want of preferment, a hundred tongues would blame his own incapacity as the cause. But the most stupid veteran that ever faltered out the thrice-told tale of a siege and a battle, and a cock and a bottle, is listened to with sympathy and reverence, when he shakes his thin locks, and talks with indignation of the boys that are put over his head. And you and I, Delaserre, foreigners both,—for what am I the better that I was originally a Scotchman, since, could I prove my descent, the English would hardly acknowledge me a countryman?-we may boast that we have fought out our preferment, and gained that by the sword which we had not money to compass otherwise. The English are a wise people. While they praise themselves, and affect to undervalue all other nations, they leave us, luckily, trap-doors and back-doors open, by which we strangers, less favoured by nature, may arrive at a share of their advantages. And thus they are, in some respects like a boastful landlord, who exalts the value and flavour of his six-years'-old mutton, while he is delighted to dispense a share of it to all the company. In short, you, whose proud family, and I, whose hard fate, made us soldiers of fortune, have the pleasant recollection, that in the British service, stop where we may upon our career, it is only for want of money to pay the turnpike, and not from our being prohibited to travel the road. If, therefore, we can persuade little Weischel to come into ours, for God's sake let him buy the ensigncy, live prudently, mind his duty, and trust to the fates for promotion.

"And now, I hope you are expiring with curiosity to learn the end of my romance. I told you I had deemed it convenient to make a few days' tour on foot among the mountains of Westmoreland, with Dudley, a young English artist, with whom I have formed some acquaintance. A fine fellow this, you must know, Delaserre—he paints tolerably, draws beautifully, converses well, and plays charmingly on the flute; and, though thus well entitled to be a coxcomb of talent, is, in fact, a modest unpretending young man. On our return from our little tour, I learned that the enemy had been reconnoitring. Mr. Mervyn's barge had crossed the lake, I was informed by my landlord, with the squire himself and a visitor.

"'What sort of person, landlord?'

"'Why, he was a dark officer-looking mon, at they called Colonel—Squoire Mervyn questioned me as close as I had been at sizes—I had guess, Mr. Dawson' (I told you that was my feigned name)—I but I tould him nought of your vagaries, and going out a-laking in the mere a-noights—not I—an I can make no sport. I'se spoil none—and Squoire Mervyn's as cross as poy-crust too, mon—he's aye maundering an my guests but land beneath his house, though it be marked for the fourth station in the Survey. Noa, noa, e'en let un smell things out o' themselves for Joe Hodges—'

"You will allow there was nothing for it after this, but paying honest Joe Hodges's bill, and departing, unless I had preferred making him my confidant, for which I felt in no way inclined. Besides, I learned that our ci-devant Colonel was on full retreat for Scotland, carrying off poor Julia along with him. I understand from those who conduct the heavy baggage, that he takes his winter' quarters at a place called Woodbourne, in—shire in Scotland. He will be all on the alert just now, so I must let him enter his entrenchments without any new alarm. And then, my good Colonel, to whom I owe so many grateful thanks, pray look to your defence.

"I protest to you, Delaserre, I often think there is a little contradiction enters into the ardour of my pursuit. I think I would rather bring this haughty insulting man to the necessity of calling his daughter Mrs. Brown, than I would wed her with his full consent, and with the king's permission to change my name for the style and arms of Mannering, though his whole fortune went with them. There is only one circumstance that chills me a little-Julia is young and romantic. I would not willingly hurry her into a step which her riper years might disapprove—no;—nor would I like to have her upbraid me, were it but with a glance of her eye, with having ruined her fortunes—far less give her reason to say, as some have not been slow to tell their lords, that, had I left her time for consideration, she would have been wiser and done better. No, Delaserre—this must not be. The picture presses close upon me, because I am aware a girl in Julia's situation has no distinct and precise idea of the value of the sacrifice she makes. She knows difficulties only by name; and, if she thinks of love and a farm, it is a ferme ornee, such as is only to be found in poetic description, or in the park of a gentleman of twelve thousand a year. She would be ill prepared for the privations of that real Swiss cottage we have so often talked of, and for the difficulties which must necessarily surround us even before we attained that haven. This must be a point clearly ascertained. Although Julia's beauty and playful tenderness have made an impression on my heart never to be erased, I must be satisfied that she perfectly understands the advantages she foregoes, before she sacrifices them for my sake.

"Am I too proud, Delaserre, when I trust that even this trial may terminate favourably to my wishes?-Am I too vain when I suppose, that the few personal qualities—which I possess, with means of competence however moderate, and the determination of consecrating my life to her happiness, may make amends for all I must call upon her to forego? Or will a difference of dress, of attendance, of style, as it is called, of the power of shifting at pleasure the scenes in which she seeks amusement,—will these outweigh, in her estimation, the prospect of domestic happiness, and the interchange of unabating affection? I say nothing of her father;—his good and evil qualities are so strangely mingled, that the former are neutralised by the latter; and that which she must regret as a daughter is so much blended with what she would gladly escape from, that I place the separation of the father and child as a circumstance which weighs little in her remarkable case. Meantime I keep up my spirits as I may. I have incurred too many hardships and difficulties to be presumptuous or confident in success, and I have been too often and too wonderfully extricated from them to be despondent.

"I wish you saw this country. I think the scenery would delight you. At least it often brings to my recollection your glowing descriptions of your native country. To me it has in a great measure the charm of novelty. Of the Scottish hills, though born among them, as I have always been assured, I have but an indistinct recollection. Indeed, my memory rather dwells upon the blank which my youthful mind experienced in gazing on the levels of the isle of Zealand, than on anything which preceded that feeling; but I am confident, from that sensation, as well as from the recollections which preceded it, that hills and rocks have been familiar to me at an early period, and that though now only remembered by contrast, And by the blank which I felt while gazing around for them in vain, they must have made an indelible impression on my infant imagination. I remember when we first mounted that celebrated pass in the Mysore country, while most of the others felt only awe and astonishment at the height and grandeur of the scenery, I rather shared your feelings and those of Cameron, whose admiration of such wild rocks was blended with familiar love, derived from early association. Despite my Dutch education, a blue hill to me is as a friend, and a roaring torrent like the sound of a domestic song that hath soothed my infancy. I never felt the impulse so strongly as in this land of lakes and mountains, and nothing grieves me so much as that duty prevents your being with me in my numerous excursions among its recesses. Some drawings I have attempted, but I succeed vilely-Dudley, on the contrary, draws delightfully, with that rapid touch which seems like magic, while I labour and blotch, and make this too heavy, and that too light, and produce at last a base caricature. I must stick to the flageolet, for music is the only one of the fine arts which deigns to acknowledge me.

"Did you know that Colonel Mannering was a draughtsman?—I believe not, for he scorned to display his accomplishments to the view of a subaltern. He draws beautifully, however. Since he and Julia left Mervyn Hall, Dudley was sent for there. The squire, it seems, wanted a set of drawings made up, of which Mannering had done the first four, but was interrupted, by his hasty departure, in his purpose of completing them. Dudley says he has seldom seen anything so masterly, though slight; and each had attached to it a short poetical description. Is Saul, you will say, among the prophets?—Colonel Mannering write poetry!—Why surely this man must have taken all the pains to conceal his accomplishments that others do to display theirs. How reserved and unsociable he appeared among us!—how little disposed to enter into any conversation which could become generally interesting! And then his attachment to that unworthy Archer, so much below him in every respect; and all this, because he was the brother of Viscount Archerfield, a poor Scottish peer! I think if Archer had longer survived the wounds in the affair of Cuddyboram, he would have told something that might have thrown light upon the inconsistencies of this singular man's character. He repeated to me more than once, 'I have that to say, which will alter your hard opinion of our late Colonel.' But death pressed him too hard; and if he owed me any atonement, which some of his expressions seemed to imply, he died before it could be made.

"I propose to make a further excursion through this country while this fine frosty weather serves, and Dudley, almost as good a walker as myself, goes with me for some part of the way. We part on the borders of Cumberland, where he must return to his lodgings in Marybone, up three pair of stairs, and labour at what he calls the commercial part of his profession. There cannot, he says, be such a difference betwixt any two portions of existence, as between that in which the artist, if an enthusiast, collects the subjects of his drawings, and that which must necessarily he dedicated to turning over his portfolio, and exhibiting them to the provoking indifference, or more provoking criticism, of fashionable amateurs. 'During the summer of my year,' says Dudley, 'I am as free as a wild Indian, enjoying myself at liberty amid the grandest scenes of nature; while, during my winters and springs, I am not only cabined, cribbed, and confined in a miserable garret, but condemned to as intolerable subservience to the humour of others, and to as indifferent company, as if I were a literal galley-slave. ' I have promised him your acquaintance, Delaserre; you will be delighted with his specimens of art, and he with your Swiss fanaticism for mountains and torrents.

"When I lose Dudley's company, I am informed—that I can easily enter Scotland by stretching across a wild country in the upper part of Cumberland; and that route I shall follow, to give the Colonel time to pitch his camp ere I reconnoitre his position.—Adieu! Delaserre—I shall hardly find another opportunity of writing till I reach Scotland."

CHAPTER XXII.

Jog on, jog on, the footpath way,
And merrily hent the stile-a:
A merry heart goes all the day,
A sad one tires in a mile-a.

Winter's Tale.

LET the reader conceive to himself a clear frosty November morning, the scene an open heath,—having for the background that huge chain of mountains in which Skiddaw and Saddleback are pre-eminent; let him look along that blind road, by which I mean the track so slightly marked by the passengers' footsteps that it can but be traced by a slight shade of verdure from the darker heath around it and, being only visible to the eye when at some distance, ceases to be distinguished while the foot is actually treading it—along this faintly-traced path advances the object of our present narrative. His firm step, his erect and free carriage, have a military air, which corresponds well with his well-proportioned limbs, and stature of six feet high. His dress is so plain and simple that it indicates nothing as to rank—it may be that of a gentleman who travels in this manner for his pleasure, or of an inferior person of whom it is the proper and usual garb. Nothing can be on a more reduced scale than his travelling equipment. A volume of Shakespeare in each pocket, a small bundle with a change of linen slung across his shoulders, an oaken cudgel in his hand, complete our pedestrian's accommodations, and in this equipage we present him to our readers.

Brown had parted that morning from his friend Dudley, and began his solitary walk towards Scotland.

The first two or three miles were rather melancholy, from want of the society to which he had of late been accustomed. But this unusual mood of mind soon gave way to the influence of his natural good spirits, excited by the exercise and the bracing effects of the frosty air. He whistled as he went along, not "from want of thought," but to give vent to those buoyant feelings which he had no other mode of expressing. For each peasant whom he chanced to meet, he had a kind greeting or a good-humoured jest; the hardy Cumbrians grinned as they passed, and said, "that's a kind heart, God bless un!" and the market-girl looked more than once over her shoulder at the athletic form, which corresponded so well with the frank and blithe address of the stranger. A rough terrier dog, his constant companion, who rivalled his master in glee, scampered at large in a thousand wheels round the heath, and came back to jump up on him, and assure him that he participated in the pleasure of the journey. Dr. Johnson thought life had few things better than the excitation produced by being whirled rapidly along in a post-chaise; but he who has in youth experienced the confident and independent feeling of a stout pedestrian in an interesting country, and during fine weather, will hold the taste of the great moralist cheap in comparison.

Part of Brown's view in choosing that unusual tract which leads through the eastern wilds of Cumberland into Scotland, had been a desire to view the remains of the celebrated Roman Wall, which are more visible in that direction than in any other part of its extent. His education had been imperfect and desultory; but neither the busy scenes in which he had been engaged, nor the pleasures of youth, nor the precarious state of his own circumstances, had diverted him from the task of mental improvement.—"And this then is the Roman Wall," he said, scrambling up to a height which commanded the course of that celebrated work of antiquity. "What a people! whose labours, even at this extremity of their empire, comprehended such space, and were executed upon a scale of such grandeur! In future ages, when the science of war shall have changed, how few traces will exist of the labours of Vauban and Coehorn, while this wonderful people's remains will even then continue to interest and astonish posterity! Their fortifications, their aqueducts, their theatres, their fountains, all their public works, bear the grave, solid, and majestic character of their language; while our modern labours, like our modern tongues, seem but constructed out of their fragments." Having thus moralised, he remembered that he was hungry, and pursued his walk to a small public-house at which he proposed to get some refreshment.

The alehouse, for it was no better, was situated in the bottom of a little dell, through which trilled a small rivulet. It was shaded by a large ash tree, against which the clay-built shed, that served the purpose of a stable, was erected, and upon which it seemed partly to recline. In this shed stood a saddled horse, employed in eating his corn. The cottages in this part of Cumberland partake of the rudeness which characterises those of Scotland. The outside of the house promised little for the interior, notwithstanding the vaunt of a sign, where a tankard of ale voluntarily decanted itself into a tumbler, and a hieroglyphical scrawl below attempted to express a promise of "good entertainment for man and horse." Brown was no fastidious traveller—he stopped and entered the cabaret [* See Note 1. Mumps's Ha'.]

The first object which caught his eye in the kitchen was a tall, stout, country-looking man, in a large jockey great-coat, the owner of the horse which stood in the shed, who was busy discussing huge slices of cold boiled beef, and casting from time to time an eye through the window, to see how his steed sped with his provender. A large tankard of ale flanked his plate of victuals, to which he applied himself by intervals. The good woman of the house was employed in baking. The fire, as is usual in that country, was on a stone hearth, in the midst of an immensely large chimney, which had two seats extended beneath the vent. On one of these sat a remarkably tall woman, in a red cloak and slouched bonnet, having the appearance of a tinker or beggar. She was busily engaged with a short black tobacco-pipe.

At the request of Brown for some food, the landlady wiped with her mealy apron one corner of the deal table, placed a wooden trencher and knife and fork before the traveller, pointed to the round of beef, recommended Mr. Dinmont's good example, and, finally, filled a brown pitcher with her home-brewed. Brown lost no time in doing ample credit to both. For a while, his opposite neighbour and he were too busy to take much notice of each other, except by a good-humoured nod as each in turn raised the tankard to his head. At length, when our pedestrian began to supply the wants of little Wasp, the Scotch storefarmer, for such was Mr. Dinmont, found himself at leisure to enter into conversation.

"A bonny terrier that, sir—and a fell [*Fiery] chield at the vermin, I warrant him—that is, if he's been weel entered, for it a' lies in that."

"Really, sir," said Brown, "his education has been somewhat neglected, and his chief property is being pleasant companion."

"Ay, sir? that's a pity, begging your pardon—it's great pity that—beast or body, education should aye be minded. I have six terriers at hame, forbye twa couple of slow-hunds, five grews, [*Greyhounds] and a wheen [*Few] other dogs. There's auld Pepper and auld Mustard, and young Pepper and young Mustard, and little Pepper and little Mustard—I had them a' regularly entered, first wi' rottens [*Rats]—then wi' stots or weasels—and then wi' the tods and brocks [*Badgers]—and now they fear naething that ever cam wi' a hairy skin on't."

"I have no doubt, sir, they are thoroughbred—but, to have so many dogs, you seem to have a very limited variety of names for them?"

"Oh, that's a fancy o' my ain to mark the breed sir; the Deuke himself has sent as far as Charlies hope to get ane o' Dandie Dinmont's Pepper and Mustard terriers—Lord, man, he sent Tam Hudson [* The real name of this veteran sportsman is now restored] the keeper, and sicken a day as we had wi' the foumarts [*Polecats] and the tods, and sicken a blythe gaedown as we had again e'en! Faith, that was a night!

"I suppose game is very plenty with you?"

"Plenty, man!—I believe there's mair hares than sheep on my farm; and for the moor-fawl, or the gray-fowl, they lie as thick as doos in a dooket—Did ye ever shoot a black-cock, man?"

"Really I had never even the pleasure to see one, except in the museum at Keswick."

"There now—I could guess that by your Southland tongue—It's very odd of these English folk that come here, how few of them has seen a black-cock! I'll tell you what—ye seem to be an honest lad, and if you'll call on me—on Dandie Dinmont—at Charlies-hope—ye shall see a black-cock, and shoot a black-cock, and eat a black-cock too, man."

"Why, the proof of the matter is the eating, to be sure, sir; and I shall be happy if I can find time to accept your invitation."

"Time, man? what ails ye to gae hame wi' me the now? How d'ye travel?"

"On foot, sir; and if that handsome pony be yours, I should find it impossible to keep up with you."

"No unless ye can walk up to fourteen mile an hour. But ye can come ower the night as far as Riccarton, where there is a public—or if ye like to stop at jockey Grieve's at the Heuch, they would be blythe to see ye, and I am just gaun to stop and drink a dram at the door wi' him, and I would tell him you're coming up—or stay—gudewife, could ye lend this gentleman the gudeman's galloway, and I'll send it ower the Waste in the morning wi' the callant?" [*Lad]

The galloway was turned out upon the fell, and was swear to catch—"Aweel, aweel, there's nae help for't, but come up the morn at ony rate.—And now, gudewife, I maun ride, to get to the Liddel or it be dark, for your Waste has but a kittle [*Ticklish] character, ye ken yourself."

"Hout fie, Mr. Dinmont, that's no like you, to gie the country an ill name—I wot, there has been nane stirred in the Waste since Sawney Culloch, the travelling-merchant, that Rowley Overdees and Jock Penny suffered for at Carlisle twa years since. There's no ane in Bewcastle would do the like o' that now—we be a' true folk now."

"Ay, Tib, that will be when the deil's blind,—and his een's no sair yet. But hear ye, gudewife, I have been through maist feck [*Part] o' Galloway and Dumfriesshire, and I have been round by Carlisle, and I was at the Staneshiebank fair the day, and I would like ill to be rubbit sae near hame, so I'll take the gate."

"Hae ye been in Dumfries and Galloway?" said the old dame, who sat smoking by the fireside, and who had not yet spoken a word.

"Troth have I, gudewife, and a weary round I've had o't."

"Then ye'll maybe ken a place they ca' Ellangowan?"

"Ellangowan, that was Mr. Bertram's—I ken the place weel eneugh.
The Laird died about a fortnight since, as I heard."

"Died!"—said the old woman, dropping her pipe, and rising and coming forward upon the floor—died?—are you sure of that?"

"Troth, am I," said Dinmont, "for it made nae sma' noise in the countryside. He died just at the roup of the stocking and furniture; it stoppit the roup, and mony folk were disappointed. They said he was the last of an auld family too, and mony were sorry—for gude blude's scarcer in Scotland than it has been."

"Dead!" replied the old woman, whom our readers have already recognised as their acquaintance Meg Merrilies—"dead! that quits a' scores. And did ye say he died without an heir?"

"Ay did he, gudewife, and the estate's sell'd by the same token; for they said, they couldna have sell'd it, if there had been an heir-male."

"Sell'd!" echoed the gipsy, with something like a scream; "and wha durst buy Ellangowan that was not of Bertram's blude?—and wha could tell whether the bonny knave-bairn may not come back to claim his ain!—wha durst buy the estate and the castle of Ellangowan?"

"Troth, gudewife, just ane o' thae writer chields that buys a' thing—they ca' him Glossin, I think."

"Glossin!—Gibbie Glossin!—that I have carried in my creels a hundred times, for his mother wasna muckle better than mysell—he to presume to buy the barony of Ellangowan!—Gude be wi' us—it is an awfu' warld!—I wished him ill—but no sic a downfa' as a' that neither—wae's me! wae's me to think o't!"—She remained a moment silent, but still opposing with her hand the farmer's retreat, who, betwixt every question, was about to turn his back, but good-humouredly stopped on observing the deep interest his answers appeared to excite.

"It will be seen and heard of—earth and sea will not hold their peace langer!—Can ye say if the same man be now the Sheriff of the county that has been sae for some years past?"

"Na, he's got some other berth in Edinburgh, they say—but gude day, gudewife, I maun ride." She followed him to his horse, and, while he drew the births of his saddle, adjusted the walise, and put on the bridle, still plied him with questions concerning Mr. Bertram's death, and the fate of his daughter; on which, however, she could obtain little information from the honest farmer.

"Did ye ever see a place they ca' Derncleugh, about a mile frae the
Place of Ellangowan?"

"I wot weel have I, gudewife,—a wild-looking den it is, wi' a wheen auld wa's o' shealins sonder—I saw it when I gaed ower the ground wi' ane that wanted to take the farm."

It was a blythe bit ance said Meg, speaking to herself,—"Did ye notice if there was an auld saugh [*Willow] tree that's maist blawn down, but yet its roots are in the earth, and it hangs ower the bit burn—mony a day hae I wrought my stocking, and sat on my sunkie [*a Stool.] under that saugh."

"Hout, deills i' the wife, wi' her saughs, and her sunkies, and Ellangowans—Godsake, woman, let me away—there's saxpence t'ye to buy half a mutchkin, instead o' clavering about thae auld-warld stories."

"Thanks to ye, gudeman—and now ye hae answered a' my questions, and never speired wherefore I asked thein, I'll gie you a bit canny [*Prudent] advice, and ye maunna speir what for neither. Tib Mumps will be out wi' the stirrup-dram in a gliffing [*Twinkling]—he'll ask ye whether ye gang ower Willie's brae, or through Conscowthart moss—tell her ony ane ye like, but be sure (speaking low and emphatically) to tak the ane ye dinna tell her." The farmer laughed and promised, and the Gipsy retreated.

"Will you take her advice?" said Brown, who had been an attentive listener to this conversation.

"That will I no—the randy quean!—Na, I had far rather Tib Mumps kenn'd which way I was gaun than her—though Tib's no muckle to lippen [*Trust] to neither, and I would advise ye on no account to stay in the house a' night."

In a moment after, Tib, the landlady, appeared with her stirrup-cup, which was taken off. She then, as Meg had predicted, inquired whether he went the hill or the moss road. He answered, the latter; and, having bid Brown good-bye, and again told him, "he depended on seeing him at Charlies-hope, the morn at latest," he rode off at a round pace.

CHAPTER XXIII.

Gallows and knock are too powerful on the highway.

Winter's Tale

The hint of the hospitable farmer was not lost on Brown. But, while he paid his reckoning, he could not avoid repeatedly fixing Iris eyes on Meg Merrilies. She was, in all respects, the same witch-like figure as when we first introduced her at Ellangowan Place. Time had grizzled her raven locks, and added wrinkles to her wild features, but her height remained erect, and her activity was unimpaired. It was remarked of this woman, as of others of the same description, that a life of action, though not of labour, gave her the perfect command of

49

her limbs and figure, so that the attitudes into which she most naturally threw herself, were free, unconstrained, and picturesque. At present, she stood by the window of the cottage, her person drawn up so as to show to full advantage her masculine stature, and her head somewhat thrown back, that the large bonnet, with which her face was shrouded, might not interrupt her steady gaze at Brown. At every gesture he made, and every tone he uttered, she seemed to give an almost imperceptible start. On his part, he was surprised to find that he could not look upon this singular figure without some emotion. "Have I dreamed of such a figure?" he said to himself, "or does this wild and singular-looking woman recall to my recollection some of the strange figures I have seen in our Indian pagodas?"

While he embarrassed himself with these discussions, and the hostess was engaged in rummaging out silver in change of half a guinea, the gipsy suddenly made two strides, and seized Brown's hand. He expected, of course, a display of her skill in palmistry, but she seemed agitated by other feelings.

"Tell me," she said, 'I tell me, in the name of God, young man, what is your name, and whence you came?"

"My name is Brown, mother, and I come from the East Indies."

"From the East Indies!" dropping his hand with a sigh; "it cannot be then—I am such an auld fool, that everything I look on seems the thing I want maist to see. But the East Indies! that cannot be—Weel, be what ye will, ye hae a face and a tongue that puts me in mind of auld times. Good-day—make haste on your road, and if ye see ony of our folk, meddle not and make not, and they'll do you nae harm."

Brown, who had by this time received his change, put a shilling into her hand, bade his hostess farewell, and, taking the route which the farmer had gone before, walked briskly on, with the advantage of being guided by the fresh hoof-prints of his horse.

Meg Merrilies looked after him for some time, and then muttered to herself, "I maun see that lad again—and I maun gang back to Ellangowan too.—The Laird's dead—aweel, death pays a' scores—he was a kind man ance.—The Sheriffs flitted, and I can keep canny in the bush—so there's no muckle hazard o' scouring the cramp-ring. [*To scour the cramp-ring, is said metaphorically for being thrown into fetters, or, generally, into prison.]—I would like to see bonny Ellangowan again or I die."

Brown, meanwhile, proceeded northward at a round pace along the moorish tract called the Waste of Cumberland. He passed a solitary house, towards which the horseman who preceded him had apparently turned up, for his horse's tread was. evident in that direction. A little farther, he seemed to have returned again into the road. Mr. Dinmont had probably made a visit there either of business or pleasure—I wish, thought Brown, the good farmer had staid till I came up; I should not have been sorry to ask him a few questions about the road, which seems to grow wilder and wilder.

In truth, nature, as if she had designed this tract of country to be the barrier between two hostile nations, has stamped upon it n character of wildness and desolation. The hills are neither high nor rocky, but the land is all heath and morass; the huts poor and mean, and at a great distance front each o,. her. Immediately around, them there is generally some little attempt at cultivation; but a half-bred foal or two, straggling about with shackles on their hind legs, to save the trouble of enclosures, intimate the farmer's chief resource to be the breeding of horses. The people, too, are of a ruder and more inhospitable class than are elsewhere to be found in Cumberland arising partly from their own habits, partly from their intermixture with vagrants and criminals, who make this wild country a refuge from justice.

So much were the men of these districts in early times the objects of suspicion and dislike to their more polished neighbours, that there was, and perhaps still exists, a by-law of the corporation of Newcastle, prohibiting any freeman of that city to take for apprentice a native of certain of these dales. It is pithily said, "Give a dog an ill name and hang him;" and it may be added, if you give a man, or race of men, an ill name, they are. very likely to do something that deserves hanging. Of this Brown had heard something, and suspected more, from the discourse between the landlady, Dinmont, and the gipsy; but he was naturally of a fearless disposition, had nothing about him that could tempt the spoiler, and trusted to get through the Waste with daylight. In this, last particular, however, he was likely to be disappointed. The way proved longer than he had anticipated, and the horizon began to grow gloomy, just as he entered upon an extensive morass.

Choosing his steps with care and deliberation, the young officer proceeded along a path that sometimes sunk between two broken black banks of moss earth, sometimes crossed narrow but deep ravines filled with a consistence between mud and water, and sometimes along heaps of gravel and stones, which had been swept together when some torrent or water-spout from the neighbouring hills overflowed the marshy ground below. He began to ponder how a horseman could make his way through such broken ground; the traces of hoofs, however, were still visible; he even thought he heard their sound at some distance, and, convinced that Mr. Dinmont's progress through the morass must be still slower than his own, he resolved to push on, in hopes to overtake him, and have the benefit of his knowledge of the country. At this moment his little terrier sprung forward, barking most furiously.

Brown quickened his pace, and, attaining the summit of a small rising ground, saw the subject of the dog's alarm. In a hollow about a gunshot below him, a man, whom he easily recognised to be Dinmont, was engaged with two others in a desperate struggle. He was dismounted, and defending himself as he best could with the butt of his heavy whip. Our traveller hastened on to his assistance; but, ere he could get up, a stroke had levelled the farmer with the earth, and one of the robbers, improving his victory, struck him some merciless blows on the head. The other villain, hastening to meet Brown, called to his companion to come along, "for that one's content," meaning, probably, past resistance or complaint. One ruffian was armed with a cutlass, the other with a bludgeon; but as the road was pretty narrow, "bar firearms," thought Brown, "and I may manage them well enough." They met accordingly, with the most murderous threats on the part of the ruffians. They soon found, however, that their near opponent was equally stout and resolute; and, after exchanging two or three blows, one of them told him to "follow his nose over the heath, in the devil's name, for they had nothing to say to him."

Brown rejected this composition, as leaving to their mercy the unfortunate man whom they were about to pillage, if not to murder outright; and the skirmish had just recommenced, when Dinmont unexpectedly recovered his senses, his feet, and his weapon, and hasted to the scene of action. As he had been no easy antagonist, even when surprised and alone, the villains did not choose to wait his joining forces with a man who had singly proved a match for them both, but fled across the bog as fast as their feet could earn, them, pursued by Wasp, who had acted gloriously during the skirmish, annoying the heels of the enemy, and repeatedly effecting a moment's diversion in his master's favour.

"Deil, but your dog's weel entered wi' the vermin now, sir!" were the first words uttered by the jolly farmer, as he came up, his head streaming with blood, and recognised his deliverer and his little attendant.

"I hope, sir, you are not hurt dangerously?"

"Oh, deil a bit-my head can stand a gey clour—nae thanks to them, though, and mony to you. But now, hinney, ye maun help me to catch the beast, and ye maun get on behind me, for we maun off like whittrets [*Weasels] before the whole clanjamfray [*Rabble] be doun upon us-the rest o' them will be no far off." The galloway was, by good fortune, easily caught, and Brown made some apology for overloading the animal.

"' Deil a fear, man," answered the proprietor, "Dumple could carry six folk if his back was lang eneugh—but God's sake, haste ye, get on, for I see some folk coming through the slack yonder, that it may be just as weel no to wait for."

Brown was of opinion that this apparition of five or six men, with whom the other villains seemed to join company, coming across the moss towards them, should abridge ceremony; he therefore mounted Dumple en croupe, and the little spirited nag cantered away with two men of great size and strength, as if they had been children of six years old. The rider, to whom the paths of these wilds seemed intimately known, pushed on at a rapid pace, managing, with much dexterity, to choose the safest route, in which he was aided by the sagacity of the galloway, who never failed to take the difficult passes exactly at the particular spot, and in the special manner, by which they could be most safely crossed. Yet, even with these advantages, the road was so broken, and they were so often thrown out of the direct course by various impediments, that they did not gain much on their pursuers. "Nevermind," said the undaunted Scotchman to his companion, "if we were ance by Withershin's Latch, the road's no near sae saft, and we'll show them fair play for't."

They soon came to the place he named, a narrow channel, through which soaked, rather than flowed, a small stagnant stream, mantled over with bright green mosses. Dinmont directed his steed towards a pass where the water appeared-to flow with more freedom over a harder bottom; but Dumple backed from the proposed crossing-place, put his head down as if to reconnoitre the swamp more nearly, stretching forward his fore-feet, and stood as fast as if he had been cut out of stone.

"Had we not better," said Brown, "dismount, and leave him to his fate—or can you, not urge him through the swamp?"

"Na, na," said his pilot, "we maun cross Dumple at no rate—he has mair sense than mony a Christian." So saying, he relaxed the reins, and shook them loosely. "Come now, lad, take your ain way o't—let's see where ye'll take us through."

Dumple, left to the freedom of his own will, trotted briskly to another part of the latch, less promising, as Brown thought, in appearance, but which the animal's sagacity or experience recommended as the safer of the two, and where, plunging in, he attained the other side with. little difficulty.

"I'm glad we're out o' that moss," said Dinmont, "where there's mair stables for horses than change-houses for men—we have the Maiden-way to help us now, at ony rate." Accordingly, they speedily gained a sort of rugged causeway so called, being the remains of an old Roman road which traverses these wild regions in a due northerly direction. Here they got on at the rate o nine or ten miles an hour, Dumple seeking no other respite than what arose from changing his pace from canter to trot. "I could gar him show mair action," said his master, "but we are twa lang-legged chields after a' and it would be a pity to stress Dumple—there wasna the like o' him at Staneshiebank fair the day."

Brown readily assented to the propriety of sparing the horse, and added, that as they were now far out of the reach of the rogues he thought Mr. Dinmont had better tie a handkerchief round his head, for fear of the cold frosty air aggravating the wound.

"What would I do that for?" answered the hardy farmer; "the best way's to let the blood barken [*Encrust] upon the cut—that saves plasters, hinney."

Brown, who in his military profession had seen a great many hard blows pass, could not help remarking, "he had never known such severe strokes received with so much apparent indifference."

"Hout tout, man—I would never be making a humdudgeon [*Fuss] about a scart on the pow-but we'll be in Scotland in five minutes now, and ye maun gang up to Charlies-hope wi' me, that's a clear case."

Brown readily accepted the offered hospitality. Night was now falling, when they came in sight of a pretty river winding its way through a pastoral country. The hills were greener and more abrupt than those which Brown had lately passed, sinking their grassy sides, at once upon the river. They had no pretensions to magnificence of height, or to romantic shapes, nor did their smooth swelling slopes exhibit either rocks or woods. Yet the view was wild, solitary, and pleasingly rural. No enclosures, no roads, almost no tillage—it seemed a land which a patriarch would have chosen to feed his flocks and herds. The remains of here and there a dismantled and ruined tower, showed that it had once harboured beings of a very different description from its present inhabitants; those free-booters, namely, to whose exploits the wars between England and Scotland bear witness. Descending by. a path towards a well-known ford, Dumple crossed the small river, and then quickening his pace, trotted about a mile briskly up its banks, and approached two or three low thatched, houses, placed with their angles to each other, with a great contempt of regularity. This was the farm-steading of Charlies-hope, or, in the language of the country, "the Town." A most furious barking was set up at their approach, by the whole three generations of Mustard and Pepper, and a number of allies, names unknown. The farmer made his well-known voice lustily heard to restore order—the door opened, and a half-dressed ewe-milker, who had done that good office, shut it in their faces, in order that she might run ben the house, to cry, "Mistress, mistress, it's the master, and another man wi' him." Dumple, turned loose, walked to his own stable-door, and there pawed and whinnied for admission, in strains which were answered by his acquaintances from the interior. Amid this bustle, Brown was fain to secure Wasp from the other dogs, who, with ardour corresponding more to their own names than to the hospitable temper of their owner, were much disposed to use the intruder roughly.

In about a minute a stout labourer was patting Dumple, and introducing him into the stable, while Mrs. Dinmont, a well-favoured buxom dame, welcomed her husband [*See Note II. Dandie Dinmont] with unfeigned rapture. "Eh, sirs! gudeman, ye hae been a weary while away!"

CHAPTER XXIV.

Liddell till now, except in Doric lays,
Tuned to her murmurs by her love-sick swains,
Unknown in song—though not a purer stream
Rolls towards the western main.
Art of Preserving Health.

The present store-farmers of the south of Scotland are a much more refined race than their fathers, and the manners I am now to describe have either altogether disappeared, or are greatly modified. Without losing the rural simplicity of manners, they now cultivate arts unknown to the former generation, not only in the progressive improvement of their possessions, but in all the comforts of life. Their houses are more commodious, their habits of life regulated so as better to keep pace with those of the civilised world, and the best of luxuries, the luxury of knowledge, has gained much ground among their hills during the last thirty years. Deep drinking, formerly their greatest failing, is now fast losing ground; and, while the frankness of their extensive hospitality continues the same, it is, generally speaking, refined in its character, and restrained in its excesses.

"Deil's in the wife," said Dandie Dinmont, shaking off his spouse's embrace, but gently and with a look of great affection;—"deil's in ye, Ailie—d'ye no see the stranger gentleman?"

Ailie turned to make her apology—"Troth, I was sae weel pleased to see the gudeman, that—But, gude gracious! what's the matter wi' ye baith?"—for they were now in her little parlour, and the candle showed the streaks of blood which Dinmont's wounded head had plentifully imparted to the clothes of his companion as well as to his own. "Ye've been fighting again, Dandie, wi' some o' the Bewcastle horse-coupers! Wow, man, a married man, a bonny family like yours, should ken better what a father's life's worth in the warld."—The tears stood in the good woman's eyes as she spoke.

"Whisht! whisht! gudewife," said her husband, with a smack that had much more affection than ceremony in it; "never mind—never mind—there's a gentleman that will tell you, that just when I had ga'en up to Lourie Lowther's, and had bidden the drinking of twa cheerers, and gotten just in again upon the moss, and was whigging cannily [*Cautiously] awa hame, twa land-loupers jumpit out of a peat-bog on me as I was thinking, and got me down, and knevelled [*Beat] me sair aneuch, or I could gar my whip walk about their lugs—and troth, gudewife, if this honest gentleman hadna come up, I would have gotten mair licks than I like, and lost mair siller than I could weel spare; so ye maun be thankful to him for it, under God." With that he drew from his side-pocket a large greasy leather pocket-book, and bade the gudewife lock it up in her kist. [*Chest]

"God bless the gentleman, and e'en God bless him wi' a' my heart—but what can we do for him, but to gie him the meat and quarters we wadna refuse to the poorest body on earth—unless (her eye directed to the pocket-book, but with a feeling of natural propriety which made the inference the most delicate possible), unless there was ony other way—" Brown saw, and estimated at its due rate, the mixture of simplicity and grateful generosity which took the downright way of expressing itself, yet qualified with so much delicacy; he was aware his own appearance, plain at best, and now torn and spattered with blood, made him an object of pity at least, and perhaps of charity. He hastened to say his name was Brown, a captain in the—regiment of cavalry, travelling for pleasure, and on foot, both from motives of independence and economy and he begged his kind landlady would look at her husband's wounds, the state of which he had refused to permit him to examine. Mrs. Dinmont was used to her husband's broken beads more than to the presence of a captain of dragoons. She therefore glanced at a tablecloth not quite clean, and conned over her proposed supper a minute or two, before, patting her husband on the shoulder, she bade him sit down for "a hard-headed loon, that was aye bringing himself and other folk into collie-shangies." [*Quarrels]

When Dandie Dinmont, after executing two or three caprioles, and cutting the Highland fling, by way of ridicule of his wife's anxiety, at last deigned to sit down, and commit his round, black, shaggy bullet of a head to her inspection, Brown thought he had seen the regimental surgeon look grave upon a more trifling case. The gudewife, however, showed some knowledge of chirurgery—she cut away with her scissors the gory locks, whose stiffened and coagulated clusters interfered with her operations, and clapped on the wound some lint besmeared with a vulnerary salve, esteemed sovereign by the whole dale (which afforded upon Fair nights considerable experience of such cases)—she then fixed her plaster with a bandage, and, spite of her patient's resistance, pulled over all a nightcap, to keep everything in its right place. Some contusions on the brow and shoulders she fomented with brandy, which the patient did not permit till the medicine had paid a heavy toll to his mouth. Mrs. Dinmont then simply, but kindly, offered her assistance to Brown.

He assured her he had no occasion for anything but the accommodation of a basin and towel.

"And that's what I should have thought of sooner," she said; "and I did think o't, but I durst na open the door, for there's a' the bairns, poor things, sae keen to see their father."

This explained a great drumming and whining at the door of the little parlour, which had somewhat surprised Brown, though his kind landlady had only noticed it by fastening the bolt as soon as she heard it begin. But on her opening the door to seek the basin and towel (for she never thought of showing the guest to a separate room), a whole tide of white-headed urchins streamed in, some from the stable, where they had been seeing Dumple, and giving him a welcome home with part of their four-hours scones; others from the kitchen, where they had been listening to auld Elspeth's tales and ballads; and the youngest half naked, out of bed, all roaring to see daddy, and to inquire what he had brought home for them from the various fairs he had visited in his peregrinations. Our knight of the broken head first kissed and hugged them all round, then distributed whistles, penny-trumpets, and Gingerbread, and, lastly, when the tumult of their joy and welcome got beyond bearing, exclaimed to his guest—"This is a' the gudewife's fault, Captain—she will gie the bairns a' their ain way."

"Me! Lord help me," said Ailie, who at that instant entered with the basin and ewer, "how can I help it?—I have naething else to gie them, poor things!"

Dinmont then exerted himself, and, between coaxing, threats, and shoving, cleared the room of all the intruders, excepting a boy and girl, the two eldest of the family, who could, as he observed, behave themselves "distinctly." For the same reason, but with less ceremony, all the dogs were kicked out, excepting the venerable patriarchs, old Pepper and Mustard, whom frequent castigation and the advance of years had inspired with such a share of passive hospitality, that, after mutual explanation and remonstrance in the shape of some growling, they admitted Wasp, who had hitherto judged it safe to keep beneath his master's chair, to a share of a dried wedder's skin, which, with the wool uppermost and unshorn, served all the purposes of a Bristol hearth-rug.

The active bustle of the mistress (so she was called in the kitchen, and the gudewife in the parlour) had already signed the fate of a couple of fowls, which, for want of time to dress them otherwise, soon appeared reeking from the gridiron-or brander, as Mrs. Dinmont denominated it. A huge piece of cold beef-ham, eggs, butter, cakes, and barley-meal bannocks in plenty, made up the entertainment, which was to be diluted with home-brewed ale of excellent quality, and a case-bottle of brandy. Few soldiers would find fault with such cheer after a day's hard exercise, and a skirmish to boot; accordingly Brown did. great honour to the eatables. While the gudewife partly aided, partly instructed, a great stout servant girl, with cheeks as red as her top-knot, to remove the supper matters, and supply sugar and hot water (which, in the damsel's anxiety to gaze upon an actual live captain, she was in some danger of forgetting), Brown took an opportunity to ask his host whether he did not repent of having neglected the gipsy's hint.

"Wha kens?" answered he;" they're queer deevils;—maybe I might just have 'scaped ae gang to' meet the other. And yet I'll no say that neither; for if that randy wife was coming to Charlies-hope, she should have a pint bottle o' brandy and a pound o' tobacco to wear her through the winter. They're queer deevils, as my auld father used to say-they're warst where they're warst guided. After a', there's baith guid and ill about the gipsies."

This, and some other desultory conversation, served as a "I shoeing-horn" to draw on another cup of ale and another cheerer, as Dinmont termed it in his country phrase, of brandy-and-water. Brown then resolutely declined all further conviviality for that evening, pleading his own weariness and the effects of time skirmish—being well aware that it would have availed nothing to have remonstrated with his host on the danger that excess might have occasioned to his own raw wound and bloody coxcomb. A very small bedroom, but a very clean bed, received the traveller, and the sheets made good the courteous vaunt of the hostess, "that they would be as pleasant as he could find ony gate, for they were washed wi' the fairy-well water, and bleached on the bonny white gowans, and bittled [*Beaten with wooden pestle.] by Nelly and herself, and what could woman, if she was a queen, do mair for them?"

They indeed rivalled snow in whiteness, and had, besides, a pleasant fragrance from the manner in which they had been bleached. Little Wasp, after licking his master's hand to ask leave, couched himself on the coverlet at his feet; and the traveller's senses were soon lost in grateful oblivion.

CHAPTER XXV.

—Give ye, Britons then Your sportive fury, pitiless to
pour Loose on the nightly robber of the fold. Him from
his craggy winding haunts unearth'd, Let all the thunder of
the chase pursue.

THOMSON'S Seasons.

Brown rose early in the morning, and walked out to look at the establishment of his new friend. All was rough and neglected in the neighbourhood of the house;—a paltry garden, no pains taken to make the vicinity dry or comfortable, and a total absence of all those little neatnesses which give the eye so much pleasure in looking at an English farm-house. There were, notwithstanding, evident signs that this arose only from want of taste, or ignorance, not from poverty, or the negligence which attends it. On the contrary, a noble cow-house, well filled with good milk-cows, a feeding-house, with ten bullocks of the most approved breed, a stable, with two good teams of horses, the appearance of domestics, active, industrious, and apparently contented with their lot; in a word, an air of liberal though sluttish plenty indicated the wealthy farmer. The situation of the house above the river formed a gentle declivity, which relieved the inhabitants of the nuisances that might otherwise have stagnated around it. At a little distance was the whole band of children, playing and building houses with peats around a huge doddered oak-tree, which was called Charlie's Bush, from some tradition respecting an old freebooter who had once inhabited the spot. Between the farm-house and the hill-pasture was a deep morass, termed in that country a slack—it had once been the defence of a fortalice, of which no vestiges now remained, but which was said to have been inhabited by the same doughty hero we have now alluded to. Brown endeavoured to make some acquaintance with the children, but "the rogues fled from him like quicksilver"—though the two eldest stood peeping when they had got to some distance. The traveller then turned his course towards the hill, crossing the foresaid swamp by a range of stepping-stones, neither the broadest nor steadiest that could be imagined. He had not climbed far up the hill when he met a man descending.

He soon recognised his worthy host, though a maud, as it is called, or a gray shepherd's-plaid, supplied his travelling jockey-coat, and a cap, faced with wild-cat's fur, more commodiously covered his bandaged head than a hat would have done. As he appeared through the morning mist, Brown, accustomed to judge of men by their thews and sinews, could not help admiring his height, the breadth of his shoulders, and the steady firmness of his step. Dinmont internally paid the same compliment to Brown, whose athletic form he now perused somewhat more at leisure than he had done formerly. After the usual greetings of the morning, the guest inquired whether his host found any inconvenient consequences from the last night's affray.

"I had maist forgotten't," said the hardy Borderer but I think this morning, now that I am fresh and sober, if you and I were at the Withershin's Latch, wi' ilka ane a gude oak souple in his hand, we wadna turn back, no for half a dizzen o' yon scaff-raff." [*Rabble.]

"But are you prudent, my good sir," said Brown, "not to take an hour or two's repose after receiving such severe contusions?"

"Confusions!" replied the farmer, laughing in derision; "Lord, Captain, naething confuses my head—I ance jumped up and laid the dogs on the fox after I had tumbled from the tap o' Christenbury Craig, and that might have confused me to purpose. Na, naething confuses me, unless it be a screed o' drink at an orra [*Occasional] time. Besides, I behooved to be round the hirsel this morning, and see how the herds were coming on—they're apt to be negligent wi' their footballs, and fairs, and trysts, when ane's away. And there I met wi' Tam o' Todshaw, and a wheen o' the rest o' the billies on the water side; they're a' for a fox-hunt this morning,—ye'll gang? I'll gie ye Dumple, and take the brood mare mysell."

"But I fear I must leave you this morning, Mr. Dinmont," replied
Brown.

"The fient a bit o' that," exclaimed the Borderer—"I'll no part wi' ye at ony rate for a fortnight mair—Na, na; we dinna meet sic friends as you on a Bewcastle moss every night."

Brown had not designed his journey should be a speedy one; he therefore readily compounded with this hearty invitation, by agreeing to pass a week at Charlies-hope.

On their return to the house, where the gudewife presided over an ample breakfast, she heard news of the proposed fox-hunt, not indeed with approbation, but without alarm or surprise. "Dand! ye're the auld man yet—naething will make ye take warning till ye're brought hame some day wi' your feet foremost."

"Tut, lass" answered Dandie, "ye ken yourself I am never a prin the waur [*a pin the worse.] o' my rambles."

So saying, he exhorted Brown to be hasty in despatching his breakfast, as, "the frost having given way, the scent would lie this morning primely."

Out they sallied accordingly for Otterscopescaurs, the farmer leading the way. They soon quitted the little valley, and involved themselves among hills as steep as they could be without being precipitous. The sides often presented gullies, down which, in the winter season, or after heavy rain, the torrents descended with great fury. Some dappled mists still floated along the peaks of the hills, the remains of the morning clouds, for the frost had broken up with a smart shower. Through these fleecy screens Were seen a hundred little temporary streamlets, or rills, descending the sides of the mountains like silver threads. By small sheep-tracks along these steeps, over which Dinmont trotted with the most fearless confidence, they at length drew near the scene of sport, and began to see other men, both on horse and foot, making toward the place of rendezvous. Brown was puzzling himself to conceive how a fox-chase could take place among hills, where it was barely possible for a pony, accustomed to the ground, to trot along, but where, quitting the track for half a yard's breadth, the rider might be either bogged, or precipitated down the bank This wonder was not diminished when he came to the place of action.

They had gradually ascended very high, and now found themselves on a mountain ridge, overhanging a glen of great depth, but extremely narrow. Here the sportsmen had collected, with an apparatus which would have shocked a member of the Pychely Hunt; for, the object being the removal of a noxious and destructive animal, as well as the pleasures of the chase, poor Reynard was allowed much less fair play than when pursued in form through an open country. The strength of his habitation, however, and the nature of the ground by which it was surrounded on all sides, supplied what was wanting in the courtesy of his pursuers. The sides of the glen were broken banks of earth, and rocks of rotten stone, which sunk sheer down to the little winding stream below, affording here and there a tuft of scathed brushwood, or a patch of furze. Along the edges of this ravine, which, as we have said, was very narrow, but of profound depth, the hunters on horse and foot ranged themselves; almost every farmer had with him; it least a, brace of large and fierce greyhounds, of the race of those deer-dogs which were formerly used in that country, but greatly lessened in size from being crossed with the common breed. The huntsman, a sort of provincial officer of the district, who receives a certain supply of meal, and a reward for every fox he destroys, was already at the bottom of the dell, whose echoes thundered to the chiding of two or three brace of fox-hounds. Terriers, including the whole generation of Pepper and Mustard, were also in attendance, having been sent forward under the care of a shepherd. Mongrel, whelp, and cur of low degree, filled up the burden of the chorus. The spectators on the brink of the ravine, or glen, held their greyhounds in leash in readiness to slip them at the fox, as soon as the activity of the party below should force him to abandon his cover.

The scene, though uncouth to the eye of a professed sportsman, had something in it wildly captivating. The shifting figures on the mountain ridge, having the sky for their background, appeared to move in the air. The dogs, impatient of their restraint, and maddened with the baying beneath, sprung here and there, and strained at the slips, which prevented them from joining their companions. Looking down, the view was equally striking. The thin mists were not totally dispersed in the glen, so that it was often through their gauzy medium that the eye strove to discover the motions of the hunters below. Sometimes a breath of wind made the scene visible, the blue rill glittering as it twined itself through its rude and solitary dell. They then could see the shepherds springing with fearless activity from one dangerous point to another, and cheering the dogs on the scent, the whole so diminished by depth and distance that they looked like pigmies. Again the mists close over them, and the only signs of their continued exertions are the halloos of the men, and the clamours of the hounds, ascending as it were out of the bowels of the earth. When the fox, thus persecuted from one stronghold to another, was at length obliged to abandon his valley, and to break away for a more distant retreat, those who watched his motions' from the top slipped their greyhounds, which, excelling the fox in swiftness, and equalling him in ferocity and spirit, soon brought the plunderer to his life's end.

In this way, without any attention to the ordinary rules and decorums of sport, but apparently as much to the gratification bath of bipeds and quadrupeds as if all due ritual had been followed, four foxes were killed on this active morning; and even Brown himself, though he had seen the princely reports of India, and ridden a-tiger-hunting upon an elephant with the Nabob of Arcot, professed to have received an excellent morning's amusement. When the sport was given up for the day, most of the sportsmen, according to the established hospitality of the country, went to dine at Charlies-hope.

During their return homeward, Brown rode for a short time beside the Huntsman, and asked him some questions concerning the mode in which he exercised his profession. The man showed an unwillingness to meet his eye, and a disposition to be rid of his company and conversation, for which Brown could not easily account. He was a thin, dark, active fellow, well framed for the hardy profession which he exercised. But his face had not the frankness of the jolly hunter; he was down-looked, embarrassed, and avoided the eyes of those who looked hard at him. After some unimportant observations on the success of the day, Brown gave him a trifling gratuity, and rode on with his landlord. They found the gudewife prepared for their reception—the fold and the poultry-yard furnished the entertainment, and the kind and hearty welcome made amends for all deficiencies in elegance and fashion.

CHAPTER XXVI.

The Elliots and Armstrongs did convene,

They were a gallant company.

Ballad of Johnnie Armstrong.

WITHOUT noticing the occupations of an intervening day or two, which, as they consisted of the ordinary silvan amusements of shooting and coursing, have nothing sufficiently interesting to detain the reader, we pass to one in some degree peculiar to Scotland, which may be called a sort of salmon-hunting. This long-shafted trident called a waster, [*Or leister. The long spear is used for striking; but there is a shorter, which is cast from the hand, and with which an experienced sportsman hits the fish with singular dexterity.] is much practised at the mouth of the Esk, and in the other salmon rivers of Scotland. The sport is followed by day and night, but most commonly in the latter, when the fish are discovered by means of torches, or fire-grates, filled with blazing fragments of tar-barrels, which shed a strong though partial light upon the water. On the present occasion, the principal party were embarked in a crazy boat upon a part of the river which was enlarged and deepened by the restraint of a mill-wear, while others, like the ancient Bacchanals in their gambols, ran along the banks, brandishing their torches and spears, and pursuing the salmon, some of which endeavoured to escape up the stream, while others, shrouding themselves under roots of trees, fragments of stones, and large rocks, attempted to conceal themselves from the researches of the fishermen. These the party in the boat detected by the slightest indications; the twinkling of a fin, the rising of an air-bell, was sufficient to point out to these adroit sportsmen in what direction to use their weapon.

The scene was inexpressibly animating to those accustomed to it; but as Brown was not practised to use the spear, he soon tired of making efforts, which were attended with no other consequences than jarring his arms against the rocks at the bottom of the river, upon which, instead of the devoted salmon, he often bestowed his blow. Nor did he relish, though he concealed feelings which would not have been understood, being quite so near the agonies of the expiring salmon, as they lay flapping about in the boat, which they moistened with their blood. He therefore requested to be put ashore, and, from the top of a heugh or broken bank, enjoyed the scene much more to his satisfaction. Often he thought of his friend Dudley the artist, when he observed the effect produced by the strong red glare on the romantic banks under which the boat glided. Now the light diminished to a distant star that seemed to twinkle on the waters, like those which, according to the legends of the country, the water-kelpy sends for the purpose of indicating the watery grave of his victims. Then it advanced nearer, brightening and enlarging as it again approached, till the broad flickering flame rendered bank, and rock, and tree, visible as it passed, tinging them with its own red glare of dusky light, and resigning them gradually to darkness, or to pale moonlight, as it receded. By this light also were seen the figures in the boat, now holding high their weapons, now stooping to strike, now standing upright, bronzed, by the same red glare, into a colour which might have befitted the regions of Pandemonium.

Having amused himself for some time with these effects of light and shadow, Brown strolled homewards towards the farmhouse, gazing in his way at the persons engaged in the sport, two or three of whom are generally kept together, one holding the torch, the others with their spears, ready to avail themselves of the light it affords to strike their prey. As he observed one man struggling with a very weighty salmon which he had speared, but was unable completely to raise from the water, Brown advanced close to the bank to see the issue of his exertions. The man who held the torch in this instance was the huntsman, whose sulky demeanour Brown had already noticed with surprise.—"Come here, sir! come here, sir! look at this ane! He turns up a side like a sow."—Such was the cry from the assistants when some of them observed Brown advancing.

"Ground the waster weel, man! ground the waster weel!—haud him down—ye haena the pith o' a cat"—were the cries of advice, encouragement, and expostulation, from those who were on the bank, to the sportsman engaged with the salmon, who stood up to his middle in water, jingling among broken ice, struggling against the force of the fish and the strength of the current, and dubious in what manner he should attempt to secure his booty. As Brown came to the edge of the bank, he called out—"Hold up your torch, friend huntsman!" for he had already distinguished his dusky features by the strong light cast upon them by the blaze. But the fellow no sooner heard his voice, and saw, or rather concluded, it was Brown who approached him, than, instead of advancing his light, he let it drop, as if accidentally, into the water.

"The deil's in Gabriel said the spearman, as the fragments of glowing wood floated half blazing, half sparkling, but soon extinguished, down the stream—the deil's in the man! —I'll never master him without the light—and a braver kipper, could I but land him, never reisted abune a pair o' cleeks." [*See Note III. Lum Cleeks.]—Some dashed into the water to lend their assistance, and the fish, which was afterwards found to weigh nearly thirty pounds, was landed in safety.

The behaviour of the huntsman struck Brown, although he had no recollection of his face, nor could conceive why he should, as it appeared he evidently did, shun his observation.—Could he be one of the footpads he had encountered a few days before?—The supposition was not altogether improbable, although unwarranted by any observation he was able to make upon the man's figure and face. To be sure the villains wore their hats much slouched, and had loose coats, and their size was not in any way so peculiarly discriminated as to enable him to resort to that criterion. He resolved to speak to his host Dinmont on the subject, but for obvious reasons concluded it were best to defer the explanation until a cool hour in the morning.

The sportsmen returned loaded with fish, upwards of one hundred salmon having been killed within the range of their sport. The best were selected for the use of the principal farmers, the others divided among their shepherds, cottars, dependants, and others of inferior rank who attended. These fish, dried in the turf smoke of their cabins, or shealings, formed a savoury addition to the mess of potatoes, mixed with onions, which was the principal part of their winter food. In the meanwhile a liberal distribution of ale and whisky was made among them, besides what was called a kettle of fish,—two or three salmon, namely, plunged into a cauldron, and boiled for their supper. Brown accompanied his jolly landlord and the rest of his friends into the large and smoky kitchen, where this savoury mess reeked on an oaken table, massive enough to have dined Johnnie Armstrong and his merry men. All was hearty cheer and huzza, and jest and clamorous laughter, and bragging alternately, and raillery between whiles. Our traveller looked earnestly around for the dark countenance of the fox-hunter; but it was nowhere to be seen.

At length he hazarded a question concerning him. "That was an awkward accident, my lads, of one of you, who dropped his torch in the water when his companion was struggling with the large fish."

"Awkward!" returned a shepherd, looking up (the same stout young fellow who had speared the salmon), "he deserved his paikes [*Punishment] for't—to put out the light when the fish was on ane's witters! [*The barbs of the spear]—I'm well convinced Gabriel drapped the roughies [*When dry splinters, or branches, are used as fuel to supply the light for burning the water, as it is called, they are termed, as in the text, Roughies. When rags, dipped in tar, are employed, they are called Hards, probably from the French.] in the water on purpose-he doesna like to see onybody do a thing better than himself."

"Ay," said another, "he's sair shamed o' himself, else he would have been up here the night—Gabriel likes a little o' the gude thing as weel as ony o' us."

"Is he of this country?" said Brown.

"Na, na, he's been but shortly in office, but he's a fell hunter-he's frae down the country, some gate on the Dumfries side."

"And what's his name, pray?"

"Gabriel."

"But Gabriel what?"

"Oh, Lord kens that; we dinna mind folk's after-names muckle here, they run sae muckle into clans."

"Ye see, sir," said an old shepherd, rising, and speaking very slow, "the folks hereabout are a' Armstrongs and Elliats, [* See Note IV. Clan Surnames.] and sic like—twa or three given names—and so, for distinction's sake, the lairds and farmers have the names of their places that they live at—as for example, Tam o' Todshaw, Will o' the Flat, Hobbie o' Sorbietrees, and our good master here, o' the Charlies-hope.—Aweel, sir, and then the inferior sort o' people, ye'll observe, are kend by sorts o' by-names some o' them, as Glaiket Christie, and the Deuke's Davie, or maybe, like this lad Gabriel, by his employment; as for example, Tod Gabble, or Hunter Gabble. He's no been lang here, sir, and I dinna think onybody kens him by ony other name. But it's no right to rin him doun ahint his back, for he's a fell fox-hunter, though he's maybe no just sae clever as some o' the folk hereawa wi' the waster."

After some further desultory conversation, the superior sportsmen retired to conclude the evening after their own manner, leaving the others to enjoy themselves, unawed by their presence. That evening, like all those which Brown had passed at Charlies-hope, was spent in much innocent mirth and conviviality. The latter might have approached to the verge of riot but for the good women; for several of the neighbouring mistresses (a phrase of a signification how different from what it bears in more fashionable life!) had assembled at Charlies hope to witness the event of this memorable evening. Finding the punch-bowl was so often replenished, that there was some danger of their gracious presence being forgotten, they rushed in valorously upon the recreant revellers, headed by our good Mistress Ailie, so that Venus speedily routed Bacchus. The fiddler and piper next made their appearance, and the best part of the night was gallantly consumed in dancing to their music.

An otter-hunt the next day, and a badger-baiting the day after, consumed the time merrily.—I hope our traveller will not sink in the reader's estimation, sportsman though he may be, when I inform him, that on this last occasion, after young Pepper had lost a fore-foot, and Mustard the second had been nearly throttled, he begged, as a particular and personal favour of Mr. Dinmont, that the poor badger, who had made so gallant a defence, should he permitted to retire to his earth without further molestation.

The farmer, who would probably have treated this request with supreme contempt had it come from any other person, was contented, in Brown's case, to express the utter extremity of his wonder. "Weel," he said, "that's queer aneugh!—But since ye take his part, deil a tyke shall meddle wi' him mair in my day—we'll e'en mark him, and ca' him the Captain's brock-and I'm sure I'm glad I can do onything to oblige you—but, Lord save us, to care about a brock!" [*Badger] After a week spent in rural sport, and distinguished by the most frank attentions on the part of his honest landlord, Brown bade adieu to the banks of the Liddel, and the hospitality of Charlies-hope. The children, with all of whom he had now become an intimate and a favourite, roared manfully in full chorus at his departure, and he was obliged to promise twenty times, that he would soon return and play over all their favourite tunes upon the flageolet till they had got them by heart.—"Come back again, Captain," said one little sturdy fellow, "and Jenny will be your wife." Jenny was about eleven years old—she ran and hid herself behind her mammy.

"Captain, come back," said a little fat roll-about girl of six, holding her mouth up to be kissed, "and I'll be your wife my ainsell."

"They must be of harder mould than I," thought Brown, "who could part from so many kind hearts with indifference. "The good dame too, with matron modesty, and an affectionate simplicity that marked the olden time, offered her cheek to the departing guest—"It's little the like of us can do," she said, "little indeed—but yet—if there were but anything—"

"Now, my dear Mrs. Dinmont, you embolden me to make a request—would you but have the kindness to weave me, or work me, just such a gray plaid as the goodman wears?" He had learned the language and feelings of the country even during the short time of his residence, and was aware of the pleasure the request would confer.

"A tait o' woo' [*Tuft of wool] would be scarce amang us," said the gudewife, brightening, "if ye shouldna hae that, and as gude a tweel as ever cam aff a pirn. I'll speak to Johnnie Goodsire, the weaver at the Castletown, the morn. Fare ye wee], sir!—and may ye be just as happy yourself as ye like to see a' body else—and that would be a sair wish to some folk." I must not omit to mention, that our traveller left his trusty attendant Wasp to be a guest at Charlies-hope for a season. He foresaw that he might prove a troublesome attendant in the event of his being in any situation where secrecy and concealment might he necessary. He, was therefore consigned to the care of the eldest boy, who promised, in the words of the old song, that he should have A bit of his supper, a bit of his bed, and that he should be engaged in none of those perilous pastimes in which the race of Mustard and Pepper had suffered frequent mutilation. Brown now prepared for his journey, having taken a temporary farewell of his trusty little companion.

There is an old prejudice in these hills in favour of riding. Every farmer rides well, and rides the whole day. Probably the extent of their large pasture farms, and the necessity of surveying them rapidly, first introduced this custom; or a very zealous antiquary might derive it from the times of the Lay o the Last Minstrel, when twenty thousand horsemen assembled at the light of the beacon-fires. [*It would be affectation to alter this reference. But the reader will understand it was inserted to keep up the author's incognito, as he was not likely to be suspected of quoting his own works. This explanation is also applicable to one or two similar passages, in this and the other novels, introduced for the same reason.] But the truth is undeniable; they like to be on horseback, and can be with difficulty convinced that any one chooses walking from other motives than those of convenience or necessity. Accordingly, Dinmont insisted upon mounting his guest, and accompanying him on horseback as far as the nearest town in Dumfriesshire, where he had directed his baggage to be sent, and from which he proposed to pursue his intended journey towards Woodbourne, the residence of Julia Mannering.

Upon the way he questioned his companion concerning the character of the fox-hunter; but gained little information, as he had been called to that office while Dinmont was making the round of the Highland fairs. "He was a shake-rag like fellow," he said, "and, he dared to say, had gipsy blood in his veins—but at ony rate he was nane o' the smacks [*Rogues] that had been on their quarters in the moss—he would ken them weel if he saw them again. There are some no bad folk amang the gipsies too, to be sic a gang," added Dandie; "if ever I see that auld randle-tree of a wife again, I'll gie her something to buy tobacco—I have a great notion she meant me very fair after a'."

When they were about finally to part, the good farmer held Brown long by the hand, and at length said, "Captain, the woo's sae weel up the year that it's paid a' the rent, and we have naething to do wi' the rest o' the siller when Ailie has had her new gown, and the bairns their bits o' duds [*Clothes]—now I was thinking of some safe hand to put it into, for it's ower muckle to ware on brandy and sugar—now I have heard that you army gentlemen can sometimes buy yoursells up a step; and if a hundred or twa would help ye on such an occasion, the bit scrape o' your pen would be as good to me as the siller, and ye might just take yere ane time o' settling it—it wad be a great convenience to me." Brown, who felt the full delicacy that wished to disguise the conferring an obligation under the show of asking a favour, thanked his grateful friend most heartily, and assured him he would have recourse to his purse, without scruple, should circumstances ever render it convenient for him. And thus they parted with many expressions of mutual regard.

CHAPTER XXVII.

If thou hast any love of mercy in thee,
Turn me upon my face that I may die.
Joanna Baillie.

Our traveller hired a post-chaise at the place where he separated from Dinmont, with the purpose of proceeding to Kippletringan, there to inquire into the state of the family at Woodbourne, before he should venture to make his presence in the country known to Miss Mannering. The stage was a long one of eighteen or twenty miles, and the road lay across the country. To add to the inconveniences of the journey, the snow began to fall pretty quickly. The postilion, however, proceeded on his journey for a good many miles, without expressing doubt or hesitation. It was not until the night was completely set in that he intimated his apprehensions whether he was in the right road. The increasing snow rendered this intimation rather alarming, for as it drove full in the lad's face, and lay whitening all around him, it served in two different ways to confuse his knowledge of the count and to diminish the chance of his recovering the right track. Brown then himself got out and looked round, not, it may be well imagined, from any better hope than that of seeing some house at which he might make inquiry. But none appeared—he could therefore only tell the lad to drive steadily on. The road on which they were, ran through plantations of considerable extent and depth, and the traveller therefore conjectured that there must be a gentleman's house at no great distance. At length, after struggling wearily on for about a mile, the post-boy stopped, and protested his horses would not budge a foot farther "but he saw," he said, "a light among the trees, which must proceed from a house; the only way was to inquire the road there." Accordingly, he dismounted, heavily encumbered with a long greatcoat, and a pair of boots which might have rivalled in thickness the sevenfold shield of Ajax. As in this guise he was plodding forth upon his voyage of discovery, Brown's impatience prevailed, and, jumping out of the carriage, he desired the lad to stop where he was, by the horses, and he would himself go to the house—a command which the driver most joyfully obeyed.

Our traveller groped along the side of the enclosure from which the light glimmered, in order to find some mode of approaching in that direction, and after proceeding for some space, at length found a stile in the hedge, and a pathway leading into the plantation, which in that place was of great extent. This promised to lead to the light which was the object of his search, and accordingly Brown proceeded in that direction, but soon totally lost sight, of it among the trees. The path, which at first seemed broad and well marked by the opening of the wood through which it winded, was now less easily distinguishable, although the whiteness of the snow afforded some reflected light to assist his search. Directing himself as much as possible through the more open parts of the wood, he proceeded almost a mile without either recovering a view of the light, or seeing anything resembling a habitation. Still, however, he thought it best to persevere in that direction. It must surely have been a light in the hut of a forester, for it shone too steadily to be the glimmer of an ignis fatuus. The ground at length became broken, and declined rapidly, and although Brown conceived he still moved along what had once at least been a pathway, it was now very unequal, and the snow concealing those breaches and inequalities, the traveller had one or two falls in consequence. He began now to think of turning back, especially as the falling snow, which his impatience had hitherto prevented his attending to, was coming on thicker and faster.

Willing, however, to make, a last. effort, he still advanced a little way, when, to his great delight, he beheld the light opposite at no great distance, and apparently upon a level with him. He quickly found that this last appearance was deception, for the ground continued so rapidly to sink, as made it obvious there was a deep dell or ravine of some kind, between him and the object of his search. Taking every precaution to preserve his footing, he continued to, descend, until he reached the bottom of a very steep and narrow glen, through which winded a small rivulet, whose course was then almost choked with snow. He now found himself embarrassed among the ruins of cottages, whose black gables, rendered more distinguishable by the contrast with the whitened surface from which they rose, were still standing; the sidewalls had long since given way to time, and, piled in shapeless heaps, and covered with snow offered frequent and embarrassing obstacles to—our traveller's progress. Still, however, he persevered, crossed the rivulet, not without some trouble, and at length, by exertions which became both painful and perilous, ascended its opposite and very rugged bank, until he came on a level with the building from' which the gleam proceeded.

It was difficult, especially by so imperfect a light, to discover the nature of this edifice; but it seemed a square building of small size, the upper part of which was totally ruinous. It had, perhaps, been the abode, in former. times, of some lesser proprietor, or a place of strength and concealment, in case of need, for one of greater importance. But only the lower vault remained, the arch of which formed the roof in the present state of the building. Brown first approached the place from whence the light proceeded, which was a long narrow slit or loophole, such as usually are to be found in old castles. Impelled by curiosity to reconnoitre the interior of this strange place before he entered, Brown gazed in at this aperture. A scene of greater desolation could not well be imagined. There was a fire upon the floor, the smoke of which, after circling through the apartment, escaped by a hole broken in the arch above. The walls, seen by this smoky light, had the rude and waste appearance of a ruin of three centuries old at least. A cask or two, with some broken boxes and packages, lay about the place in confusion. But the inmates chiefly occupied Brown's attention. Upon a lair composed of straw with a blanket stretched over it, lay a figure, so stilly, that, except that it was not dressed in the ordinary habiliments of the grave, Brown would have concluded it to be a corpse. On a steadier view he perceived it was only on the point of becoming so, for he heard one or two of these low, deep, and hard-drawn sighs, that precede dissolution when the frame is tenacious of life. A female figure, dressed in a long cloak, sat on a stone by this miserable couch; her elbows rested upon her knees, and her face, averted from the light of an iron lamp beside her, was bent upon that of the dying person. She moistened his mouth from time to time with some liquid, and between whiles sung, in a low monotonous cadence, one of those prayers, or rather spells, which, in some parts of Scotland and the north of England, are used by the vulgar and ignorant to speed the passage of a parting spirit, like the tolling, of the bell in catholic days. She accompanied this dismal sound with a slow rocking motion of her body to and fro, as if to keep time with her song. The words ran nearly thus—

   Wasted, weary, wherefore stay,
Wrestling thus with earth and clay?
From the body pass away;—
Hark! the mass is singing,
   From thee doff thy mortal weed,
Mary Mother be thy speed,
Saints to help thee at thy need;—
Hark! the knell is ringing.

Fear not snow-drift driving fast
Sleet, or hail, or levin blast;
Soon the shroud shall lap thee fast,
And the sleep be on thee cast
That shall ne'er know waking.

Haste thee, haste thee, to be gone,
Earth flits fast, and time draws on,—
Gasp thy gasp, and groan thy groan,
Day is near the breaking.

The songstress paused, and was answered by one or two deep and hollow groans, that seemed to proceed from the very agony of the mortal strife. "It will not be," she muttered to herself—"He cannot pass away with that on his mind—it tethers him here—

"Heaven cannot abide it,
Earth refuses to hide it."

[*See Note V. Gipsy Superstitions.]

I must open the door;" and, rising, she faced towards the door of the apartment, observing heedfully not to turn back her head, and, withdrawing a bolt or two (for, notwithstanding the miserable appearance of the place, the door was cautiously secured), she lifted the latch, saying,

"Open lock end strife, Come death, and pass life." Brown, who had by this time moved from his post, stood before her as she opened the door. She stepped back a pace, and he entered, instantly recognising, but with no comfortable sensation, the same gipsy woman whom he had met in Bewcastle. She also knew him at once, and her attitude, figure, and the anxiety of her countenance assumed the appearance of the well-disposed ogress of a fairy tale, warning a stranger not to enter the dangerous castle of her husband. The first words she spoke (holding up her hands in a reproving manner) were, "Said I not to ye, Make not, meddle not?—Beware of the redding straik! [*The redding straik, namely, a blow received by a peacemaker who interfere betwixt two combatants, to red or separate them, is proverbially said to be the most dangerous blow a man can receive.] you are come to no house o' fairstrae [*Natural] death." So saying, she raised the lamp, and turned its light on the dying man, whose rude and harsh features were now convulsed with the last agony. A roll of linen about his head was stained with blood, which had soaked also through the blankets and the straw. It was, indeed, under no natural disease that the wretch was suffering. Brown started back from this horrible object, and, turning to the gipsy, exclaimed, "Wretched woman, who has done this?"

"They that were permitted," answered Meg Merrilies, while she scanned with a close and keen glance the features of the expiring man.—"He has had a sair struggle—but it's passing—I kenn'd he would pass when you came in.—That was the death-ruckle—he's dead."

Sounds were now heard at a distance, as of voices. "They are coming," said she to Brown; "you are a dead man if ye had as mony lives as hairs." Brown eagerly looked round for some weapon of defence. There was none near. He then rushed to the door, with the intention of plunging among the trees, and making his escape by flight, from what he now esteemed a den of murderers, but Merrilies held him with a masculine grasp. "Here," she said, "here be still and you are safe—stir not, whatever you see or hear, and nothing shall befall you."

Brown, in these desperate circumstances, remembered this woman's intimation formerly, and thought he had no chance of safety but in obeying her. She caused him to couch down among a parcel of straw on the opposite side of the apartment from the corpse, covered him carefully, and flung over him two or three old sacks which lay about the place. Anxious to observe what was to happen, Brown arranged, as softly as he could, the means of peeping from under the coverings by which he was hidden, and awaited with a throbbing heart the issue of this strange and most unpleasant adventure. The old gipsy, in the meantime, set about arranging the dead body, composing its limbs, and straightening the arms by its side. "Best to do this," she muttered, "ere he stiffen." She placed on the dead man's breast a trencher, with salt sprinkled upon it, set one candle at the head, and another at the feet of the body, and lighted both. Then she resumed her song, and awaited the approach of those whose voices had been heard without.

Brown was a soldier, and a brave one; but he was also a man, and at this moment his fears mastered his courage so completely that the cold drops burst out from every pore. The idea of being dragged out of his miserable concealment by wretches, whose trade was that of midnight murder, without weapons or the slightest means of defence, except entreaties, which would be only their sport, and cries for help, which could never reach other ear than their own—his safety entrusted to the precarious compassion of a being associated with these felons, and whose trade of rapine and imposture must have hardened her against every human feeling—the bitterness of his emotions almost choked him. He endeavoured to read in her withered and dark countenance, as the lamp threw its light upon her features, something that promised those feelings of compassion, which, females, even in their most degraded state, can seldom altogether smother. There was no such touch of humanity about this woman. The interest, whatever it was, that determined her in his favour, arose not from the impulse of compassion, but from some internal, and probably capricious, association of feelings, to which he had no clew. It rested, perhaps, on a fancied likeness, such as Lady Macbeth found to her father in the sleeping monarch. Such were the reflections that passed in rapid succession through Brown's mind, as he gazed from his hiding-place upon this extraordinary personage. Meantime the gang did not yet approach, and he was almost prompted to resume his original intention of attempting an escape from the hut, and cursed internally his own irresolution, which had consented to his being cooped up where he had neither room for resistance nor flight.

Meg Merrilies seemed equally on the watch. She bent her ear to every sound that whistled round the old walls. Then she turned again to the dead body, and found something new to arrange or alter in its position. "He's a bonny corpse, she muttered to herself, "and weel worth the streaking."—And in this dismal occupation she appeared to feel a sort of professional pleasure, entering slowly into all the minutiae, as if with the skill and feelings of a connoisseur. A long dark-coloured sea-cloak,—Which she dragged out of a corner, was disposed for a pall. The face she left bare, after closing the mouth and eyes, and arranged the capes of the cloak so as to hide the bloody bandages, and give the body, as she muttered, a mair decent appearance."

At once three or four men, equally ruffians in appearance and dress rushed into the hut. "Meg, ye limb of Satan, how dare you leave the door open?" was the first salutation of the party.

"And wha ever heard of a door being barred when a man was in the dead-thraw?—how d'ye think the spirit was to get awa through bolts and bars like thae?

"Is he dead, then?" said one who went to the side of the couch to look at the body.

"Ay, ay—dead enough," said another—"but here's what shall give him a rousing lykewake." So saying, he fetched a keg of spirits from a corner, while Meg hastened to display pipes and tobacco. From the activity with which she undertook the task, Brown conceived good hope of her fidelity towards her guest. It was obvious that she wished to engage the ruffians in their debauch, to prevent the discovery which might take place if, by accident, any of their should approach too nearly the place of Brown's concealment.

CHAPTER XXVIII.

Nor board nor garner own we now,
  Nor roof nor latched door,
Nor kind mate, bound by holy vows
  To bless a good man's store.
Noon lulls us in a gloomy den,
  And night is grown our day;
Uprouse ye, then, my merry men!
  And use it as ye may.

  JOANNA BAILLIE.

Brown could now reckon his foes—they were five in number; two of them were very powerful men, who appeared to be either real seamen, or strollers who assumed that character; the other three, an old man and two lads, were slighter made, and, from their black hair and dark complexion, seemed to belong to Meg's tribe. They passed from one to another the cup out of which they drank their spirits. "Here's to his good voyage!" said one of the seamen, drinking; "a squally night he's got, however, to drift through the sky in."

We omit here various execrations with which these honest gentlemen garnished their discourse, retaining only such of their expletives as are least offensive.

"'A does not mind wind and weather—'A has had many a north-easter in his day."

"He had his last yesterday," said another gruffly; "and now old Meg may pray for his last fair wind, as she's often done before."

"I'll pray for nane o' him," said Meg, "nor for you neither, you randy dog. The times are sair altered since I was a kinchin-mort. [*Girl.] Men were men then, and fought other in the open field, and there was nae milling in the darkmans. [*Murder by night.] And the gentry had kind hearts, and would have given baith lap and pannel [*Liquor and food] to ony puir gipsy; and there was not one, from Johnnie Faa the upright man, [*The leader (and greatest rogue) of the gang.] to little Christie that was in the panniers, would cloyed a dud [*Stolen a rag] from them. But ye are a' altered from the gude auld rules, and no wonder that you scour the cramp-ring, and trine to the cheat [*Get imprisoned and hanged.] sae often. Yes, ye are a' altered-you'll cat the gudeman's meat, drink his drink, sleep on the strammel [*Straw] in his barn, and break his house and cut his throat for his pains! There's blood on your hands, too, ye dogs—mair than ever came there by fair fighting. See how ye'll die then—lang it was ere he died—he strove, and strove sair, and could neither die nor live;—but you—half the country will see how ye'll grace the woodie."

The party set up a hoarse laugh at Meg's prophecy. "What made you come back here, ye auld beldame?" said one of the gipsies; "could ye not have staid where you were, and spaed fortunes to the Cumberland flats?—Bing out and tour, [*Go out and watch] ye auld devil, and see that nobody has scented; that's a' you're good for now."

"Is that a' I am good for now?" said the indignant matron. "I was good for mair than that in the great fight between our folk and Patrico Salmon's; if I had not helped you with these very fambles (holding up her hands), Jean Baillie would have frummagem'd you, [*Throttled you] ye feckless do-little!"

There was here another laugh at the expense of the hero who had received this amazon's assistance.

"Here, mother," said one of the sailors, "here's a cup of the right for you, and never mind that bully-huff."

Meg drank the spirits, and, withdrawing herself from further conversation, sat down before the spot where Brown lay bid, in such a posture that it would have been difficult for any one to have approached it without her rising. The men, however, showed no disposition to disturb her.

They closed around the fire, and held deep consultation together; but the low tone in which they spoke, and the cant language which they used, prevented Brown from understanding much of their conversation. He gathered in general, that they expressed great indignation against some individual. "He shall have his gruel,"—said one, and then whispered something very low into the ear of his comrade.

"I'll have nothing to do with that," said the other

"Are you turned hen-hearted, Jack?"

"No, by G-d, no more than yourself,—but I won't—it was something like that stopped all the trade fifteen or twenty years ago you have heard of the 'Loup'?"

"I have heard him (indicating the corpse by a jerk of his head) tell about that job. G-d, how he used to laugh when he showed us how he fetched him off the perch!"

"Well, but it did up the trade for one while," said Jack.

"How should that be?" asked the surly villain.

"Why," replied Jack, "the people got rusty about it, and would not deal, and they had bought so many brooms [*Got so many warrants out] that—"

"Well for all that," said the other. "I think we should be down upon the fellow one of these darkmans, and let him get it well."

"But old Meg's asleep now," said another; "she grows a driveller, and is afraid of her shadow. She'll sing out, [*To sing out or whistle in the cage, is when a rogue, being apprehended, peaches against his comrades.] some of these odd-come-shortlies, if you ,don't look sharp."

"Never fear," said the old gipsy man Meg's true-bred; she's the last in the gang that will start—but she has some queer ways, and often cuts queer words."

With more of this gibberish, they continued the conversation, rendering it thus, even to each other, a dark obscure dialect, eked out by significant nods and signs, but never expressing distinctly, or in plain language, the subject on which it turned. At length one of them, observing Meg was still fast asleep, or appeared to be so, desired one of the lads "to hand in the black Peter, that they might flick it open."

The boy stepped to the door, and brought in a portmanteau, which Brown instantly recognised for his own. His thoughts immediately turned to the unfortunate lad he had left with the carriage. Had the ruffians murdered him? was the horrible doubt that crossed his mind. The agony of his attention grew yet keener, and while the villains pulled out and admired the different articles of his clothes and linen, he eagerly listened for some indication that might intimate the fate of the postilion. But the ruffians were too much delighted with their prize, and too much busied in examining its contents, to enter into any detail concerning the manner in which they had acquired it. The portmanteau contained various articles of apparel, a pair of pistols, a leathern case with a few papers, and some money, etc. etc. At any other time it would have provoked Brown excessively to see the unceremonious manner in which the thieves shared his property, and made themselves merry at the expense or the owner. But the moment was too perilous to admit any thoughts but what had immediate reference to self-preservation.

After a sufficient scrutiny into the portmanteau, and an equitable division of its contents, the ruffians applied themselves more closely to the serious occupation of drinking, in which they spent the greater part of the night. Brown was for some time in great hopes that they would drink so deep as to render themselves insensible, when his escape would have been an easy matter. But their dangerous trade required precautions inconsistent with such unlimited indulgence, and they stopped short on this side of absolute intoxication. Three of them at length composed themselves to rest, while the fourth watched. He was relieved in—this duty by one of the others, after a vigil of two hours. When the second watch had elapsed, the sentinel awakened the whole, who, to Brown's inexpressible relief, began to make some preparations as if for departure, bundling up the various articles which each had appropriated. Still, however, there remained something to be done. Two of them, after some rummaging, which not a little alarmed Brown, produced a mattock and shovel, another took a pickaxe from behind the straw on which the dead body was extended. With these implements two of them left the hut, and the remaining three, two of whom were the seamen, very strong men, still remained in garrison.

After the space of about half an hour, one of those who had departed again returned, and whispered the others. They wrapped up the dead body in the sea-cloak which had served as a pall, and went out, bearing it along with them. The aged sibyl then arose from her real or feigned slumbers. She first went to the door, as if for the purpose of watching the departure of her late inmates, then returned, and commanded Brown, in a low and stifled voice, to follow her instantly. He obeyed; but, on leaving the hut, he would willingly have repossessed himself of his money, or papers at least, but this she prohibited in the most peremptory manner. It immediately occurred to him that the suspicion of having removed anything, of which he might repossess himself, would fall upon this woman, by whom, in all probability, his life had been saved. He therefore immediately desisted from his attempt, contenting himself with seizing a cutlass, which one of the ruffians had flung aside among the straw. On his feet, and possessed of this weapon, he already found himself half delivered from the dangers which beset him. Still, however, he felt stiffened and cramped, both with the cold, and by the constrained and unaltered position which he had occupied all night. But as he followed the gipsy from the door of the hut, the fresh air of the morning, and the action of walking, restored circulation and activity to his benumbed limbs.

The pale light of a winter's morning was rendered more clear by the snow, which was lying all around, crisped by the influence of a severe frost. Brown cast a hasty glance at the landscape around him, that he might be able again to know the spot. The little tower, of which only a single vault remained, forming the dismal apartment in which he had spent this remarkable night, was perched on the very point of a projecting rock overhanging the rivulet. It was accessible only on one side, and that from the ravine or glen below. On the other three sides the bank was precipitous, so that Brown had on the preceding evening escaped more dangers than one; for, if he had attempted to go round the building, which was once his purpose, he must have been dashed to pieces. The dell was so narrow that the trees met in some places from the opposite sides. They were now loaded with snow instead of leaves, and thus formed a sort of frozen canopy over the rivulet beneath, which was marked by its darker colour, as it soaked its way obscurely through wreaths of snow. In one place, where the glen was a little wider, leaving a small piece of flat ground between the rivulet and the bank, were situated the ruins of the hamlet in which Brown had been involved on the preceding evening. The ruined gables, the insides of which were japanned with turf-smoke, looked yet blacker, contrasted with the patches of snow which had been driven against them by the wind, and with the drifts which lay around them.

Upon this wintry and dismal scene, Brown could only at present cast a very hasty glance; for his guide, after pausing an instant, as if to permit him to indulge his curiosity, strode hastily before him down the path which led into the glen. He observed, with some feelings of suspicion, that she chose a track already marked by several feet, which he could only suppose were those of the depredators who had spent the night in the vault. A moment's recollection, however, put his suspicions to rest. —It was not to be thought that the woman, who might have delivered him up to her gang when in a state totally defenceless, would have suspended her supposed treachery until he was armed, and in the open air, and had so many better chances of defence or escape. He therefore followed his guide in confidence and silence. They crossed the small brook at the same place where it previously had been passed by those who had gone before. The footmarks then proceeded through the ruined village, and from thence down the glen, which again narrowed to a ravine, after the small opening in which they were situated. But the gipsy no longer followed the same track: she turned aside, and led the way by a very rugged and uneven path up the bank which overhung the village. Although the snow in many places bid the pathway, and Rendered the footing uncertain and unsafe, Meg proceeded with a firm and determined step, which indicated an intimate knowledge of the ground she traversed. At length they gained the top of the bank, though by a passage so steep and intricate, that Brown, though convinced it was the same by which he had descended on the night before, was not a little surprised how he had accomplished the task without breaking his neck. Above, the country opened wide and unenclosed for about a mile or two on the one hand, and on the other were thick plantations of considerable extent.

Meg, however, still led the way along the bank of the ravine out of which they had ascended, until she heard beneath the murmur of voices. She then pointed to a deep plantation of trees at some distance.

"The road to Kippletringan," she said, is on the other side of these enclosures—Make the speed ye can; there's mair rests on your life than other folk's. But you have lost all—stay." She fumbled in an immense pocket, from which she produced a greasy purse—"Many's the awmous your house has gi'en Meg and hers—and she has lived to pay it back in a small degree;"—and she placed the purse in his hand.

"The woman is insane," thought Brown; but it was no time to debate the point, for the sounds he heard in the ravine below probably proceeded from the banditti. "How shall I repay this money," he said "or how acknowledge the kindness you have done me?"

"I hae twa boons to crave," answered the sibyl, speaking low and hastily; one, that you will never speak of what you have seen this night; the other, that you will not leave this country till you see me again, and that you leave word at the Gordon Arms where you are to be heard of; and when I next call for you, be it in church or market, at wedding or at burial, Sunday or Saturday, meal-time or fasting, that ye leave everything else and come with me."

"Why, that will do you little good, mother."

"But 'twill do yourself muckle, and that's what I'm thinking o'.—I am not mad, although I have had eneugh to make me sae—I am not mad, nor doating, nor drunken—I know what I am asking, and I know it has been the will of God to preserve you in strange dangers, and that I shall be the instrument to set you in your father's seat again.—Sae give me your promise, and mind that you owe your life to me this blessed night."

"There's wildness in her manner, certainly," thought Brown; "and yet it is more like the wildness of energy than of madness."

"Well, mother, since you do ask so useless and trifling a favour, you have my promise. It will at least give me an opportunity to repay your money with additions. You are an uncommon kind of creditor, no doubt, but—"

"Away, away, then!" said she, waving her hand. "Think not about the goud—it's a' your ain; but remember your promise, and do not dare to follow me or look after me." So saying, she plunged again into the dell, and descended it with great agility, the icicles and snow-wreaths showering down after her as she disappeared.

Notwithstanding her prohibition, Brown endeavoured to gain some point of the bank from which he might, unseen, gaze down into the glen and with some difficulty (for it must be conceived that the utmost caution was necessary), he succeeded. The spot which he attained for this purpose was the point of a projecting rock, which rose precipitously from among the trees. By kneeling down among the snow, and stretching his head cautiously forward, he could observe what was going on in the bottom of the dell. He saw, as he expected, his companions of the last night, now joined by two or three others. They had cleared away the snow from the foot of the rock, and dug a deep pit, which was designed to serve the purpose of a grave. Around this they now stood, and lowered into it something wrapped in a naval cloak, which Brown instantly concluded to be the dead body of the man he had seen expire. They then stood silent for half a minute, as if under some touch of feeling for the loss of their companion. But if they experienced such, they did not long remain under its influence, for all hands went presently to work to fill up the grave; and Brown, perceiving that the task would be soon ended, thought it best to take the gipsy-woman's hint, and walk as fast as possible until he should gain the shelter of the plantation.

Having arrived under cover of the trees, his first thought was of the gipsy's purse. He had accepted it without hesitation, though with something like a feeling of degradation, arising from the character of the person by whom he was thus accommodated. But it relieved him from a serious though temporary' embarrassment. His money, excepting a very few shillings, was in his portmanteau, and that was in possession of Meg's friends. Some time was necessary to write to his agent, or even to apply to his good host at Charlies-hope, who would gladly have supplied him. In the meantime, he resolved to avail himself of Meg's subsidy, confident he should have a speedy opportunity of replacing it with a handsome gratuity. "It can be but a trifling sum," he said to himself, "and I dare say the good lady may have a share of my bank-notes to make amends."

With these reflections he opened the leathern purse, expecting to find at most three or four guineas. But how much was he surprised to discover that it contained, besides a considerable quantity of gold pieces, of different coinages and various countries, the joint amount of which could not be short of a hundred pounds, several valuable rings and ornaments set with jewels, and, as appeared from the slight inspection he had time to give them, of very considerable value.

Brown was equally astonished and embarrassed by the circumstances in which he found himself, possesses, as he now appeared to be, of property to a much greater amount than his own, but which had been obtained in all probability by the same nefarious means through which he had himself been plundered. His first thought was to inquire after the nearest justice of peace, and to place in his hands the treasure of which he had thus unexpectedly become the depositary, telling, at the same time, his own remarkable story. But a moment's consideration brought several objections to this mode of procedure. In the first place, by observing this course, he should break his promise of silence, and might probably by that means involve the safety, perhaps the life, of this woman, who had risked her own to preserve his, and who had voluntarily endowed him with this treasure,—a generosity which might thus become the means of her ruin. This was not to be thought of. Besides, he was a stranger, and, for a time at least, unprovided with means of establishing his own character and credit to the satisfaction of a stupid or obstinate country magistrate.—"I will think over. . .,the matter more maturely," he said; "Perhaps there may be a regiment quartered at the county town, in which 'case my knowledge of the service, and acquaintance with many officers of the army, cannot fail to establish my situation and character by evidence which a civil judge could not sufficiently estimate.—And then I shall have the commanding officer's assistance in; managing matters so as to screen—this unhappy madwoman, whose mistake or prejudice has been so fortunate for me. A civil magistrate might think himself obliged to send out warrants for her at once, and the consequence in case of her being taken is pretty evident. No, she has been upon honour with me if she were the devil, and I will be equally upon honour with her—she shall have the privilege of a court-martial, where the point of honour can qualify strict law. Besides I may see her at this place, Kipple-Couple—what did she call it?—and then I can make restitution to her, and e'en let the law claim its own when it can secure her. In the meanwhile, however, I cut rather an awkward figure for one who has the honour to bear his Majesty's commission, being little better than the receiver of stolen goods."

With these reflections, Brown took from the gipsy's treasure three or four guineas, for the purpose of his immediate expenses, and tying up the rest in the purse which contained them, resolved not again to open it, until he could either restore it to her by whom it was given, or put it into the hands of some public functionary. He next thought of the cutlass, and his first impulse was to leave it in the plantation. But when he considered the risk of meeting with these ruffians, he could not resolve on parting with his arms. His walking-dress, though plain, had so much of a military character as suited not amiss with his having such a weapon. Besides, though the custom of wearing swords by persons out of uniform had been gradually becoming antiquated, it was not yet so totally forgotten as to occasion any particular remark towards those who chose to adhere to it. Retaining, therefore, his weapon of defence, and placing the purse of the gipsy in a private pocket, our traveller strode gallantly on through the wood in search of the promised high road.

CHAPTER XXIX.

All school-days' friendship, childhood innocence,
We, Hermia, like two artificial gods,
Have with our needles created both one flower,

Both on one sampler, sitting on one cushion,
Both warbling of one song, both in one key,
As if our hands, our sides, voices, and minds,
Had been incorporate.
  A Midsummer Nights Dream.

JULIA MANNERING TO MATILDA MARCHMONT.

How can you upbraid me, my dearest Matilda, with abatement in friendship, or fluctuation in affection? Is it possible for me to forget that you are the chosen of my heart, in whose faithful bosom I have deposited every feeling which your poor Julia dares to acknowledge to herself? And you do me equal injustice in upbraiding me with exchanging your friendship for that of Lucy Bertram. I assure you she has not the materials I must seek for in a bosom confidante. She is a charming girl, to be sure, and I like her very much, and I confess our forenoon and evening engagements have left me less time for the exercise of my pen than our proposed regularity of correspondence demands. But she is totally devoid of elegant accomplishments, excepting the knowledge of French and Italian, which she acquired from the most grotesque monster you ever beheld, whom my father has engaged as a kind of librarian, and whom he patronises, I believe, to show his defiance of the world's opinion. Colonel Mannering seems to have formed a determination, that nothing shall be considered as ridiculous, so long as it appertains to or is connected with him. I remember in India he had picked up somewhere a little mongrel cur, with bandy legs, a long back, and huge flapping ears. Of this uncouth creature he chose to make a favourite, in despite of all taste and opinion; and I remember one instance which he alleged, of what he called Brown's petulance, was, that he had criticised severely the crooked legs and drooping ears of Bingo. On my word, Matilda, I believe he nurses his high opinion of this most awkward of all pedants upon a similar principle. He seats the creature at table, where he pronounces a grace that sounds like the scream of the man in the square that used to cry mackerel, flings his meat down his throat by shovelfuls, like a dustman loading his cart, and apparently without the most distant perception of what he is swallowing,—then bleats forth another unnatural set of tones, by way of returning thanks, stalks out of the room, and immerses himself among a parcel of huge worm-eaten folios that are as uncouth as himself! I could endure the creature well enough, had I anybody to laugh at him along with me; but Lucy Bertram, if I but verge on the border of a jest affecting this same Mr. Sampson (such is the horrid man's horrid name), looks so piteous, that it deprives me of all spirit to proceed, and my father knits his brow, flashes fire from his eye, bites his lip, and says something that is extremely rude, and uncomfortable to my feelings.

"It was not of this creature, however, that I meant to speak to you—only that, being a good scholar in the modern, as well as the ancient languages, he has contrived to make Lucy Bertram mistress of the former, and she has only, I believe, to thank her own good sense or obstinacy, that the Greek, Latin (and Hebrew, for aught I know), were not added to her acquisitions. And thus she really has a great fund of information, and I assure you I am daily surprised at the power which she seems to possess of amusing herself by recalling and arranging the subjects of her former reading. We read together every morning, and I begin to like Italian much better than when we were teased by that conceited animal Cicipici,—this is the way to spell his name, and not Chichipichi—you see I grow a connoisseur.

"' But perhaps I like Miss Bertram more for the accomplishments she wants, than for the knowledge she possesses. She knows nothing of music whatever, and no more of dancing than is here common to the meanest peasants, who, by the way, dance with great zeal and spirit. So that I am instructor in my turn, and she takes with great gratitude lessons from me upon the harpsichord, and I have even taught her some of La Pique's steps, and you know he thought me a promising scholar.

"In the evening papa often reads, and I assure you he is the best reader of poetry you ever heard—not like that actor, who made a kind of jumble between reading and acting, staring, and bending his brow, and twisting his face, and gesticulating as if he were on the stage, and dressed out in all his costume. My father's manner is quite different—it is the reading of a gentleman, who produces effect by feeling, taste, and inflection of voice, not by action or mummery. Lucy Bertram rides remarkably well, and I can now accompany her on horseback, having become emboldened by example. We walk also a good deal in spite of the cold—So, upon the whole I have not quite so much time for writing as I used to have.

"Besides, my love, I must really use the apology of all stupid correspondents, that I have nothing to say. My hopes, my fears, my anxieties about Brown are of a less interesting cast, since I know that he is at liberty, and in health. Besides, I must own, I think that by this time the gentleman might have given me some intimation what he was doing. Our intercourse may, be an imprudent one, but it is not very complimentary to me, that Mr. Vanbeest Brown should be the first to discover that such is the case, and. to break off in consequence. I can promise him that we might not differ much in opinion should that happen to be his, for I have sometimes thought I have behaved extremely foolishly in that matter. Yet I have so good an opinion of poor Brown, that I cannot but think there is something extraordinary in his silence.

"To return to Lucy Bertram—No, my dearest Matilda, she can never, never rival you in my regard, so that all your affectionate jealousy on that account is without foundation. She is, to be sure, a very pretty, a very sensible, a very affectionate girl, and I think there are few persons to whose consolatory friendship I could have recourse more freely in what are called the real evils of life. But then these so seldom come in one's way, and one wants a friend who will sympathise with distresses of sentiment, as well as with actual misfortune. Heaven knows, and you know, my dearest Matilda, that these diseases of the heart require the balm of sympathy and affection as much as the evils of a more obvious and determinate character. Now Lucy Bertram has nothing of this kindly sympathy—nothing at all, my dearest Matilda. Were I sick of a fever, she would sit up night after night to nurse me with the most unrepining patience; but with the fever of the heart, which my Matilda has soothed so often, she has no more sympathy than her old tutor. And yet, what provokes me is, that the demure monkey actually has a lover of her own, and that their mutual affection (for mutual I take it to be) has a great deal of complicated and romantic interest. She was once, you must know, a great heiress, but was ruined by the prodigality of her father, and the villainy of a horrid man in whom he confided. And one of the handsomest young gentlemen in the country is attached to her; but as he is heir to a great estate, she discourages his addresses on account of the disproportion of their fortune.

"But with all this moderation, and self-denial, and modesty, and so forth, Lucy is a sly girl—I am sure she loves young Hazlewood, and I am sure he has some guess of that, and would probably bring her to acknowledge it too, if my father or she would allow him an opportunity. But you must know the Colonel is always himself in the way to pay Miss Bertram those attentions which afford the best indirect opportunities for a young gentleman in Hazlewood's situation. I would have my good papa take care that he does not himself pay the usual penalty of meddling folks. I assure you, if I were Hazlewood, I should look on his compliments, his bowings, his cloakings, his shawlings, and his handings, with some little suspicion; and truly I think Hazlewood does so too at some odd times. Then imagine what a silly figure your poor Julia makes on such occasions! Here is my father making the agreeable to my friend; there is young Hazlewood watching every word of her lips, and every motion of her eye; and I have not the poor satisfaction of interesting a human being—not even the exotic monster of a parson, for even he sits with his mouth open, and his huge round goggling eyes fixed like those of a statue, admiring—Mess Baartram!

"All this makes me sometimes a little nervous, and sometimes a little mischievous. I was so provoked at my father and the lovers the other day for turning me completely out of their thoughts and society, that I began an attack on Hazlewood, from which it was impossible for him, in common civility, to escape. He insensibly became warm in his defence—I assure you, Matilda, he is a very clever, as well as a very handsome young man, and I don't think I ever remember having seen him to the same advantage—when, behold, in the midst of our lively conversation, a very soft sigh from Miss Lucy reached my not ungratified ears. I was greatly too generous to prosecute my victory any further, even if I had not been afraid of papa. Luckily for me, he had at that moment got into a long description of the peculiar notions and manners of a certain tribe of Indians, who live far up the country, and was illustrating them by making drawings on Miss Bertram's work-patterns, three of which he utterly damaged, by introducing among the intricacies of the pattern his specimens of Oriental costume. But I believe she thought as little of her own gown at the moment as of the India turbans and cummerbands. However, it was quite as well for me that he did not see all the merit of my little manoeuvre, for he is as sharp-sighted as a hawk, and a sworn enemy to the slightest shade of coquetry.

"Well, Matilda, Hazlewood heard this same half-audible sigh, and instantly repented his temporary attentions to such an unworthy object as your Julia, and, with a very comical expression of consciousness, drew near to Lucy's work-table. He made some trifling observation, and her reply was one in which nothing but an ear as acute as that of a lover, or a curious observer like myself, could have distinguished anything more cold and dry than usual. But it conveyed reproof to the self-accusing hero, and he stood abashed accordingly. You will admit that I was called upon in generosity to act as mediator. So I mingled in the conversation, in the quiet tone of an unobserving and uninterested third party, led them into their former habits of easy chat, and, after having served awhile as the channel of communication through which they chose to address each other, set them down to a pensive game at chess, and very dutifully went to tease papa, who was still busied with his drawings. The chess-players, you must observe, were placed near the chimney, beside a little work-table, which held the board and men, the Colonel, at some distance, with lights upon a library table,—for it is a large old-fashioned room, with several recesses, and hung with grim tapestry, representing what it might have puzzled the artist himself to explain.

'Is chess a very interesting game, papa?'

'I am told so,' without honouring me with much of his notice. "'I should think so, from the attention Mr. Hazlewood and Lucy are bestowing on it.'

"He raised his head hastily, and held his pencil suspended for an instant. Apparently he saw nothing that excited his suspicions, for he was resuming the folds of a Mahratta's turban in tranquility, when I interrupted him with—'How old is Miss Bertram, sir?'

'How should I know, Miss? about your own age, I suppose.'

"'Older, I should think, sir. You are always telling me how much more decorously she goes through all the honours of the tea-table—Lord, papa, what if you should give her a right to preside once and for ever!'

'Julia, my, dear,' returned papa 'you are either a fool outright, or you are more disposed to make mischief than I have yet believed you.'

"'Oh, my. dear. sir! put your best construction upon it—I would not be thought. a. fool for all the world. '

'Then why do you talk like one?' said my father.

'Lord, sir, I am sure there is nothing so foolish in what I said just now—everybody knows you are a very handsome man' (a smile was just visible), 'that is, for your time of life' (the dawn was over-cast), 'which is far from being advanced, and I am sure I don't know why you should not please yourself, if you have a mind. I am sensible I am but a thoughtless girl, and if a graver companion could render you more happy—'

"There was a mixture of displeasure and grave affection in the manner in which my father took my hand, that was a severe reproof to me for trifling with his feelings. 'Julia,' he said, 'I bear with much of your petulance, because I think I have in some degree deserved it, by neglecting to superintend your education sufficiently closely. Yet I would not have you give it the rein upon a subject so delicate. If you do not respect the feelings of your surviving parent towards the memory of her whom you have lost, attend at least to the sacred claims of misfortune; and observe, that the slightest hint of such a jest reaching Miss Bertram's ears would at once induce her to renounce her present asylum, and go forth, without a protector, into a world she has already felt so unfriendly.'

'What could I say to this, Matilda?—I only cried heartily, begged pardon, and promised to be a good girl in future. And so here am I neutralised again, for I cannot, in honour, or common good-nature, tease poor Lucy by interfering with Hazlewood, although she has so little confidence in me; and neither can I, after this grave appeal, venture again upon such delicate ground with papa. So I burn little rolls of paper, and sketch Turks' heads upon visiting cards with the blackened end—I assure you I succeeded in making a superb Hyder-Ally last night—and I jingle on my unfortunate harpsichord, and begin at the end of a grave book and read it backward.—After all, I begin to be very much vexed about Brown's silence. Had he been obliged to leave the country, I am sure he would at least have written to me—Is it possible that my father can have intercepted his letters? But no—that is contrary to all his principles—I don't think he would open a letter addressed to me to-night, to prevent my jumping out of window to-morrow—What an expression I have suffered to escape my pen! I should be ashamed of it, even to you, Matilda, and used in jest. But I need not take much merit for acting as I ought to do; this same Mr. Vanbeest Brown is by no means so very ardent a lover as to hurry the object of his attachment into such inconsiderate steps. He gives one full time to reflect, that must be admitted. However, I will not blame him unheard, nor permit myself to doubt the manly firmness of a character which I have so often extolled to you. Were he capable of doubt, of fear, of the shadow of change, I should have little to regret.

"And why, you will say, when I expect such steady and unalterable constancy from a lover, why should I be anxious about what Hazlewood does, or to whom he offers his attentions?—I ask myself the questions a hundred times a day, and it only receives the very silly answer, that one does not like to be neglected, though one would not encourage a serious infidelity.

"I write all these trifles, because you say that they amuse you,—and yet I wonder how they should. I remember, in our stolen voyages to the world of fiction, you always admired the grand and the romantic—tales of knights, dwarfs, giants, and distressed damsels, soothsayers, visions, beckoning ghosts, and bloody hands,—whereas I was partial to the involved intrigues of private life, or at furthest, to so much only of the supernatural as is conferred by the agency of an Eastern genie or a beneficent fairy. You would have loved to shape your course of life over the broad ocean, with its dead calms and howling tempests, its, tornadoes, and its billows mountain-high,—whereas I should like to trim my little pinnace to a brisk breeze in some inland lake or tranquil bay where there was just difficulty of navigation sufficient to give interest and to require skill, without any sensible degree of danger. So that, upon the whole, Matilda, I think you should have had my father, with his pride of arms and of ancestry, his chivalrous point of honour, his high talents, and his abstruse and mystic studies—You should have had Lucy Bertram too for your friend, whose fathers, with names which alike defy memory and orthography, ruled over this romantic country, and whose birth took place, as I have been indistinctly informed, under circumstances of deep and peculiar interest—You should have had, too, our Scottish residence, surrounded by mountains, and our lonely walks to haunted ruins—And I should have had, in exchange, the lawns and shrubs, and greenhouses, and conservatories, of Pine Park, with your, good, quiet, indulgent aunt, her chapel in the morning, her nap after dinner, her hand at whist in the evening, not forgetting her fat coach-horses and fatter coachman. Take notice, however, that Brown is not included in this proposed barter of mine—his good-humour,

lively conversation, and open gallantry, suit my plan of life, as well as his athletic form, handsome features, and high spirit, would accord with a character of chivalry. So as we cannot change altogether out and out, I think we must e'en abide as we are."

CHAPTER XXX.

I renounce your defiance; if you parley so roughly I'll
barricado my gates against you.—Do you see yon bay
window? Storm,—I care not, serving the good Duke of
Norfolk.

Merry Devil of Edmonton.

JULIA MANNERING TO MATILDA MARCHMC)NT.

"I rise from a sick-bed, my dearest Matlida, to communicate the strange and frightful scenes which have just passed. Alas! how little we ought to jest with futurity! I closed my letter to you in high spirits, with some flippant remarks on your taste for the romantic and extraordinary in fictitious narrative. How little I expected to have had such events to record in the course of a few days! and to witness scenes of terror, or to contemplate them in description, is as different, my dearest Matilda, as to bend over the brink, of a precipice holding by the frail tenure of a half-rotted shrub, or to admire the same precipice as represented in the landscape of Salvator. But I will not anticipate my narrative.

"The first part of my story is frightful enough, though it had nothing to interest my feelings. You must know that this country is particularly favourable to the commerce of a set of desperate men from the Isle of Man, which is nearly opposite. These smugglers are numerous, resolute, and formidable, and have at different times become the dread of the neighbourhood when any one has interfered with their contraband trade. The local magistrates, from timidity or worse motives, have become shy of acting against them, and impunity has rendered them equally daring and desperate. With all this, my father, a stranger in the land, and invested with no official authority, had, one would think, nothing to do. But it must be owned, that, as he himself expresses it, he was born when Mars was lord of his ascendant, and that strife and bloodshed find him out in circumstances and situations the most retired and pacific.

"About eleven o'clock on last Tuesday morning, while Hazlewood and my father were proposing to walk to a little lake about three miles' distance, for the purpose of shooting wild ducks, and while Lucy and I were busied with arranging our plan of work and study for the day, we were alarmed by the sound of horses' feet, advancing very fast up the avenue. The ground was hardened by a severe frost, which made the clatter of the hoofs sound yet louder and sharper. In a moment, two or three men, armed, mounted, and each leading a spare horse loaded with packages, appeared on the lawn, and, without keeping upon the road, which makes a small sweep, pushed right across for the door of the house. Their appearance was in the utmost degree hurried and disordered, and they frequently looked back like men who apprehended a close and deadly pursuit. My father and Hazlewood hurried to the front door to demand who they were, and what was their business. They were revenue officers, they stated, who had seized these horses, loaded with contraband articles, at a place about three miles off. But the smugglers had been reinforced, and were now pursuing them with the avowed purpose of recovering the goods, and putting to death the officers who had presumed to do their duty. The men said that their horses being loaded, and the pursuers gaining ground upon them, they had fled to Woodbourne, conceiving, that as my father had served the king, he would not refuse to protect the servants of government, when threatened to be murdered in the discharge of their duty.

"My father, to whom, in his enthusiastic feelings of military loyalty, even a dog would be of importance if he came in the king's name, gave prompt orders for securing the goods in the hall, arming the servants, and defending the house in case it should be necessary. Hazlewood seconded him with great spirit, and even the strange animal they call Sampson stalked out of his den, and seized upon a fowling-piece, which my father had laid aside, to take what they call a rifle-gun, with which they shoot tigers, etc., in the east. The piece went off in the awkward hands of the poor parson, and very nearly shot one' of the excisemen. At this unexpected and involuntary explosion of his weapon, the Dominie (such is his nickname) exclaimed, 'Prodigious!' which is his usual ejaculation when astonished. But no power could force the man to part with his discharged piece, so they were content to let him retain it, with the precaution of trusting him with no ammunition. This (excepting the alarm occasioned by the report) escaped my notice at the time, you may easily believe; but in talking over the scene afterwards, Hazlewood made us very merry with the Dominie's ignorant but zealous valour.

"When my father had got everything into proper order for defence, and his people stationed at the windows with their firearms, he wanted to order us out of danger—into the cellar, I believe—but we could not be prevailed upon to stir. Though terrified to death, I have so much of his own spirit that I would look upon the peril which. threatens us rather than hear it rage around me without knowing its nature or its progress. Lucy, looking as pale as a marble statue, and keeping her eyes fixed on Hazlewood, seemed not even to hear the prayers with which he conjured her to leave the front of the house. But, in truth, unless the hall-door should be forced, we were in little danger; the windows being almost blocked up with cushion's and pillows, and, what the Dominie most lamented, with folio volumes. , brought hastily from the library, leaving only spaces through which the defenders might fire upon the assailants.

"My father had now made his dispositions, and we sat in breathless expectation in the darkened apartment, the men remaining all silent upon their posts, in anxious contemplation probably of the approaching danger. My father, who was quite at home in such a scene, walked from one to another, and reiterated his orders, that no one should presume to fire until he gave the word. Hazlewood, who seemed to catch courage from his eye, acted as his aide-de-camp, and displayed the utmost alertness in bearing his directions from one place to another, and seeing them properly carried into execution. Our force, with the strangers included, might amount to about twelve men.

"At length the silence of this awful period of expectation was broken by a sound, which, at a distance, was like the rushing of a stream of water, but, as it approached, we distinguished the thick-beating clang of a number of horses advancing very fast. I had arranged a loophole for myself, from which I could see the approach of the enemy. The noise increased and came nearer, and at length thirty horsemen and more rushed upon the lawn. You never saw such horrid wretches! Notwithstanding the severity of the season, they were most of them stripped to their shirts and trousers, with silk handkerchiefs knotted about their heads, and all well armed with carbines, pistols, and cutlasses. I, who am a soldier's daughter, and accustomed to see war from my infancy, was never so terrified in my life as by the savage appearance of these ruffians, their horses reeking with the speed at which they had ridden, and their furious exclamations of rage and disappointment, when they saw themselves baulked of their prey. They paused, however, when they saw the preparations made to receive them, and appeared to hold a moment's consultation among themselves. At length, one of the party, his face blackened with gunpowder by way of disguise, came forward with a white handkerchief on the end of his carbine, and asked to speak with Colonel Mannering. My father, to my infinite terror, threw open a window near which he was posted, and demanded what he wanted. 'We want our goods, which we have been robbed of by these sharks,' said the fellow; 'and our lieutenant bids me say, that if they are delivered, we'll go off for this bout without clearing scores with the rascals who took them; but if not, we'll burn the house, and have the heart's blood every one in it.'—a threat which he. repeated more than once, graced by a fresh variety of imprecations, and the most horrid denunciations that cruelty could suggest.

"'And which is your lieutenant?' said my father in reply.

"'That gentleman on the gray horse,' said the miscreant, I with the red handkerchief bound about his brow.'

"'Then be pleased to tell that gentleman, that it he, and the scoundrels who are with him, do not ride off the lawn this instant, I will fire upon them without ceremony." So saying, my father shut the window, and broke short the conference.

"The fellow no sooner regained his troop, than with a loud hurra, or rather a savage yell, they fired a volley against our garrison. The glass of the windows was shattered in every direction, but the precautions already noticed saved the party within from suffering. Three such volleys were fired without a shot being returned from within. My father then observed them getting hatchets and crows, probably to assail the hall-door, and called aloud, 'Let none fire but Hazlewood and me—Hazlewood, mark the ambassador.' He himself aimed at the man on the gray horse, who fell on receiving his shot. Hazlewood was equally successful. He shot the spokesman, who had dismounted, and was advancing with an axe in his hand. Their fall discouraged the rest, who began to turn round their horses; and a few shots fired at them soon sent them off, bearing along with them their slain or wounded companions. We could not observe that they suffered any further loss. Shortly after their retreat a party of soldiers made their appearance, to my infinite relief. These men were quartered at a village some miles distant, and had marched on the first rumour of the skirmish. A part of them escorted the terrified revenue officers and their seizure to a neighbouring seaport as a place of safety, and at my earnest request two or three files remained with us for that and the following day, for the security of the house from the vengeance of these banditti.

"Such, dearest Matilda, was my first alarm. I must not forget to add, that the ruffians left, at a cottage on the roadside, the man whose face was blackened with powder, apparently because he was unable to bear transportation. He died in about half an hour after. On examining the corpse, it proved to be that of a profligate boor in the neighbourhood, a person notorious as a poacher and—smuggler. We I received many messages of congratulation from the neighbouring families, and it was generally allowed that a few such instances of spirited resistance would greatly check the presumption of these lawless men. My father distributed rewards among his servants, and praised Hazlewood's courage and coolness to the skies. Lucy and I came in for a share of his applause, because we had stood fire with firmness, and had not disturbed him with screams or expostulations. As for the Dominie, my father took an opportunity of begging to exchange snuff-boxes with him. The honest gentleman was much flattered with the proposal, and extolled the beauty, of his new snuff-box excessively. 'It looked,' he said, 'as well as if it were real gold from Ophir. '—Indeed it would be odd if it should not, being formed in fact of that very metal: but, to do this honest creature justice, I believe the knowledge of its real value would not enhance his sense of my father's kindness supposing it, as he does, to be pinchbeck gilded. He has had a hard task replacing the folios which were used in the barricade, smoothing out the creases And dog-ears, and repairing the other disasters they have sustained during their service in the Fortification. He brought us some pieces of lead and bullets which these ponderous tomes had intercepted during the action, and which he had extracted with great care; and, were I in spirits, I could give you a comic account of his astonishment at the apathy with which we heard of the wounds and mutilation suffered by Thomas Aquinas, or the venerable Chrysostom. But I am not in spirits, and I have yet another and a more interesting incident to communicate. I feel, however, so much fatigued with my present exertion, that I cannot resume the pen till to-morrow. I will detain this letter notwithstanding, that you may not feel any anxiety upon account of your own

"JULIA MANNERING."

CHAPTER XXXI.

Here's a good world! -Knew you of this fair work?

King John

JULIA MANNERING TO MATILDA MARCHMONT.

"I must take tip the thread of my story, my dearest Matilda, where
I broke off yesterday.

"For two or three days we talked of nothing but our siege and its probable consequences, and dinned into my father's unwilling ears a proposal to go to Edinburgh, or at least to Dumfries, where there is remarkably good society, until the resentment of these outlaws should blow over. He answered with great composure, that he had no mind to have his landlord's house and his own property at Woodbourne destroyed; that, with our good leave, he had usually been esteemed competent to taking measures for the safety or protection of his family; that if he remained quick at home, he conceived the welcome the villains had received was not of a nature to invite a second visit, but should he show any signs of alarm, it would be the sure way to incur the very risk which we were afraid of. Heartened by his arguments, and by the extreme indifference with which he treated the supposed danger, we began to grow a little bolder, and to walk about as usual Only the gentlemen were sometimes invited to take their guns when they attended us, and I observed that my father for several nights paid particular attention to having the house properly secured and required his domestics to keep their arms in readiness in case of necessity.

"But three days ago chanced an occurrence, of a nature which alarmed me more by far than. the attack of the smugglers.

"I told you there was a small lake at some distance from Woodbourne, where the gentlemen sometimes go to shoot wild-fowl. I happened at breakfast to say I should like to see this place in its present frozen state, occupied by skaters and curlers, as they call those who play a particular sort of game upon the ice. There is snow on the ground, but frozen so hard that I thought Lucy and I might venture to that distance, as the footpath leading there was well beaten by the repair of those who frequented it for pastime. Hazlewood instantly offered to attend us, and we stipulated that he should take his fowling-piece. He laughed a good deal at the idea of going a-shooting in the snow; but, to relieve our tremors, desired that a groom, who acts as gamekeeper occasionally, should follow us with his gun. As for Colonel Mannering, he does not like crowds or sights of any kind where human figures make up the show, unless indeed it were a military review— so he declined the party.

"We set out unusually early, on a fine frosty, exhilarating morning, and we felt our minds, as well as our nerves, braced by the elasticity of the pure air. Our walk to the lake was delightful, or at least the difficulties were only such as diverted us, a slippery descent for instance, or a frozen ditch to cross, which made Hazlewood's assistance absolutely necessary. I don't think Lucy liked her walk the less for these occasional embarrassments.

"The scene upon the lake was beautiful. One side of it is bordered by a steep crag, from which hung a thousand enormous icicles all glittering in the sun; on the other side was a little wood, now exhibiting that fantastic appearance which the pine-trees present when their branches are loaded with snow. On the frozen bosom of the lake itself were a multitude of moving figures, some flitting along with the velocity of swallows, some sweeping in the most graceful circles, and others deeply interested in a less active pastime, crowding round the spot where the inhabitants of two rival parishes contended for the prize at curling,—an honour of no small importance, if we were to judge from the anxiety expressed both by the players and bystanders. We walked round the little lake, supported by Hazlewood, who lent us each an arm. He spoke, poor fellow, with great kindness, to old and. young, and seemed deservedly popular among the assembled crowd. At length we thought of retiring.

"Why do I mention these trivial occurrences?"—not, Heaven knows, from the interest I can now attach to them—but because, like a drowning man who catches at a brittle twig, I seize every apology for delaying the subsequent and dreadful part of my narrative. But, it must be communicated—I must have the sympathy of at least one friend under this heart-rending calamity.

"We were returning home by a footpath, which led through a plantation of firs. Lucy had quitted Hazlewood's arm—it is only the plea of absolute necessity which reconciles her to accept his assistance. I still leaned upon his other arm. Lucy followed us close, and the servant was two or three paces behind us. Such was our position, when at once, and as if he had started out of the earth, Brown stood before us at a short turn of the road! He was very plainly, I might say coarsely, dressed, and his whole appearance had in it something wild and agitated. I screamed between surprise and terror—Hazlewood mistook the nature of my alarm, and, when Brown advanced towards me as if to speak, commanded him haughtily to stand back, and not to alarm the lady. Brown replied, with equal asperity, he had no occasion to take lessons from him how to behave to that or any other lady. I rather believe that Hazlewood, impressed with the idea that he belonged to the band of smugglers, and had some bad purpose in view, heard and understood him imperfectly. He snatched the gun from the servant, who had come up on a line with us, and, pointing the muzzle at Brown, commanded him to stand off at his peril. My screams, for my terror prevented my finding articulate language, only hastened the catastrophe. Brown, thus menaced, sprung upon Hazlewood, grappled with him, and had nearly succeeded in wrenching the fowling-piece from his grasp, when the gun went off in the struggle, and the contents were lodged in Hazlewood's shoulder, who instantly fell. I saw no more, for the whole scene reeled before my eyes, and I fainted away; but, by Lucy's report, the unhappy perpetrator of this action gazed a moment on the scene before him, until her screams began to alarm the people upon the lake, several of whom now came in sight. He then bounded over a hedge, which divided the footpath from the plantation, and has not since been heard of. The servant made no attempt to stop or secure him, and the report he made of the matter to those who came up to us, induced them rather to exercise their humanity in recalling me to life, than show their courage by pursuing a desperado, described by the groom as a man of tremendous personal strength, and completely armed.

"Hazlewood was conveyed home, that is, to Woodbourne, in safety—I trust his wound will prove in no respect dangerous, though he suffers much. But to Brown the consequences must be most disastrous. He is already the object of my father's resentment, and he has now incurred danger from the law of the country, as well as from the clamorous vengeance of the father of Hazlewood, who threatens to move heaven and earth against the author of his son's wound. How will he be able to shroud himself from the vindictive activity of the pursuit? how to defend himself, if taken, against the severity of laws which I am told may even affect his life? and how can I find means to warn him of his danger? Then poor Lucy's ill-concealed grief, occasioned by her lover's wound, is another source of distress to me, and everything round me appears to bear witness against that indiscretion which has occasioned this calamity.

"For two days I was very ill indeed. The news that Hazlewood was recovering, and that the person who bad shot him was nowhere to be traced, only that for certain he was one of the leaders of the gang of smugglers, gave me some comfort. The suspicion and pursuit being directed towards those people, must naturally facilitate Brown's escape, and, I trust, has, ere this, ensured it. But patrols of horse and foot traverse the country in all directions, and I am tortured by a thousand confused and unauthenticated rumours of arrests and discoveries.

"Meanwhile, my greatest source of comfort is the generous candour of Hazlewood, who persists in declaring, that with whatever intentions the person by whom he was wounded approached our party, he is convinced the gun went off in the struggle by accident, and that the injury he received was undesigned. The groom, on the other hand, maintains that the piece was wrenched out of Hazlewood's hands, and deliberately pointed at his body, and Lucy inclines to the same opinion—I do not suspect them of wilful exaggeration, yet such is the fallacy of human testimony, for the unhappy shot was most unquestionably discharged unintentionally. Perhaps it would be the best way to confide the whole secret to Hazlewood—but he is very young, and I feel the utmost repugnance to communicate to him my folly. I once thought of disclosing the mystery to Lucy, and began by asking what she recollected of the person and features of the man whom we had so unfortunately met— but she ran out into such a horrid description of a hedge-ruffian, that I was deprived of all courage and disposition to own my attachment to one of such appearance as she attributed to him. I must say Miss Bertram is strangely biased by her prepossessions, for there are few handsomer men than poor Brown. I had not seen him for a long time, and even in his strange and sudden apparition on this unhappy occasion, and under every disadvantage, his form seems to me, on reflection, improved in grace, and his features in expressive dignity.—Shall we ever meet again? Who can answer that question?—Write to me, kindly, my dearest Matilda—but when did you otherwise?—yet, again, write to me soon, and write to me, kindly. I am not in a situation to profit by advice or reproof, nor have I my usual spirits to parry them by raillery. I feel the terrors of a child, who has, in heedless sport, put in motion some powerful piece of machinery; and, while he beholds wheels revolving, chains clashing, cylinders rolling around him, is equally astonished at the tremendous powers which his weak agency has called into action, and terrified for the consequences which he is compelled to await, without the possibility of averting them.

"I must not omit to say that my father is very kind and affectionate. The alarm which I have received forms a sufficient apology for my nervous complaints. My hopes are, that Brown has made his escape into the sister kingdom of England, or perhaps to Ireland, or the Isle of Man. In either case he may wait the issue of Hazlewood's wound with safety and with patience, for the communication of these countries with Scotland, for the purpose of justice, is not (thank Heaven) of an intimate nature. The consequences of his being apprehended would be terrible at this moment. I endeavour to strengthen my mind by arguing against the possibility of such a calamity. Alas! how soon have sorrows and friars, real as well as severe, followed the uniform and tranquil state of existence at which so lately I was disposed to repine! But I will not oppress you any longer with my complaints. Adieu, my dearest Matilda! JULIA MANNERING."

CHAPTER XXXII.

> A man may see how this world goes with no eyes.—Look with thine ears: See how yon justice rails upon yon simple thief. Hark in
> thine ear—change places; and, handy-dandy, which is the justice, which is the thief? King Lear.

Among those who took the most lively interest in endeavouring to discover the person by whom young Charles Hazlewood had been waylaid and wounded, was Gilbert Glossin, Esquire, late writer in —, now Laird of Ellangowan, and one of the worshipful commission of justices of the peace for the county of—. His motives for exertion on this occasion were manifold; but we presume that our readers, from what they already know of this gentleman, will acquit him of being actuated by any zealous or intemperate love of abstract justice.

The truth was, that this respectable personage felt himself less at ease than he had expected, after his machinations put him in possession of his benefactor's estate. His reflections within doors, where so much occurred to remind him of former times, were not always the self-congratulations of successful stratagem. And when he looked abroad, he could not but be sensible that he was excluded from the society of the gentry of the county, to whose rank he conceived he had raised himself. He was not admitted to their clubs, and at meetings of a public nature, from which he could not be altogether excluded, he found himself thwarted and looked upon with coldness and contempt. Both principle and prejudice co-operated in creating this dislike; for the gentlemen of the county despised him for the lowness of his birth, while they hated him for the means by which he had raised his fortune. With the common people his reputation stood still worse. They would neither yield him the territorial appellation of Ellangowan, nor the usual compliment of Mr. Glossin;—with them he was bare Glossin, and so incredibly was his vanity interested by this trifling circumstance, that he was known to give half a crown to a beggar, because he had thrice called him Ellangowan, in beseeching him for a penny. He therefore felt acutely the general want of respect, and particularly when he contrasted his own character and reception in society with those of Mr. MacMorlan, who, in far inferior worldly circumstances, was beloved and respected both by rich and poor, and was slowly but securely laying the foundation of a moderate fortune, with the general goodwill and esteem of all who knew him.

Glossin, while he repined internally at what he would fain have called the prejudices and prepossessions of the country, was too wise to make any open complaint, He was sensible his elevation was too recent to be immediately forgotten, and the means by which he had attained it too odious to be soon forgiven. But time, thought he, diminishes wonder and palliates misconduct. With the dexterity, therefore, of one who made his fortune by studying the weak points of human nature, he determined to lie by for opportunities to make himself useful even to those who most disliked him; trusting that his own abilities, the disposition of country gentlemen to get into quarrels, when a lawyer's advice becomes precious, and a thousand other contingencies, of which, with patience and address, he doubted not to be able to avail himself, would soon place him in a more important and respectable light to his neighbours, and perhaps raise him to the eminence sometimes attained by a shrewd, worldly, bustling man of business, when, settled among a generation of country gentlemen, he becomes, in Burns's language, The tongue of the trump to them a'. [*The tongue of the trump is the wire of the Jew's harp, that which gives sound to the whole instrument.] The attack on Colonel Mannering's house, followed by the accident of Hazlewood's wound, appeared to Glossin a proper opportunity to impress upon the country at large the service which could he rendered by an active magistrate (for he had been in the commission for some time), well acquainted with the law, and no less so with the haunts and habits of the illicit traders. He had acquired the latter kind of experience by a former close alliance with some of the most desperate smugglers, in consequence of which he had occasionally acted, sometimes as partner, sometimes as legal adviser, with these persons. But the connection had been dropped many years; nor, considering how short the race of eminent characters of this description, and the frequent circumstances which occur to make them retire from particular scenes of action, had he the least reason to think that his present researches could possibly compromise any old friend who might possess means of retaliation. The having been concerned in these practices abstractedly, was a circumstance which, according to his opinion, ought in no respect to interfere with his now using his experience in behalf of the public, or rather to further his own private views. To acquire the good opinion and countenance of Colonel Mannering would be no small object to a gentleman who was much disposed to escape from Coventry; and to gain the favour of old Hazlewood, who was a leading man in the county, was of more importance still. Lastly, if he should succeed in discovering, apprehending, and convicting the culprits, he would have the satisfaction of mortifying, and in some degree disparaging, Mac-Morlan, to whom, as Sheriff-substitute of the county, this sort of investigation properly belonged, and who would certainly suffer in public opinion should the voluntary exertions of Glossin be more successful than his own.

Actuated by motives so stimulating, and well acquainted with the lower retainers of the law, Glossin set every spring in motion to detect and apprehend, if possible, some of the gang who had attacked Woodbourne, and more particularly the individual who had wounded Charles Hazlewood. He promised high rewards, he suggested various schemes, and used his personal interest among his old acquaintances who favoured the trade, urging that they had better make sacrifice of an understrapper or two than incur the odium of having favoured such atrocious proceedings. But for some time all these exertions were in vain. The common people of the country either favoured or feared the smugglers too much to afford any evidence against them. At length, this busy magistrate obtained information, that a man, having the dress and appearance of the person who had wounded Hazlewood, had lodged on the evening before the rencontre at the Gordon Arms in Kippletringan. Thither Mr. Glossin immediately went, for the purpose of interrogating our old acquaintance, Mrs. Mac-Candlish.

The reader may remember that Mr. Glossin did not, according to this good woman's phrase, stand high in her books. She therefore attended his summons to the parlour slowly and reluctantly, and, on entering the room, paid her respects in the coldest possible manner. The dialogue then proceeded as follows:-

"A fine frosty morning, Mrs. Mac-Candlish."

"Ay, sir; the morning's weel eneugh," answered the landlady dryly.

"Mrs. Mac-Candlish, I wish to know if the justices are to dine here as usual after the business of the court on Tuesday?"

"I believe—fancy sae, sir—as usual"—(about to leave the room).

"Stay a moment, Mrs. Mac-Candlish—why, you are in a prodigious hurry, my good friend!—I have been thinking a club dining here once a month would be a very pleasant thing."

"Certainly, sir; a club of respectable gentlemen."

"True, true," said Glossin, "I mean landed proprietors and gentlemen of weight in the county; and I should like to set such a thing a-going."

The short dry cough with which Mrs. Mac-Candlish received this proposal, by no means indicated any dislike to the overture abstractedly considered, but inferred much doubt how far it would succeed under the auspices of the gentleman by whom it was proposed. It was not a cough negative, but a cough dubious, and as such Glossin felt it; but it was not his cue to take offence.

"Have there been brisk doings on the road, Mrs. Mac-Candlish? plenty of company, I suppose?"

"Pretty weel, sir,—but I believe I am wanted at the bar."

"No, no,—stop one moment, cannot you, to oblige an old customer?—Pray, do you remember a remarkably tall young man, who lodged one night in your House last week?"

"Troth, sir, I canna weel say—I never take heed whether my company be lang or short, if they make a lang bill."

"And if they do not, you can do that for them, eh, Mrs. Mac-Candlish?—ha, ha, ha!—But this young man that I inquire after was upwards of six feet high, had a dark frock, with metal buttons, light-brown hair unpowdered, blue eyes, and a straight nose, travelled on foot, had no servant or baggage.—you surely can remember having seen such a traveller?"

"Indeed, sir," answered Mrs. Mac-Candlish, bent on baffling his inquiries, "I canna charge my memory about the matter—there's mair to do in a house like this, I trow, than to look after passengers' hair, or their een, or noses either."

"Then, Mrs. Mac-Candlish, I must tell you in plain terms, that this person suspected of having been guilty of a crime; and it is in consequence of these suspicions that I, as a magistrate, require this information from you,—and if you refuse to answer my questions, I must put you upon your oath."

"Troth, sir, I am no free to swear [*Some of the strict dissenters decline taking an oath before a civil magistrate]—we aye gaed to the Antiburgher meeting—it's very true, in Bailie Mac-Candlish's time (honest man), we keepit the kirk, whilk was most seemly in his station, as having office—, but after his being called to a better place than Kippletringan, I hae gaen back to worthy Maister MacGrainer. And so ye see, sir, I am no clear to swear without speaking to the minister—especially against ony sackless puir young thing that's gaun through the country, stranger and freendless like."

"I shall relieve your scruples, perhaps, without troubling Mr. Mac-Grainer, when I tell you that this fellow whom I Inquire after is the man who shot your young friend Charles Hazlewood."

"Gudeness! wha could hae thought the like o' that o' him?— na, if it had been for debt, or e'en for a bit tuilzie [*Scuffle] wi' the gauger, the deil o' Nelly Mac-Candlish's tongue should ever hae wranged him. But if he really shot young Hazlewood—But I canna think it, Mr. Glossin; this will be same o' your skits [*Tricks] now—I canna think it o' sae douce a lad;—na, na, this is just some a' your auld s 'kits.—Ye'll he for having a horning or a caption after him."

"I see you have no confidence in me, Mrs. Mac-Candlish;— but look at these declarations, signed by the persons who saw the crime committed, and judge yourself if the description of the ruffian be not that of your guest."

He put the papers into her hand, which she perused very carefully, often taking off her spectacles to cast her eyes up to Heaven, or perhaps to wipe a tear from them, for young Hazlewood was an especial favourite with the good dame. "Aweel, aweel," she said, when she had concluded her examination, "since it's e'en sae, I gie him up, the villain —But oh, we are erring mortals!—I never saw a face I liked better, or a lad that was mair douce and canny—I thought he had been some gentleman under trouble.—But I gie him up, the villain!—to shoot Charles Hazlewood— and before the young ladies, poor innocent things!—I gie him up.

"So you admit, then, that such a person lodged here the night before this vile business?"

"Troth did he, sir, and a' the house were taen wi' him, he was sic a frank, pleasant young man, It wasna for his spending, I'm sure, for he just had a mutton-chop, and a mug of ale, and maybe a glass or twa o' wine-and I asked him to drink tea wi' mysell, and didna put that into the bill; and he took nae supper, for he said he was defeat [*Exhausted] wi' travel a' the night afore—I dare say now it had been on some hellicat errand or other."

"Did you by any chance learn his name?"

"I wot weel did I," said the landlady, now as eager to communicate her evidence as formerly desirous to suppress it. "He tell'd me his name was Brown, and he said it was likely that an auld woman like a gipsy wife might be asking for him—Ay, ay! tell me your company, and I'll tell you wha ye are! Oh, the villain!—Aweel, sir, when he gaed away in the morning, he paid his bill very honestly, and gae something to the chamber-maid, nae doubt, for Grizy has naething frae me, by twa pair o' new shoon ilka year, and maybe a bit compliment at Hansel Monanday—"Here Glossin found it necessary to interfere, and bring the good woman back to the point.

"Ou than, he just said, if there comes such a person to inquire after Mr. Brown, you will say I am gone to look at the skaters on Loch Creeran, as you call it, and I will be back here to dinner—But he never came back—though I expected him sae faithfully, that I gae a look to making the friar's chicken mysell, and to the crappit-heads [*Haddock-heads stuffed] too, and that's what I dinna do for ordinary, Mr. Glossin—But little did I think what skating wark he was gaun about—to shoot Mr. Charles, the innocent lamb!"

Mr. Glossin, having, like a prudent examinator, suffered. his witness, to give. vent to all her surprise and indignation, now began to inquire whether the suspected person had left any property or papers about the inn.

"Troth, he put a parcel—a sma' parcel, under my charge, and he gave me some siller, and desired me to get him half a dozen ruffled sarks, and Peg Pasley's in bands wi' them e'en now—they may serve him to gang up the Lawnmarket I in, the scoundrel!" [*The procession of the criminals to the gallows of old took that direction, moving, as the schoolboy rhyme had it, Up the Lawnmarket, Down the West Bow, Up the lang ladder, And down the little tow.] Mr. Glossin then demanded to see the packet, but here mine hostess demurred.

"She didna ken—she wad not say but justice should take its course but when a thing, was trusted to ane in her way, doubtless they were responsible—but she suld cry in Deacon Bearcliff, and if Mr. Glossin liked to tak an inventar o' the property, and gie her a receipt before the Deacon—or, what she wad like muckle better, an it could, be scaled up and left in Deacon Bearclift's hands, it wad mak her mind easy—She was for naething but justice on a' sides."

Mrs. Mac-Candlish's natural sagacity and acquired suspicion being inflexible, Glossin sent for Deacon Bearcliff, to speak "anent the villain that had shot Mr. Charles Hazlewood." The Deacon accordingly made his appearance, with his wig awry, owing to the hurry with which, at this summons of the Justice, he had exchanged it for the Kilmarnock cap with which he usually attended his customers. Mrs. MacCandlish then produced the parcel deposited with her by Brown, in which was found the gipsy's purse. On perceiving the value of the miscellaneous contents, Mrs. Mac-Candlish internally congratulated herself upon the precautions she had taken before delivering them up to Glossin, while he, with an appearance of disinterested candour, was the first to propose they should be properly inventoried, and deposited with Deacon Bearcliff, until they should be sent to the Crown Office. "He did not" he observed, "like to be personally responsible for articles which seemed of considerable value, and had doubtless been acquired by the most nefarious practices."

He then examined the paper in which the purse had been wrapt up. It was the back of a letter addressed to V. Brown, Esquire, but the rest of the address was torn away. The landlady,—now as eager to throw light upon the criminal's escape as she had formerly been desirous of withholding it, for the miscellaneous contents of the purse argued strongly to her mind that all was not right,—Mrs. Mac-Candlish, I say, now gave Glossin to understand, that her postilion and hostler had both seen the stranger upon the ice that day when young Hazlewood was wounded.

Our reader's old acquaintance, Jock Jabos, was first summoned, and admitted frankly that he had seen and conversed upon the ice that morning with a stranger, who, he understood, had lodged at the Gordon Arms the night before.

"What turn did your conversation take?" said Glossin.

"Turn?—ou, we turned nae gate at a', but just keepit straight forward upon the ice like."

"Well, but what did ye speak about?"

"Ou, he just asked questions like ony ither stranger," answered. the postilion, possessed, as it seemed, with the refractory and uncommunicative spirit which had left his mistress.

"But about what?" said Glossin.

"Ou, just about the folk that was playing at the curling, and about auld Jock Stevenson that was at the cock, and about the leddies, and sic like."

"What ladies? and what did he ask about them, Jock?" said the interrogator.

"What leddies? ou, it was Miss Jowlia Mannering and Miss Lucy Bertram, that ye ken fu' weel yourself, Mr. Glossin—they were walking wi' the young Laird of Hazlewood upon the ice."

""And what did you tell him about them?" demanded Glossin.

"Tut, we just said that was Miss Lucy Bertram of Ellangowan, that should ance have had a great estate in the country—and that was Miss Jowlia Mannering, that was to be married to young Hazlewood—See as she was hinging on his arm—we just spoke about our country clashes like—he was a very frank man."

"Well, and what did he say in answer?"

"Ou, he just stared at the young leddies very keen like, and asked if it was for certain that the marriage was to be between Miss Mannering and young Hazlewood—and I answered him that it was for positive and absolute certain, as I had an undoubted right to say sae—for my third cousin Jean Clavers (she's a relation o' your ain, Mr. Glossin, ye wad ken Jean lang syne?), she's sib [*Related] to the housekeeper at Woodbourne, and she's tell'd me mair than ance that there was naething could be mair likely."

"And what did the stranger say when you told him all this?" said Glossin.

"Say?" echoed the postilion, "he said naething at a'—he just stared at them as they walked round the loch upon the ice, as if he could have eaten them, and he never took his ee aff them, or said another word, or gave another glance at the Bonspiel, [*playing match] though there was the finest fun amang the curlers ever was seen—and he turned round and gaed aff the loch by the kirk-stile through Woodbourne fir-plantings, and we saw nae mair o' him."

"Only think," said Mrs. Mac-Candlish, "what a hard heart he maun hae had, to think o' hurting the poor young gentleman in the very presence of the leddy he was to be married to!"

"Oh, Mrs. Mac-Candlish,' said Glossin, "there's been many cases such as that on the record—,doubtless he was seeking revenge where it would be deepest and sweetest."

"God pity us!" said Deacon Bearcliff, "we're puir frail creatures when left to oursells!—ay, he forgot wha said, 'Vengeance is mine, and I will repay it.'"

"Weel, aweel, sirs," said Jabos, whose hard-headed and uncultivated shrewdness seemed sometimes to start the game when others beat the bush—"Weel, weel, ye may be a' mista'en yet—I'll never believe that a man would lay a plan to shoot another wi' his ain gun. Lord help me, I was the keeper's assistant down at the Isle mysell, and I'll uphaud it, the biggest man in Scotland shouldna take a gun frae me or I had weized the slugs through him, though I'm but sic a little feckless [*Spiritless] body, fit for naething but the outside o' a saddle and the fore-end o' a poschay—na, na, nae living man wad venture on that. I'll wad ma best buckskins, and they were new coft [*Bought] at Kirkcudbright fair, it's been a chance job after a'. But if ye hae naething mair to say to me, I am thinking I maun gang and see my beasts fed." And he departed accordingly.

69

The hostler, who had accompanied him, gave evidence to the same purpose. He and Mrs. MacCandlish were then re-interrogated, whether Brown had no arms with him on that unhappy morning. "None," they said, "but an ordinary bit cutlass or hanger by his side."

"Now," said the Deacon, taking Glossin by the button (for, in considering this intricate subject, he had forgot Glossin's new accession of rank)—"this is but doubtfu' after a', Maister Gilbert—for it was not Sae dooms [*Absolutely] likely that he would go down into battle wi' sic sma' means."

Glossin extricated himself from the Deacon's grasp, and from the discussion, though not with rudeness; for it was his present interest to buy golden opinions from all sorts of people. He inquired the price of tea and sugar, and spoke of providing himself for the year; he gave Mrs. Mac-Candlish directions to have a handsome entertainment in readiness for a party of five friends, whom he intended to invite to dine with him at the Gordon Arms next Saturday week; and, lastly, he gave a half-crown to Jock Jabos, whom the hostler had deputed to hold his steed.

"Weel," said the Deacon to Mrs. Mac-Candlish, as he accepted her offer of a glass of bitters at the bar, "the deil's no sae ill as he's ca'd. It's pleasant to see a gentleman pay the regard to the business o' the county that Mr. Glossin does."

"Ay, 'deed is't, Deacon," answered the landlady and yet I wonder our gentry leave their ain wark to the like o' him. —But as lang as silver's current, Deacon, folk maunna look ower nicely at what king's head's on't."

"I doubt Glossin will prove but shand [*Cant expression for base coin] after a', mistress," said Jabos, as he passed through the little lobby beside the bar; "but this is a gude half-crown ony way."

CHAPTER XXXIII.

A man that apprehends death to be no more dreadful but as a
drunken sleep; careless, reckless, and fearless of what's
past, present, or to come; insensible of mortality, and
desperately mortal.

Measure for Measure.

Glossin had made careful minutes of the information derived from these examinations. They threw little light upon the story, so far as he understood its purport; but the better informed reader has received, through means of this investigation, an account of Brown's proceedings, between the moment when we left him upon his walk to Kippletringan, the time when, stung by jealousy, he so rashly and unhappily presented himself before Julia Mannering, and well-nigh brought to a fatal termination the quarrel which his appearance occasioned.

Glossin rode slowly back to Ellangowan, pondering on what he had heard, and more and more convinced that the active and successful prosecution of this mysterious business was an opportunity of ingratiating himself with Hazlewood and Mannering to be on no account neglected. Perhaps, also, he felt his professional acuteness interested in bringing it to a successful close. It was, therefore, with great pleasure that, on his return to his house from Kippletringan, he heard his servants announce hastily, "that Mac-Guffog, the thief-taker, and twa or three concurrents, had a man in hands in the kitchen waiting for his honour."

He instantly jumped from horseback, and hastened into the house. "Send my clerk here directly; ye'll find him copying the survey of the estate in the little green parlour. Set things to rights in my study, and wheel the great leathern chair up to the writing-table—set a stool for Mr. Scrow. —Scrow (to the clerk, as he entered the presence-chamber), hand down Sir George Mackenzie on Crimes; open it at the section Vis Publica et Privata, and fold down a leaf at the passage 'anent the bearing of unlawful weapons.' Now lend me a hand off with my muckle-coat, and hang it up in the lobby, and bid them bring up the prisoner—I trow I'll sort him— but stay, first send up Mac-Guffog.— Now, Mac-Guffog, where did ye find this chield?"

Mac-Guffog, a stout bandy-legged fellow, with a neck like a bull, a face like a—firebrand, and a most portentous squint of the left eye, began, after various contortions by way of courtesy to the justice, to tell his story, eking it out by sundry sly nods and knowing winks, which appeared to bespeak an intimate correspondence of ideas between the narrator and his principal auditor. "Your honour sees I went down to yon place that your honour spoke o', that's kept by her that your honour kens o', by the sea-side.— So, says she, what are you wanting here? Ye'll be come wi' a broom in your pocket frae Ellangowan?—So, says I, deil a broom will come frae there awa, for ye ken, says I, his honour Ellangowan himself in former times—"

"Well, well," said Glossin, "no occasion to be particular, tell the essentials."

"Weel, so we sat niffering [*Bargaining] about some brandy that I said I wanted, till he came in."

"Who?"

"He!" pointing with his thumb inverted to the kitchen, where the prisoner was in custody. "So he had his griego wrapped close round him, and I judged he was not dry-handed [*Unarmed]—so I thought it was best to speak proper, and so he believed I was a Manks man, and I kept aye between him and her, for fear she had whistled. [*Given information to the party concerned] And then we began to drink about, and then I betted he would not drink out a quartern of Hollands without drawing breath—and then he tried it—and just then Slounging Jock and Dick Spur'em came in, and we clinked the darbies [*Handcuffs] on him, took him as quiet as a lamb—and now he's had his bit sleep out, and is as fresh as a May gowan, to answer what your honour likes to speer." [*Inquire] This narrative, delivered with a wonderful quantity of gesture and grimace, received at the conclusion the thanks and praises which the narrator expected.

"Had he no arms?" asked the Justice.

"Ay, ay, they are never without barkers and slashers."

"Any papers?"

"This bundle," delivering a dirty pocket-book. "Go downstairs, then, Mac-Guffog,. and be in waiting." The officer left the room.

The clink of irons was immediately afterwards heard upon the stair, and in two or three minutes a man was introduced, handcuffed and fettered. He was thick, brawny, and muscular, and although his shagged and grizzled hair marked an age somewhat advanced, and his stature was rather low, he appeared, nevertheless, a person whom few would have chosen to cope with in personal conflict. His coarse and savage features were still flushed, and his eye still reeled under the influence of the strong potation which had proved the immediate cause of his seizure. But the sleep, though short, which MacGuffog had allowed him, and still more a sense of the peril of his situation, had restored to him the full use of his faculties. The worthy judge, and the no less estimable captive, looked at each other steadily for a long time without speaking. Glossin apparently recognised his prisoner, but seemed at a loss how to proceed with his investigation. At length he broke silence.

"Soh, Captain, this is you?—you have been a stranger on this coast for some years."

"Stranger?" replied the other; "strange enough, I think—for hold me der deyvil, if I been ever here before."

"That won't pass, Mr. Captain."

"That must pass, Mr. Justice—sapperment!"

"And who will you be pleased to call yourself, then, for the present," said Glossin, "just until I shall bring some other folks to refresh your memory, concerning who you are, or at least who you have been?"

"What bin I?—donner and blitzen! I bin Jans Janson, from Cuxhaven—what sall Ich bin?"

Glossin took from a case which was in the apartment a pair of small pocket pistols, which he loaded with ostentatious care. "You may retire, "said he to his clerk," and carry the people with You, Scrow—but wait in the lobby within call."

The clerk would have offered some remonstrances to his patron on the danger of remaining alone with such a desperate character, although ironed beyond the possibility of active exertion, but Glossin waved him off impatiently. When he had left the room, the justice took two short turns through the apartment, then drew his chair opposite to the prisoner, so as to confront him fully, placed the pistols before him in readiness, and said in a steady voice, "You are Dirk Hatteraick of Flushing, are you not?"

The prisoner turned his eye instinctively to the door, as if he apprehended some one was listening. Glossin rose, opened the door, so that from the chair in which his prisoner sat he might satisfy himself there was no eavesdropper within hearing, then shut it, resumed his seat, and repeated his question, "You are Dirk Hatteraick, formerly of the Yungfrauw Haagenslaapen are you not?"

"Tousand deyvils!—and if you know that, why ask me?" said the prisoner.

"Because I am surprised to see you in the very last place where you ought to be, if you regard your safety," observed Glossin coolly.

"Der deyvil!—no man regards his own safety that speaks so to me!"

"What? unarmed, and in irons!—well said, Captain!" replied Glossin ironically. "But, Captain, bullying won't do—you'll hardly get out of this country without accounting for a little accident that happened at Warroch Point a few years ago."

Hatteraick's looks grew black as midnight.

"For my part," continued Glossin, "I have no particular wish to be hard upon an old acquaintance—but I must do my duty—I shall send you off to Edinburgh in a post-chaise and four this very day."

"Poz donner! you would not do that?" said Hatteraick,—in a lower and more humbled tone; "why, you had the matter of half a cargo in bills on Vanbeest and Vanbruggen."

"It is so long since, Captain Hatteraick," answered Glossin superciliously, "that I really forget how I was recompensed for my trouble."

"Your trouble? your silence, you mean."

"It was an affair in the course of business," said Glossin, "and I have retired from business for some time."

"Ay, but I have a notion that I could make you go steady about, and try the old course again," answered Dirk Hatteraick. "Why, man, hold me der deyvil, but I meant to visit you, and tell you something that concerns you."

"Of the boy?" said Glossin eagerly.

"Yaw, Mynheer," replied the Captain coolly.

"He does not live, does he?"

"As lifelich as you or I," said Hatteraick.

"Good God!—But in India?" exclaimed Glossin.

"No, tousand deyvils, here on this dirty coast of yours," rejoined the prisoner.

"But, Hatteraick, this,—that is, if it be true, which I do not believe,—this will ruin us both, for he cannot but remember your neat job; and for me—it will be productive of the worst consequences. It will ruin us both, I tell you."

"I tell you," said the seaman, "it will ruin none but you—for I am done up already, and if I must strap for it, all shall out."

"Zounds!" said the justice impatiently, "what brought you back to this coast like a madman?"

"Why, all the gelt was gone, and the house was shaking, and I thought the job was clayed over and forgotten," answered the worthy skipper.

"Stay—what can be done?" said Glossin anxiously. I dare not discharge you—but might you not be rescued in the way—ay sure—a word to Lieutenant Brown,—and I would send the people with you by the coast-road."

"No, no! that won't do—Brown's dead-shot—laid in the locker, man—the devil has the picking of him."

"Dead?—shot?—at Woodbourne, I suppose?" replied Glossin.

"Yaw, Mynheer."

Glossin paused—the sweat broke upon his brow with the agony of his feelings, while the hard-featured miscreant who sat opposite, coolly rolled his tobacco in his cheek, and squirted the juice into the fire-grate. "It would be ruin," said Glossin to himself, "absolute ruin, if the heir should reappear—and then what might be the consequence of conniving with these men?—yet there is so little time to take measures—Hark you, Hatteraick; I can't set you at liberty—but I can put you where you may set yourself at liberty—I always like to assist an old friend. I shall confine you in the old castle for tonight, and give these people double allowance of grog. Mac-Guffog will fall in the trap in which he caught you. The stanchions on the window of the strong room, as they call it, are wasted to pieces, and it is not above twelve feet from the level of the ground without, and the snow lies thick."

"But the darbies," said Hatteraick, looking upon his fetters.

"Hark ye," said Glossin, going to a tool-chest, and taking out a small file, "there's a friend for you, and you know the road to the sea by the stairs." Hatteraick shook his chains in ecstasy, as if he were already at liberty, and strove to extend his lettered hand towards his protector. Glossin laid his finger upon his lips with a cautious glance at the door, and then proceeded in his instructions. "When you escape, you had better go to the Kaim of Dernecleugh."

"Donner! that howff is blown."

"The devil!—well, then, you may steal my skiff that lies on the beach there, and away. But you must remain snug at the Point of Warroch till I come to see you."

"The Point of Warroch?" said Hatteraick, his countenance again falling; "what, in the cave, I suppose?—I would rather it were anywhere else;—es spuckt da!—they say for certain that he walks—But, donner and blitzen! I never shunned him alive, and I won't shun him dead—Strafe mich helle! it shall never be said Dirk Hatteraick feared either dog or devil!—So I am to wait there till I see you?"

"Ay, ay," answered Glossin, "and now I must call in the men." He did so, accordingly.

"I can make nothing of Captain Janson, as he calls himself, Mac-Guffog, and it's now too late to bundle him off to the county jail. Is there not a strong room up yonder in the old castle?"

"Ay is there, sir; my uncle the constable ance kept a man there for three days in auld Ellangowan's time. But there was an unco dust about it—it was tried in the Inner House afore the Feifteen."

"I know all that, but this person will not stay there very long—it's only a makeshift for a night, a mere lock-up house till further examination. There is a small room through which it opens, you may light a fire for yourselves there, and I'll send you plenty of stuff to make you comfortable. But be sure you lock the door upon the prisoner; and, hark ye, let him have a fire in the strongroom too, the season requires it. Perhaps he'll make a clean breast to-morrow."

With these instructions, and with a large allowance of food and liquor, the justice dismissed his party to keep guard for the night in the old castle, under the full hope and belief that they would neither spend the night in watching, nor prayer.

There was little fear that Glossin himself should that night sleep over-sound. His situation was perilous in the extreme, for the schemes of a life of villainy seemed at once to be crumbling around and above him. He laid himself to rest, and tossed upon his pillow for a long time in vain. At length he fell asleep, but it was only to dream of his patron,—now, as he had last seen him, with the paleness of death upon his features, then again transformed into all the vigour and comeliness of youth, approaching to expel him from the mansion-house of his fathers. Then he dreamed, that after wandering long over a wild heath, he came at length to an inn, from which sounded the voice of revelry; and that when he entered, the first person he met was Frank Kennedy, all smashed and gory, as he had lain on the beach at Warroch Point, but with a reeking punch-bowl in his hand. Then the scene changed to a dungeon, where he heard Dirk Hatteraick, whom he imagined to be under sentence of death, confessing his crimes to a clergyman.—"After the bloody deed was done," said the penitent, "we retreated into a cave close beside, the secret of which was known but to one man in the country; we were debating what to do with the child, and we thought of—giving it up to the gipsies, when we heard the cries of the pursuers hallooing to each other. One man alone came straight to our cave, and it was that man who knew the secret—but we made him our friend at the expense of half the value of the goods saved. By his, advice we carried off the child to Holland in our consort, which came the following night to take us from the coast. That man was—"

"No, I deny it!—it was not I!" said Glossin, in half-uttered accents; and, struggling in his agony to express his denial more distinctly, he awoke.

It was, however, conscience chat had, prepared this mental phantasmagoria. The truth was, that, knowing much better than any other person the haunts of the smugglers, he had, while the others were searching in different directions, gone straight to the cave, even before he had learned the murder of Kennedy, whom he expected to find their prisoner. He came upon them with some idea of mediation, but found them in the midst of their guilty terrors, while the rage, which had hurried them on to murder, began, with all but Hatteraick, to sink into remorse and fear. Glossin was then indigent and greatly in debt, but he was already possessed of Mr. Bertram's ear, and, aware of the facility of his disposition, he saw no difficulty in enriching himself at his expense, provided the heir-male were removed, in which case the estate became the unlimited property of the weak and prodigal father. Stimulated by present gain and the prospect of contingent advantage, he accepted the bribe which the smugglers offered in their terror, and connived at, or rather encouraged, their intention of carrying away the child of his benefactor, who, if left behind, was old enough to have described the scene of blood which he had witnessed. The only palliative which the ingenuity of Glossin could offer to his conscience was, that the temptation was great, and came suddenly upon him, embracing as it were the very advantages on which his mind had so long rested, and promising to relieve him from distresses which must have otherwise speedily overwhelmed him. Besides, he endeavoured to think that self-preservation rendered his conduct necessary. He was, in some degree, in the power of the robbers, and pleaded hard with his conscience, that, had he declined their offers, the assistance which he could have called for, though not distant, might not have arrived in time to save him from men, who, on less provocation, had just committed murder.

Galled with the anxious forebodings of a guilty conscience, Glossin now arose, and looked out upon the night. The scene which we have already described in the third chapter of this story, was now covered with snow, and the brilliant, though waste, whiteness of the land, gave to the sea by contrast a dark and livid tinge. A landscape covered with snow, though abstractedly it may be called beautiful, has, both from the association of cold and barrenness, and from its comparative infrequency, a wild, strange, and desolate appearance. Objects, well known to us in their common state, have either disappeared, or are so strangely varied and disguised, that we seem gazing on an unknown world. But it was not with such reflections that the mind of this bad man was occupied. His eye was upon the gigantic and gloomy outlines of the old castle, where, in a flanking tower of enormous size and thickness, glimmered two lights, one from the window of the strong room, where Hatteraick was confined, the other from that of the adjacent apartment occupied by his keepers. "Has he made his escape, or will he be able to do so?—Have these men watched, who never watched before, in order to complete my ruin?—If morning finds him there, he must be committed to prison; Mac-Morlan or some other person will take the matter up—he will be detected—convicted—and will tell all in revenge!—"

While these racking thoughts glided rapidly through Glossin's mind, he observed one of the lights obscured, as by an opaque body placed at the window. What a moment of interest!—"He has got clear of his irons!—he is working at the stanchions of the window—they are surely quite decayed, they must give way—O God! they have fallen outward; I heard them clink among the stones!—the noise cannot fail to wake them—furies seize his Dutch awkwardness!—The light burns free again—they have torn him from the window, and are binding him in the room!—No! he had only retired an instant on the alarm of the falling bars—he is at the window again—and the light is quite obscured now—he is getting out!—"

A heavy sound, as of a body dropped from a height among the snow, announced that Hatteraick had completed his escape, and shortly after Glossin beheld a dark figure, like a shadow, steal along the whitened beach, and reach the spot where the skiff lay. New cause for fear! "His single strength will be unable to float her," said Glossin to himself; "I must go to the rascal's assistance. But no! he has got her off, and now, thank God, her sail is spreading itself against the moon—ay, he has got the breeze now—would to Heaven it were a tempest, to sink him to the bottom!"

After this last cordial wish, he continued watching the progress of the boat as it stood away towards the Point of Warroch, until he could no longer distinguish the dusky sail from the gloomy waves over which it glided. Satisfied then that the immediate danger was averted, he retired with somewhat more composure to his guilty pillow.

CHAPTER XXXIV.

Why dost not comfort me, and help me out
From this unhallowed and blood-stained hole?

Titus Andronicus

On the next morning, great was the alarm and confusion of the officers, when they discovered the escape of their prisoner. Mac-Guffog appeared before Glossin with a head perturbed with brandy and fear, and incurred a most severe reprimand for neglect of duty—The resentment of the justice appeared only to be suspended by his anxiety to recover possession of the prisoner, and the thief-takers, glad to escape from his awful and incensed presence, were sent off in every direction (except the right one) to recover their prisoner, if possible. Glossin particularly recommended a careful search at the Kaim of Dernecleugh, which was occasionally occupied under night by vagrants of different descriptions. Having thus dispersed his myrmidons in various directions, he himself hastened by devious paths through the Wood of Warroch, to his appointed interview with Hatteraick, from whom he hoped to learn at more leisure than last night's conference admitted, the circumstances attending the return of the heir of Ellangowan to his native country.

With manoeuvres like those of a fox when he doubles to avoid the pack, Glossin strove to approach the place of appointment in a manner which should leave no distinct track of his course. "Would to Heaven it would snow," he said, looking upward, "and hide these footprints. Should one of the officers light upon them, he would run the scent up, like a bloodhound, and surprise us.—I must get down upon the sea-beach, and contrive to creep along beneath the rocks."

And accordingly, he descended from the cliffs with some difficulty, and scrambled along between the rocks and the advancing tide; now looking up to see if his motions were watched from the rocks above him, now casting a jealous glance to mark if any boat appeared upon the sea, from which his course might be discovered.

But even the feelings of selfish apprehension were for a time superseded, as Glossin passed the spot where Kennedy's body had been found. It was marked by the fragment of rock which had been precipitated from the cliff above, either with the body or after it. The mass was now encrusted with small shell-fish, and tasselled with tangle and seaweed; but still its shape and substance were different from those of the other rocks which lay scattered around. His voluntary walks, it will readily be believed, had never led to this spot; so that finding himself now there for the first time after the terrible catastrophe, the scene at once recurred to his mind with all its accompaniments of horror. He remembered how, like a guilty thing, gliding from the neighbouring place of concealment, he had mingled with eagerness, yet with caution, among the terrified group who surrounded the corpse, dreading lest any one should ask from whence he came. He remembered, too, with what conscious fear he had avoided gazing upon that ghastly spectacle. The wild scream of his patron, "My bairn! my bairn!" again rang in his ears. "Good God!" he exclaimed, "land is all I have gained worth the agony of that moment, and the thousand anxious fears and horrors which have since embittered my life!—Oh how I wish that I lay where that wretched man lies, and that he stood here in life and health!—But these regrets are all too late."

Stifling, therefore, his feelings, he crept forward to the cave, which was so near the spot where the body was found, that the smugglers might have heard from their hiding-place the various conjectures of the bystanders concerning the fate of their victim. But nothing could be more completely concealed than the entrance to their asylum. The opening, not larger than that of a fox-earth, lay in the face of the cliff directly behind a large black rock, or rather upright stone, which served at once to conceal it from strangers, and as a mark to point out its situation to those who used it as a place of retreat. The space between the stone and the cliff was exceedingly narrow, and being heaped with sand and other rubbish, the most minute search would not have discovered the mouth of the cavern, without removing those substances which the tide had drifted before it. For the purpose of further concealment, it was usual with the contraband traders who frequented this haunt, after they had entered, to stuff the mouth with withered seaweed loosely piled together as if carried there by the waves. Dirk Hatteraick had not forgotten this precaution.

Glossin, though a bold and hardy man, felt his heart throb, and his knees knock together, when he prepared to enter this den of secret iniquity, in order to hold conference with a felon, whom he justly accounted one of the most desperate and depraved of men. "But he has no interest to injure me," was his consolatory reflection. He examined his pocket-pistols, however, before removing the weeds and entering the cavern, which he did upon hands and knees. The passage, which at first was low and narrow, just admitting entrance to a man in a creeping posture, expanded after a few yards into a high arched vault of considerable width. The bottom, ascending gradually, was covered with the purest sand. Ere Glossin had got upon his feet, the hoarse yet suppressed voice of Hatteraick growled through the recesses of the cave.

"Hagel and donner!—be'st du?"

"Are you in the dark?"

"Dark? der deyvil! ay," said Dirk Hatteraick; "where should I have a glim?"

"I have brought light;" and Glossin accordingly produced a tinder-box, and lighted a small lantern.

"You must kindle some fire too, for hold mich der deyvil, Ich bin ganz gefrorne!"

"It is a cold place to be sure," said Glossin, gathering together some decayed staves of barrels and pieces of wood, which had perhaps lain in the cavern since Hatteraick was there last.

"Cold? Snow-wasser and hagel! it's perdition—I could only keep myself alive by rambling up and down this d-d vault, and thinking about the merry rouses we have had in it."

The flame then began to blaze brightly, and Hatteraick hung his bronzed visage, and expanded his hard and sinewy hands over it, with an avidity resembling that of a famished wretch to whom food is exposed. The light showed his savage and stern features, and the smoke, which in his agony of cold he seemed to endure almost to suffocation, after circling round his head, rose to the dim and rugged roof of the cave, through which it escaped by some secret rents or clefts in the rock; the same doubtless that afforded air to the cavern when the tide was in, at which time the aperture to the sea was filled with water.

"And now I have brought you some breakfast," said Glossin, producing some cold meat and a flask of spirits. The latter Hatteraick eagerly seized upon, and applied to his mouth; and, after a hearty draught, he exclaimed with great rapture, "Das schmeckt! That is good—that warms the liver!"—Then broke into the fragment of a High-Dutch song,

"Saufen Bier, und Brante-wein, Schmeissens alle die Fenstern ein; Ich ben liederlich, Du bist liederlich; Sind wir nicht liederlich Leute a!"

"Well said, my hearty Captain!" cried Glossin, endeavouring to catch the tone of revelry—

"Gin by pailfuls, wine in rivers,
Dash the window-glass to shivers!
For three wild lads were we, brave boys,
And three wild lads were we;
Thou on the land, and I on the sand,
And jack on the gallows-tree!"

That's it, my bully-boy! Why, you're alive again now!—And now let us talk about our business."

"Your business, if you please," said Hatteraick; hagel and donner!—mine was done when I got out of the bilboes."

"Have patience, my good friend;—I'll convince you our interests are just the same."

Hatteraick gave a short dry cough, and Glossin, after a pause, proceeded. "How came you to let the boy escape?"

"Why, fluch and blitzen! he was no charge of mine. Lieutenant Brown gave him to his cousin that's in the Middleburgh house of Vanbeest and Vanbruggen, and told him some goose's gazette about his being taken in a skirmish with the land-sharks—he gave him for a foot-boy. Me let him escape!—the bastard kinchin should have walked the plank ere I troubled myself about him."

"Well, and was he bred a foot-boy then?"

"Nein, nein; the kinchin got about the old man's heart, and he gave him his own name, and bred him up in the office, and then sent him to India—I believe he would have packed him back here, but his nephew told him it would do up the free trade for many a day, if the youngster got back to Scotland."

"Do you think the younker knows much of his own origin now?"

"Deyvil!" replied Hatteraick, "how should I tell what he knows now? But he remembered something of it long. When he was but ten years old, he persuaded another Satan's limb of an English bastard like himself to steal my lugger's khan—boat—what do you call it—to return to his country, as he called it—fire him! Before we could overtake them, they had the skiff out of channel as far as the Deurloo—the boat might have been lost."

"I wish to Heaven she had—with him in her" ejaculated Glossin.

"Why, I was so angry myself, that, sapperment! I did give him a tip over the side—but split him—the comical little devil swam like a duck; so I made him swim astern for a mile to teach him manners, and then took him in when he was sinking.—By the knocking Nicholas! he'll plague you, now he's come over the herring-pond! When he was so high, he had the spirit of thunder and lightning."

"How did he get back from India?"

"Why, how should I know?—the house there was done up, and that gave us a shake at Middleburgh, I think—so they sent me again to see what could be done among my old acquaintances here—for we held old stories were done away and forgotten. So I had got a pretty trade on foot within the last two trips; but that stupid houndsfoot schelm, Brown, has knocked it on the head again, I suppose, with getting himself shot by the colonel-man.

"Why were you not with them?"

"Why, you see—sapperment! I fear nothing—but it was too far within land, and I might have been scented."

"True. But to return to this youngster—"

"Ay, ay, donner and blitzen! he's your affair," said the Captain.

"—How do you really know that he is in this country?"

"Why, Gabriel saw him up among the hills."

"Gabriel! who is he?"

A fellow from the gipsies, that, about eighteen years since, was pressed on board that d-d fellow Pritchard's sloop-of-war. It was he came off and gave us warning that the Shark was coming round upon us the day Kennedy was done; and he told us how Kennedy had given the information. The gipsies and Kennedy had some quarrel besides. This Gab went to the East Indies in the same ship with your younker, and, sapperment! knew him well, though the other did not remember him. Gab kept out of his eye though, as he had served the States against England, and was a deserter to boot; and he sent us word directly, that we might know of his being here—though it does not concern us a rope's end."

"So, then, really, and in sober earnest, he is actually in this country, Hatteraick, between friend and friend?" asked Glossin seriously.

"Wetter and donner, yawl What do you take me for?"

"For a bloodthirsty, fearless miscreant!" thought Glossin internally; but said aloud, "And which of your people was it that shot young Hazlewood?"

"Sturm-wetter!" said the Captain, "do ye think we were mad?-none of us, man—Gott! the country was too hot for the trade already with that d-d frolic of Brown's, attacking what you call Woodbourne House."

"Why, I am told," said Glossin, "it was Brown who shot Hazlewood?"

"Not our lieutenant, I promise you; for he was laid six feet deep at Derncleugh the day before the thing happened.—Tausend deyvils, man I do ye think that he could rise out of the earth to shoot another man?"

A light here began to break upon Glossin's confusion of ideas. "Did you not say that the younker, as you call him, goes by the name of Brown

"Of Brown? yaw-Vanbeest Brown; old Vanbeest Brown, of our Vanbeest and Vanbruggen, gave him his own name—he did."

"Then," said Glossin, rubbing his hands, "it is he, by Heaven, who has committed this crime!"

"And what have we to do with that?" demanded Hatteraick.

Glossin paused, and, fertile in expedients, hastily ran over his project in his own mind, and then drew near the smuggler with a confidential air. "You know, my dear Hatteraick, it is our principal business to get rid of this young man?"

"Umph!" answered Dirk Hatteraick-.

"Not," continued Glossin—"not that I would wish any personal harm to him—if—if—if we can do without. Now, he is liable to be seized upon by justice, both as bearing the same name with your lieutenant, who was engaged in that affair at Woodbourne, and for firing at young Hazlewood with intent to kill or wound."

"Ay, ay," said Dirk Hatteraick; "but what good will that do you? He'll be loose again as soon as he shows himself to carry other colours."

"True, my dear Dirk; well noticed, my friend Hatteraick! But there is ground enough for a temporary imprisonment till he fetch his proofs from England or elsewhere, my good friend. I understand the law, Captain Hatteraick, and I'll take it upon me, simple Gilbert Glossin of Ellangowan, justice of peace for the county of—, to refuse his bail, if he should offer the best in the country, until he is brought up for a second examination—now where d'ye think I'll incarcerate him?

"Hagel and wetter! what do I care?"

"Stay, my friend—you do care a great deal. Do you know your goods, that were seized and carried to Woodbourne, are now lying in the Custom-house at Portanferry?" (a small fishing-town).—"Now I will commit this younker—"

"When you have caught him?"

"Ay, ay, when I have caught him; I shall not be long about that—I will commit him to the Workhouse, or Bridewell, which you know is beside the Custom-house."

"Yaw, the Rasp-house; I know it very well."

"I will take care that the red-coats are dispersed through the country; you land at night with the crew of your lugger, receive your own goods, and carry the younker Brown with you back to Flushing. Won't that do?"

"Ay, carry him to Flushing," said the Captain, "or—to America?"

"Ay, ay, my friend."

"Or—to Jericho?"

"Psha! Wherever you have a mind."

"Ay, or—pitch him overboard?"

"Nay, I advise no violence."

"Nein, nein—you leave that to me. Sturm-wetter! I know you of old. But, hark ye, what am I, Dirk Hatteraick, to be the better of this?"

"Why, is it not your interest as well as mine?" said Glossin; "besides, I set you free this morning."

"You set me free!—Donner and deyvil! I set myself free. Besides, it was all in the way of your profession, and happened a long time ago, ha, ha, ha!"

"Pshaw! pshaw! don't let us jest; I am not against making a handsome compliment—but it's your affair as well as mine."

"What do you talk of my affair? is it not you that keep the bouncer's whole estate from him? Dirk Hatteraick never touched a stiver of his rents."

"Hush-hush—I tell you it shall be a joint business."

"Why, will ye give me half the kit?"

"What, half the estate?—d'ye mean . Ye should set up house together at Ellangowan, and take the barony, ridge about?"

"Sturm-wetter, no! but you might give me half the value—half the gelt. Live with you? Nein—I would have a lusthaus of mine own on the Middleburgh dyke, and a blumengarten like a burgomaster's."

"Ay, and a wooden lion at the door, and a painted sentinel in the garden, with a pipe in his mouth!—But, hark ye, Hatteraick; what will all the tulips, and flower-gardens, and pleasure-houses in the Netherlands do for you, if you are hanged here in Scotland?"

Hatteraick's countenance fell. "Der deyvil! hanged?"

"Ay, hanged, meinheer Captain. The devil can scarce save Dirk Hatteraick from being hanged for a murderer and kidnapper, if the younker of Ellangowan should settle in this country, and if the gallant Captain chances to be caught here re-establishing his fair trade! And I won't say, but, as peace is now so much talked of, their High Mightinesses may not hand him over to oblige their new allies, even if he remained in faderland."

"Poz bagel blitzen and donner! I—I doubt you say true."

"Not," said Glossin, perceiving he had made the desired impression, "not that I am against being civil;" and he slid into Hatteraick's passive hand a bank-note of some value.

"Is this all?" said the smuggler; "you had the price of half a cargo for winking at our job, and made us do your business too."

"But, my good friend, you forget—in this case you will recover all your own goods."

"Ay, at the risk of all our own necks—we could do that without you."

"I doubt that, Captain Hatteraick," said Glossin dryly, "because you would probably find a dozen red-coats at the Custom-house, whom it must be my business, if we agree about this matter, to have removed. Come, come, I will be as liberal as I can, but you should have a conscience."

"Now strafe mich der deyfel!—this provokes me more than all the rest.—You rob and you murder, and you want me to rob and murder, and play the silver-cooper, or kidnapper, as you call it, a dozen times over, and then, hagel and wind-sturm! you speak to me of conscience!—Can you think of no fairer way of getting rid of this unlucky lad?"

"No, meinheer; but as I commit him to your charge—"

"To my charge—to the charge of steel and gunpowder! and—well, if it must be, it must—but you have a tolerably good guess what's like to come of it."

"Oh, my dear friend, I trust no degree of severity will be necessary," replied Glossin.

"Severity!" said the fellow, with a kind of groan, I wish you had had my dreams when I first came to this dog-hole, and tried to sleep among the dry seaweed.—First, there was that d-d fellow there, with his broken back, sprawling as he did when I hurled the rock over atop on him—ha, ha, you would have sworn he was lying on the floor where you stand, wriggling like a crushed frog—and then—"

"Nay, my friend," said Glossin, interrupting him, what signifies going over this nonsense?—If you are turned chicken-hearted, why, the game's up, that's all—the game's up with us both."

"Chicken-hearted?—No. I have not lived so long upon the account to start at last, neither for Devil nor Dutchman."

Well then, take another schnaps—the cold's at your heart still.—And now tell me, are any of your old crew with you?"

"Nein—all dead, shot, hanged, drowned, and damned. Brown was the last—all dead, but Gipsy Gab, and he would go off the country for a spill of money—or he'll be quiet for his own sake—or old Meg, his aunt, will keep him quiet for hers."

"Which Meg?"

"Meg Merrilies, the old devil's limb of a gipsy witch."

"Is she still alive?"

"Yaw."

"And in this country?"

"And in this country. She was at the Kaim of Derncleugh, at Vanbeest Brown's last wake, as they call it, the other night, with two of my people, and some of her own blasted gipsies."

"That's another breaker ahead, Captain! Will she not squeak, think ye?"

"Not she—she won't start—she swore by the salmon, [*The great and inviolable oath of the strolling tribes] if we did the kinchin no harm, she would never tell how the gauger got it. Why, man, though I gave her a wipe with my hanger in the heat of the matter, and cut her arm, and though she was so long after in trouble about it up at your borough-town there, der deyvil! old Meg was as true as steel."

"Why, that's true, as you say," replied Glossin. "And yet if she could be carried over to Zealand, or Hamburg, or—or—anywhere else, you know, it were as well."

Hatteraick jumped upright upon his feet, and looked at Glossin from head to heel.—"I don't see the goat's foot," he said, "and yet he must be the very deyvil!—But Meg Merrilies is closer yet with the Kobold than you are—ay, and I had never such weather as after having drawn her blood. Nein, nein, I'll meddle with her no more-she's a witch of the fiend—a real deyvil's kind—but that's her affair. Donner and wetter! I'll neither make nor meddle— that's her work.—But for the rest—why, if I thought the trade would not suffer, I would soon rid you of the younker, if you send me word when he's under embargo."

In brief and undertones the two worthy associates concerted their enterprise, and agreed at which of his haunts Hatteraick should be heard of. The stay of his lugger on the coast was not difficult, as there were no king's vessels there at the time.

CHAPTER XXXV.

You are one of those that will not serve God if the devil bids you—Because we come to do you service, you think we are ruffians.
Othello.

When Glossin returned home, he found, among other letters and papers sent to him, one of considerable importance. It was signed by Mr. Protocol, an attorney in Edinburgh, and, addressing him as the agent for Godfrey Bertram, Esq., late of Ellangowan, and his representatives, acquainted him with the sudden death of Mrs. Margaret Bertram of Singleside, requesting him to inform his clients thereof, in case they should judge it proper to have any person present for their interest at opening the repositories of the deceased. Mr. Glossin perceived at once that the letter-writer was unacquainted with the breach which had taken place between him and his late patron. The estate of the deceased lady should by rights as he well knew, descend to Lucy Bertram, but it was a thousand to one that the caprice of the old lady might have altered its destination. After running over contingencies and probabilities in his fertile mind, to ascertain what sort of personal advantage might accrue to him from this incident, he could not perceive any mode of availing himself of it, except in so far as it might go to assist his plan of recovering, or rather creating, a character, the want of which he had already experienced, and was likely to feel yet more deeply. "I must place myself," he thought, "on strong ground, that, if anything goes wrong with Dirk Hatteraick's project, I may have prepossessions in my favour at least."—Besides, to do Glossin justice, bad as he was, he might feel some desire to compensate to Miss Bertram in a small degree, and in a case in which his own interest did not interfere with hers, the infinite mischief which he had occasioned to her family. He therefore resolved early the next morning to ride over to Woodbourne.

It was not without hesitation that he took this step, having the natural reluctance to face Colonel Mannering, which fraud and villainy have to encounter honour and probity. But he had great confidence in his own savoir faire. His talents were naturally acute, and by no means confined to the line of his profession. He had at different times resided a good deal in England, and his address was free both from country rusticity and professional pedantry; so that he had considerable powers both of address and persuasion, joined to an unshaken effrontery, which he affected to disguise under plainness of manner. Confident, therefore, in himself, he appeared at Woodbourne about ten in the morning, and was admitted as a gentleman come to wait upon Miss Bertram.

He did not announce himself until he was at the door of the breakfast-parlour, when the servant, by his desire, said aloud—"Mr. Glossin, to wait upon Miss Bertram. "Lucy, remembering the last scene of her father's existence, turned as pale as death, and had well-nigh fallen from her chair. Julia Mannering flew to her assistance, and they left the room together. There remained Colonel Mannering, Charles Hazlewood, with his arm in a sling, and the Dominie, whose gaunt visage and wall-eyes assumed a most hostile aspect on recognising Glossin.

That honest gentleman, though somewhat abashed by the effect of his first introduction, advanced with confidence, and hoped he did not intrude upon the ladies. Colonel Mannering, in a very upright and stately manner, observed, that he did not know to what he was to impute the honour of a visit from Mr. Glossin.

"Hem! hem! I took the liberty to wait upon Miss Bertram, Colonel
Mannering, on account of a matter of business."

"If it can be communicated to Mr. Mac-Morlan, her agent, sir, I believe it will be more agreeable to Miss Bertram."

"I beg pardon, Colonel Mannering," said Glossin, making a wretched attempt at an easy demeanour; "you are a man of the world—there are some cases in which it is most prudent for all parties to treat with principals."

"Then," replied Mannering, with a repulsive air, "if Mr. Glossin will take the trouble to state his object in a letter, I will answer that Miss Bertram pays proper attention to it."

"Certainly," stammered Glossin; "but there are cases in which a viva voce conference—Hem! I perceive—I know—Colonel Mannering has adopted some prejudices which may make may visit appear intrusive, but I submit to his good sense, whether he ought to exclude me from a hearing without knowing the purpose of my visit, or of how much consequence it may be to the young lady whom he honours with his protection."

"Certainly, sir, I have not the least intention to do so," replied the Colonel. "I will learn Miss Bertram's pleasure on the subject, and acquaint Mr. Glossin, if he can spare time to wait for her answer." So saying, he left the room.

Glossin had still remained standing in the midst of the apartment. Colonel Mannering had made not the slightest motion to invite him to sit, and indeed had remained standing himself during their short interview. When he left the room, however, Glossin seized upon a chair, and threw himself into it with an air between embarrassment and effrontery. He felt the silence of his companions disconcerting and oppressive, and resolved to interrupt it.

"A fine day, Mr. Sampson." The Dominie answered with something between an acquiescent grunt and an indignant groan.

"You never come down to see your old acquaintance on the Ellangowan property, Mr. Sampson—You would find most of the old stagers still stationary there. I have too much respect for—the late family to disturb old residenters, even under pretence of improvement. Besides, it's not my way—I don't like it—I believe, Mr. Sampson, Scripture particularly condemns those who oppress the poor—, and remove landmarks."

"Or who devour the substance of orphans." subjoined the Dominie. "Anathema, Maranatha!" So saying, he rose, shouldered the folio which he had been perusing, faced to the right about, and marched out of the room with the strides of a grenadier.

Mr. Glossin, no way disconcerted, or at least, feeling it necessary not to appear so, turned to young Hazlewood, who was apparently busy with the newspaper.—"Any news, sir?" Hazlewood raised his eyes, looked at him, and pushed the paper towards him, as if to a stranger in a coffee-house, then rose, and was about to leave the room. "I beg pardon, Mr. Hazlewood—but I can't help wishing you joy of getting so easily over that infernal accident."

This was answered by a sort of inclination of the head as slight and stiff as could be imagined. Yet it encouraged our man of law to proceed. "I can promise You, Mr. Hazlewood, few people have taken the interest in that matter which I have done, both for the sake of the country, and on account of my particular respect for your family, which has so high a stake in it; indeed, so very high a stake, that, as Mr. Featherhead is turning old now, and as there's a talk, since his last stroke, of his taking the Chiltern Hundreds', it might be worth your while to look about you. I speak as a friend, Mr. Hazlewood, and as one who understands the roll; and if in going over it together—"

"I beg pardon, sir, but I have no views in which your assistance could be useful."

"Oh very well—perhaps you are right—it's quite time enough, and I love to see a young gentleman cautious. But I was talking of your wound—I think I have got a clew to that business—I think I have—and if I don't bring the fellow to condign punishment!—"

"I beg your pardon, sir, once more; but your zeal outruns my wishes. I have every reason to think the wound was accidental—certainly it was not premeditated. Against ingratitude and premeditated treachery, should you find any one guilty of them, my resentment will be as warm as your own." This was Hazlewood's answer.

"Another rebuff," thought Glossin I must try him upon the other tack.—"Right, sir; very nobly said! I would have no more mercy on an ungrateful man than I would on a woodcock—And now we talk of sport (this was a sort of diverting of the conversation which Glossin had learned from his former patron), I see you often carry a gun, and I hope you will be soon able to take the field again. I observe you confine yourself always to your own side of the Hazleshaws burn. I hope, my dear sir, you will make no scruple of following your game to the Ellangowan bank. I believe it is rather the best exposure of the two for woodcocks, although both are capital."

As this offer only excited a cold and constrained bow, Glossin was obliged to remain silent, and was presently afterwards somewhat relieved by the entrance of Colonel Mannering.

"I have detained you some time, I fear, sir," said he, addressing Glossin; "I wished to prevail upon Miss Bertram to see you, as, in my opinion, her objections ought to give way to the necessity of hearing in her own person what is stated to be of importance that she should know. But I find that circumstances of recent occurrence, and not easily to be forgotten, have rendered her so utterly repugnant to a personal interview with Mr. Glossin, that it would be cruelty to insist upon it: and she has deputed me to receive his commands, or proposal, or, in short, whatever he may wish to say to her."

"Hem, hem! I am sorry, sir—I am very sorry, Colonel Mannering, that Miss Bertram should suppose—that any prejudice, in short—or idea that anything on my part—"

"Sir," said the inflexible Colonel, "where no accusation is made, excuses or explanations are unnecessary. Have you any objection to communicate to me, as Miss Bertram's temporary guardian, the circumstances which you conceive to interest her?"

"None, Colonel Mannering; she could not choose a more respectable friend, or one with whom I, in particular, would more anxiously wish to communicate frankly."

"Have the goodness to speak to the point, sir, if you please."

"Why, sir, it is not so easy all at once—but Mr. Hazlewood need not leave the room,—I mean so well to Miss Bertram, that I could wish the whole world to hear my part of the conference."

"My friend Mr. Charles Hazlewood will not probably be anxious, Mr. Glossin, to listen to what cannot concern him—and now, when he has left us alone, let me pray you to be short and explicit in what you have to say. I am a soldier, sir, somewhat impatient of forms and introductions." So saying he drew himself up in his chair, and waited for Mr. Glossin's communication.

"Be pleased to look at that letter," said Glossin, putting Protocol's epistle into Mannering's hand, as the shortest way of stating his business.

The Colonel read it, and returned it, after pencilling the name of the writer in his memorandum-book. "This, sir, does not seem to require much discussion—I will see that Miss Bertram's interest is attended to."

"But, sir,—but, Colonel Mannering," added Glossin, there is another matter which no one can explain but myself. This lady—this Mrs. Margaret Bertram, to my certain knowledge, made a general settlement of her affairs in Miss Lucy Bertram's favour while she lived with my old friend, Mr. Bertram, at Ellangowan. The Dominie—that was the name by which my deceased friend always called that very respectable man Mr. Sampson—he and I witnessed the deed. And she had full power at that time to make such a settlement, for she was in fee of the estate of Singleside even then, although it was life-rented by an elder sister. It was a whimsical settlement of old Singleside's, sir; he pitted the two cats his daughters against each other, ha, ha, ha!"

"Well, sir," said Mannering, without the slightest smile of sympathy, "but to the purpose. You say that this lady had power to settle her estate on Miss Bertram, and that she did so?"

"Even so, Colonel," replied Glossin. "I think I should understand the law—I have followed it for many years, and though I have given it up to retire upon a handsome competence, I did not throw away that knowledge which is pronounced better than house and land, and which I take to be the knowledge of the law, since, as our common rhyme has it,

"'Tis most excellent,

To win the land that's gone and spent.

No, no, I love the smack of the whip—I have a little, a very little law yet, at the service of my friends."

"Glossin ran on in this manner, thinking he had made a favourable impression on Mannering. The Colonel indeed reflected that this might be a most important crisis for Miss Bertram's interest, and resolved that his strong inclination to throw Glossin out at window, or at door, should not interfere with it. He put a strong curb on his temper, and resolved to listen with patience at least, if without complacency. He therefore let Mr. Glossin get to the end of his self-congratulations, and then asked him if he knew where the deed was?"

"I know—that is, I think—I believe I can recover it—In such cases custodiers have sometimes made a charge."

"We won't differ as to that, sir," said the Colonel, taking out his pocket-book.

"But, my dear sir, you take me so very short—I said some persons might make such a claim—I mean for payment of the expenses of the deed, trouble in the affair, etc. But I, for my own part, only wish Miss Bertram and her friends to be satisfied that I am acting towards her with honour. There's the paper, sir! It would have been a satisfaction to me to have delivered it into Miss Bertram's own hands, and to have wished her joy of the prospects which it opens. But since her prejudices on the subject are invincible, it only remains for me to transmit her my best wishes through you, Colonel Mannering, and to express that I shall willingly give my testimony in support of that deed when I shall be called upon. I have the honour to wish you a good morning, sir."

This parting speech was so well got up, and had so much the tone of conscious integrity unjustly suspected, that even Colonel Mannering was staggered in his bad opinion. He followed him two or three steps, and took leave of him with more politeness (though still cold and formal) than he had paid during his visit. Glossin left the house half pleased with the impression he had made, half mortified by the stern caution and proud reluctance with which he had been received. "Colonel Mannering might have had more politeness," he said to himself—"it is not every man that can bring a good chance of 400L a year to a penniless girl. Singleside must be up to 400L a year now—there's Reilageganbed, Gillifidget, Loverless, Liealone, and the Spinster's Knowe—good 400L a year. Some people might have made their own of it in my place—and yet, to own the truth, after much consideration, I don't see how that is possible."

Glossin was no sooner mounted and gone, than the Colonel despatched a groom for Mr. Mac-Morlan, and, putting the deed into his hand, requested to know if it was likely to be available to his friend Lucy Bertram. Mac-Morlan perused it with eyes that sparkled with delight, snapped his fingers repeatedly, and at length exclaimed, "Available!—it's as tight as a glove—naebody could make better wark than Glossin, when he didna let down a steek on purpose.—But (his countenance falling) the auld b——, that I should say so, might alter at pleasure!"

"Ah! And how shall we know whether she has done so?"

"Somebody must attend on Miss Bertram's part, when the repositories of the deceased are opened."

"Can you go?" said the Colonel. "I fear I cannot," replied Mac-Morlan; "I must attend a jury trial before our court."

"Then I will go myself," said the Colonel; "I'll set out to-morrow. Sampson shall go with me—he is witness to this settlement. But I shall want a legal adviser?"

"The gentleman that was lately Sheriff of this county is high in reputation as a barrister; I will give you a card of introduction to him."

"What I like about you, Mr. Mac-Morlan," said the Colonel, "is, that you always come straight to the point. Let me have it instantly—shall we tell Miss Lucy her chance of becoming an heiress?"

"Surely, because you must have some powers from her, which I will instantly draw out. Besides, I will be caution for her prudence, and that she will consider it only in the light of a chance."

Mac-Morlan judged well. It could not be discerned from Miss Bertram's manner that she founded exulting hopes upon the prospect thus unexpectedly opening before her. She did indeed, in the course of the evening, ask Mr. Mac-Morlan, as if by accident, what might be the annual income of the Hazlewood property; but shall we therefore aver for certain that she was considering whether an heiress of four hundred a year might be a suitable match for the young Laird?

CHAPTER XXXVI.

Give me a cup of sack, to make mine eyes look red—For I must speak in passion, and I will do it in King Cambyses' vein. Henry IV. Part 1

MANNERING, with Sampson for his companion, lost no time in his journey to Edinburgh. They travelled in the Colonel's post-chariot, who, knowing his companion's habits of abstraction, did not choose to lose him out of his own sight, far less to trust him on horseback, where, in all probability, a knavish stable-boy might with little address have contrived to mount him with his face to the tail. Accordingly, with the aid of his valet, who attended on horseback, he contrived to bring Mr. Sampson safe to an inn in Edinburgh,—for hotels in those days there were none,—without any other accident than arose from his straying twice upon the road. On one occasion he was recovered by Barnes, who understood his humour, when, after engaging in close colloquy with the schoolmaster of Moffat, respecting a disputed quantity in Horace's 7th Ode, Book ll., the dispute led on to another controversy, concerning the exact meaning of the word Malobathro, in that lyric effusion. His second escapade was made for the purpose of visiting the field of Rullion-green, which was dear to his Presbyterian predilections. Having got out of the carriage for an instant, he saw the sepulchral monument of the slain at the distance of about a mile, and was arrested by Barnes in his progress up the Pentland Hills, having on both occasions forgot his friend, patron, and fellow-traveller, as completely as if he had been in the East Indies. On being reminded that Colonel Mannering was waiting for him, he uttered his usual ejaculation of "Prodigious!—I was oblivious," and then strode back to his post. Barnes was surprised at his master's patience on both occasions, knowing by experience how little he brooked neglect or delay; but the Dominie was in every respect a privileged person. His patron and he were never for a moment in each other's way, and it seemed obvious that they were formed to be companions through life. If Mannering wanted a particular book, the Dominie could bring it; if he wished to have accounts summed up, or checked, his assistance was equally ready; if he desired to recall a particular passage in the classics, he could have recourse to the Dominie as to a dictionary; and all the while, this walking statue was neither presuming when noticed, nor sulky when left to himself. To a proud, shy, reserved man, and such in many respects was Mannering, this sort of living catalogue, and animated automaton, had all the advantages of a literary dumb-waiter.

As soon as they arrived in Edinburgh, and were established at the George Inn near Bristol Port, then kept by old Cockburn (I love to be particular), the Colonel desired the waiter to procure him a guide to Mr. Pleydell's, the advocate, for whom he had a letter of introduction from Mr. Mac-Morlan. He then commanded Barnes to have an eye to the Dominie, and walked forth with a chairman, who was to usher him to the man of law.

The period was near the end of the American war. The desire of room, of air, and of decent accommodation, had not as yet made very much progress in the capital of Scotland. Some efforts had been made on the south side of the town towards building houses within themselves, as they are emphatically termed; and the New Town on the north, since so much extended, was then just commenced. But the great bulk of the better classes, and particularly those connected with the law, still lived in flats or dungeons of the Old Town. The manners also of some of the veterans of the law had not admitted innovation. One or two eminent lawyers still saw their clients in taverns, as was the general custom fifty years before; and although their habits were already considered as old-fashioned by the younger barristers, yet the custom of mixing wine and revelry with serious business was still maintained by those serious counsellors, who loved the old road, either because it was such, or because they had got too well used to it to travel any other. Among those praisers of the past time, who with ostentatious obstinacy affected the manners of a former generation, was this same Paulus Pleydell, Esq., otherwise a good scholar, an excellent lawyer, and a worthy man.

Under the guidance of his trusty attendant, Colonel Mannering, after threading a dark lane or two, reached the High Street, then clanging with the voices of oyster-women and the bells of pie-men; for it had, as his guide assured him, just "chappit [*struck] eight upon the Tron." It was long since Mannering had been in the street of a crowded metropolis, which, with its noise and clamour, its sounds of trade, of revelry and of licence, its variety of lights, and the eternally changing bustle of its hundred groups, offers, by night especially, a spectacle, which, though composed of the most vulgar materials when they are separately considered, has, when they are combined, a striking and powerful effect on the imagination. The extraordinary height of the houses was marked by lights, which, glimmering irregularly along their front, ascended so high among the attics, that they seemed at length to twinkle in the middle sky. This coup d'oeil, which still subsists in a certain degree, was then more imposing, owing to the uninterrupted range of buildings on each side, which, broken only at the space where the North Bridge joins the main street, formed a superb and uniform Place, extending from the front of the Luckenbooths to the head of the Canongate, and corresponding in breadth and length to the uncommon height of the buildings on either side.

Mannering had not much time to look and to admire. His conductor hurried him across this striking scene, and suddenly dived with him into a very steep paved lane. Turning to the right, they entered a scale-staircase, as it is called, the state of which, so far as it could be judged of by one of his senses, annoyed Mannering's delicacy not a little. When they had ascended cautiously to a considerable height, they heard a heavy rap at a door, still two stories above them. The door opened, and immediately ensued the sharp and worrying bark of a dog, the squalling of a woman, the screams of an assaulted cat, and the hoarse voice of a man, who cried in a most imperative tone, Will ye, Mustard? will ye?—down, sir! down!"

"Lord preserve us!" said the female voice, "an he had worried our cat, Mr. Pleydell would ne'er hae forgi'en me!"

"Aweel, my doo, [*dove] the cat's no a prin the waur—so he's no in, ye say?"

"Na, Mr. Pleydell's ne'er in the house on Saturday at e'en," answered the female voice.

"And the morn's Sabbath too," said the querist "I dinna ken what will be done."

By this time Mannering appeared, and found a tall strong countryman, clad in a coat of pepper-and-salt coloured mixture, with huge metal buttons, a glazed hat and boots, and a large horsewhip beneath his arm, in colloquy with a slipshod damsel—I, who had in one hand the lock of the door, and in the other a pail of whiting, or camstane, as it is called, mixed with water—a circumstance which indicates Saturday night in Edinburgh.

"So Mr. Pleydell is not at home, my good girl?" said Mannering.

"Ay, sir, he's at hame, but he's no in the house: he's aye out on
Saturday at e'en."

"But, try good girl, I am a stranger, and my business express—Will you tell me where I can find him?"

"His honour," said the chairman, "will be at Clerihugh's about this time—Hersell could hae tell'd ye that, but she thought ye wanted to see his house."

"Well, then, show me to this tavern—I suppose he will see me, as I come on business of some consequence?"

"I dinna ken, sir," said the girl; "he disna like to be disturbed on Saturdays wi' business—but he's aye civil to strangers."

"I'll gang to the tavern too," said our friend Dinmont, "for I am a stranger also, and on business e'en sic like."

"Na," said the handmaiden, "an he see the gentleman, he'll see the simple body too—but, Lord's sake, dinna say it was me sent ye there!"

"Atweel, I am a simple body, that's true, hinny, but I am no come to steal ony o' his skeel for naething," said the farmer in his honest pride, and strutted away downstairs, followed by Mannering and the cadie. Mannering could not help admiring the determined stride with which the stranger who preceded them divided the press, shouldering from him, by the mere weight and impetus of his motion, both drunk and sober passengers. "He'll be a Teviotdale tup tat ane," said the chairman, "tat's for keeping ta crown o' ta causeway tat gate—he'll no gang far or he'll get somebody to bell ta cat wi' him."

His shrewd augury, however, was not fulfilled. Those who recoiled from the colossal weight of Dinmont, on looking up at his size and strength, apparently judged him too heavy metal to be rashly encountered, and suffered him to pursue his course unchallenged. Following in the wake of this first-rate, Mannering proceeded till the farmer made a pause, and, looking back to the chairman, said, "I'm thinking this will be the close, friend?"

"Ay, ay," replied Donald, "tat's ta close."

Dinmont descended confidently, then turned into a dark alley— then up a dark stair—and then into an open door. While he was whistling shrilly for the waiter, as if he had been one of his collie dogs, Mannering looked round him, and could hardly conceive how a gentleman of a liberal profession, and good society, should choose such a scene for social indulgence. Besides the miserable entrance, the house itself seemed paltry and half ruinous. The passage in which they stood had a window to the close, which admitted a little light during the daytime, and a villainous compound of smells at all times, but more especially towards evening. Corresponding to this window was a borrowed light on the other side of the passage, looking into the kitchen, which had no direct communication with the free air, but received in the daytime, at second hand, such straggling and obscure light as found its way from the lane through the window opposite. At present, the interior of the kitchen was visible by its own huge fires—a sort of Pandemonium, where men and women, half undressed, were busied in baking, broiling, roasting oysters, and preparing devils on the gridiron; the mistress of the place, with her shoes slipshod, and her hair straggling like that of Megaera from under a round-eared cap, toiling, scolding, receiving orders, giving them, and obeying them all at once, seemed the presiding enchantress of that gloomy and fiery region.

Loud and repeated bursts of laughter, from different quarters of the house, proved that her labours were acceptable, and not unrewarded by a generous public. With some difficulty a waiter was prevailed upon to show Colonel Mannering and Dinmont the room where their friend, learned in the law, held his hebdomadal carousals. The scene which it exhibited, and particularly the attitude of the counsellor himself, the principal figure therein, struck his two clients with amazement.

Mr. Pleydell was a lively, sharp-looking gentleman, with a professional shrewdness in his eye, and, generally speaking, a professional formality in his manners. But this, like his three-tailed wig and black coat, he could slip off on a Saturday evening, when surrounded by a party of jolly companions, and disposed for what he called his altitudes. On the present occasion, the revel had lasted since four o'clock, and, at length, under the direction of a venerable compotater, who had shared the sports and festivity of three generations, the frolicsome company had begun to practise the ancient and now forgotten pastime of High-jinks. This game was played in several different ways. Most frequently the dice were thrown by the company, and those upon whom the lot fell were obliged to assume and maintain, for a time, a certain fictitious character, or to repeat a certain number of fescennine verses in a particular order. If they departed from the characters assigned, or if their memory proved treacherous in the repetition, they incurred forfeits, which were either compounded for by swallowing an additional bumper, or by paying a small sum towards the reckoning. At this sport the jovial company were closely engaged, when Mannering entered the room.

Mr. Counsellor Pleydell, such as we have described him, was enthroned as a monarch, in an elbow-chair, placed, on the dining-table, his scratch wig on one side, his head crowned with a bottle-slider, his eye leering with an expression betwixt fun and the effects of wine, while his court around him resounded with such crambo scraps of verse as these .

Where is Gerunto now? and what's become of him?

Gerunto's drowned because he could not swim, etc. etc.

Such, O Themis, were anciently the sports of thy Scottish children! Dinmont was first in the room. He stood aghast a moment,—and then exclaimed, "It's him, sure enough-Deil o' the like o' that ever saw!"

At the sound of "Mr. Dinmont and Colonel Mannering wanted to speak to you, sir," Pleydell turned his head, and blushed a little when he saw the very genteel figure of the English stranger. He was, however, of the opinion of Falstaff, "Out, ye villains, play out the play!" wisely judging it the better way to appear totally unconcerned. "Where be our guards?" exclaimed this second Justinian; "see ye not a stranger knight from foreign parts arrived at this our court of Holyrood—with our bold yeoman Andrew Dinmont, who has succeeded to the keeping of our royal flocks within the forest of Jedwood, where, thanks to our royal care in the administration of justice, they feed as safe as if they were within the bounds of Fife? Where be our heralds, our pursuivants, our Lyon, our Marchmount, our Carrick, and our Snowdown? Let the strangers be placed at our board, and regaled as beseemeth their quality, and this our high holiday—to-morrow we will hear their tidings."

"So please you, my liege, to-morrow's Sunday," said one of the company.

"Sunday, is it? then we will give no offence to the assembly of the kirk—on Monday shall be. their audience."

Mannering, who had stood at first uncertain whether to advance or retreat, now resolved to enter for the moment into the whim of the scene, though internally fretting at Mac-Morlan for sending him to consult with a crack-brained humorist. He therefore advanced with three profound congees, and craved permission to lay his credentials at the feet of the Scottish monarch, in order to be perused at his best leisure. The gravity with which he accommodated himself to the humour of the moment, and the deep and humble inclination with which he at first declined, and then accepted, a seat presented by the master of the ceremonies, procured him three rounds of applause.

"Deil hae me, if they arena a' mad thegither!" said Dinmont, occupying with less ceremony a seat at the bottom of the table, "or else they hae taen Yule before it comes, and are gaun a-guisarding."

A large glass of claret was offered to Mannering, who drank it to the health of the reigning prince. "You are, I presume to guess," said the monarch, "that celebrated Sir Miles Mannering, so renowned in the French wars, and may well pronounce to us if the wines of Gascony lose their flavour in our more northern realm."

Mannering, agreeably flattered by this allusion to the fame of his celebrated ancestor, replied, by professing himself only a distant relation of the preux chevalier, and added, "that in his opinion the wine was superlatively good."

"It's owre cauld for my stamach," said Dinmont, setting down the glass (empty, however).

"We will correct that quality," answered King Paulus, the first of the name; "we have not forgotten that the moist and humid air of our valley of Liddel inclines to stronger potations.—Seneschal, let our faithful yeoman have a cup of brandy; it will be more germain to the matter."

"And now," said Mannering, "since we have unwarily intruded upon your majesty at a moment of mirthful retirement, be pleased to say when you will indulge a stranger with an audience on those affairs of weight which have brought him to your northern capital."

The monarch opened Mac-Morlan's letter, and, running it hastily over, exclaimed, with his natural voice and. manner, "Lucy Bertram of Ellangowan, poor dear lassie!"

"A forfeit! a forfeit!" exclaimed a dozen voices; his majesty has forgot his kingly character."

"Not a whit! not a whit!" replied the king; "I'll be judged by this courteous knight. May not a monarch love a maid of low degree? Is not King Cophetua and the Beggar-maid, an adjudged case in point?"

"Professional! professional!—another forfeit," exclaimed the tumultuary nobility.

"Had not our royal predecessors," continued the monarch, exalting his sovereign voice to drown these disaffected clamours,—"Had they not their Jean Logies, their Bessie Carmichaels, their Oliphants, their Sandilands, and their Weirs, and shall it be denied to us even to name a maiden whom we delight to honour? Nay, then, sink state and perish sovereignty! for, like a second Charles V., we will abdicate, and seek in the private shades of life those pleasures which are denied to a throne."

So saying, he flung away his crown, and sprung from his exalted station with more agility than could have been expected from his age, ordered lights and a wash-hand basin and towel, with a cup of green tea, into another room, and made a sign to Mannering to accompany him. In less than two minutes he washed his face and hands, settled his wig in the glass, and, to Mannering's great surprise, looked quite a different man from the childish Bacchanal he bad seen a moment before.

"There are folks," he said, "Mr. Mannering, before whom one should take care how they play the fool—because they have either too much malice, or too little wit, as the poet says. The best compliment I can pay Colonel Mannering, is to show I am not ashamed to expose myself before him—and truly I think it is a compliment I have not spared to-night on your good-nature.—But what's that great strong fellow wanting?"

Dinmont, who had pushed after Mannering into the room, began with a scrape with his foot and a scratch of his head in unison. "I am Dandie Dinmont, sir, of the Charlies-hope—the Liddesdale lad—ye'll mind me?—it was for me ye won yon grand plea."

"What plea, you loggerhead" said the lawyer "d'ye think I can remember all the fools that come to plague me?"

"Lord, sir, it was the grand plea about the grazing o' the Langtae
Head!" said the farmer.

"Well, curse thee, never mind; give me the memorial [*The Scottish memorial corresponds to the English brief.] and come to me on Monday at ten," replied the learned counsel.

"But, sir, I haena got ony distinct memorial."

"No memorial, man?" said Pleydell.

"Na, sir, nae memorial," answered Dandie "for your honour said before, Mr. Pleydell, ye'll mind, that ye liked best to bear us hill-folk tell our ain tale by word o' mounts"

"Beshrew my tongue that said so!" answered the counsellor; "it will cost my ears a dinning.—Well, say in two words what you've got to say—you see the gentleman waits."

"Ou, sir, if the gentleman likes he may play his ain spring first; it's a' ane to Dandie."

"Now, you looby," said the lawyer, "cannot you conceive that your business can be nothing to Colonel Mannering, but that he may not choose to have these great ears of thine regaled with his matters?"

"Aweel, sir, just as you and he like—so ye see to my business," said Dandie, not a whit disconcerted by the roughness of this reception. "We're at the auld wark o' the marches again, Jock o' Dawston Cleugh and me. Ye see we march on the tap o' Touthop Rigg after we pass the Pomoragrains; for the Pomoragrains, and Slackenspool, and Bloodylaws, they come in there, and they belang to the Peel; but after ye pass Pomoragrains at a muckle great saucer-headed cutlugged stane, that they ca' Charlie's Chuckie, there Dawston Cleugh and Charlies-hope they march. Now, I say, the march rins on the tap o' the hill where the wind and water shears; but Jock o' Dawston Cleugh again, he contravenes that, and says, that it hauds down by the auld drove-road that gaes awa by the Knot o' the Gate ower to Keeldar Ward—and that makes an unco [*Uncommon] difference."

"And what difference does it make, friend?" said Pleydell. "How many sheep will it feed?"

"Ou, no mony," said Dandie, scratching his head, it's lying high and exposed—it may feed a hog, or aiblins [*Perhaps] twa in a good year."

"And for this grazing, which may be worth about five shillings a year, you are willing to throw away a hundred pound or two?"

"Na, sir, it's no for the value of the grass," replied Dinmont; "it's for justice."

"My good friend," said Pleydell, "justice, like charity, should begin at home. Do you justice to your wife and family, and think no more about-the matter."

Dinmont still lingered, twisting his hat in his hand-" It's no for that, sir—but I would like ill to be bragged wi' him—he threeps [*Declares] he'll bring a score o' witnesses and mair—and I'm sure there's as mony will swear for me as for him, folk that lived a' their days upon the Charlies-hope, and wadna like to see the land lose its right."

"Zounds, man, if it be a point of honour," said the lawyer, "why don't your landlords take it up?"

"I dinna ken, sir" (scratching his head again), "there's been nae election-dusts lately, and the lairds are unco neighbourly, and Jock and me canna get them to yoke thegither about it a' that we can say—but if ye thought we might keep up the rent—"

"No! no! that will never do," said Pleydell,—"confound you, why don't you take good cudgels and settle it?"

"Odd, sir," answered the farmer, "we tried that three times already—that's twice on the land add ance at Lockerby fair.—But I dinna ken—we're baith gey good at single-stick, and it couldna weel be judged."

"Then take broadswords, and be d-d to you, as your fathers did before you," said the counsel learned in the law.

"Aweel, sir, if ye think it wadna be again the law, it's a' ane to
Dandie."

"Hold! Hold!" exclaimed Pleydell, "we shall have another Lord Soulis' mistake—Pr'ythee, man, comprehend me; I wish you to consider how very trifling and foolish a lawsuit you wish to engage in."

"Ay, sir?" said Dandie, in a disappointed tone. "So ye winna take on wi' me, I'm doubting?"

"Me! not I—go home, go home, take a pint and agree." Dandie looked but half contented, and still remained stationary. "Anything more, my friend?"

"Only, sir, about the succession of this leddy that's dead, auld
Miss Margaret Bertram o' Singleside."

"Ay, what about her?" said the counsellor, rather surprised.

"Ou, we have nae connection at a' wi' the Bertrams," said Dandie,—"they were grand folk by the like o' us.—But Jean Liltup, that was auld Singleside's housekeeper, and the mother of these twa young ladies that are gane—the last o' them's dead at a ripe age, I trow—Jean Liltup came out o' Liddel water, and she was as near our connection as second cousin to my mother's half-sister—She drew up wi' Singleside, nae doubt, when she was his housekeeper, and it was a sair vex and grief to a' her kith and kin. But he acknowledged a marriage, and satisfied the kirk—and now I wad ken frae you if we hae not some claim by law?"

"Not the shadow of a claim."

"Aweel, we're nae puirer," said Dandie,—"but she may hae thought on us if she was minded to make a testament.—Weel, sir, I've said my say—I'se e'en wish you good-night, and—"putting his hand in his pocket.

"No, no, my friend; I never take fees on Saturday nights, or without a memorial—away with you, Dandie." And Dandie made his reverence, and departed accordingly.

CHAPTER XXXVII.

But this poor farce has neither truth, nor art,
To please the fancy or to touch the heart.
Dark but not awful, dismal but yet mean,
With anxious bustle moves the cumbrous scene,
Presents no objects tender or profound,
But spreads its cold unmeaning gloom around.
Parish Register.

"Your majesty," said Mannering, laughing, "has solemnised your abdication by an act of mercy and charity—That fellow will scarce think of going to law."

"Oh, you are quite wrong," said the experienced lawyer. "The only difference is, I have lost my client and my fee. He'll never rest till he finds somebody to encourage him to commit the folly he has predetermined—No! no! I have only shown you another weakness of my character—I always speak truth of a Saturday night."

"And sometimes through the week, I should think," said Mannering, continuing the same tone.

"Why, yes; as far as my vocation will permit. I am, as Hamlet says, indifferent honest, when my clients and their solicitors do not make me the medium of conveying their double-distilled lies to the bench. But oportet vivere! it is a sad thing.—And now to our business. I am glad my old friend MacMorlan has sent you to me; he is an active, honest, and intelligent man, long Sheriff-substitute of the county of—under me, and still holds the office. He knows I have a regard for that unfortunate family of Ellangowan, and for poor Lucy. I have not seen her since she was twelve years old, and she was then a sweet pretty girl under the management of a very silly father. But my interest in her is of an early date. I was called upon, Mr. Mannering, being then Sheriff of that county, to investigate the particulars of a murder which had been committed near Ellangowan the day on which this poor child was born; and which, by a strange combination that I was unhappily not able to trace, involved the death or abstraction of her only brother, a boy of about five years old. No, Colonel, I shall never forget the misery of the house of Ellangowan that morning!—the father half distracted—the mother dead in premature travail—the helpless infant, with scarce any one to attend it, coming wawling and crying into this miserable world at such a moment of unutterable misery. We lawyers are not of iron, sir, or of brass, any more than you soldiers are of steel. We are conversant with the crimes and distresses of civil society, as you are with those that occur in a state of war, and to do our duty in either case a little apathy is perhaps necessary—But the devil take a soldier whose heart can be as hard as his sword, and his dam catch the lawyer who bronzes his bosom instead of his forehead!—But come, I am losing my Saturday at e'en—will you have the kindness to trust me with these papers which relate to Miss Bertram's business? — and stay—to-morrow you'll take a bachelor's dinner with an old lawyer,—I insist upon it, at three precisely—and come an hour sooner.—The old lady is to be buried on Monday; it is the orphan's cause, and we'll borrow an hour from the Sunday to talk over this business—although I fear nothing can be done if she has altered her settlement—unless perhaps it occurs within the sixty days, and then if Miss Bertram can show that she possesses the character of heir-at-law, why—

"But, hark! my lieges are impatient of their inter-regnum—I do not invite you to rejoin us, Colonel; it would be a trespass on your complaisance, unless you had begun the day with us, and gradually glided on front wisdom to mirth, and from mirth to—to—to—extravagance.—Good-night-Harry, go home with Mr. Mannering to his lodging-Colonel, I expect you at a little past two to-morrow."

The Colonel returned to his inn, equally surprised at the childish frolics in which he had found his learned counsellor engaged, at the candour and sound sense which he had in a moment summoned up to meet the exigencies of his profession, and at the tone of feeling which he displayed when he spoke of the friendless orphan.

In the morning, while the Colonel and his most quiet and silent of all retainers, Dominie Sampson, were finishing the breakfast which Barnes had made and poured out, after the Dominie had scalded himself in the attempt, Mr. Pleydell was suddenly ushered in. A nicely dressed bob-wig, upon every hair of which a zealous and careful barber had bestowed its proper allowance of powder; a well-brushed black suit, with very clean shoes and gold buckles and stock-buckle; a manner rather reserved and formal than intrusive, but, withal, showing only the formality of manner, by no means that of awkwardness; a countenance, the expressive and somewhat comic features of which were in complete repose,—all showed a being perfectly different from the choice spirit of the evening before. A glance of shrewd and piercing fire in his eye was the only marked expression which recalled the man of "Saturday at e'en."

"I am come," said he, with a very polite address, "to use my regal authority in your behalf in spirituals as well as temporals—can I accompany you to the Presbyterian kirk, or Episcopal meeting-house?—Tros Tyriusve" a lawyer, you know, is of both religions, or rather I should say of both forms—or can I assist in passing the forenoon otherwise? You'll excuse my old-fashioned importunity—I was born in a time when a Scotchman was thought inhospitable if he left a guest alone a moment, except when he slept—but I trust you will tell me at once if I intrude."

"Not at all, my dear sir," answered Colonel Mannering—"I am delighted to put myself under your pilotage. I should wish much to hear some of your Scottish preachers whose talents have done such honour to your country—your Blair, your Robertson, or your Henry; and I embrace—your kind offer with all my heart.—Only," drawing the lawyer a little aside, and turning his eye towards Sampson, "my worthy friend there in the reverie is a little helpless and abstracted, and my servant, Barnes, who is his pilot in ordinary, cannot well assist him here, especially as he has expressed his determination of going to some of your darker and more remote places of worship."

The lawyer's eye glanced at Dominie Sampson. "A curiosity worth preserving—and I'll find you a fit custodier.—Here you, sir (to the waiter), go to Luckie Finlayson's in the Cowgate for Miles Macfin the cadie, he'll be there about this time, and tell him I wish to speak to him."

The person wanted soon arrived. "I will commit your friend to this man's charge," said Pleydell; "he'll attend him, or conduct him, wherever he chooses to go, with a happy indifference as to kirk or market, meeting or court of justice, or any other place whatever—and bring him safe home at whatever hour you appoint; so that Mr. Barnes there may be left to the freedom of his own will."

This was easily arranged, and the Colonel committed the Dominie to the charge of this man while they should remain in Edinburgh.

"And now, sir, if you please, we shall go to the Greyfriars church, to hear our historian of Scotland, of the Continent, and of America."

They were disappointed—he did not preach that morning.—"Never mind," said the counsellor, "I have a moment's patience, and we shall do very well."

The colleague of Dr. Robertson ascended the pulpit. [*This was the celebrated Dr. Rescan, a distinguished clergyman, and a most excellent man.] His external appearance was not prepossessing. A remarkably fair complexion, strangely contrasted with a black wig without a grain of powder; a narrow chest and a stooping posture; hands which, placed like props on either side of the pulpit, seemed necessary rather to support the person than to assist the gesticulation of the preacher,—no gown, not even that of Geneva, a tumbled band, and a gesture which seemed scarce voluntary, were the first circumstances which struck a stranger. "The preacher seems a very ungainly person," whispered Mannering to his new friend.

"Never fear; he's the son of an excellent Scottish lawyer [*The father of Dr. Erskine was an eminent lawyer, and his Institutes of the Law of Scotland are to this day the text-hook of students of that science.]—he'll show blood, I'll warrant him."

The learned counsellor predicted truly. A lecture was delivered, fraught with new, striking, and entertaining views of Scripture history—a sermon, in which the Calvinism of the Kirk of Scotland was ably supported, yet made the basis of a sound system of practical morals, which should neither shelter the sinner under the cloak of speculative faith or of peculiarity of opinion, nor leave him loose to the waves of unbelief and schism. Something there was of an antiquated turn of argument and metaphor, but it only served to give zest and peculiarity to the style of elocution. The sermon was not read—a scrap of paper containing the heads of the discourse was occasionally referred to, and the enunciation, which at first seemed imperfect and embarrassed, became, as the preacher warmed in his progress, animated and distinct, and although the discourse could not be quoted as a correct specimen of pulpit eloquence, yet Mannering had seldom heard so much learning, metaphysical acuteness, and energy of argument, brought into the service of Christianity.

"Such," he said, going out of the church, "must have been the preachers, to whose uncaring minds, and acute, though sometimes rudely exercised talents, we own the Reformation."

"And yet that reverend gentleman," said Pleydell, "whom I love for his father's sake and his own, has nothing of the sour or pharisaical pride which has been imputed to some of the early fathers of the Calvinistic Kirk of Scotland. His colleague and he differ, and head different parties in the kirk, about particular points of church discipline; but without for a moment losing personal regard or respect for each other, or suffering malignity to interfere in an opposition, steady, constant, and apparently conscientious on both sides."

"And you, Mr. Pleydell, what do you think of their points of difference?"

"Why, I hope, Colonel, a plain man may go to heaven without thinking about them at all—besides, inter nos, I am a member of the suffering and Episcopal Church of Scotland—the shadow of a shade now, and fortunately so—but I love to pray where my fathers prayed before me, without thinking worse of the Presbyterian forms, because they do not affect me with the same associations." And with this remark they parted until dinner-time.

From the awkward access to the lawyer's mansion, Mannering was induced to form very moderate expectations of the entertainment which he was to receive. The approach looked even more dismal by daylight than on the preceding evening. The houses on each side of the lane were so close, that the neighbours might have shaken hands with each other from the different sides, and occasionally the space between was traversed by wooden galleries, and thus entirely closed up. The stair, the scale-stair, was not well cleaned; and on entering the house, Mannering was struck with the narrowness and meanness of the wainscoted passage. But the library, into which he was shown by an elderly respectable looking man-servant, was a complete contrast to these unpromising appearances. It was a well-proportioned room, hung with a portrait or two of Scottish characters of eminence, by Jamieson, the Caledonian Vandyke, and surrounded with books, the best editions of the best authors, and, in particular, an admirable collection of classics.

"These," said Pleydell, "are my tools of trade. A lawyer without history or literature is a mechanic, a mere working mason; if he possesses some knowledge of these, he may venture to call himself an architect."

But Mannering was chiefly delighted with the view from the windows, which commanded that incomparable prospect of the ground between Edinburgh and the sea; the Firth of Forth, with its islands; the embayment which is terminated by the Law of North Berwick; and the varied shores of Fife to the northward, indenting with a hilly outline the clear blue horizon.

When Mr. Pleydell had sufficiently enjoyed the surprise of his guest, he called his attention to Miss Bertram's affairs. "I was in hopes," he said, "though but faint, to have discovered some means of ascertaining her indefeasible right to this property of Singleside; but my researches have been in vain. The old lady was certainly absolute fiar, and might dispose of it in full right of property. All that we have to hope is, that the devil may not have tempted her to alter this very proper settlement. You must attend the old girl's funeral to-morrow, to which you will receive an invitation, for I have acquainted her agent with your being here on Miss Bertram's part; and I will meet you afterwards at the house she inhabited, and be present to see fair play at the opening of the settlement. The old cat had a little girl, the orphan of some relation, who lived with her as a kind of slavish companion. I hope she has had the conscience to make her independent, in consideration of the peine forte et dure to which she subjected her during her lifetime."

Three gentlemen now appeared, and were introduced to the stranger. They were men of good sense, gaiety, and general information, so that the day passed very pleasantly over; and Colonel Mannering assisted, about eight o'clock at night, in discussing the landlord's bottle, which was, of course, a magnum. Upon his return to the inn, he found a card inviting him to the funeral of Miss Margaret Bertram, late of Singleside, which was to proceed from her own house to the place of interment in the Greyfriars churchyard, at one o'clock afternoon.

At the appointed hour, Mannering went to a small house in the suburbs to the southward of the city, where he found the place of mourning, indicated, as usual in Scotland, by two rueful figures with long black cloaks, white crapes and hatbands, holding in their hands poles, adorned with melancholy streamers of the same description. By two other mutes, who, from their visages, seemed suffering under the pressure of some strange calamity, he was ushered into the dining-parlour of the defunct, where the company were assembled for the funeral.

In Scotland, the custom, now disused in England, of inviting the relations of the deceased to the interment, is universally retained. On many occasions this has a singular and striking effect, but it degenerates into mere empty form and grimace, in cases where the defunct has had the misfortune to live unbeloved and die unlamented. The English service for the dead, one of the most beautiful and impressive parts of the ritual of the church, would have, in such cases, the effect of fixing the attention, and uniting the thoughts and feelings of the audience present, in an exercise of devotion so peculiarly adapted to such an occasion. But according to the Scottish custom, if there be not real feeling among the assistants, there is nothing to supply the deficiency, and exalt or rouse the attention; so that a sense of tedious form, and almost hypocritical restraint, is too apt to pervade the company assembled for the mournful solemnity. Mrs. Margaret Bertram was unluckily one of those whose good qualities had attached no general friendship. She had no near relations who might have mourned from natural affection, and therefore her funeral exhibited merely the exterior trappings of sorrow.

Mannering, therefore, stood among this lugubrious company of cousins in the third, fourth, fifth, and sixth degree, composing his countenance to the decent solemnity of all who were around him, and looking as much concerned on Mrs. Margaret Bertram's account, as if the deceased lady of Singleside had been his own sister or mother. After a deep and awful pause, the company began to talk aside under their breaths, however, and as if in the chamber of a dying person.

"Our poor friend," said one grave gentleman, scarcely opening his mouth, for fear of deranging the necessary solemnity of his features, and sliding his whisper from between his lips, which were as little unclosed as possible,—"Our poor friend has died well to pass in the world."

"Nae doubt," answered the person addressed, with half-closed eyes; "poor Mrs. Margaret was aye careful of the gear."

"Any news to-day, Colonel Mannering?" said one of the gentlemen whom he had dined with the day before, but in a tone which might, for its impressive gravity, have communicated the death of his whole generation.

"Nothing particular, I believe, sir," said Mannering, in the cadence which was, he observed, appropriated to the house of mourning.

"I understand," continued the first speaker emphatically, and with the air of one who is well informed—"I understand there is a settlement."

"And what does little Jenny Gibson get?"

"A hundred, and the auld repeater."

"That's but sma' gear, puir thing; she had a sair time o't with the auld leddy. But it's ill waiting for deadfolk's shoon."

"I am afraid," said the politician, who was close by Mannering," we have not done with your old friend Tippoo Saib yet—I doubt he'll give the Company more plague; and I am told, but you'll know for certain that East India Stock is not rising."

"I trust it will, sir, soon."

"Mrs. Margaret," said another person, mingling in the conversation, "had some India bonds. I know that, for I drew the interest for her—it would be desirable now for the trustees and legatees to have the Colonel's advice about the time and mode of converting them into money. For my part I think—But there's Mr. Mortcloke to tell us they are gaun to lift."

Mr. Mortcloke the undertaker did accordingly, with a visage of professional length and most grievous solemnity, distribute among the pall-bearers little cards, assigning their respective situations in attendance upon the coffin. As this precedence is supposed to be regulated by propinquity to the defunct, the undertaker, however skilful a master of these lugubrious ceremonies, did not escape giving some offence. To be related to Mrs. Bertram was to be of kin to the lands of Singleside, and was a propinquity of which each relative present at that moment was particularly jealous. Some murmurs there were on the occasion, and our friend Dinmont gave more open offence, being unable either to repress his discontent, or to utter it in the key properly modulated to the solemnity. "I think ye might hae at least gi'en me a leg o' her to carry," he exclaimed, in a voice considerably louder than propriety admitted; "God! an it hadna been for the rigs o' land, I would hae gotten her a' to carry mysell, for as many gentles as are here."

A score of frowning and reproving brows were bent upon the unappalled yeoman, who, having given vent to his displeasure, stalked sturdily downstairs with the rest of the company, totally disregarding the censures of those whom his remarks had scandalised.

And then the funeral pomp set forth; saulies with their batons, and gumphions of tarnished white crape, in honour of the well-preserved maiden fame of Mrs. Margaret Bertram. Six starved horses, themselves the very emblems of mortality, well cloaked and plumed, lugging along the hearse with its dismal emblazonry, crept in slow state towards the place of interment, preceded by Jamie Duff, an idiot, who, with weepers and cravat made of white paper, attended on every funeral, and followed by six mourning coaches, filled with the company. Many of these now gave more free loose to their tongues, and discussed with unrestrained earnestness the amount of the succession, and the probability of its destination. The principal expectants, however, kept a prudent silence, indeed, ashamed to express hopes which might prove fallacious; and the agent, or man of business, who alone knew exactly how matters stood, maintained a countenance of mysterious importance, as if determined to preserve the full interest of anxiety and suspense.

At length they arrived at the churchyard gates, and from thence, amid the gaping of two or three dozen of idle women with infants in their arms, and accompanied by some twenty children, who ran gambolling and screaming alongside of the sable procession, they finally arrived at the burial-place of the Singleside family. This was a square enclosure in the Greyfriars churchyard, guarded on one side by a veteran angel, without a nose, and having only one wing, who had the merit of having maintained his post for a century, while his comrade cherub, who had stood sentinel on the corresponding pedestal, lay a broken trunk among the hemlock, burdock, and nettles, which grew in gigantic luxuriance around the walls of the mausoleum. A moss-grown and broken inscription informed the reader, that in the Year 1650 Captain Andrew Bertram, first of Singleside, descended of the very ancient and honourable house of Ellangowan, had caused this monument to be erected for himself and his descendants. A reasonable number of scythes and hour-glasses, and death's heads, and cross-bones, garnished the following sprig of sepulchral poetry, to the memory of the founder of the mausoleum;—

Nathaniel's heart, Bezaleel's hand. If ever any had, These boldly do I say had he, Who lieth in this bed.

Here then, amid the deep black fat loam into which her ancestors were now resolved, they deposited the body of Mrs. Margaret Bertram; and 'like soldiers returning from a military funeral, the nearest relations who might be interested in the settlements of the lady, urged the dog-cattle of the hackney coaches to all the speed of which they were capable, in order to put an end to further suspense on that interesting topic.

CHAPTER XXXVIII.

Die and endow a college or a cat

Pope

There is a fable told by Lucian, that while a troop of monkeys, well drilled by an intelligent manager, were performing a tragedy with great applause, the decorum of the whole scene was at once destroyed, and the natural passions of the actors called forth into very indecent and active emulation, by a wag who threw a handful of nuts upon the stage. In like manner, the approaching crisis stirred up among the expectants feelings of a nature very different from those, of which, under the superintendence of Mr. Mortcloke, they had but now been endeavouring to imitate the expression. Those eyes which were lately devoutly cast up to heaven, or with greater humility bent solemnly upon earth, were now sharply and alertly darting their glances through shuttles, and trunks, and drawers, and cabinets, and all the odd corners of an old maiden lady's repositories. Nor was their search without interest, though they did not find the will of which they were in quest.

Here was a promissory note for 20L by the minister of the nonjuring chapel. interest marked as paid to Martinmas last, carefully folded up in a new set of words to the old tune of "Over the Water to Charlie".—there, was a curious love correspondence between the deceased and a certain Lieutenant O'Kean of a marching regiment of foot; and tied up with the letters was a document, which at once explained to the relatives why a connection that boded them little good had been suddenly broken off, being the Lieutenant's bond for two hundred pounds upon which no interest whatever appeared to have been paid. Other bills and bonds to a larger amount, and signed by better names (I mean commercially) than those of the worthy divine and gallant soldier, also occurred in the course of their researches, besides a hoard of coins of every size and denomination, and scraps of broken gold and silver, old earrings, hinges of cracked snuff-boxes, mounting of spectacles, etc., etc., etc. Still no will made its appearance, and Colonel Mannering began full well to hope that the settlement which he had obtained from Glossin contained the ultimate arrangement of the old lady's affairs. But his friend Pleydell, who now came into the room, cautioned him against entertaining this belief.

"I am well acquainted with the gentleman," he said, "who is conducting the search, and I guess from his manner that he knows something more of the matter than any of us." Meantime, while the search proceeds, let us take a brief glance at one or two of the company, who seem most interested.

Of Dinmont, who, with his large hunting-whip under his arm, stood poking his great round face over the shoulder of the homme d'affaires, it is unnecessary to say anything. That thin-looking oldish person, in a most correct and gentleman-like suit of mourning is Mac-Casquil, formerly of Drumquag, who was ruined by having a legacy bequeathed to him of two shares in the Ayr bank. His hopes on the present occasion are founded on a very distant relationship, upon his sitting in the same pew with the deceased every Sunday, and upon his playing at cribbage with her regularly on the Saturday evenings—taking great care never to come off a winner. That other coarse-looking man, wearing his own greasy hair tied in a leathern cue more greasy still, is a tobacconist, a relation of Mrs. Bertram's mother, who, having a good stock in trade when the colonial war broke out, trebled the price of his commodity to all the world, Mrs. Bertram alone excepted, whose tortoiseshell snuff-box was weekly filled with the best rappee at the old prices, because the maid brought it to the shop with Mrs. Bertram's respects to her cousin Mr. Quid. That young fellow, who has not had the decency to put off his boots and buckskins, might have stood as forward as most of them in the graces of the old lady, who loved to look upon a comely young man; but it is thought he has forfeited the moment of fortune, by sometimes neglecting her tea-table when solemnly invited; sometimes appearing there, when he had been dining with blither company; twice treading upon her cat's tail, and once affronting her parrot.

To Mannering, the most interesting of the group was the poor girl, who had been a sort of humble companion of the deceased, as a subject upon whom she could at all times expectorate her bad humour. She was for form's sake dragged into the room by the deceased's favourite female attendant, where, shrinking into a corner as soon as possible, she saw with wonder and affright the intrusive researches of the strangers amongst those recesses to which from childhood she had looked with awful veneration. This girl was regarded with an unfavourable eye by, all the competitors, honest Dinmont only excepted; the rest conceived they should find in her a formidable competitor, whose claims might at least encumber and diminish their chance of succession. Yet she was the only person present who seemed really to feel sorrow for the deceased. Mrs. Bertram had been her protectress, although from selfish motives, and her capricious tyranny was forgotten at the moment while the tears followed each other fast down the cheeks of her frightened and friendless dependant. "There's ower muckle saut water there, Drumquag," said the tobacconist to the ex-proprietor, "to bode ither folk muckle gude. Folk seldom greet that gate but they ken what it's for. Mr. MacCasquil only replied with a nod, feeling the propriety of asserting his superior gentry in presence of Mr. Pleydell and Colonel Mannering.

"Very queer if there suld be nae will after a', friend," said Dinmont, who began to grow impatient, to the man of business.

"A moment's patience, it you please—she was a good and prudent woman, Mrs. Margaret Bertram—a good, and prudent and well-judging woman, and knew how to choose friends and depositories—she may have put her last will and testament, or rather her mortis causa settlement, as it relates to heritage, into the hands of some safe friend."

"I'll bet a rump and dozen," said Pleydell, whispering to the Colonel, "he has got it in his own pocket;"—then addressing the man of law, "Come, sir, we'll cut this short if you please-here is a settlement of the estate of Singleside, executed several years ago, in favour of Miss Lucy Bertram of Ellangowan—"The company stared fearfully wild. "You, I presume, Mr. Protocol, can inform us if there is a later deed?"

"Please to favour me, Mr. Pleydell;"—and so saying, he took the deed out of the learned counsel's hand, and glanced his eve over the contents.

"Too cool," said Pleydell, "too cool by half—he has another deed in his pocket still."

"Why does he not show it then, and be d-d to him!" said the military gentleman, whose patience began to wax threadbare.

"Why, how should I know?" answered the barrister,—"why does a cat not kill a mouse when she takes him?—the consciousness of power and the love of teasing, I suppose. —Well, Mr. Protocol, what say you to that deed?"

"Why, Mr. Pleydell, the deed is a well-drawn deed, properly authenticated and tested in forms of the statute."

"But recalled or superseded by another of posterior date in your possession, eh?" said the counsellor.

"Something of the sort, I confess, Mr. Pleydell," rejoined the man of business, producing a bundle tied with tape, and sealed at each fold and ligation with black wax. "That deed, Mr. Pleydell, which you produce and found upon, is dated 1st June 17—; but this"—breaking the seals and unfolding the document slowly—"is dated the 20th—no, I see it is the 21st, of April of this present year, being ten years posterior."

"Marry, hang her, brock!" said the counsellor, borrowing an exclamation from Sir Toby Belch, "just the month in which Ellangowan's distresses became generally public. But let us hear what she has done."

Mr. Protocol accordingly, having required silence, began to read the settlement aloud in a slow, steady, business—like tone. The group around, in whose eyes hope alternately awakened and faded, and who were straining their apprehensions to get at the drift of the testator's meaning through the mist of technical language in which the conveyance had involved it, might have made a study for Hogarth.

The deed was of an unexpected nature. It set forth with conveying and disposing all and whole the estate and lands of Singleside and others, with the lands of Loverless, Liealone, Spinster's Knowe, and heaven knows what beside, "to and in favours of (here the reader softened his voice to a gentle and modest piano) Peter Protocol, clerk to the signet, having the fullest confidence in his capacity and integrity—(these are the very words which my worthy deceased friend insisted upon my inserting)—But in TRUST always" (here the reader recovered his voice and style, and the visages of several of the bearers, which had attained a longitude that Mr. Mortcloke might have envied, were perceptibly shortened), "in TRUST always, and for the uses, ends, and purposes herein after-mentioned."

In these "uses, ends, and purposes," lay the cream of the affair. The first was introduced by a preamble setting forth, that the testatrix was lineally descended from the ancient house of Ellangowan, her respected great-grandfather, Andrew Bertram, first of Singleside, of happy memory, having been second son to Allan Bertram, fifteenth Baron of Ellangowan. It proceeded to state, that Henry Bertram, son and heir of Godfrey Bertram, now of Ellangowan, had been stolen from his parents in infancy, but that she, the testatrix, was well assured that he was yet alive in foreign parts, and by the providence of heaven would be restored to the possessions of his ancestors—in which case the said Peter Protocol was bound and obliged, like as he bound and obliged himself, by acceptance of these presents, to denude himself of the said lands of Singleside and others, and of all the other effects thereby conveyed (excepting always a proper gratification for his own trouble) to and in favour of the said Henry Bertram upon his return to his native country. And during the time of his residing in foreign parts, or in case of his never again returning to Scotland, Mr. Peter Protocol, the trustee, was directed to distribute the rents of the land, and the interest of the other funds (deducting always a proper gratification for his trouble in the premises), in equal portions, among four charitable establishments pointed out in the will. The power of management, of letting leases, of raising and lending out money, in short, the full authority of a proprietor, was vested in this confidential trustee, and, in the event of, his death, went to certain official persons named in the deed. There were only two legacies; one of a hundred pounds to a favourite waiting-maid, another of the like sum to Janet Gibson (whom the deed stated to have been supported by the charity of the testatrix) for the purpose of binding her an apprentice to some honest trade.

A settlement in mortmain is in Scotland termed a mortification, and in one great borough (Aberdeen, if I remember rightly) there is a municipal officer who takes care of these public endowments, and is thence called the Master of Mortifications. One would almost presume that the term had its origin in the effect which such settlements usually produce upon the kinsmen of those by whom they are executed. Heavy at least was the mortification which befell the audience, who, in the late Mrs. Margaret Bertram's parlour, had listened to this unexpected destination of the lands of Singleside. There was a profound silence after the deed had been read over.

Mr. Pleydell was the first to speak. He begged to look at the deed, and having satisfied himself that it was correctly drawn and executed, he returned it without any observation, only saying aside to Mannering, "Protocol is not worse than other people, I believe; but this old lady has determined that, if he do not turn rogue, it shall not be for want of temptation."

"I really think," said Mr. Mac-Casquil of Drumquag, who, having gulped down one half of his vexation, determined to give vent to the rest, "I really think this is an extraordinary case! I should like now to know from Mr. Protocol, who, being sole and unlimited trustee, must have been consulted upon this occasion; I should like, I say, to know, how Mrs. Bertram could possibly believe in the existence of a boy, that a' the world kens was murdered many a year since?"

"Really, sir," said Mr. Protocol, "I do not conceive it is possible for me to explain her motives more than she has done herself. Our excellent deceased friend was a good woman, sir—a pious woman—and might have grounds for confidence in the boy's safety which are not accessible to us, sir."

"Hout," said the tobacconist, "I ken very weel what were her grounds for confidence. There's Mrs. Rebecca (the maid) sitting there, has tell'd me a hundred times in my ain shop, there was nae kenning how her leddy wad settle her affairs, for an auld gipsy witch wife at Gilsland had possessed her with a notion, that the callant—Harry Bertram ca's she him?—would come alive again some day after a'—ye'll no deny that, Mrs. Rebecca?—though I dare to say ye forgot to put your mistress in mind of what ye promised to say when I gied ye mony a half-crown—But ye'll no deny what I am saying now, lass?"

"I ken naething at a' about it," answered Rebecca doggedly, and looking straight forward with the firm countenance of one not disposed to be compelled to remember more than was agreeable to her.

"Weel said, Rebecca! ye're satisfied wi' your ain share ony way," rejoined the tobacconist.

The buck of the second-head, for a buck of the first-head he was not, had hitherto been slapping his boots with his switch-whip, and looking like a spoiled child that has lost its supper. His murmurs, however, were all vented inwardly, or at most in a soliloquy such as this—"I am sorry, by G-d, I ever plagued myself about her—I came here, by G-d, one night to drink tea, and I left King, and the Duke's rider, Will Hack. They were toasting a round of running horses; by G-d, I might have got leave to wear the jacket as well as other folk, if I had carried it on with them— and she has not so much as left me that hundred!"

"We'll make the payment of the note quite agreeable," said Mr. Protocol, who had no wish to increase at that moment the odium attached to his office—"and now, gentlemen, I fancy we have no more to wait for here, and—I shall put the settlement of my excellent and worthy friend on record to-morrow, that every gentleman may examine the contents, and have free access to take an extract; and"—he proceeded to lock up the repositories of the deceased with more speed than he had opened them—"Mrs. Rebecca, ye'll be so kind as to keep all right here until we can let the house—I had an offer from a tenant this morning, if such a thing should be, and if I was to have any management."

Our friend Dinmont, having had his hopes as well as another, had hitherto sat sulky enough in the armchair formerly appropriated to the deceased, and in which she would have been not a little scandalised to have seen this colossal specimen of the masculine gender lolling at length. His employment had been rolling up, into the form of a coiled snake, the long lash of his horsewhip, and then by a jerk causing it to unroll itself into the middle of the floor. The first words he said when he had digested the shock, contained a magnanimous declaration, which he probably was not conscious of having uttered aloud—"Weel-blude's thicker than water—she's welcome to the cheeses and the hams just the same." But when the trustee had made the above-mentioned motion for the mourners to depart, and talked of the house being immediately let, honest Dinmont got upon his feet, and stunned the company with this blunt question, "And what's to come o' this poor lassie then, Jenny Gibson? Sae mony o' us as thought oursells sib to the family when the gear was parting, we may do something for her amang us surely."

This proposal seemed to dispose most of the assembly instantly to evacuate the premises, although upon Mr. Protcol's motion they had lingered as if around the grave of their disappointed hopes. Drumquag said, or rather muttered, something of having a family of his own, and took precedence, in virtue of his gentle blood, to depart as fast as possible. The tobacconist sturdily stood forward, and scouted the motion—"A little huzzie, like that, was weel eneugh provided for already; and Mr. Protocol at ony rate was the proper person to take direction of her, as he had charge of her legacy;" and after uttering such his opinion in a steady and decisive tone of voice, he also left the place. The buck made a stupid and brutal attempt at a jest upon Mrs. Bertram's recommendation that the poor girl should be taught some honest trade; but encountered a scowl from Colonel Mannering's darkening eye (to whom, in his ignorance of the tone of good society, he had looked for applause) that made him ache to the very backbone. He shuffled downstairs, therefore, as fast as possible.

Protocol, who was really a good sort of man, next expressed his intention to take a temporary charge of the young lady, under protest always, that his so doing should be considered as merely eleemosynary; when Dinmont at length got up, and, having shaken his huge dreadnought greatcoat, as a Newfoundland dog does his shaggy hide when he comes out of the water, ejaculated, "Weel, deil hae me then, if ye hae ony fash [*Trouble] wi' her, Mr. Protocol, if she likes to gang hame wi' me, that is. Ye see, Ailie and me we're weel to pass, and we would like the lassies to hae a wee bit mair lair than oursells, and to be neighbour-like—that wad we. —And ye see Jenny canna miss but to ken manners, and the like o' reading books, and sewing seams—having lived sae lang wi' a grand lady like Lady Singleside; or if she disna ken onything about it, I'm jealous that our bairns will like her a' the better. And I'll take care o' the bits o' claes, and what spending siller she maun hae, so the—hundred pound may rin on in your hands, Mr. Protocol, and I'll be adding something till't, till she'll maybe get a Liddesdale joe that wants something to help to buy the hirsel. [*The stock of sheep]—What d'ye say to that, hinny? I'll take out a ticket for ye in the fly to Jethart—odd, but ye maun take a powny after that o'er the Limestane-rig—deil a wheeled carriage ever gaed into Liddesdale. [*The roads of Liddesdale, in Dandie Dinmont's days, could not he said to exist, and the district was only accessible through a succession of tremendous morasses. About thirty years ago, the author himself was the first person who ever drove a little open carriage into these wilds: the excellent roads by which they are now traversed being then in some progress. The people stared with no small wonder at a sight which many of them had never witnessed in their lives before.]—And I'll be very glad if Mrs. Rebecca comes wi' you, hinny, and stays a month or twa while ye're stranger like."

While Mrs. Rebecca was curtseying, and endeavouring to make the poor orphan girl curtsey instead of crying, and while Dandie, in his rough way, was encouraging them both, old Pleydell had recourse to his snuff-box. It's meat and drink to me, now, Colonel," he said, as he recovered himself, "to see a clown like this—I must gratify him in his own way,—must assist him to ruin himself—there's no help for it. Here, you Liddesdale—Dandie—Charlies-hope-what do they call you?"

The farmer turned, infinitely gratified even by this sort of notice; for in his heart, next to his own landlord, he honoured a lawyer in high practice.

"So you will not be advised against trying that question about your marches?"

"No—no, sir—naebody likes to lose their right, and to be laughed at down the haill water. But since your honour's no agreeable, and is maybe a friend to the other side like, we maun try some other advocate."

"There—I told you so, Colonel Mannering!—Well, sir, if you must needs be a fool, the business is to give you the luxury of a lawsuit at the least possible expense, and to bring you off conqueror if possible. Let Mr. Protocol send me your papers, and I will advise him how to conduct your cause. I don't see, after all, why you should not have your lawsuits too, and your feuds in the Court of Session, as well as your forefathers had their manslaughters and fire-raisings."

"Very natural, to be sure, sir. We wad just take the auld gate as readily, if it werena for the law. And as the law binds us, the law should loose us. Besides, a, man's aye the better thought o' in out country for having been afore the Feifteen."

"Excellently argued, my friend! Away with you, and send your papers to me.—Come, Colonel, we have no more to do here."

"God, we'll ding [*Defeat] Jock o' Dawston Cleugh now after a'!" said Dinmont, slapping his thigh in great exultation.

CHAPTER XXXIX.

—I am going to the parliament;

You understand this bag: If you have any business Depending there, be short, and let me hear it, And pay your fees. Little French Lawyer.

"SHALL you be able to carry this honest fellow's cause for him?" said Mannering.

"Why, I don't know; the battle is not to the strong, but he shall come off triumphant over Jock of Dawston if we can make it out. I owe him something. It is the pest of our profession that we seldom see the best side of human nature. People come to us with every selfish feeling newly pointed and grinded; they turn down the very caulkers of their animosities and prejudices, as smiths do with horses' shoes in a white frost. Many a man has come to my garret Yonder, that I have at first longed to pitch out at the window, and yet, at length, have discovered that he was only doing as I might have done in his case, being very angry, and, of course, very unreasonable. I have now satisfied myself, that if our profession sees more of human folly and human roguery than others, it is because we witness them acting in that channel in which they can most freely vent themselves. In civilised society, law is the chimney through which all that smoke discharges itself that used to circulate through the whole house, and put every one's eyes out—no wonder, therefore, that the vent itself should sometimes get a little sooty. But we will take care our Liddesdale-man's cause is well conducted and well argued, so all unnecessary expense will be saved—he shall have his pineapple at wholesale price."

"Will you do me the pleasure," said Mannering, as they parted, "to dine with me at my lodgings? my landlord says he has a bit of red-deer venison, and some excellent wine."

"Venison—eh?" answered the counsellor alertly, but presently added—"But no! it's impossible—and I can't ask you home neither. Monday's a sacred day—so's Tuesday—and Wednesday, we are to be heard in the great teind case in presence—but stay—it's frosty weather, and if you don't leave town, and that venison would keep till Thursday—"

"You will dine with me that day?"

"Under certification."

"Well, then, I will indulge a thought I had of spending a week here; and if the venison will not keep, why, we will see what else our landlord can do for us."

"Oh, the venison will keep," said Pleydell; "and now good-bye—look at these two or three notes, and deliver them if you like the addresses. I wrote them for you this morning—farewell; my clerk has been waiting this hour to begin a d-d information."—And away walked Mr. Pleydell with great activity, diving through closes and ascending covered stairs, in order to attain the High Street by an access, which, compared to the common route, was what the Straits of Magellan are to the more open, but circuitous passage round Cape Horn.

On looking at the notes of introduction which Pleydell had thrust into his hand, Mannering was gratified with seeing that they were addressed to some of the first literary characters of Scotland. "To David Hume, Esq." "To John Home, Esq." "To Dr. Ferguson." "To Dr. Black." "To Lord Kaimes." "To Mr. Hutton." "To John Clerk, Esq., of Eldin." "To Adam Smith, Esq." "To Dr. Robertson."

"Upon my word, my legal friend has a good selection of acquaintances—these are names pretty widely blown indeed—an East-Indian must rub up his faculties a little, and put his mind in order, before he enters this sort of society."

Mannering gladly availed himself of these introductions; and we regret deeply it is not in our power to give the reader an account of the pleasure and information which he received, in admission to a circle never closed against strangers of sense and information, and which has perhaps at no period been equalled, considering the depth and variety of talent which it embraced and concentrated.

Upon the Thursday appointed, Mr. Pleydell made his appearance at the inn where Colonel Mannering lodged. The venison proved in high order, the claret excellent, and the learned counsel, a professed amateur in the affairs of the table, did distinguished honour to both. I am uncertain, however, if even the good cheer gave him more satisfaction than the presence of Dominie Sampson, from whom, in his own juridical style of wit, he contrived to extract great amusement, both for himself and one or two friends whom the Colonel regaled on the same occasion. The grave and laconic simplicity of Sampson's answers to the insidious questions of the barrister, placed the bonhomie of his character in a more luminous point of view than Mannering had yet seen it. Upon the same occasion he drew forth a strange quantity of miscellaneous and abstruse, though, generally speaking, useless learning. The lawyer afterwards compared his mind to the magazine of a pawnbroker, stowed with goods of every description, but so cumbrously piled together, and in such total disorganisation, that the owner can never lay his hands upon any one article at the moment he has occasion for it.

As for the advocate himself, he afforded at least as much exercise to Sampson as he extracted amusement from him. When the man of law began to get into his altitudes, and his wit, naturally shrewd and dry, became more lively and poignant, the Dominie looked upon him with that sort of surprise with which we can conceive a tame bear might regard his future associate, the monkey, on their being first introduced to each other. It was Mr. Pleydell's delight to state in grave and serious argument some position which he knew the Dominie would be inclined to dispute. He then beheld with exquisite pleasure the internal labour with which the honest man arranged his ideas for reply, and tasked his inert and sluggish powers to bring up all the heavy artillery of his learning for demolishing the schismatic or heretical opinion which had been stated—when, behold, before the ordnance could be discharged, the foe had quitted the post, and appeared in a new position of annoyance on the Dominie's flank or rear. Often did he exclaim "Prodigious!" when, marching up to the enemy in full confidence of victory, he found the field evacuated, and it may be supposed that it cost him no little labour to attempt a new formation. "He was like a native Indian army," the Colonel said, "formidable by numerical strength and size of ordnance, but liable to be thrown into irreparable confusion by a movement to take them in flank."—On the whole, however, the Dominie, though somewhat fatigued with these mental exertions, made at unusual speed and upon the pressure of the moment, reckoned this one of the white days of his life, and always mentioned Mr. Pleydell as a very erudite and fa-ce-ti-ous person.

By degrees the rest of the party dropped off, and left these three gentlemen together. Their conversation turned to Mrs. Bertram's settlements. "Now what could drive it into the noddle of that old harridan," said Pleydell, "to disinherit poor Lucy Bertram, under pretence of settling her property on a boy who has been so long dead and gone?—I ask your pardon, Mr. Sampson, I forgot what an affecting case this was for you—I remember taking your examination upon it—and I never had so much trouble to make any one speak three words consecutively—You may talk of your Pythagoreans, or your silent Brahmins, Colonel,—go to, I tell you this learned gentleman beats them all in taciturnity—but the words of the wise are precious, and not to be thrown away lightly."

"Of a surety," said the Dominie, taking his blue-checked handkerchief from his eyes, "that was a bitter day with me indeed; ay, and a day of grief hard to be borne—but He giveth strength who layeth on the load."

Colonel Mannering took this opportunity to request Mr. Pleydell to inform him of the particulars attending the loss of the boy; and the counsellor, who was fond of talking upon subjects of criminal jurisprudence, especially when connected with his own experience, went through the circumstances at full length. "And what is your opinion upon the result of the whole?"

"Oh, that Kennedy was murdered: it's an old case which has occurred on that coast before now—the case of Smuggler versus Exciseman."

"What then is your conjecture concerning the fate of the child?

"Oh, murdered too, doubtless," answered Pleydell. "He was old enough to tell what he had seen, and these ruthless scoundrels would not scruple committing a second Bethlehem massacre if they thought their interest required it."

The Dominie groaned deeply, and ejaculated, "Enormous!"

"'Yet there was mention of gipsies in the business too, counsellor," said Mannering, "and from what that vulgar-looking fellow said after the funeral—"

"Mrs. Margaret Bertram's idea that the child was alive was founded upon the report of a gipsy," said Pleydell, catching at the half-spoken hint—"I envy you the concatenation, Colonel—it is a shame to me not to have drawn the same conclusion. We'll follow this business tip instantly—Here, hark ye, waiter, go down to Luckie Wood's in the Cowgate; ye'll find my clerk Driver; he'll be set down to High-jinks by this time (for we and our retainers, Colonel, are exceedingly regular in our irregularities); tell him to come here instantly, and I will pay his forfeits."

"He won't appear in character, will he?" said Mannering.

"Ah! no more of that, Hal, an thou lovest me," said Pleydell. "But we must have some news from the land of Egypt, if possible. Oh, if I had but hold of the slightest thread of this complicated skein, you should see how I would unravel it!—I would work the truth out of your Bohemian, as the French call them, better than a Monitoire, or a Plainte de Tournelle; I know how to manage a refractory witness."

While Mr. Pleydell was thus vaunting his knowledge of his profession, the waiter re-entered with Mr. Driver, his mouth still greasy with mutton pies, and the froth of the last draught of twopenny yet unsubsided on his upper lip, with such speed had he obeyed the commands of his principal.—"Driver, you must go instantly and find out the woman who was old Mrs. Margaret Bertram's maid. Inquire for her everywhere, but if you find it necessary to have recourse to Protocol, Quid the tobacconist, or any other of these folks, you will take care not to appear yourself, but send some woman of your acquaintance—I dare say you know enough that may be so condescending as to oblige you. When you have found her out, engage her to come to my chambers to-morrow at eight o'clock precisely."

"What shall I say to make her forthcoming?" asked the aide-de-camp.

"Anything you choose," replied the lawyer. "Is it my business to make lies for you, do you think? But let her be in praesentia by eight o'clock, as I have said before." The clerk grinned, made his reverence, and exit.

"That's a useful fellow," said the counsellor "I don't believe his match ever carried a process. He'll write to my dictating three nights in the week without sleep, or, what's the same thing, he writes as well and correctly when he's asleep as when he's awake. Then he's such a steady fellow—some of them are always changing their alehouses, so that they have twenty cadies sweating after them, like the bare-headed captains traversing the taverns of East-Cheap in search of Sir John Falstaff. But this is a complete fixture-he has his winter seat by the fire, and his summer seat by the window, in Luckie Wood's, betwixt which seats are his only migrations; there he's to be found at all times when he is off duty. It is my opinion he never puts off his clothes or goes to sleep—sheer ale supports him under everything. It is meat, drink, and clothing, bed, board, and washing."

"And is he always fit for duty upon a sudden turn-out? I should distrust it, considering his quarters."

"Oh, s drink never disturbs him, Colonel; he can write for hours after he cannot speak. I remember being called suddenly to draw an appeal case. I had been dining, and it was Saturday night, and I had ill will to begin to it—however, they got me down to Clerihugh's, and there we sat birling till I had a fair tappit hen, [*See Note VI. Tappit Hen.] under my belt, and then they persuaded me to draw the paper. Then we had to seek Driver, and it was all that two men could do to bear him in, for, when found, he was, as it happened, both motionless and speechless. But no sooner was his pen put between his fingers, his paper stretched before him, and he heard my voice, than he began to write like a scrivener—and, excepting that we were obliged to have somebody to dip his pen in the ink, for he could not see the standish, I never saw a thing scrolled more handsomely."

"But how did your joint production look the next morning?" said the
Colonel.

"Wheugh! capital—not three words required to be altered; [* See Note VII. Convivial Habits of the Scottish Bar.] it was sent off by that day's post. But you'll come and breakfast with me to-morrow, and hear this woman's examination?"

"Why, your hour is rather early."

"Can't make it later. If I were not on the boards of the Outer House precisely as the nine-hours bell rings, there would be a report that I had got an apoplexy, and I should feel the effects of it all the rest of the session."

"Well, I will make an exertion to wait upon you."

Here the company broke up for the evening.

In the morning Colonel Mannering appeared at the counsellor's chambers, although cursing the raw air of a Scottish morning in December. Mr. Pleydell had got Mrs. Rebecca installed on one side of his fire, accommodated her with a cup of chocolate, and was already deeply engaged in conversation with her. "Oh no, I assure you, Mrs. Rebecca, there is no intention to challenge your mistress's will; and I give you my word of honour that your legacy is quite safe. You have deserved it by your conduct to your mistress, and I wish it had been twice as much."

"Why, to be sure, sir, it's no right to mention what is said before ane—ye heard how that dirty body Quid cast up to me the bits o' compliments he gied me, and tell'd owre again ony loose cracks [*Gossip] I might hae had wi' him; now if ane was talking loosely to your honour, there's nae saying what might come o't."

"I assure you, my good Rebecca, my character and your own age and appearance are your security, if you should talk as loosely as an amatory poet."

"Aweel, if your honour thinks I am safe-the story is just this.—Ye see, about a year ago, or no just sae lang, my leddy was advised to go to Gilsland for a while for her spirits were distressing her sair. Ellangowan's troubles began to be spoken o' publicly, and sair vexed she was—or she was proud o' her family. For Ellangowan himsell and her, they sometimes 'greed, and sometimes no—but at last they didna 'gree at a' for twa or three year—for he was aye wanting to borrow siller, and that was what she couldna bide at no hand, and she was aye wanting it paid back again, and that the Laird he liked as little. So, at last, they were clean aff thegither. And then some of the company at Gilsland tells her that the estate was to be sell'd; and ye wad hae thought she had taen an ill will at Miss Lucy Bertram frae that moment, for mony a time she cried to me, 'O Becky, O Becky, if that useless peenging thing o' a lassie there, at Ellangowan, that canna keep her ne'er-do-weel father within bounds—if she had been but a lad-bairn, they couldna hae sell'd the auld inheritance for that fool-body's debt;'—and she would rin on that way till I was just wearied and sick to hear her ban the puir lassie, as if she wadna hae been a lad-bairn, and keepit the land, if it had been in her will to change her sect. And ae day at the spae-well below the craig at Gilsland, she was seeing a very bonny family o' bairns—they belonged to ane MacCrosky—and she broke out—'Is not it an odd like thing that ilka waf carlfe [*Every insignificant churl] in the country has a son and heir, and that the house of Ellangowan is without male succession?' There was a gipsy wife stood ahint and heard her—a muckle sture [*Strong] fearsome-looking wife she was as ever I set een on.—'Wha is it,' says she, 'that dare say the house of Ellangowan will perish without male succession?' My mistress just turned on her—she was a high-spirited woman, and aye ready wi' an answer to a' body. 'It's me that says it,' says she, 'that may say it with a sad heart.' Wi' that the gipsy wife gripped till her hand; 'I ken you weel eneugh,' said she, 'though ye kenna me—But as sure as that sun's in heaven, and as sure as that water's rinning to the sea, and as sure as there's an ee that sees, and an ear that hears us baith—Harry Bertram, that was thought to perish at Warroch Point, never did die there—he was to have a weary weird [*Cruel fate] o't till his ane-an-twentieth year, that was aye said o' him—but if ye live and I live, ye'll hear mair o' him this winter before the snaw lies twa days on the Dun of Singleside—I want nane o' your siller,' she said, 'to make ye think I am blearing [*Moistening] your ee—fare ye weel till after Martimas;'—and there she left us standing."

"Was she a very tall woman?" interrupted Mannering.

"Had she black hair, black eyes, and a cut above the brow?" added the lawyer.

"She was the tallest woman I ever saw, and her hair was as black as midnight, unless where it was gray, and she had a scar abune the brow, that ye might hae laid the lith [*joint] of your finger in. Naebody that's seen her will ever forget her; and I am morally sure that it was on the ground o' what that gipsy-woman said that my mistress made her will, having taen a dislike at the young leddy o' Ellangowan, and she liked her far waur after she was obliged to send her 20L—for she said, Miss Bertram, no content wi' letting the Ellangowan property pass into strange hands, owing to her being a lass and no a lad, was coming, by her poverty, to be a burden and a disgrace to Singleside too.—But I hope my mistress's is a good will for a' that, for it would be hard an me to lose the wee bit legacy—I served for little fee and bountith, weel I wot."

The counsellor relieved her fears on this head, then inquired after Jenny Gibson, and understood she had accepted Mr. Dinmont's offer; "and I have done sae mysell too, since he was sae discreet as to ask me," said Mrs. Rebecca; they are very decent folk the Dinmonts, though my lady didna dow to hear muckle about the friends on that side the house. But she liked the Charlies-hope hams, and the cheeses, and the muir-fowl, that they were aye sending, and the lamb's-wool hose and mittens—she liked them weel eneugh."

Mr. Pleydell now dismissed Mrs. Rebecca. When she was gone, "I think I know the gipsy woman," said the lawyer.

"I was just going to say the same," replied Mannering.

"And her name—" said Pleydell.

"Is Meg Merrilies," answered the Colonel.

"Are you avised of that?" said the counsellor, looking at his military friend with a comic expression of surprise.

Mannering answered that he had known such a woman when he was at Ellangowan upwards of twenty years before; and then made his learned friend acquainted with all the remarkable particulars of his first visit there.

Mr. Pleydell listened with great attention, and then replied, "I congratulated myself upon having made the acquaintance of a profound theologian in your chaplain; but I really did not expect to find a pupil of Albumazar or Messabala in his patron. I have a notion, however, this gipsy could tell us some more of the matter than she derives from astrology or second-sight—I had her through hands once, and could then make little of her, but I must write to Mac-Morlan to stir heaven and earth to find her out. I will gladly come to—shire myself to assist at her examination—I am still in the commission of the peace there, though I have ceased to be Sheriff—I never had anything more at heart in my life than tracing that murder, and the fate of the child. I must write to the Sheriff of Roxburghshire too, and to an active justice of peace in Cumberland."

"I hope when you come to the country you will make Woodbourne your headquarters?"

"Certainly; I was afraid you were going to forbid me—but we must go to breakfast now, or I shall be too late."

On the following day the new friends parted, And the Colonel rejoined his family without any adventure worthy of being detailed in these chapters.

CHAPTER XL.

Can no rest find me, no private place secure me, But still
my miseries like bloodhounds haunt me? Unfortunate young
man, which way now guides thee, Guides thee from death? The
country's laid around for thee.

Women Pleased.

Our narrative now recalls us for a moment to the period when young Hazlewood received his wound. That accident had no sooner happened, than the consequences to Miss Mannering and to himself rushed upon Brown's mind. From the manner in which the muzzle of the piece was pointed when it went off, he had no great fear that the consequences would be fatal. But an arrest in a strange country, and while he was unprovided with any means of establishing his rank and character, was at least to be avoided. He therefore resolved to escape for the present to the neighbouring coast of England, and to remain concealed there, if possible, until he should receive letters from his regimental, friends, and remittances from his agent; and then to resume his own character, and offer to young Hazlewood and his friends any explanation or satisfaction they might desire. With this purpose he walked stoutly forward, after leaving the spot where the accident had happened, and reached without adventure the village which we have called Portanferry (but which the reader will in vain seek for under that name in the county map). A large open boat was just about to leave the quay, bound for the little seaport of Allonby, in Cumberland. In this vessel Brown embarked, and resolved to make that place his temporary abode, until he should receive letters and money from England.

In the course of their short voyage he entered into some conversation with the steersman, who was also owner of the boat, a jolly old man, who had occasionally been engaged in the smuggling trade, like most fishers on the coast. After talking about objects of less interest, Brown endeavoured to turn the discourse toward the Mannering family. The sailor had heard of the attack upon the house at Woodbourne, but disapproved of the smugglers' proceedings.

"Hands off is fair play; zounds, they'll bring the whole country down upon them—na, na! when I was in that way I played at giff-gaff [*Give and take] with the officers—here a cargo taen—vera weel, that was their luck;—there another carried clean through, that was mine,—na, na! hawks shouldna pike out hawks' een."

"And this Colonel Mannering?" said Brown.

"Troth, he's nae wise man neither, to interfere—no that I blame him for saving the gaugers' lives—that was very right; but it wasna like a gentleman to be fighting about the poor folk's pocks o' tea and brandy kegs—however, he's a grand man and an officer man, and they do what they like wi' the like o' us."

"And his daughter," said Brown, with a throbbing heart, "is going to be married into a great family too, as I have heard?"

"What, into the Hazlewoods'?" said the pilot. "Na, na, that's but idle clashes-every Sabbath day, as regularly as it came round, did the young man ride hame wi' the daughter of the late Ellangowan—and my daughter Peggy's in the service up at Woodbourne, and she says she's sure young Hazlewood thinks nae mair of Miss Mannering than you do."

Bitterly censuring his own precipitate adoption of a contrary belief, Brown yet heard with delight that the suspicions of Julia's fidelity, upon which he had so rashly acted, were probably void of foundation. How must he in the meantime be suffering in her opinion? or what could she suppose of conduct, which must have made him appear to her regardless alike of her peace of mind, and of the interests of their affection? The old man's connection with the family at Woodbourne seemed to offer a safe mode of communication, of which he determined to avail himself.

"Your daughter is a maid-servant at Woodbourne?—I knew Miss Mannering in India, and though I am at present in an inferior rank of life, I have great reason to hope she would interest herself in my favour. I had a quarrel unfortunately with her father, who was my commanding officer, and I am sure the young lady would endeavour to reconcile him to me. Perhaps your daughter could deliver a letter to her upon she subject, without making mischief between her father and her?"

The old man, a friend to smuggling of every kind, readily answered for the letter's being faithfully and secretly delivered; and, accordingly, as soon as they arrived at Allonby, Brown wrote to Miss Mannering, stating the utmost contrition for what had happened through his rashness, and conjuring her to let him have an opportunity of pleading his own cause, and obtaining forgiveness for his indiscretion. He did not judge it safe to go into any detail concerning the circumstances by which he had been misled, and upon the whole endeavoured to express himself with such ambiguity, that if the letter should fall into wrong hands, it would be difficult either to understand its real purport, or to trace the writer. This letter the old man undertook faithfully to deliver to his daughter at Woodbourne: and, as his trade would speedily again bring him or his boat to Allonby, he promised further to take charge of any answer with which the young lady might entrust him.

And now our persecuted traveller landed at Allonby, and sought for such accommodations as might at once suit his temporary poverty, and his desire of remaining as much unobserved as possible. With this view he assumed the name and profession of his friend Dudley, having command enough of the pencil to verify his pretended character to his host of Allonby. His baggage he pretended to expect front Wigton; and keeping himself as much within doors as possible, awaited the return of the letters which he had sent to his agent, to Delaserre, and to his Lieutenant-Colonel. From the first he requested a supply of money; he conjured Delaserre, if possible, to join him in Scotland; and from the Lieutenant-Colonel he required such testimony of his rank and conduct in the regiment as should place his character as a gentleman and officer beyond the power of question. The inconvenience of being run short in his finances struck him so strongly, that he wrote to Dinmont on that subject, requesting a small temporary loan, having no doubt that, being within sixty or seventy miles of his residence, he should receive a speedy as well as favourable answer to his request of pecuniary accommodation, which was owing, as he stated, to his having been robbed after their parting. And then, with impatience enough, though without any serious apprehension, he waited the answers of these various letters.

It must be observed, in excuse of his correspondents, that the post was then much more tardy than since Mr. Palmer's ingenious invention has taken place; and with respect to honest Dinmont in particular, as he rarely received above one letter a quarter (unless during the time of his being engaged in a lawsuit, when he regularly sent to the post-town), his correspondence usually remained for a month or two sticking in the postmaster's window, among pamphlets, gingerbread, rolls, or ballads, according to the trade which the said postmaster exercised. Besides, there was then a custom, not yet wholly obsolete, of causing a letter, from one town to another, perhaps within the distance of thirty miles, perform a circuit of two hundred miles before delivery; which had the combined advantage of airing the epistle thoroughly, of adding some pence to the revenue of the post-office, and of exercising the patience of the correspondents. Owing to these circumstances, Brown remained several days in Allonby without any answers whatever, and his stock of money, though husbanded with the utmost economy, began to wear very low, when he received, by the hands of a young fisherman, the following letter—

"You have acted with the most cruel indiscretion, you have shown how little I can trust to your declarations that my peace and happiness are dear to you; and your rashness has nearly occasioned the death of a young man of the highest worth and honour. Must I say more?—must I add, that I have been myself ill in consequence of your violence and its effects? And, alas! need I say still further, that I have thought anxiously upon them as they are likely to affect you, although you have given me such slight cause to do so? The C. is gone from home for several days; Mr. H. is almost quite recovered; and I have reason to think that the blame is laid in a quarter different from that where it is deserved. Yet do not think of venturing here. Our fate has been crossed by accidents of a nature too violent and terrible to permit me to think of renewing a correspondence which has so often threatened the most dreadful catastrophe. Farewell, therefore, and believe that no one can wish your happiness more sincerely than J. M."

This letter contained that species of advice, which is frequently given for the precise purpose that it may lead to a directly opposite conduct from that which it recommends. At least so thought Brown, who immediately asked the young fisherman if he came from Portanferry.

"Ay," said the lad; "I am auld Willie Johnstone's son, and I got that letter frae my sister Peggy, that's laundry-maid at Woodbourne."

"My good friend, when do you sail?"

"With the tide this evening."

"I'll return with you; but as I do not desire to go to Portanferry,
I wish you could put me on shore somewhere on the coast."

"We can easily do that," said the lad.

Although the price of provisions, etc., was then very moderate, the discharging his lodgings, and the expense of his living, together with that of a change of dress, which safety as well as a proper regard to his external appearance rendered necessary, brought Brown's purse to a very low ebb. He left directions at the post-office that his letters should be forwarded to Kippletringan, whither he resolved to proceed, and reclaim the treasure which he had deposited in the hands of Mrs. Mac-Candlish. He also felt it would be his duty to assume his proper character as soon as he should receive the necessary evidence for supporting it, and, as an officer in the king's service, give and receive every explanation which might be necessary with young Hazlewood. If he is not very wrong-headed indeed, he thought, he must allow the manner in which I acted to have been the necessary consequence of his own overbearing conduct.

And now we must suppose him once more embarked on the Solway frith. The wind was adverse, attended by some rain, and they struggled against it without much assistance from the tide. The boat was heavily laden with goods (part of which were probably contraband), and laboured deep in the sea. Brown, who had been bred a sailor, and was indeed skilled in most athletic exercises, gave his powerful and effectual assistance in rowing, or occasionally in steering the boat, and his advice in the management, which became the more delicate as the wind increased, and, being opposed to the very rapid tides of that coast, made the voyage perilous. At length, after spending the whole night upon the frith, they were at morning within sight of a beautiful bay upon the Scottish coast. The weather was now more mild. The snow, which had been for some time waning, had given way entirely under the fresh gale of the preceding night. The more distant hills, indeed, retained their snowy mantle, but all the open country was cleared, unless where a few white patches indicated that it had been drifted to an uncommon depth. Even under its wintry appearance, the shore was highly interesting. The line of sea-coast, with all its varied curves, indentures, and embayments, swept away from the sight on either hand, in that varied, intricate, yet graceful and easy line, which the eye loves so well to pursue. And it was no less relieved and varied in elevation than in outline by the different forms of the shore; the beach in some places being edged by steep rocks, and in others rising smoothly from the sands in easy and swelling slopes. Buildings of different kinds caught and reflected the wintry sunbeams of a December morning, and the woods, though now leafless, gave relief and variety to the landscape. Brown felt that lively and awakening interest which taste and sensibility always derive from the beauties of nature, when opening suddenly to the eye, after the dulness and gloom of a night voyage. Perhaps,—for who can presume to analyse that inexplicable feeling which binds the person born in a mountainous country to his native hills,—perhaps some early associations, retaining their effect long after the cause was forgotten, mingled in the feelings of pleasure with which he regarded the scene before him.

"And what," said Brown to the boatman, "is the name of that fine cape, that stretches into the sea with its sloping banks and hillocks of wood, and forms the right side of the bay?"

"Warroch Point," answered the lad.

"And that old castle, my friend, with the modern house situated just beneath it? It seems at this distance a very large building."

"That's the Auld Place, sir; and that's the New Place below it.
We'll land you there if you like."

"I should like it of all things. I must visit that ruin before I continue my journey."

"Ay, it's a queer auld bit," said the fisherman and that highest tower is a gude landmark as far as Ramsay in Man, and the Point of Ayr—there was muckle fighting about the place lang syne."

Brown would have inquired into further particulars, but a fisherman is seldom an antiquary. His boatman's local knowledge was summed up in the information already given, "that it was a grand landmark, and that there had been muckle fighting about the bit lang syne."

"I shall learn more of it," said Brown to himself, "when I get ashore."

The boat continued its course close under the point upon which the castle was situated, which frowned from the summit of its rocky site upon the still agitated waves of the bay beneath. "I believe," said the steersman, "ye'll get ashore here as dry as ony gate. [*Any place] There's a place where their berlins and galleys, as they ca'd them, used to lie in lang syne, but it's no used now, because it's ill carrying gudes up the narrow stairs, or ower the rocks. Whiles of a moon-light night I have landed articles there, though."

While he thus spoke, they pulled round a point of rock, and found a very small harbour, partly formed by nature, partly by the indefatigable labour of the ancient inhabitants of the castle, who, as the fisherman observed, had found it essential for the protection of their boats and small craft, thou-h it could not receive vessels of any burden. The two points of rock which formed the access approached each other so nearly, that only one boat could enter at a time-. On each side were still remaining two immense iron rings, deeply morticed into the solid rock. Through these, according to tradition, there was nightly drawn a huge chain, secured by an immense padlock, for the protection of the haven, and the armada which it contained. A ledge of rock had, by the assistance of the chisel and pick-axe, been formed into a sort of quay. The rock was of extremely hard consistence, and the task so difficult, that, according to the fisherman, a labourer who wrought at the work might in the evening have carried home in his bonnet all the shivers which he had struck from the mass in the course of the day. This little quay communicated with a rude staircase, already repeatedly mentioned, which descended from the old castle. There was also a communication between the beach and the quay, by scrambling over the rocks.

"Ye had better land here," said the lad, "for the surfs running high at the Shellicoat-stane, and there will no be a dry thread amang us or we get the cargo out.—Na! na! (in answer to an offer of money) ye have wrought for your passage, and wrought far better than ony o' us. Gude day to ye. . I wuss ye weel."

So saying, he pushed off in order to land his cargo on the opposite side of the bay; and Brown, with a small bundle in his hand, containing the trifling stock of necessaries which he had been obliged to purchase at Allonby, was left on the rocks beneath the ruin.

And thus, unconscious as the most absolute stranger, and in circumstances which, if not destitute, were for the present highly embarrassing; without the countenance of a friend within the circle of several hundred miles; accused of a heavy crime, and, what was as bad as all the rest, being nearly penniless, did the harassed wanderer for the first time, after the interval of so many years, approach the remains of the castle, where his ancestors had exercised all but regal dominion.

CHAPTER XLI.

—Yes, ye moss-green walls, Ye towers defenceless, I
revisit ye Shame-stricken! Where are all your trophies
now? Your thronged courts, the revelry, the tumult, That
spoke the grandeur of my house, the homage Of neighbouring
Barons?

Mysterious Mother.

Entering the castle of Ellangowan by a postern door-way, which showed symptoms of having been once secured with the most jealous care, Brown (whom, since he has set font upon the property of his fathers, we shall hereafter call by his father's name of Bertram) wandered from one ruined apartment to another, surprised at the massive strength of some parts of the building, the rude and impressive magnificence of others, and the great extent of the whole. In two of these rooms, close beside each other, he saw signs of recent habitation. In one small apartment were empty bottles, half-gnawed bones, and dried fragments of bread. In the vault which adjoined, and which was defended by a strong door, then left open, he observed a considerable quantity of straw, and in both were the relies of recent fires. How little was it possible for Bertram to conceive, that such trivial circumstances were closely connected with incidents affecting his prosperity, his honour, perhaps his life!

After satisfying his curiosity by a hasty glance through the interior of the castle, Bertram now advanced through the great gateway which opened to the land, and paused to look upon the noble landscape which it commanded. Having in vain endeavoured to guess the position of Woodbourne, and having nearly ascertained that of Kippletringan, he turned to take a parting look at the stately ruins which he had just traversed. He admired the massive and picturesque effect of the huge round towers, which, flanking the gateway, gave a double portion of depth and majesty to the high yet gloomy arch under which it opened. The, carved stone escutcheon of the ancient family, bearing for their arms three wolves' heads, was hung diagonally beneath the helmet and crest, the latter being a wolf couchant pierced with an arrow. On either side stood as supporters, in full human size, or larger, a salvage man proper, to use the language of heraldry, wreathed and cinctured, and holding in his hand an oak-tree eradicated, that is, torn up by the roots.

"And the powerful barons who owned this blazonry," thought Bertram, pursuing the usual train of ideas which flows upon the mind at such scenes,—"do their posterity continue to possess the lands which they had laboured to fortify so strongly? or are they wanderers, ignorant perhaps even of the fame or power of their forefathers, while their hereditary possessions are held by a race of strangers? Why is it?" he thought, continuing to follow out the succession of ideas which the scene prompted, "why is it that some scenes awaken thoughts, which belong as it were to dreams of early and shadowy recollection, such as my old Brahmin Moonshie would have ascribed to a state of previous existence? Is it the visions of our sleep that float confusedly in our memory, and are recalled by the appearance of such real objects as in any respect correspond to the phantoms they presented to our imagination? How often do we find ourselves in society which we have never before met, and yet feel impressed with a mysterious and ill-defined consciousness, that neither the scene, the speakers, nor the subject are entirely new; nay, feel as if we could anticipate that part of the conversation which has not yet taken place! It is even so with me while I gaze upon that ruin; nor can I divest myself of the idea, that these massive towers, and that dark gateway, retiring through its deep-vaulted and ribbed arches, and dimly lighted by the courtyard beyond, are not entirely strange to me. Can it be that they have been familiar to me in infancy, and that I am to seek in their vicinity those friends of whom my childhood has still a tender though faint remembrance, and whom I early exchanged for such severe taskmasters? Yet Brown, who I think would not have deceived me, always told me I was brought off from the eastern coast, after a skirmish in which my father was killed; and I do remember enough of a horrid scene of violence to strengthen his account."

It happened that the spot upon which young Bertram chanced to station himself for the better viewing the castle, was nearly the same on which his father had died. It was marked by a large old oak-tree, the only one on the esplanade, and which, having been used for executions by the barons of Ellangowan, was called the justice Tree. It chanced, and the coincidence was remarkable, that Glossin was this morning engaged with a person, whom he was in the habit of consulting in such matters, concerning some projected repairs, and a large addition to the house of Ellangowan, and that, having no great pleasure in remains so intimately connected with the grandeur of the former inhabitants, he had resolved to use the stones of the ruinous castle in his new edifice. Accordingly he came up the bank, followed by the land-surveyor mentioned on a former occasion, who was also in the habit of acting as a sort of architect in case of necessity. In drawing the plans, etc., Glossin was in the custom of relying upon his own skill. Bertram's back was towards them as they came up the ascent, and he was quite shrouded by the branches of the large tree, so that Glossin was not aware of the presence of the stranger till he was close upon him.

"Yes, sir, as I have often said before to you, the Old Place is a perfect quarry of hewn stone, and it would be better for the estate if it were all down, since it is only a den for smugglers. "At this instant Bertram turned short round upon Glossin at the distance of two yards only, and said—"Would you destroy this fine old castle, sir?"

His face, person, and voice, were so exactly those of his father in his best days, that Glossin, hearing his exclamation, and seeing such a sudden apparition in the shape of his patron, and on nearly the very spot where he had expired, almost thought the grave had given up its dead! —He staggered back two or three paces, as if he had received a sudden and deadly wound. He instantly recovered, however, his presence of mind, stimulated by the thrilling reflection that it was no inhabitant of the other world which stood before him, but an injured man, whom the slightest want of dexterity on his part might lead to acquaintance with his rights, and the means of asserting them to his utter destruction. Yet his ideas were so much confused by the shock he had received, that his first question partook of the alarm.

"In the name of God how came you here?" said Glossin.

"How came I here?" repeated Bertram, surprised at the solemnity of the address. "I landed a quarter of an hour since in the little harbour beneath the castle, and was employing a moment's leisure in viewing these fine ruins. I trust there is no intrusion?"

"Intrusion, sir?—no, sir," said Glossin, in some degree recovering his breath, and then whispered a few words into his companion's ear, who immediately left him, and descended towards the house. "Intrusion, sir?—no, sir,—you or any gentleman are welcome to satisfy your curiosity."

"I thank you, sir," said Bertram. "'They call this the Old Place,
I am informed?"

"Yes, sir; in distinction to the New Place, my house there below."

Glossin, it must be remarked, was, during the following dialogue, an the one hand eager to learn what local recollections young Bertram had retained of the scenes of his infancy, and, on the other, compelled to be extremely cautious in his replies, lest he should awaken or assist, by some name, phrase, or anecdote, the slumbering train of association. He suffered, indeed, during the whole scene, the agonies which he so richly deserved; yet his pride and interest, like the fortitude of a North American Indian, manned him to sustain the tortures inflicted at once by the contending stings of a guilty conscience, of hatred, of fear, and of suspicion.

"I wish to ask the name, sir," said Bertram, "of the family to whom this stately ruin belongs?"

It is my property, sir; my name is Glossin."

"Glossin—Glossin?" repeated Bertram, as if the answer were somewhat different from what he expected : "I beg your pardon, Mr. Glossin; I am apt to be very absent.—May I ask if the castle has been long in your family?"

"It was built, I believe, long ago, by a family called MacDingawaie," answered Glossin; suppressing for obvious reasons the more familiar sound of Bertram, which might have awakened the recollections which he was anxious to lull to rest, and slurring with an evasive answer the question concerning the endurance of his own possession.

"And how do you read the half-defaced motto, sir," said Bertram, "which is upon that scroll above the entablature with the arms?"

"I—I—I really do not exactly know," replied Glossin.

"I should be apt to make it out, 'Our Right makes our Might.' "

"I believe it is something of that kind," said Glossin.

"May I ask, sir," said the stranger, "if it is your family motto?"

"N-n-no—no—not ours. That is, I believe, the motto of the former people—mine is—mine is—in fact I have had some correspondence with Mr. Cumming of the Lyon Office in Edinburgh about mine. He writes me the Glossins anciently bore for a motto, 'He who takes it, makes it.' "

"If there be any uncertainty, sir, and the case were mine," said Bertram, "I would assume the old motto, which seems to me the better of the two."

Glossin, whose tongue by this time clove to the roof of his mouth, only answered by a nod.

"It is odd enough," said Bertram, fixing his eye upon the arms and gateway, and partly addressing Glossin, partly as it were thinking aloud—"it is odd the tricks which our memory plays us. The remnants of an old prophecy, or song, or rhyme, of some kind or other, return to my recollection on hearing that motto—stay—it is a strange jingle of sounds:

The dark shall be light,

And the wrong made right,

When Bertram's right and Bertram's might

Shall meet on—

I cannot remember the last line—on some particular height— height is the rhyme, I am sure; but I cannot hit upon the preceding word."

"Confound your memory," muttered Glossin, "you remember by far too much of it!"

"There are other rhymes connected with these early recollections," continued the young man : "Pray, sir, is there any song current in this part of the world respecting a daughter of the King of the Isle of Man eloping with a Scottish knight?"

"I am the worst person in the world to consult upon legendary antiquities," answered Glossin.

"I could sing such a ballad," said Bertram, "from one end to another, when I was a boy. You must know I left Scotland, which is my native country, very young, and those who brought me up discouraged all my attempts to preserve recollection of my native land, on account, I believe, of a boyish wish which I had to escape from their charge."

"Very natural," said Glossin, but speaking as if his utmost efforts were unable to unseal his lips beyond the width of a quarter of an inch, so that his whole utterance was a kind of compressed muttering, very different from the round, bold, bullying voice with which he usually spoke. Indeed his appearance and demeanour during all this conversation seemed to diminish even his strength and stature; so that he appeared to wither into the shadow of himself, now advancing one foot, now the other, now stooping and wriggling his shoulders, now fumbling with the buttons of his waistcoat, now clasping his hands together,—in short, he was the picture of a mean-spirited shuffling rascal in the very agonies of detection. To these appearances Bertram was totally inattentive,—being dragged on as it were by the current of his own associations. Indeed, although he addressed Glossin, he was not so much thinking of him, as arguing upon the embarrassing state of his own feelings and recollection. "Yes," he said, "I preserved my language among the sailors, most of whom spoke English, and when I could get into a corner by myself, I used to sing all that song over from beginning to end—I have forgot it all now—but I remember the tune well, though I cannot guess what should at present so strongly recall it to my memory."

He took his flageolet from his pocket, and played a simple melody. Apparently the tune awoke the corresponding associations of a damsel, who, close beside a fine spring about half-way down the descent, and which had once supplied the castle with water, was engaged in bleaching linen. She immediately took up the song:

"Are these the Links of Forth, she said, Or are they the crooks of Dee. Or the hannie woods of Warroch Head That I so fain would see?"

"By heaven," said Bertram, "it is the very ballad. I must learn these words from the girl."

"Confusion!" thought Glossin; "if I cannot put a stop to this, all will be out. Oh, the devil take all ballads, and ballad-makers, and ballad-singers! and that d-d jade too, to set up her pipe!—You will have time enough for this on some other occasion," he said aloud; "at present"—(for now he saw his emissary with two or three men coming up the bank),—"at present we must have some more serious conversation together."

"How do you mean, sir?" said Bertram, turning short upon him, and not liking the tone which he made use of.

"Why, sir, as to that—I believe your name is Brown?" said Glossin.

"And what of that, sir?"

Glossin looked over his shoulder to see how near his party had approached; they were coming fast on.

"Vanbeest Brown? if I mistake not."

"And what of that, sir?" said Bertram, with increasing astonishment and displeasure.

"Why, in that case," said Glossin, observing his friends had now got upon the level space close beside them—"in that case you are my prisoner in the king's name!"—At the same time he stretched his hand towards Bertram's collar, while two of the men who had come up seized upon his arms; he shook himself, however, free of their grasp by a violent effort, in which he pitched the most pertinacious down the bank, and, drawing his cutlass, stood on the defensive, while those who had felt his strength recoiled from his presence, and gazed at a safe distance. "Observe," he called out at the same time, "that I have no purpose to resist legal authority; satisfy me that you have a magistrates warrant, and are authorised to make this arrest, and I will obey it quietly; but let no man who loves his life venture to approach me, till I am satisfied for what crime, and by whose authority, I am apprehended."

Glossin then caused one of the officers show a warrant for the apprehension of Vanbeest Brown, accused of the crime of wilfully and maliciously shooting at Charles Hazlewood, younger of Hazlewood, with an intent to kill, and also of other crimes and misdemeanours, and which appointed him, having been so apprehended, to be brought before the next magistrate for examination. The warrant being formal, and the fact such as he could not deny, Bertram threw down his weapon, and submitted himself to the officers, who, flying on him with eagerness corresponding to their former pusillanimity, were about to load him with irons, alleging the strength and activity which he had displayed, as a justification of this severity. But Glossin was ashamed or afraid to permit this unnecessary insult, and directed the prisoner to be treated with all the decency, and even respect, that was consistent with safety. Afraid, however, to introduce him into his own house, where still further subjects of recollection might have been suggested, and anxious at the same time to cover his own proceedings by the sanction of another's authority, he ordered his carriage (for he had lately set up a carriage) to be got ready, and in the meantime directed refreshments to be given to the prisoner and the officers, who were consigned to one of the rooms in the old castle, until the means of conveyance for examination before a magistrate should be provided.

CHAPTER XLII.

—Bring in the evidence—Thou robed man of justice,
take thy place, And thou, his yoke-fellow of equity, Bench
by his side—you are of the commission, Sit you too.
King Lear.

While the carriage was getting ready, Glossin had a letter to compose, about which. he wasted no small time. It was to his neighbour, as he was fond of calling him, Sir Robert Hazlewood of Hazlewood, the head of an ancient and powerful interest in the county, which had in the decadence of the Ellangowan family gradually succeeded to much of their Authority and influence. The present representative of the family was an elderly man, dotingly fond of his own family, which was limited to an only son and daughter, and stoically indifferent to the fate of all mankind besides. For the rest, he was honourable in his general dealings, because he was afraid to suffer the censure of the world, and just from a better motive. He was presumptuously over-conceited on the score of family pride and importance, a feeling considerably enhanced by his late succession to the title of a Nova Scotia Baronet; and he hated the memory of the Ellangowan family, though now a memory only, because a certain baron of that house was traditionally, reported to have caused the founder of the Hazlewood family hold his stirrup until he mounted into his saddle. In his general department he was pompous and important, affecting a specious of florid elocution, which often became ridiculous from his misarranging the triads and quaternions with which he loaded his sentences.

To this personage Glossin was now to write in such a conciliatory style as might be most acceptable to his vanity and family pride, and the following was the form of his note.

"Mr. Gilbert Glossin" (he longed to add of Ellangowan, but prudence prevailed, and he suppressed that territorial designation)—"Mr. Gilbert Glossin has the honour to offer his most respectful compliments to Sir Robert Hazlewood, and to inform him, that he has this morning been fortunate enough to secure the person who wounded Mr. C. Hazlewood. As Sir Robert Hazlewood may probably choose to conduct the examination of this criminal himself, Mr. G. Glossin will cause the mail to be carried to the inn at Kippletringan, or to Hazlewood House, as Sir Robert Hazlewood may be pleased to direct : And, with Sir Robert Hazlewood's permission, Mr. G. Glossin will attend him at either of these places with the proofs and declarations which he has been so fortunate as to collect respecting this atrocious business."

Addressed,

"Sir Robert Hazlewood of Hazlewood, Bart. "Hazlewood House, &c. &c.

"Elln. Gn,
Tuesday."

This note he despatched by a servant on horseback, and having given the man some time to get ahead, and desired him to ride fast, he ordered two officers of justice to get into the carriage with Bertram; and he himself, mounting his horse, accompanied them at a slow pace to the point where the roads to Kippletringan and Hazlewood House separated, and there awaited the return of his messenger, in order that his farther route might be determined by the answer he should receive from the Baronet. In about half an hour his servant returned with the following answer, handsomely folded, and scaled with the Hazlewood arms, having the Nova Scotia badge depending from the shield.

"Sir Robert Hazlewood of Hazlewood returns Mr. G. Glossin's compliments, and thanks him for the trouble he has taken in a matter affecting the safety of Sir Robert's family. Sir R. H. requests Mr. G. G. will have the goodness to bring the prisoner to Hazlewood House for examination, with the other proofs or declarations which he mentions. And after the business is over, in case Mr. G. G. is not otherwise engaged, Sir R. and Lady Hazlewood request his company to dinner."

Addressed,

"Mr. Gilbert Glossin, &c.

Hazlewood House,
Tuesday."

"Soh!" thought Mr. Glossin, "here is one finger in at least, and that I will make the means of introducing my whole hand. But I must first get clear of this wretched young fellow.—I think I can manage Sir Robert. He is dull and pompous, and will be alike disposed to listen to my suggestions upon the law of the case, and to assume the credit of acting upon them as his own proper motion. So I shall have the advantage of being the real magistrate, without the odium of responsibility."

As he cherished these hopes and expectations the carriage approached Hazlewood House, through a noble avenue of old oaks, which shrouded the ancient abbey-resembling building so called. It was a large edifice built at different periods, part having actually been a priory, upon the suppression of which, in the time of Queen Mary, the first of the family had obtained a gift of the house and the surrounding lands from the crown. It was pleasantly situated in a large deer-park, on the banks of the river we have before mentioned. The scenery around was of a dark, solemn, and somewhat melancholy cast, according well with the architecture of the house. Everything appeared to be kept in the highest possible order, and announced the opulence and rank of the proprietor.

As Mr. Glossin's carriage stopped at the door of the hall, Sir Robert reconnoitred the new vehicle from the windows. According to his aristocratic feelings, there was a degree of presumption in this novus homo, this Mr. Gilbert Glossin, late writer in—, presuming to set up such an accommodation at all; but his wrath was mitigated when he observed that the mantle upon the panels only bore a plain cypher of G. G. This apparent modesty was indeed solely owing to the delay of Mr. Cumming of the Lyon Office, who, being at that time engaged in discovering and matriculating the arms of two commissaries from North America, three English-Irish peers, and two great Jamaica traders, had been more slow than usual in finding an escutcheon for the new Laird of Ellangowan. But his delay told to the advantage of Glossin in the opinion of the proud Baronet.

While the officers of justice detained their prisoner in a sort of steward's room, Mr. Glossin was ushered into what was called the great oak-parlour, a long room, panelled with well-varnished wainscot, and adorned with the grim portraits of Sir Robert Hazlewood's ancestry. The visitor, who had no internal consciousness of worth to balance that of meanness of birth, felt his inferiority, and by the depth of his bow and the obsequiousness of his demeanour, showed that the Laird of Ellangowan was sunk for the time in the old and submissive habits of the quondam retainer of the law. He would have persuaded himself, indeed, that he was only humouring the pride of the old Baronet, for the purpose of turning it to his own advantage; but his feelings were of a mingled nature, and he felt the influence of those very prejudices which he pretended to flatter.

The Baronet received his visitor with that condescending parade which was meant at once to assert his own vast superiority, and to show the generosity and courtesy with which he could waive it, and descend to the level of ordinary conversation with ordinary men. He thanked Glossin for his attention to a matter in which "young Hazlewood" was so intimately concerned, and, pointing to his family pictures, observed, with a gracious smile, "Indeed these venerable gentlemen, Mr. Glossin, are as much obliged as I am in this case, for the labour, pains, care, and trouble which you have taken in their behalf; and I have no doubt, were they capable of expressing themselves, would join me, sir, in thanking you for the favour you have conferred upon the house of Hazlewood, by taking care, and trouble, sir, and interest, in behalf of the young, gentleman who is to continue their name and family."

Thrice bowed Glossin, and each time more profoundly than before; once in honour of the knight who stood upright before him, once in respect to the quiet personages who patiently hung upon the wainscot, and a third time in deference to the young gentleman who was to carry on the name and family. Roturier as he was, Sir Robert was gratified by the homage which he rendered, and proceeded in a tone of gracious familiarity: "And now, Mr Glossin, my exceeding good friend, you must allow me to avail myself of your knowledge of law in our proceedings in this matter. I am not much in the habit of acting as a justice of the peace; it suits better with other gentlemen, whose domestic and family affairs require less constant superintendence, attention, and management than mine."

Of course, whatever small assistance Mr. Glossin could render was entirely at Sir Robert Hazlewood's service; but, as Sir Robert Hazlewood's name stood high in the list of the faculty, the said Mr. Glossin could not presume to hope it could be either necessary or useful.

"Why, my good sir, you will understand me only to mean, that I am something deficient in the practical knowledge of the ordinary details of justice-business. I was indeed educated to the bar, and might boast perhaps at one time, that I had made some progress in the speculative, and abstract, and abstruse doctrines of our municipal code; but there is in the present day so little opportunity of a man of family and fortune rising to that eminence at the bar, which is attained by adventurers who are as willing to plead for John a Nokes as for the first noble of the land, that I was really early disgusted with practice. The first case, indeed, which was laid on my table, quite sickened me; it respected a bargain, sir, of tallow, between a butcher and. a candle-maker; and I found it was expected that I should grease my mouth, not only with their vulgar names, but with all the technical terms and phrases, and peculiar language, of their dirty arts. Upon my honour, my good sir, I have never been able to bear the smell of a tallow-candle since."

Pitying, as seemed to be expected, the mean use to which the Baronet's faculties had been degraded on the melancholy occasion, Mr, Glossin offered to officiate as clerk or assessor, or in any way in which he could be most useful. "And with a view to possessing you of the whole business, and in the first place, there will, I believe, be no difficulty in proving the main fact, that this was the person who fired the unhappy piece. Should he deny it, it can be proved by Mr. Hazlewood, I presume."

"Young Hazlewood is not at home to-day, Mr. Glossin."

"But we can have the oath of the servant who attended him," said the ready Mr. Glossin; "indeed I hardly think the fact will be disputed. I am more apprehensive, that, from the too favourable and indulgent manner in which I have understood that Mr. Hazlewood has been pleased to represent the business, the assault may be considered as accidental, and the injury as unintentional, so that the fellow may be immediately set at liberty, to do more mischief."

"I have not the honour to know the gentleman who now holds the office of king's advocate," replied Sir Robert gravely; "but I presume, sir—nay, I am confident, that he will consider the mere fact of having wounded young Hazlewood of Hazlewood, even by inadvertency, to take the matter in its mildest and gentlest, and in its most favourable and improbable light, as a crime which will be too easily atoned by imprisonment, and as more deserving of deportation."

"Indeed, Sir Robert," said his assenting brother in justice, "I am entirely of your opinion; but, I don't know how it is, I have observed the Edinburgh gentlemen of the bar, and even the officers of the crown, pique themselves upon an indifferent administration of justice, without respect to rank and family; and I should fear—"

"How, sir; without respect to rank and family? Will you tell me that doctrine can be held by men of birth and legal education? No, sir; if a trifle stolen in the street is termed mere pickery, but is elevated into sacrilege if the crime be committed in a church, so, according to the just gradations of society, the guilt of an injury is enhanced by the rank of the person to whom it is offered, done, or perpetrated, sir."

Glossin bowed low to this declaration ex cathedra, but observed, that in case of the very worst, and of such unnatural doctrines being actually held as he had already hinted, "the law had another hold on Mr. Vanbeest Brown."

"Vanbeest Brown! is that the fellow's name? Good God! that young Hazlewood of Hazlewood should have had his life endangered, the clavicle of his right shoulder considerably lacerated and dislodged, several large drops or slugs deposited in the acromion process, as the account of the family surgeon expressly bears, and all by an obscure wretch named Vanbeest Brown!"

"Why, really, Sir Robert, it is a thing which one can hardly bear to think of; but, begging ten thousand pardons for resuming what I was about to say, a person of the same name is, as appears from these papers (producing Dirk Hatteraick's pocket-book), mate to the smuggling vessel who offered such violence at Woodbourne, and I have no doubt that this is the same individual; which, however, your acute discrimination will easily be able to ascertain."

"The same, my good sir, he must assuredly be—it would be injustice even to the meanest of the people, to suppose there could be found among them two persons doomed to bear a name so shocking to one's ears as this of Vanbeest Brown."

"True, Sir Robert; most unquestionably; there cannot be a shadow of doubt of it. But you see further, that this circumstance accounts for the man's desperate conduct. You, Sir Robert, will discover the motive for his crime—you, I say, will discover it without difficulty, on your giving your mind to the examination; for my part, I cannot help suspecting the moving spring to have been revenge for the gallantry with which Mr. Hazlewood, with all the spirit of his renowned forefathers, defended the house at Woodbourne against this villain and his lawless companions."

"I will inquire into it, my good sir," said the learned Baronet. "Yet even now I venture to conjecture that I shall adopt the solution or explanation of this riddle, enigma, or mystery, which you have in some degree thus started. Yes! revenge it must be—and, good Heaven! entertained by and against whom?—entertained, fostered, cherished, against young Hazlewood of Hazlewood, and in part carried into effect, executed, and implemented, by the hand of Vanbeest Brown! These are dreadful days indeed, my worthy neighbour (this epithet indicated a rapid advance in the Baronet's good graces)—days when the bulwarks of society are shaken to their mighty base, and that rank, which forms, as it were, its highest grace and ornament, is mingled and confused with the viler parts of the architecture. Oh, my good Mr. Gilbert Glossin, in my time, sir, the use of swords and pistols, and such honourable arms, were reserved by the nobility and gentry to themselves, and the disputes of the vulgar were decided by the weapons which nature had given them, or by cudgels cut, broken, or hemmed out of the next wood. But now, sir, the clouted [*Patched] shoe of the peasant galls the kibe of the courtier. The lower ranks have their quarrels, sir, and their points of honour, and their revenges, which they must bring, forsooth, to fatal arbitrament. But well, well! it will last my time—let us have in this fellow, this Vanbeest Brown, and make an end of him at least for the present."

CHAPTER XLIII.

—'Twas he ye Gave heat unto the injury, which returned, Like a petard ill lighted, into the bosom Of him gave fire to't. Yet I hope his hurt Is not so dangerous but he may recover. Fair Maid of the Inn.

The prisoner was now presented before the two worshipful magistrates. Glossin, partly from some compunctious visitings, and partly out of his cautious resolution to suffer Sir Robert Hazlewood to be the ostensible manager of the whole examination, looked down upon the table, and busied himself with reading and, arranging the papers respecting the business, only now and then throwing in a skilful catchword as prompter, when he saw the principal, and apparently most active magistrate, stand in need of a hint. As for Sir Robert Hazlewood, he assumed on his part a happy mixture of the austerity of the justice, combined with the display of personal dignity appertaining to the baronet of ancient family.

"There, constables, let him stand there at the bottom of the table.—Be so good as look me in the face, sir, and raise your voice as you answer the questions which I am going to put to you."

"May I beg, in the first place, to know, sir, who it is that takes the trouble to interrogate me?" said the prisoner; "for the honest gentlemen who have brought me here have not been pleased to furnish any information upon that point."

"And pray, sir," answered Sir Robert, "what has my name and quality to do with the questions I am about to ask you?"

"Nothing, perhaps, sir," replied Bertram but it may considerably influence my disposition to answer them."

"Why, then, sir, you will please to be informed that you are in presence of Sir Robert Hazlewood of Hazlewood, and another justice of peace for this county—that's all."

As this intimation produced a less stunning effect upon the prisoner than he had anticipated, Sir Robert proceeded in his investigation with an increasing dislike to the object of it.

"Is your name Vanbeest Brown, sir?"

"It is," answered the prisoner.

"So far well;—and how are we to design you further, sir?" demanded the justice.

"Captain in his Majesty's regiment of horse," answered Bertram.

The Baronet's ears received this intimation with astonishment; but he was refreshed in courage by an incredulous look from Glossin, and by hearing him gently utter a sort of interjectional whistle, in a note of surprise and contempt. "I believe, my friend," said Sir Robert, "we shall find for you, before we part, a more humble title."

"If you do, sir," replied his prisoner, "I shall willingly submit to any punishment which such an imposture shall be thought to deserve."

"Well, sir, we shall see," continued Sir Robert. "Do you know young Hazlewood of Hazlewood?"

"I never saw the gentleman who I am informed bears that name excepting once, and I regret that it was under very unpleasant circumstances."

"You mean to acknowledge, then," said the Baronet, "that you inflicted upon young Hazlewood of Hazlewood that wound which endangered his life, considerably lacerated the clavicle of his right shoulder, and deposited, as the family surgeon declares, several large drops. or slugs in the acromion process?"

"Why, sir," replied Bertram, "I can only say I am equally ignorant of and sorry for the extent of the damage which the young gentleman has sustained. I met him in a narrow path, walking with two ladies and a servant, and before I could either pass them or address them, this young Hazlewood took his gun from his servant, presented it against my body, and commanded me in the most haughty tone to stand back. I was neither inclined to submit to his authority, nor to leave him in possession of the means to injure me, which he seemed disposed to use with such rashness. I therefore closed with him for the purpose of disarming him; and just as I had nearly effected my purpose, the piece went off accidentally, and, to my regret then and since, inflicted upon the young gentleman a severer chastisement than I desired, though I am glad to understand it is like to prove no more than his unprovoked folly deserved."

"And so, sir," said the Baronet, every feature swollen with offended dignity,—"You, sir, admit, sir, that it was your purpose, sir, and your intention, sir, and the real jet and object of your assault, sir, to disarm young Hazlewood of Hazlewood of his gun, sir, or his fowling-piece, or his fuzee, or whatever you please to call it, sir, upon the king's highway, sir?—I think this will do, my worthy neighbour! I think he should stand committed?"

"You are by far the best judge, Sir Robert," said Glossin, in his most insinuating tone; "but if I might presume to hint, there was something about these smugglers."

"Very true, good sir.—And besides, sir, you, Vanbeest Brown, who call yourself a captain in his Majesty's service, are no better or worse than a rascally mate of a smuggler!"

"Really, sir," said Bertram, "you are an old gentleman, and acting under some strange delusion, otherwise I should be very angry with you."

"Old gentleman, sir! strange delusion, sir!" said Sir Robert, colouring with indignation. "I protest and declare—Why, sir, have you any papers or letters that can establish your pretended rank, and estate, and commission?"

"None at present, sir," answered Bertram; "but in the return of a post or two—"

"And how do you, sir," continued the Baronet, "if you are a captain in his Majesty's service, how do you chance to be travelling in Scotland without letters of introduction, credentials, baggage, or anything belonging to your pretended rank, estate, and condition, as I said before?"

"Sir," replied the prisoner, "I had the misfortune to be robbed of my clothes and baggage."

"Oho! then you are the gentleman who took a post-chaise from—to Kippletringan, gave the boy the slip on the road, and sent two of your accomplices to beat the boy and bring away the baggage?"

"I was, sir, in a carriage as you describe, was obliged to alight in the snow, and lost my way endeavouring to find the road to Kippletringan. The landlady of the inn will inform you that on my arrival there the next day, my first inquiries were after the boy."

"Then give me leave to ask where you spent the night—not in the snow, I presume? you do not suppose that will pass, or be taken, credited, and received?"

"I beg leave," said Bertram, his recollection turning to the gipsy female, and to the promise he had given her, "I beg leave to decline answering that question."

"I thought as much," said Sir Robert.—"Were you not during that night in the ruins of Derncleugh?—in the ruins of Derncleugh, sir?"

"I have told you that I do not intend answering that question," replied Bertram.

"Well, sir, then you will stand committed, sir." said Sir Robert, "and be sent to prison, sir, that's all, sir.—Have the goodness to look at these papers; are you the Vanbeest Brown who is there mentioned?"

It must be remarked that Glossin had shuffled among the papers some writings which really did belong to Bertram, and which had been found by the officers in the old vault where his portmanteau was ransacked.

"Some of these papers," said Bertram, looking over them, "are mine, and were in my portfolio when it was stolen from the post-chaise. They are memoranda of little value, and, I see, have been carefully selected as affording no evidence of my rank or character, which many of the other papers would have established fully. They are mingled with ship-accounts and other papers, belonging apparently to a person of the same name."

"And wilt thou attempt to persuade me, friend," demanded Sir Robert, "that there are two persons in this country, at the same time, of thy very uncommon and awkwardly sounding name?"

"I really do not see, sir, as there is an old Hazlewood and a young Hazlewood, why there should not be an old and a young Vanbeest Brown. And, to speak seriously, I was educated in Holland, and I know that this name, however uncouth it may sound in British ears—"

Glossin, conscious that the prisoner was now about to enter upon dangerous ground, interfered, though the interruption was unnecessary, for the purpose of diverting the attention of Sir Robert Hazlewood, who was speechless and motionless with indignation at the presumptuous comparison implied in Bertram's last speech. In fact, the veins of his throat and of his temples swelled almost to bursting, and he sat with the indignant and disconcerted air of one who has received a mortal insult from a quarter to which he holds it unmeet and indecorous to make any reply. While with a bent brow and an angry eye he was drawing in his breath slowly and majestically, and puffing it forth again with deep and solemn exertion, Glossin stepped in to his assistance. "I should think now, Sir Robert, with great submission, that this matter may be closed. One of the constables, besides the pregnant proof already produced, offers to make oath, that the sword of which the prisoner was this morning deprived (while using it, by the way, in resistance to a legal warrant) was a cutlass taken from him in a fray between the officers and smugglers, just previous to their attack upon Woodbourne. And yet," he added, "I would not have you form any rash construction upon that subject; perhaps the young man can explain how he came by that weapon."

"That question, sir," said Bertram, "I shall also leave unanswered."

"There is yet another circumstance to be inquired into, always under Sir Robert's leave," insinuated Glossin. "This prisoner put into the hands of Mrs. Mac-Candlish of Kippletringan a parcel containing a variety of gold coins and valuable articles of different kinds. Perhaps, Sir Robert, you might think it right to ask, how he came by property of a description which seldom occurs?"

"You, sir, Mr. Vanbeest Brown, sir, you hear the question, sir, which the gentleman asks you?"

"I have particular reasons for declining to answer that question," answered Bertram.

"Then I am afraid, sir," said Glossin, who had brought matters to the point he desired to reach, "our duty must lay us under the necessity to sign a warrant of committal."

"As you please, sir," answered Bertram; "take care, however, what you do. Observe that I inform you that I am a captain in his Majesty's—regiment, and that I am just returned from India, and therefore cannot possibly be connected with any of those contraband traders you talk of; that my Lieutenant-Colonel is now at Nottingham, the Major, with the officers of my corps, at Kingston-upon-Thames.

I offer before you both to submit to any degree of ignominy, if, within the return of the Kingston and Nottingham posts, I am not able to establish these points. Or you may write to the agent for the regiment, if you please, and—"

"This is all very well," said Glossin, beginning to fear lest the firm expostulation of Bertram should make some impression on Sir Robert, who would almost have died of shame at committing such a solecism as sending a captain of horse to jail—"This is all very well, sir; but is there no person nearer whom you could refer to?"

"There are only two persons in this country who know anything of me," replied the prisoner. "One is a plain Liddesdale sheep-farmer, called Dinmont of Charlies-hope; but he knows nothing more of me than what I told him, and what I now tell you."

"Why, this is well enough, Sir Robert!" said Glossin, "I suppose he would bring forward this thick-skulled fellow to give his oath of credulity, Sir Robert, ha, ha, ha!"

"And what is your other witness, friend?" said the Baronet.

"A gentleman whom I have some reluctance to mention, because of certain private reasons; but under whose command I served some time in India, and who is too much a man of honour to refuse his testimony to my character as a soldier and gentleman."

"And who is this doughty witness, pray, sir?" said Sir Robert,—"some half-pay quarter-master or sergeant, I suppose?"

"Colonel Guy Mannering, late of tile—regiment, in which, as I told you, I have a troop."

"Colonel Guy Mannering!" thought Glossin,—"who the devil could have guessed this?"

"Colonel Guy Mannering!" echoed the Baronet, considerably shaken in his opinion,—"My good sir,"—apart to Glossin, "the young man with a dreadfully plebeian name, and a good deal of modest assurance, has nevertheless something of the tone, and manners, and feeling of a gentleman, of one at least who has lived in good society—they do give commissions very loosely, and carelessly, and inaccurately, in India—I think we had better pause till Colonel Mannering shall return; he is now, I believe, at Edinburgh."

"You are in every respect the best judge, Sir Robert," answered Glossin, "in every possible respect. I would only submit to you, that we are certainly hardly entitled to dismiss this man upon an assertion which cannot be satisfied by proof, and that we shall incur a heavy responsibility by detaining him in private custody, without committing him to a public jail. Undoubtedly, however, you are the best judge, Sir Robert;—and I would only say, for my own part, that I very lately incurred severe censure by detaining a person in a place which I thought perfectly secure, and under the custody of the proper officers. The man made his escape, and I have no doubt my own character for attention and circumspection as a magistrate has in some degree suffered—I only hint this—I will join in any step you, Sir Robert, think most advisable." But Mr. Glossin was well aware that such a hint was of power sufficient to decide the motions of his self-important, but not self-relying colleague. So that Sir Robert Hazlewood summed up the business in the following speech, which proceeded partly upon the supposition of the prisoner being really a gentleman, and partly upon the opposite belief that he was a villain and an assassin.

"Sir, Mr. Vanbeest Brown—I would call you Captain Brown if there was the least reason, or cause, or grounds to suppose that you are a captain, or had a troop in the very respectable corps you mention, or indeed in any other corps in his Majesty's service, as to which circumstance I beg to be understood to give no positive, settled, or unalterable judgment, declaration, or opinion. I say therefore, sir, Mr. Brown, we have determined, considering the unpleasant predicament in which you now stand, having been robbed, as you say, an assertion as to which I suspend my opinion, and being possessed of much and valuable treasure, and of a brass-handled cutlass besides, as to your obtaining which you will favour us with no explanation—I say, sir, we have determined and resolved, and made up our minds, to commit you to jail, or rather to assign you an apartment therein, in order that you may be forthcoming upon Colonel Mannering's return from Edinburgh."

"With humble submission, Sir Robert," said Glossin, "may I inquire if it is your purpose to send this young gentleman to the county jail?—for if that were not your settled intention, I would take the liberty to hint, that there would be less hardship in sending him to the Bridewell at Portanferry, where he can be secured without public exposure; a circumstance which, on the mere chance of his story being really true, is much to be avoided."

"Why, there is a guard of soldiers at Portanferry, to be sure, for protection of the goods in the Custom-house; and upon the whole, considering everything, and that the place is comfortable for such a place, I say all things considered, we will commit this person, I would rather say authorise him to be detained, in the workhouse at Portanferry."

The warrant was made out accordingly, and Bertram was informed he was next morning to be removed to his place of confinement, as Sir Robert had determined he should not be taken there under cloud of night, for fear of rescue. He was, during the interval, to be detained at Hazlewood House.

"It cannot be so hard as my imprisonment by the Looties in India," he thought; "nor can it last so long. But the deuce take the old formal dunderhead, and his more sly associate, who speaks always under his breath,—they cannot understand a plain man's story when it is told them."

In the meanwhile Glossin took leave of the Baronet, with a thousand respectful bows and cringing apologies for not accepting his invitation to dinner, and venturing to hope he might be pardoned in paying his respects to him, Lady Hazlewood, and young Mr. Hazlewood, on some future occasion.

"Certainly, sir," said the Baronet, very graciously. I hope our family was never at any time deficient in civility to our neighbours; and when I ride that way, good Mr. Glossin, I will convince you of this by calling at your house as familiarly as is consistent—that is, as can be hoped or expected."

"And now," said Glossin to himself, "to find Dirk Hatteraick and his people,—to get the guard sent off from the Custom-house,—and then for the grand cast of the dice. Everything must depend upon speed. How lucky that Mannering has betaken himself to Edinburgh! His knowledge of this young fellow is a most perilous addition to my dangers,"—here he suffered his horse to slacken his pace—"What if I should try to compound with the heir?—It's likely he might be brought to pay a round sum for restitution, and I could give up Hatteraick—But no, no, no! there were too many eyes on me, Hatteraick himself, and the gipsy sailor, and that old hag—No, no! I must stick to my original plan. "And with that he struck his spurs against his horse's flanks, and rode forward at a hard trot to put his machines in motion.

CHAPTER XLIV.

A prison is a house of care, A place where none can thrive,
A touchstone true to try a friend, A grave for one alive.
Sometimes a place of right, Sometimes a place of wrong,
Sometimes a place of rogues and thieves, And honest men
among. Inscription on Edinburgh Tollbooth.

Early on the following morning, the carriage which had brought Bertram to Hazlewood House, was, with his two silent and surly attendants, appointed to convey him to his place of confinement at Portanferry. This building adjoined to the Custom-house established at that little seaport, and both were situated so close to the sea-beach that it was necessary to defend the back part with a large and strong rampart or bulwark of huge stones, disposed in a slope towards the surf, which often reached and broke upon them. The front was surrounded by a high wall, enclosing a small courtyard, within which the miserable inmates of the mansion were occasionally permitted to take exercise and air. The prison was used as a House of Correction, and sometimes as a chapel of case to the county jail, which was old, and far from being conveniently situated with reference to the Kippletringan district of the county, Mac-Guffog, the officer by whom Bertram had at first been apprehended, and who was now in attendance upon him, was keeper of this palace of little-ease. He caused the carriage to be drawn close up to the outer gate, and got out himself to summon the warders. The noise of his rap alarmed some twenty or thirty ragged boys, who left off sailing their mimic sloops and frigates in the little pools of salt water left by the receding tide, and hastily crowded round the vehicle to see what luckless being was to be delivered to the prison-house out of "Glossin's braw new carriage." The door of the courtyard, after the heavy clanking of many chains and bars, was opened by Mrs. MacGuffog, an awful spectacle, being a woman for strength and resolution capable of maintaining order among her riotous inmates, and of administering the discipline of the house, as it was called, during the absence of her husband, or when he chanced to have taken an overdose of the creature. The growling voice of this Amazon, which rivalled in harshness the crashing music of her own bolts and bars, soon dispersed in every direction the little varlets who had thronged around her threshold, and she next addressed her amiable helpmate:—

"Be sharp, man, and get out the swell, canst thou not?"

"Hold your tongue and be d-d, you—," answered her loving husband, with two additional epithets of great energy, but which we beg to be excused from repeating. Then, addressing Bertram:

"Come, will you get out, my handy lad, or must we lend you a lift?"

Bertram came out of the carriage, and, collared by the constable as he put his foot on the ground, was dragged, though he offered no resistance, across the threshold, amid the continued shouts of the little sans-culottes, who looked on at such distance as their fear of Mrs. Mac-Guffog permitted. The instant his foot had crossed the fatal porch, the portress again dropped her chains, drew her bolts, and turning with both hands an immense key, took it from the lock, and thrust it into a huge side-pocket of red cloth.

Bertram was now in the small court already mentioned. Two or three prisoners were sauntering along the pavement, and deriving as it were a feeling of refreshment from the monetary glimpse with which the opening door had extended their prospect to the other side of a dirty street. Nor can this he thought surprising, when it is considered, that, unless on such occasions, their view was confined to the grated front of their prison, the high and sable walls of the courtyard, the heaven above them, and the pavement beneath their feet; a sameness of landscape, which, to use the poet's expression, "lay like a load on the wearied eye," and had fostered in some a callous and dull misanthropy, in others that sickness of the heart which induces him who is immured already in a living grave, to wish for a sepulchre yet more calm and sequestered.

Mac-Guffog, when they entered the courtyard, suffered Bertram to pause for a minute, and look upon his companions in affliction. When he had cast his eye around, on faces on which guilt, and despondence, and low excess, had fixed their stigma; upon the spendthrift, and the swindler, and the thief, the bankrupt debtor, the "moping idiot, and the madman gay," whom a paltry spirit of economy congregated to share this dismal habitation, he felt his heart recoil with inexpressible loathing from enduring the contamination of their society even for a moment.

"I hope, sir," he said to the keeper "you intend to assign me a place of confinement apart?"

"And what should I be the better of that?"

"Why, sir I can but be detained here a day or two, and it would be very disagreeable to me to mix in the sort of company this place affords."

"And what do I care for that?"

"Why, then, sir, to speak to your feelings," said Bertram, "I shall be willing to make you a handsome compliment for this indulgence."

"Ay, but when, Captain? when and how? that's the question, or rather, the twa questions," said the jailor.

"When I am delivered, and get my remittances from England," answered the prisoner.

Mac-Guffog shook his head incredulously. "Why, friend, you do not pretend to believe that I am really a malefactor?" said Bertram.

"Why, I no ken," said the fellow; "but if you are on the account, ye're nae sharp ane, that's the daylight o't."

"And why do you say I am no sharp one?"

"Why, wha but a crack-brained greenhorn wad hae let them keep up the siller that ye left at the Gordon Arms?" said the constable. "Deil fetch me, but I wad have held it out o' their wames [*Bellies] Ye had nae right to be strippit o' your money and sent to jail without a mark to pay your fees—; they might have keepit the rest o' the articles for evidence. But why, for a blind bottle-head, did not ye ask the guineas? and I kept winking and nodding a' the time, and the donnert [*Stupid] deevil wad never ance look my way!"

"Well, sir," replied Bertram, "if I have a title to have that property delivered up to me, I shall apply for it; and there is a good deal more than enough to pay any demand you can set up."

"I dinna ken a bit about that," said Mac-Guffog; "ye may be here lang eneugh. And then the giving credit maun be considered in the fees. But, however, as ye do seem to be a chap by common, though my wife says I lose by my good-nature, if ye gie me an order for my fees upon that money—I dare say Glossin will make it forthcoming—I ken something about an escape from Ellangowan—ay, ay, he'll be glad to carry me through, and be neighbour-like."

"Well, sir," replied Bertram," if I am not furnished in a day or two otherwise, you shall have such—an order."

"Weel, weel, then ye shall be put up like a prince," said Mac-Guffog. "But mark ye me, friend, that we may have nae colly-shangie [*Quarrel] afterhend, these are the fees I always charge a swell that must have his libken to himsell—Thirty shillings a week for lodgings, and a guinea for garnish; half-a-guinea a week for a single bed,—and I dinna get the whole of it, for I must gie half-a-crown out of it to Donald Laider that's in for sheep-stealing, that should sleep with you by rule, and he'll expect clean strae, and maybe some whisky beside. So I make little upon that."

"Well, sir, go on."

"Then for meat and liquor, ye may have the best, and I never charge abune twenty per cent. ower tavern price for pleasing a gentleman that way—and that's little eneugh for sending in and sending out, and wearing the lassie's shoon out. And then if ye're dowie, I will sit wi' you a gliff [*Twinkling] in the evening mysell, man, and help ye out wi' your bottle.—I have drunk mony a glass wi' Glossin, man, that did you up, though he's a justice now. And then I'se warrant ye'll be for fire thir cauld nights, or if ye want candle, that's an expensive article, for it's against the rules. And now I've tell'd ye the head articles of the charge, and I dinna think there's muckle mair, though there will aye be some odd expenses ower and abune."

"Well, sir, I must trust to your conscience, if ever you happened to hear of such a thing—I cannot help myself."

"Na, na, sir," answered the cautious jailor, "I'll no permit you to be saying that—I'm forcing naething upon ye;—an ye dinna like the price ye needna take the article—I force no man; I was only explaining what civility was; but if ye like to take the common run of the house, it's a' one to me—I'll be saved trouble, that's a'."

"Nay, my friend, I have, as I suppose you may easily guess, no inclination to dispute your terms upon such a penalty," answered Bertram. "Come, show me where I am to be, for I would fain be alone for a little while."

"Ay, ay, come along then, Captain," said the fellow, with a contortion of visage which he intended to be a smile; "and I'll tell you now,—to show you that I have a conscience, as ye ca't, d—n me if I charge ye abune sixpence a day for the freedom o' the court, and ye may walk in't very near three hours a day, and play at pitch-and-toss and handba', and what not."

With this gracious promise, he ushered Bertram into the house, and showed him up a steep and narrow stone staircase, at the top of which was a strong door, clenched with iron and studded with nails. Beyond this door was a narrow passage or gallery, having three cells on each side, wretched ,vaults, with iron bed-frames and straw mattresses. But at the farther end was a small apartment, of rather a more decent appearance, that is, having less the air of a place of confinement, since, unless for the large lock and chain upon the door, and the crossed and ponderous stanchions upon the window, it rather resembled the "worst inn's worst room." It was designed as a sort of infirmary for prisoners whose state of health required some indulgence; and, in fact, Donald Laider, Bertram's destined chum, had been just dragged out of one of the two beds which it contained, to try whether clean straw and whisky might not have a better chance to cure his intermitting fever. This process of ejection had been carried into force by Mrs. Mac-Guffog while her husband parleyed with Bertram in the courtyard, that good lady having a distinct presentiment of the manner in which the treaty must necessarily terminate. Apparently the expulsion had not taken place without some application of the strong hand, for one of the bed-posts of a sort of tent-bed was broken down, so that the tester and curtains hung forward into the middle of the narrow chamber, like the banner of a chieftain, half-sinking amid the confusion of a combat.

"Never mind that being out o' sorts, Captain," said Mrs. Mac-Guffog, who now followed them into the room; then, turning her back to the prisoner, with as much delicacy as the action admitted, she whipped from her knee her ferret garter, and applied it to splicing and fastening the broken bed-post—then used more pins than her apparel could well spare to fasten up the bed-curtains in festoons—then shook the bed-clothes into something like form—then flung over all a tattered patchwork quilt, and pronounced that things were now "something purpose-like."

"And there's your bed, Captain," pointing to a massy four-posted bulk, which, owing to the inequality of the floor that had sunk considerably (the house, though new, having been built by contract), stood on three legs, and held the fourth aloft as if pawing the air, and in the attitude of advancing like an elephant passant upon the panel of a coach—"There's your bed and the blankets; but if ye want sheets, or bowster, or pillow, or ony sort o' nappery for the table, or for your hands, ye'll hae to speak to me about it, for that's out o' the gudeman's line (Mac-Guffog had by this time left the room, to avoid, probably, any appeal which might he made to him upon this new exaction), and he never engages for onything like that."

"In God's name," said Bertram, "let me have what is decent, and make any charge you please."

"Aweel, aweel, that's sune settled; we'll no excise you neither, Though we live sae near the Custom-house. And I maun see to get you some fire and some dinner too, I'se warrant; but your dinner will be but a puir ane the day, no expecting company that would be nice and fashious."—So saying, and in all haste, Mrs. Mac-Guffog fetched a scuttle of live coals, and having replenished "the rusty grate, unconscious of a fire" for months before, she proceeded with unwashed hands to arrange the stipulated bed-linen (alas, how different from Ailie Dinmont's!), and muttering to herself as she discharged her task, seemed, in inveterate spleen of temper, to grudge even those accommodations for which she was to receive payment. At length, however, she departed, grumbling between her teeth, that "she wad rather lock up a haill ward than be fiking about thae niff-naffy [*Fastidious] gentles that gae sae muckle fash [*Trouble] wi' their fancies."

When she was gone, Bertram found himself reduced to the alternative of pacing his little apartment for exercise, or gazing out upon the sea in such proportions as could be seen from the narrow panes of his window, obscured by dirt and by close iron-bars, or reading over the records of brutal wit and black-guardism which despair had scrawled upon the half-whitened walls. The sounds were as uncomfortable as the objects of sight; the sullen dash of the tide, which was now retreating, and the occasional opening and shutting of a door, with all its accompaniments of jarring bolts and creaking hinges, mingling occasionally with the dull monotony of the retiring ocean. Sometimes, too, he could hear the hoarse growl of the keeper, or the shriller strain of his helpmate, almost always in the tone of discontent, anger, or insolence. At other times the large mastiff, chained in the court-yard, answered with furious bark the insults of the idle loiterers who made a sport of incensing him.

At length the tedium of this weary space was broken by the entrance of a dirty-looking serving wench, who made some preparations for dinner by laying a half-dirty cloth upon a whole-dirty deal table. A knife and fork, which had not been worn out by over-cleaning, flanked a cracked delf plate; a nearly empty mustard-pot, placed on one side of the table, balanced a salt-cellar, containing an article of a grayish, or rather a blackish mixture, upon the other, both of stone-ware, and bearing too obvious marks of recent service. Shortly after, the same Hebe brought up a plate of beef-collops, done in the frying-pan, with a huge allowance of grease floating in an ocean of lukewarm water; and having added a coarse loaf to these savoury viands, she requested to know what liquors the gentleman chose to order. The appearance of this fare was not very inviting; but Bertram endeavoured to mend his commons by ordering wine, which he found tolerably good, and, with the assistance of some indifferent cheese, made his dinner chiefly off the brown loaf. When his meal was over, the girl presented her master's compliments, and, if agreeable to the gentleman, he would help him to spend the evening. Bertram desired to be excused, and begged, instead of this gracious society, that he might be furnished with paper, pen, ink, and candles. The light appeared in the shape of one long broken tallow-candle, inclining over a tin candlestick coated with grease; as for the writing materials, the prisoner was informed that he might have them the next day if he chose to send out to buy them. Bertram next desired the maid to procure him a book, and enforced his request with a shilling; in consequence of which, after long absence, she reappeared with two odd volumes of the Newgate Calendar, which she had borrowed from Sam Silverquill, an idle apprentice, who was imprisoned under a charge of forgery. Having laid the books on the table she retired, and left Bertram to studies which were not ill adapted to his present melancholy situation.

CHAPTER XLV.

But if thou shouldst he dragg'd in scorn
To yonder ignominious tree,
Thou shalt not want one faithful friend
To share the cruel fates' decree.
　　Shenstone.

Plunged in the gloomy reflections which were naturally excited by his dismal reading, and disconsolate situation, Bertram, for the first time in his life, felt himself affected with a disposition to low spirits. "I have been in worse situations than this too," he said;—"more dangerous, for here is no danger; more dismal in prospect, for my present confinement must necessarily be short; more intolerable for the time, for here, at least, I have fire, food, and shelter. Yet, with reading these bloody tales of crime and misery, in a place so corresponding to the ideas which they excite, and in listening to these sad sounds, I feel a stronger disposition to melancholy than in my life I ever experienced. But I will not give way to it.—Begone, thou record of guilt and infamy!" he said, flinging the book upon the spare bed; "a Scottish jail shall not break, on the very first day, the spirits which have resisted climate, and want, and penury, and disease, and imprisonment, in a foreign land. I have fought many a hard battle with dame Fortune, and she shall not beat me now if I can help it."

Then bending his mind to a strong effort, he endeavoured to view his situation in the most favourable light. Delaserre must soon be in Scotland; the certificates from his commanding officer must soon arrive; nay, if Mannering were first applied to, who could say but the effect might be a reconciliation between them? He had often observed, and now remembered, that when his former colonel took the part of any one, it was never by halves, and that he seemed to love those persons most who had lain under obligation to him. In the present case, a favour, which could be asked with honour and granted with readiness, might be the means of reconciling them to each other. From this his feelings naturally turned towards Julia; and, without very nicely measuring the distance between a soldier of fortune, who expected that her father's attestation would deliver him from confinement, and the heiress of that father's wealth and expectations, he was building the gayest castle in the clouds, and varnishing it with all the tints of a summer-evening sky, when his labour was interrupted by a loud knocking at the outer gate, answered by the barking of the gaunt half-starved mastiff, which was quartered in the courtyard as an addition to the garrison. After much scrupulous precaution the gate was opened, and some person admitted. The house-door was next unbarred, unlocked, and unchained, a dog's feet pattered upstairs in great haste, and the animal was heard scratching and whining at the door of the room. Next a heavy step was heard lumbering up, and Mac-Guffog's voice in the character of pilot—"This way, this way; take care of the step;—that's the room."—Bertram's door was then unbolted, and, to his great surprise and joy, his terrier, Wasp, rushed into the apartment, and almost devoured him with caresses, followed by the massy form of his friend from Charlies-hope.

"Eh whow! Eh whow!" ejaculated the honest farmer, as he looked round upon his friend's miserable apartment and wretched accommodation—"What's this o't! what's this o't!"

"Just a trick of fortune, my good friend," said Bertram, rising and shaking him heartily by the hand, "that's all."

"But what will be done about it?—or what can be done about it?" said honest Dandie—"is't for debt, or what is't for?"

"Why, it is not for debt," answered Bertram; and if you have time to sit down, I'll tell you all I know of the matter myself."

"If I hae time?" said Dandie, with an accent on the word that sounded like a howl of derision—"Ou, what the deevil am I come here for, man, but just ance errand to see about it? But ye'll no be the waur o' something to eat, I trow;—it's getting late at e'en—I tell'd the folk at the Change, where I put up Dumple, to send ower my supper here, and the chield Mac-Guffog is agreeable to let it in—I hae settled a' that.—And now let's hear your story—Whisht, Wasp, man! wow but he's glad to see you, poor thing!"

Bertram's story, being confined to the accident of Hazlewood, and the confusion made between his own ,identity and that of one of the smugglers, who had been active in the assault of Woodbourne, and chanced to bear the same name, was soon told. Dinmont listened very attentively. "Aweel," he said, "this suld be nae sic dooms-desperate business surely—the lad's doing weel again that was hurt, and what signifies twa or three lead draps in his shouther? if ye had putten out his ee it would hae been another case. But eh, as I wuss auld Sherra Pleydell was to the fore here!—odd, he was the man for sorting them, and the queerest rough-spoken deevil too that ever ye heard!"

"But now tell me, my excellent friend, how did you find out I was here?"

"Odd, lad, queerly eneugh," said Dandie; "but I'll tell ye that after ye are done wi' our supper, for it will maybe no be sae weel to speak about it while that lang-lugged limmer o' a lass is gaun flisking in and out o' the room."

Bertram's curiosity was in some degree put to rest by the appearance of the supper which his friend had ordered, which, although homely enough, had the appetising cleanliness in which Mrs. Mac-Guffog's cookery was so eminently deficient. Dinmont also, premising he had ridden the whole day since breakfast-time, without tasting anything "to speak of," which qualifying phrase related to about three pounds of cold roast mutton which he had discussed at his midday stage,—Dinmont, I say, fell stoutly upon the good cheer, and, like one of Homer's heroes, said little, either good or bad, till the rage of thirst and hunger was appeased. At length, after a draught of home-brewed ale, he began by observing, "Aweel, aweel, that hen," looking upon the lamentable relics of what had been once a large fowl, "wasna a bad ane to be bred at a town end, though it's no like our barn-door chuckles at Charlies-hope—and I am glad to see that this vexing job hasna taen awa your appetite, Captain."

"Why, really, my dinner was not so excellent, Mr. Dinmont, as to spoil my supper."

"I dare say no, I dare say no," said Dandie:—"But now, hinny, that ye hae brought us the brandy, and the mug wi' the het water, and the sugar, and a' right, ye may steak [*Fasten] the door, ye see, for we wad hae some o' our ain cracks." [*Conversation] The damsel accordingly retired, and shut the door of the apartment, to which she added the precaution of drawing a large bolt on the outside.

As soon as she was gone, Dandie reconnoitred the premises, listened at the keyhole as if he had been listening for the blowing of an otter, and having satisfied himself that there were no eavesdroppers, returned to the table; and making himself what he called a gey stiff cheerer, poked the fire, and began his story in an undertone of gravity and importance not very usual with him.

"Ye see, Captain, I had been in Edinbro' for twa or three days, looking after the burial of a friend that we hae lost, and maybe I suld hae had something for my ride; but there's disappointments in a' things, and wha can help the like o' that? And I had a wee bit law business besides, but that's neither here nor there. In short, I had got my matters settled, and hame I cam; and the morn awa to the muirs to see what the herds had been about, and I thought I might as weel gie a look to the Tout-hope head, where Jock o' Dawston and me has the outcast about a march.—Weel, just as I was coming upon the bit I saw a man afore me that I kenn'd was nane o' our herds, and it's a wild bit to meet ony other body, so when I cam up to him, it was Tod Gabriel the fox-hunter. So I says to him, rather surprised like, 'What are ye doing up amang the craws here, without your hounds, man? are ye seeking the fox without the dogs?' So he said, 'Na, gudeman, but I wanted to see yourself.'

"'Ay,' said I, 'and ye'll be wanting eilding now, or something to pit ower the winter?'

"'Na, na,' quo' he, I it's no that I'm seeking; but ye tak an unco concern in that Captain Brown that was staying wi' you, d'ye no?'

"'Troth do I, Gabriel,' says I; 'and what about him, lad?'

"Says he, 'There's mair tak an interest in him than you, and some that I am bound to obey; and it's no just on my ain will that I'm here to tell you something about him that will no please you.'

"'Faith, naething will please me,' quo' I, 'that's no pleasing to him.'

"'And then,' quo' he, 'ye'll be ill-sorted to hear that he's like to be in the prison at Portanferry, if he disna tak a' the better care o' himself, for there's been warrants out to tak him as soon as he comes ower the water frae Allonby. And now, gudeman, an ever ye wish him weel, ye maun ride down to Portanferry, and let nae grass grow at the nag's heels; and if ye find him in confinement, ye maun stay beside him night and day, for a day or twa, for he'll want friends that hae baith heart and hand; and if ye neglect this ye'll never rue but ance, for it will be for a' your life.,

"'But, safe us, man,' quo' I, 'how did ye learn a' this? it's an unco way between this and Portanferry.'

"'Never ye mind that,' quo' he, 'them that brought us the news rade night and day, and ye maun be aff instantly if ye wad do ony gude— and sae I have naething mair to tell ye.'—Sae he sat himself doun and hirselled [*Creeping sideways in a sitting posture by means of the hands.] doun into the glen, where it wad hae been ill following him wi' the beast, and I cam back to Charlies-hope to tell the gudewife, for I was uncertain what to do. It wad look unco-like, I thought, just to be sent out on a hunt-the-gowk errand wi' a land-louper [*Vagrant] like that. But, Lord! as the gudewife set up her throat about it, and said what a shame it wad be if ye was to come to ony wrang, an I could help ye; and then in cam your letter that confirmed it. So I took to the kist, and out wi' the, pickle [*A supply.] notes in case they should be needed, and a' the bairns ran to saddle Dumple. By great luck I had taen the other beast to Edinbro', sae Dumple was as fresh as a rose Sae aff I set, and Wasp wi' me, for ye wad really hae thought he kenn'd where I was gaun, puir beast; and here I am after a trot o' sixty mile, or near by. But Wasp rade thirty of them afore me on the saddle, and the puir doggie balanced itself as ane o' the weans wad hae dune, whether I trotted or cantered."

In this strange story Bertram obviously saw, supposing the warning to be true, some intimation of danger more violent and imminent than could be likely to arise from a few days' imprisonment. At the same time it was equally evident that some unknown friend was working in his behalf. "Did you not say," he asked Dinmont, "that this man Gabriel was of gipsy blood?"

"It was e'en judged sae," said Dinmont, "and I think this maks it likely; for they aye ken where the gangs o' ilk ither I are to be found, and they can gar news flee like a footba' through the country an they like. An' I forgat to tell ye, there's been an unco inquiry after the auld wife that we saw in Bewcastle; the Sheriffs had folk ower the Limestane Edge after her, and down the Hermitage and Liddel, and a' gates, and a reward offered for her to appear, o' fifty pound sterling, nae less; and justice Forster, he's had out warrants, as I am tell'd, in Cumberland, and an unco ranging and riping [*A Searching.] they have had a' gates seeking for her; but she'll no be taen wi' them unless she likes, for a' that."

"And how comes that?" said Bertram.

"Ou, I dinna ken; I daur say it's nonsense, but they say she has gathered the fern-seed, and can gang ony gate she likes, like Jock-the-Giant-killer in the ballant, wi' his coat o'darkness and his shoon o' swiftness. Ony way she's a kind o' queen amang the gipsies; she is mair than a hundred year auld, folk say, and minds the coming in o' the moss-troopers in the troublesome times when the Stuarts were put awa. Sae, if she canna hide herself, she kens them that can hide her weel eneugh, ye needna doubt that. Odd, an I had kenn'd it had been Meg Merrilies yon night at Tibb Mumps's, I wad taen care how I crossed her."

Bertram listened with great attention to this account, which tallied so well in many points with what he had himself seen of this gipsy sibyl. After a moment's consideration, he concluded it would be no breach of faith to mention what he had seen at Derncleugh to a person who held Meg in such reverence as Dinmont obviously did. He told his story accordingly, often interrupted by ejaculations such as, "Weel, the like o' that now!" or, "Na, deil an that's no something now!"

When our Liddesdale friend had heard the whole to an end, he shook his great black head—"Weel, I'll uphaud there's baith gude and ill amang the gipsies, and if they deal wi' the Enemy, it's a' their ain business and no ours.—I ken what the streeking the corpse wad be, weel eneugh. Thae smuggler deevils, when ony o' them's killed in a fray, they'll send for a wife like Meg far eneugh to dress the corpse; odd, it's a' the burial they ever think o'! and then to be put into the ground without ony decency, just like dogs. But they stick to it, that they" be streekit, and hae an auld wife when they're dying to rhyme ower prayers, and ballants, and charms, as they ca' them, rather than they'll hae a minister to come and pray wi' them—that's an auld threep o' theirs; and I am thinking the man that died will hae been ane o' the folk that was shot when they burnt Woodbourne."

"But, my good friend, Woodbourne is not burnt," said Bertram.

"Weel, the better for them that bides in't," answered the store-farmer. "Odd, we had it up the water wi' us, that there wasna a stane on the tap o' anither. But there was fighting, ony way; I daur to say, it would he fine fun! And, as I said, Ye may take it on trust, that that's been ane o' the men killed there, and that it's been the gipsies that took your pockmanky when they fand the chaise stickin' in the snaw—they wadna pass the like a' that—it wad just come to their hand like the bowl o' a pint stoup." [*The handle of a stoup of liquor; than which, our proverb seems to infer, there is nothing comes more readily to the grasp.]

"But if this woman is a sovereign among them, why was she not able to afford me open protection, and to get me back my property?"

"Ou, wha kens? she has muckle to say wi' them, but whiles they'll tak their ain way for a' that, when they're under temptation. And then there's the smugglers that they're aye leagued wi', she maybe couldna manage them sae weel-they're aye banded thegither—I've heard that the gipsies ken when the smugglers will come aff, and where they're to land, better than the very merchants that deal wi' them. And then, to the boot o' that, she's whiles crack-brained, and has a bee in her head; they say that whether her spaeings and fortune-tellings be true or no, for certain she believes in them a' hersell, and is aye guiding herself by some queer prophecy or anither. So she disna aye gang the straight road to the well.—But deil o' sic a story as yours, wi' glamour and dead folk and losing ane's gate, I ever heard out o' the tale-books!—But whisht, I hear the keeper coming."

Mac-Guffog accordingly interrupted their discourse by the harsh harmony of the bolts and bars, and showed his bloated visage at the opening door. "Come, Mr. Dinmont, we have put off locking up for an hour to oblige ye; ye must go to your quarters."

"Quarters, man? I intend to sleep here the night. There's a spare bed in the Captain's room."

"It's impossible!" answered the keeper.

"But I say it is possible, and that I winna stir—and there's a dram t'ye."

Mac-Guffog drank off the spirits, and resumed his objection. "But it's against rule, sir; ye have committed nae malefaction."

"I'll break your head," said the sturdy Liddesdale man, "if ye say ony mair about it, and that will be malefaction eneugh to entitle me to ae night's lodging wi' you ony way."

"But I tell ye, Mr. Dinmont," reiterated the keeper, it's against rule, and I behoved to lose my post."

"Weel, Mac-Guffog," said Dandie, "I hae just twa things to say. Ye ken wha I am weel eneugh, and that I wadna loose a prisoners"

"And how do I ken that?" answered the jailor.

"Weel, if ye dinna ken that," said the resolute farmer, "ye ken this;—ye ken ye're whiles obliged to be up our water in the way o' your business; now, if ye let me stay quietly here the night wi' the Captain, I'se pay ye double fees for the room; and if ye say no, ye shall hae the best sark-fu' o' sair banes that ever ye had in your life, the first time ye set a foot by Liddel-moat!"

"Aweel, aweel, gudeman," said Mac-Guffog, "a wilfu' man maun hae his way; but if I am challenged for it by the justices, I ken wha sail bear the wyte;"—and having scaled this observation with a deep oath or two, he retired to bed, after carefully securing all the doors of the Bridewell. The bell from the town steeple tolled nine just as the ceremony was concluded.

"Although it's but early hours," said the farmer, who had observed that his friend looked somewhat pale and fatigued, "I think we had better lie down, Captain, if ye're no agreeable to another cheerer. But troth, ye're nae glass-breaker; and neither am I, unless it be a screed wi' the neighbours, or when I'm on a ramble."

Bertram readily assented to the motion of his faithful friend, but, on looking at the bed, felt repugnance to trust himself undressed to Mrs. Mac-Guffog's clean sheets.

"I'm muckle o' your opinion, Captain," said Dandie. "Odd, this bed looks as if a' the colliers in Sanquhar had been in't thegither. But it'll no win through my muckle coat. "So saying, he flung himself upon the frail bed with a force that made all its timbers crack, and in a few moments gave audible signal that he was fast asleep. Bertram slipped off his coat and boots, and, occupied the other dormitory. The strangeness of his destiny, and the mysteries which appeared to thicken around him, while he seemed alike to be persecuted and protected by secret enemies and friends, arising out of a class of people with whom he had no previous connection, for some time occupied his thoughts. Fatigue, however, gradually composed his mind, and in a short time he was as fast asleep as his companion. And in this comfortable state of oblivion we must leave them, until we acquaint the reader with some other circumstances which occurred about the same period.

CHAPTER XLVI.

—Say from whence You owe this strange intelligence? or
why Upon this blasted heath you stop our way With such
prophetic greeting?—Speak, I charge you.

Macbeth

Upon the evening of the day when Bertram's examination had taken place, Colonel Mannering arrived at Woodbourne from Edinburgh. He found his family n their usual state, which probably, so far as Julia vas concerned, would not have been the case had she learned the news of Bertram's arrest. But as, during the Colonel's absence, the two young ladies lived much retired, this circumstance fortunately had not reached Woodbourne. A letter had already made Miss Bertram acquainted with the downfall of the expectations which had been formed upon the bequest of her kinswoman. Whatever hopes that news night have dispelled, the disappointment did not prevent her from joining her friend in affording a cheerful reception to the Colonel, to whom she thus endeavoured to express the deep sense she entertained of his paternal kindness. She touched on her regret, that at such a season of the year he should have made, upon her account, a journey so fruitless.

"That it was fruitless to you, my dear," said the Colonel, "I do most deeply lament; but for, my own share, I have made some valuable acquaintances, and have spent the time I have been absent in Edinburgh with peculiar satisfaction; so that, on that score, there is nothing to be regretted. Even our friend the Dominie is returned thrice the man he was, from having sharpened his wits in controversy with the geniuses of the northern metropolis."

"Of a surety," said the Dominie, with great complacency, "I did wrestle, and was not overcome, though my adversary was cunning in his art."

"I presume," said Miss Mannering, "the conquest was somewhat fatiguing, Mr. Sampson?"

"Very much, young lady—howbeit I girded up my loins and strove against him."

"I can bear witness," said the Colonel; "I never saw an affair better contested. The enemy was like the Mahratta cavalry; he assailed on all sides, and presented no fair mark for artillery; but Mr. Sampson stood to his guns, notwithstanding, and fired away, now upon the enemy, and now upon the dust which he had raised. But we must not fight our battles over again to-night—to-morrow we shall have the whole at breakfast."

The next morning at breakfast, however, the Dominie did not make his appearance. He had walked out, a servant said, early in the morning. It was so common for him to forget his meals, that his absence never deranged the family. The housekeeper, a decent old-fashioned Presbyterian matron, having, as such, the highest respect for Sampson's theological acquisitions, had it in charge on these occasions to take care that he was no sufferer by his absence of mind, and therefore usually, waylaid him on his return, to remind him of his sublunary wants, and to minister to their relief. It seldom, however, happened that he was absent from two meals together, as was the case in the present instance. We must explain the cause of this unusual occurrence.

The conversation which Mr. Pleydell had held with Mr. Mannering on the subject of the loss of Harry Bertram, had awakened all the painful sensations which that event had inflicted upon Sampson. The affectionate heart of the poor Dominie had always reproached him, that his negligence in leaving the child in the care of Frank Kennedy had been the proximate cause of the murder of the one, the loss of the other, the death of Mrs. Bertram, and the ruin of the family of his patron. It was a subject which he never conversed upon,—if indeed his mode of speech could be called conversation at any time,—but it was often present to his imagination. The sort of hope so strongly affirmed and asserted in Mrs. Bertram's last settlement, had excited a corresponding feeling in the Dominie's bosom, which was exasperated into a sort of sickening anxiety, by the discredit with which Pleydell had treated it.—"Assuredly," thought Sampson to himself, "he is a man of erudition, and well skilled in the weighty matters of the law; but he is also a man of humorous levity and inconsistency of speech; and wherefore should he pronounce ex cathedra, as it were, on the hope expressed by worthy Madam Margaret Bertram of Singleside?"

All this, I say, the Dominie thought to himself for had he uttered half the sentence, his jaws would have ached for a month under the unusual fatigue of such a continued exertion. The result of these cogitations was a resolution to go and visit the scene of the tragedy at Warroch Point, where he had not been for many years—not, indeed, since the fatal accident had happened. The walk was a long one, for the Point of Warroch lay on the farther side of the Ellangowan property, which was interposed between it and Woodbourne. Besides, the Dominie went astray more than once, and met with brooks swollen into torrents by the melting of the snow, where he, honest man, had only the summer-recollection of little trickling rills.

At length, however, he reached the woods which he had made the object of his excursion, and traversed them with care, muddling his disturbed brains with vague efforts to recall every circumstance of the catastrophe. It will readily be supposed that the influence of local situation and association was inadequate to produce conclusions different from those which he had formed under the immediate pressure of the occurrences themselves. "With many a weary sigh, therefore, and many a groan," the poor Dominie returned from his hopeless pilgrimage, and weariedly plodded his way towards Woodbourne, debating at times in his altered mind a question which was forced upon him by the cravings of an appetite rather of the keenest, namely, whether he had breakfasted that morning or no?—It was in this twilight humour, now thinking of the loss of the child, then involuntarily compelled to meditate upon the somewhat incongruous subject of hung-beef, rolls, and butter, that his route, which was different from that which he had taken in the morning, conducted him past the small ruined—tower, or rather vestige of a tower, called by the country people the Kaim of Derncleugh.

The reader may recollect the description of this ruin in the twenty-seventh chapter of this narrative, as the vault in which young Bertram, under the auspices of Meg Merrilies, witnessed the death of Hatteraick's lieutenant. The tradition of the country added ghostly terrors to the natural awe inspired by the situation of this place, which terrors the gipsies, who so long inhabited the vicinity, had probably invented, or at least propagated, for their own advantage. It was said that, during the times of the Galwegian independence, one Hanlon MacDingawaie, brother to the reigning chief, Knarth MacDingawaie, murdered his brother and sovereign, in order to usurp the principality from his infant nephew, and that being pursued for vengeance by the faithful allies and retainers of the house, who espoused the cause of the lawful heir, he was compelled to retreat, with a few followers whom he had involved in his crime, to his impregnable tower called the Kaim of Derncleugh, where he defended himself until nearly reduced by famine, when, setting fire to the place, he and the small remaining garrison desperately perished by their own swords, rather than fall into the hands of their exasperated enemies. This tragedy, which, considering the wild times wherein it was placed, might have some foundation in truth, was larded with many legends of superstition and diablerie, so that most of the peasants of the neighbourhood, if benighted, would rather have chosen to make a considerable circuit, than pass these haunted walls. The lights, often seen around the tower when used as the rendezvous of the lawless characters by whom it was occasionally frequented, were accounted for, under authority of these tales of witchery, in a manner at once convenient for the private parties concerned, and satisfactory to the public.

Now, it must be confessed, that our friend Sampson, although a profound scholar and mathematician, had not travelled so far in philosophy as to doubt the reality of witchcraft or apparitions. Born indeed at a time when a doubt in the existence of witches was interpreted as equivalent to a justification of their infernal practices, a belief of such legends had been impressed upon the Dominie as an article indivisible from his religious faith, and perhaps it would have been equally difficult to have induced him to doubt the one as the other. With these feelings, and in a thick misty day, which was already drawing to its close, Dominie Sampson did not pass the Kaim of Derncleugh without some feelings of tacit horror.

What then was his astonishment, when, on passing the door—that door which was supposed to have been placed there by one of the latter Lairds of Ellangowan to prevent presumptuous strangers from incurring the dangers of the haunted vault—that door, supposed to be always locked, and the key of which was popularly said to be deposited with the presbytery—that door, that very door, opened suddenly, and the figure of Meg Merrilies, well known, though not seen for many a revolving year, was placed at once before the eyes of the startled Dominie! She stood immediately before him in the footpath, confronting him so absolutely, that he could not avoid her except by fairly turning back, which his manhood prevented him from thinking of.

"I kenn'd ye wad be here," she said with her harsh and hollow voice "I ken wha ye seek; but ye maun do my bidding."

"Get thee behind me!" said the alarmed Dominie—"Avoid ye!— Conjuro te, scelestissima—nequissima—spurcissima—iniquissima—atque miserrim—conjuro te!!!"—Meg stood her ground against this tremendous volley of superlatives, which Sampson hawked up from the pit of his stomach, and hurled at her in thunder. "Is the carl daft," she said, "wi' his glamour?"

"Conjuro," continued the Dominie, "abjuro contestor, atque viriliter impero tibi!"—

"What, in the name of Sathan, are ye feared for, wi' your French gibberish, that would make a dog sick? Listen, ye stickit stibbler, [*A broken-down clerical probationer.] to what I tell ye, or ye sall rue it while there's a limb o' ye hings to anither!—Tell Colonel Mannering that I ken he's seeking me. He kens, and I ken, that the blood will be wiped out, and the lost will be found,

"And Bertram's right and Bertram's might Shall meet on Ellangowan height.

Hae, there's a letter to him, I was gaun to send it in another way.—I canna write mysell; but I hae them that will baith write and read, and ride and rin for me. Tell him the time's coming now, and the weird's dreed [*The destiny is fulfilled.] and the wheel's turning. Bid him look at the stars as he has looked at them before.—Will ye mind a' this?"

"Assuredly," said the Dominie, "I am dubious—for, woman, I am perturbed at thy words, and my flesh quakes to hear thee."

"'They'll do you nae ill though, and maybe muckle gude."

"Avoid ye! I desire no good that comes by unlawful means."

"Fule-body that thou art," said Meg, stepping up to him with a frown of indignation that made her dark eyes flash like lamps from under her bent brows,—"Fule-body! if I meant ye wrang, couldna I clod [*Hurl.] ye ower that craig [*Steep rock.], and wad man ken how ye cam by your end mair than Frank Kennedy? Hear ye that, ye worricow?" [*Scarecrow.]

"In the name of all that is good," said the Dominie, recoiling, and pointing his long pewter-headed walking-cane like a javelin at the supposed sorceress,—"in the name of all that is good, bide off hands! I will not be handled woman, stand off, upon thine own proper peril!—desist, I say—I am strong—lo, I will resist!"—Here his speech was cut short; for Meg, armed with supernatural strength, (as the Dominie asserted), broke in upon his guard, put by a thrust which he made at her with his cane, and lifted him into the vault, "as easily," said he, "as I could sway a Kitchen's Atlas."

"Sit down there," she said, pushing the half-throttled preacher with some violence against a broken chair,—"sit down there, and gather your wind and your senses, ye black barrow-tram [*Limb.] o' the kirk that ye are—Are ye fou or fasting?"

"Fasting—from all but sin," answered the Dominie, who, recovering his voice, and finding his exorcisms only served to exasperate the intractable sorceress, thought it best to affect complaisance and submission, inwardly conning over, however, the wholesome conjurations which he durst no longer utter aloud. But as the Dominie's brain was by no means equal to carry on two trains of ideas at the same time, a word or two of his mental exercise sometimes escaped, and mingled with his uttered speech in a manner ludicrous enough, especially as the poor man shrunk himself together after every escape of the kind, from terror of the effect it might produce upon the irritable feelings of the witch.

Meg, in the meanwhile, went to a great black cauldron that was boiling on a fire on the floor, and, lifting the lid, an odour was diffused through the vault, which, if the vapours of a witch's cauldron could in aught be trusted, promised better things than the hell-broth which such vessels are usually supposed to contain. It was in fact the savour of a goodly stew, composed of fowls, hares, partridges, and moorgame, boiled, in a large mess with potatoes, onions, and leeks, and from the size of the cauldron, appeared to be prepared for half a dozen people at least. "So ye hae eat naething a' day?" said Meg, heaping a large portion of this mess into a brown dish, and strewing it savourily with salt and pepper. [*We must again have recourse to the contribution to Blackwood's Magazine, April 1817 :—

"To the admirers of good eating, Gipsy cookery seems to have little to recommend it. I can assure you, however, that the cook of a nobleman of high distinction, a person who never reads even a novel without an eye to the enlargement of the culinary science, has added to the Almanach des Gourmands, a certain Potage a la Meg Merrilies de Dernclough, consisting of game and poultry of all kinds, stewed with vegetables into a soup, which rivals in savour and richness the gallant messes of Comacho's wedding; and which the Baron of Bradwardine would certainly have reckoned among the Epulae, lautiores."

[The artist alluded to in this passage in Mons. Florence, cook to Henry and Charles, late Dukes of Buccleuch, and of high distinction in his profession.]

"Nothing," answered the Dominie—"scelestissima!—that is—gudewife."

"Hae then," said she, placing the dish before him, "there's what will warm your heart."

"I do not hunger—malefica—that is to say—Mrs. Merrilies!" for he said unto himself, ,the savour is sweet, but it bath been cooked by a Canidia or an Ericthoe."

"If ye dinna eat instantly, and put some saul in ye, by the bread and the salt, I'll put it down your throat wi' the cutty [*Short.] spoon, scaulding as it is, and whether ye will or no. Gape, sinner, and swallow!"

Sampson, afraid of eye of newt, and toe of frog, tigers' chaudrons, and so forth, had determined not to venture; but the smell of the stew was fast melting his obstinacy, which flowed from his chops as it were in streams of water, and the witch's threats decided him to feed. Hunger and fear are excellent casuists.

"Saul," said Hunger, "feasted with the witch of Endor."—"And," quoth Fear, "the salt which she sprinkled upon the food showeth plainly it is not a necromantic banquet, in which that seasoning never occurs."—"And, besides," says Hunger, after the first spoonful, "it is savoury and refreshing viands."

"So ye like the meat?" said the hostess. "Yea," answered the Dominie, "and I give thee thanks-sceleratissima!—which means—Mrs. Margaret."

"Aweel, eat your fill; but an ye kenn'd how it was gotten, ye' maybe wadna like it sae weel. "Sampson's spoon dropped, in the act of conveying its load to his mouth. There's been mony a moon-light watch to bring a' that trade thegither," continued Meg,—"the folk that are to eat that dinner thought little o' your game-laws."

"Is that all?" thought Sampson, resuming his spoon, and shovelling away manfully; "I will not lack my food upon that argument."

"Now, ye maun tak a dram?"

"I will," quoth Sampson—"conjuro te—that is, I thank you heartily," for he thought to himself, in for a penny, in for a pound; and he fairly drank the witch's health, in a cupful of brandy. When he had put this cope-stone upon Meg's good cheer, he felt, as he said, "mightily elevated, and afraid of no evil which could befall unto him."

"Will ye remember my errand now?" said Meg Merrilies; "I ken by the cast o' your ee that ye're anither man than when you cam in."

"I will, Mrs. Margaret," repeated Sampson stoutly "I will deliver unto him the sealed yepistle, and will add what you please to send by word of mouth."

"Then I'll make it short," says Meg. "Tell him to look at the stars without fail this night, and to do what I desire him in that letter, as he would wish

"That Bertram's right and Bertram's might

Should meet on Ellangowan height.

I have seen him twice when he saw na me; I ken when he was in this country first, and I ken what's brought him back again. Up, an' to the gate! ye're ower lang here-follow me."

Sampson followed the sibyl accordingly, who guided him about a quarter of a mile through the woods, by a shorter cut than he could have found for himself; they then entered upon the common, Meg still marching before him at a great pace, until she gained the top of a small hillock which overhung the road.

"Here," she said, "stand still here. Look how the setting sun breaks through yon cloud that's been darkening the lift a' day. See where the first stream o' light fa's—it's upon Donagild's round tower—the auldest tower in the Castle o' Ellangowan—that's no for naething!—See as it's glooming to seaward abune yon sloop in the bay—that's no for naething neither.—Here I stood on this very spot," said she, drawing herself up so as not to lose one hair-breadth of her uncommon height, and stretching out her long sinewy arm and clenched hand, "Here I stood, when I tauld the last Laird o' Ellangowan what was coming on his house—and did that fa' to the ground?—na—it bit even ower sair!—And here, where I brake the wand of peace ower him—here I stand again—to bid God bless and prosper the just heir of Ellangowan that will sune be brought to his ain; and the best laird he shall be that Ellangowan has seen for three hundred years.—I'll no live to see it, maybe; but there will be mony a blithe ee see it though mine be closed. And now, Abel Sampson, as ever ye lo'ed the house of Ellangowan, away wi' my message, to the English Colonel, as if life and death were upon your haste!"

So saying, she turned suddenly from the amazed Dominie, and regained with swift and long strides the shelter of the wood from which she had issued, at the point where it most encroached upon the common. Sampson gazed after her for a moment in utter astonishment, and then obeyed her directions,—hurrying to Woodbourne at a pace very unusual for him, exclaiming three times, "Prodigious! prodigious! prodi-gi-ous! "

CHAPTER XLVII.

—It is not madness That I have utter'd; bring me to the
test, And I the matter will re-word; which madness Would
gambol from.

Hamlet

As Mr. Sampson crossed the hall with a bewildered look, Mrs. Allan, the good housekeeper, who, with the reverent attention which is usually rendered to the clergy in Scotland, was on the watch for his return, sallied forth to meet him—" What's this o't now, Mr. Sampson, this is waur than ever!—Ye'll really do yourself some injury wi' these lang fasts—naething's sae hurtful to the stamach, Mr. Sampson;—if ye would but put some peppermint draps in your pocket, or let Barnes cut ye a sandwich."

"Avoid thee!" quoth the Dominie, his mind running still upon his interview with Meg Merrilies, and making for the dining-parlour.

"Na, ye needna gang in there, the cloth's been removed an hour syne, and the Colonel's at his wine; but just step into my room, I have a nice steak that the cook will do in a moment."

"Exorciso te!" said Sampson,—"that is, I have dined."

"Dined! it's impossible—wha can ye hae dined wi', you that gangs out nae gate?"

"With Beelzebub, I believe," said the minister.

"Na, then he's bewitched for certain," said the housekeeper, letting go her hold; "he's bewitched, or he's daft, and ony way the Colonel maun just guide him his ain gate—Wae's me! Hech, sirs! It's a sair thing to see learning bring folk to this!" And with this compassionate ejaculation, she retreated into her own premises.

The object of her commiseration had by this time entered the dining-parlour, where his appearance gave great surprise. He was mud up to the' shoulders, and the natural paleness of his hue was twice as cadaverous as usual, through terror, fatigue, and perturbation of mind. "What on earth is the meaning of this, Mr. Sampson?" said Mannering, who observed Miss Bertram looking much alarmed for her simple but attached friend.

"Exorciso,"—said the Dominie.

"How, sir?" replied the astonished Colonel.

"I crave pardon, honourable sir! but my wits—"

"Are gone a wool-gathering, I think—pray, Mr. Sampson, collect yourself, and let me know the meaning of all this."

Sampson was about to reply, but finding his Latin formula of exorcism still came most readily to his tongue, he prudently desisted from the attempt, and put the scrap of paper which he had received from the gipsy into Mannering's hand, who broke the seal and read it with surprise. "This seems to be some jest," he said, "and a very dull one."

"It came from no jesting person," said Mr. Sampson.

"From whom then did it come?" demanded Mannering.

The Dominie, who often displayed some delicacy of recollection in cases where Miss Bertram had an interest, remembered the painful circumstances connected with Meg Merrilies, looked at the young ladies, and remained silent. "We will join you at the tea-table in an instant, Julia," said the Colonel; "I see that Mr. Sampson wishes to speak to me alone.—And now they are gone, what, in heaven's name, Mr. Sampson, is the meaning of all this?"

"It may be a message from Heaven," said the Dominie, "but it came by Beelzebub's postmistress. It was that witch, Meg Merrilies, who should have been burned with a tar-barrel twenty years since, for a harlot, thief, witch, and gipsy."

"Are you sure it was she?" said the Colonel with great interest.

"Sure, honoured sir?—Of a truth she is one not to be forgotten—the like o' Meg Merrilies is not to be seen in any land."

The Colonel paced the room rapidly, cogitating with himself. "To send out to apprehend her—but it is too distant to send to Mac-Morlan, and Sir Robert Hazlewood is a pompous coxcomb; besides the chance of not finding her upon the spot, or that the humour of silence that seized her, before may again return;—no, I will not, to save being thought a fool, neglect the course she points out. Many of her class set out by being impostors, and end by becoming enthusiasts, or hold a kind of darkling conduct between both lines, unconscious almost when they are cheating themselves, or when imposing on others.—Well, my course is a plain one at any rate; and if my efforts are fruitless, it shall not be owing to over-jealousy of my own character for wisdom."

With this he rang the bell, and ordering Barnes into his private sitting-room, gave him some orders, with the result of which the reader may be made hereafter acquainted. We must now take up another adventure, which is also to be woven into the story of this remarkable day.

Charles Hazlewood had not ventured to make a visit at Woodbourne during the absence of the Colonel. Indeed Mannering's whole behaviour had impressed upon him an opinion that this would be disagreeable; and such was the ascendency which the successful soldier and accomplished gentleman had attained over the young man's conduct, that in no respect would he have ventured to offend him. He saw, or thought he saw, in Colonel Mannering's general conduct, an approbation of his attachment to Miss Bertram. But then he saw still more plainly the impropriety of any attempt at a private correspondence, of which his parents could not be supposed to approve, and he respected this barrier interposed betwixt them, both on Mannering's account, and as he was the liberal and zealous protector of Miss Bertram. "No," said he to himself, "I will not endanger the comfort of my Lucy's present retreat, until I can offer her a home of her own."

With this valorous resolution, which he maintained, although his horse, from constant habit, turned his head down the avenue of Woodbourne, and although he himself passed the lodge twice every day, Charles Hazlewood withstood a strong inclination to ride down, just to ask how the young ladies were, and whether he could be of any service to them during Colonel Mannering's absence. But on the second occasion he felt the temptation so severe, that he resolved not to expose himself to it a third time; and, contenting himself with sending hopes and inquiries, and so forth, to Woodbourne, he resolved to make a visit long promised to a family at some distance, and to return in such time as to be one of the earliest among Mannering's visitors, who should congratulate his safe arrival from his distant and hazardous expedition to Edinburgh. Accordingly, he made out his visit, and having arranged matters so as to be informed within a few hours after Colonel Mannering reached home, he finally resolved to take leave of the friends with whom he had spent the intervening time, with the intention of dining at Woodbourne, where he was in a great measure domesticated; and this (for he thought much more deeply on the subject than was necessary) would, he flattered himself, appear a simple, natural, and easy mode of conducting himself.

Fate, however, of which lovers make so many complaints, was, in this case, unfavourable to Charles Hazlewood. His horse's shoes required an alteration, in consequence of the fresh weather having decidedly commenced. The lady of the house, where he was a visitor, chose to indulge in her own room till a very late breakfast hour. His friend also insisted on showing him a litter of puppies, which his favourite pointer bitch had produced that morning. The colours had occasioned some doubts about the paternity, a weighty question of legitimacy, to the decision of which Hazlewood's opinion was called in as arbiter between his friend and his groom, and which inferred in its consequences, which of the litter should be drowned, which saved. Besides, the Laird himself delayed our young lover's departure for a considerable time, endeavouring, with long and superfluous rhetoric, to insinuate to Sir Robert Hazlewood, through the medium of his son, his own particular ideas respecting the line of a meditated turnpike road. It is greatly to the shame of our young lover's apprehension, that after the tenth reiterated account of the matter, he could not see the advantage to be obtained by the proposed road passing over the Lang-hirst, Windyknowe, the Goodhouse-park, Hailziecroft, and then crossing the river at Simon's Pool, and so by the road to Kippletringan; and the less eligible line pointed out by the English surveyor, which would go clear through the main enclosures at Hazlewood, and cut within a mile, or nearly so, of the house itself, destroying the privacy and pleasure, as his informer contended, of the grounds.

In short, the adviser (whose actual interest was to have the bridge built as near as possible to a farm of his own) failed in every effort to attract young Hazlewood's attention, until he mentioned by chance that the proposed line was favoured by "that fellow Glossin," who pretended to take a lead in the county. On a sudden young Hazlewood became attentive and interested; and having satisfied himself which was the line that Glossin patronised, assured his friend it should not be his fault if his father did not countenance any other instead of that. But these various interruptions consumed the morning. Hazlewood got on horseback at least three hours later than he intended, and, cursing fine ladies, pointers, puppies, and turnpike acts of parliament, saw himself detained beyond the time when he could, with propriety, intrude upon the family at Woodbourne.

He had passed, therefore, the turn of the road which led to that mansion, only edified by the distant appearance of the blue smoke, curling against the pale sky of the winter evening, when he thought he beheld the Dominie taking a footpath for the house through the woods. He called after him, but in vain; for that honest gentleman, never the most susceptible of extraneous impressions, had just that moment parted from Meg Merrilies, and was too deeply wrapt up in pondering upon her vaticinations, to make any answer to Hazlewood's call. He was, therefore, obliged to let him proceed without inquiry after the health of the young ladies, or, any other fishing question, to which he might, by good chance, have had an answer returned wherein Miss Bertram's name might have been mentioned. All cause for haste was now over, and, slackening the reins—upon his horse's neck, he permitted the animal to ascend at his own leisure the steep sandy track between two high banks, which, rising to a considerable height, commanded, at length, an extensive view of the neighbouring country.

Hazlewood was, however, so far from eagerly looking. forward to this prospect, though it had the recommendation that great part of the land was his father's, and must necessarily be his own, that his head still turned backward towards the chimneys of Woodbourne, although at every step his horse made the difficulty of employing his eyes in that direction become greater. From the reverie in which he was sunk, be was suddenly roused by a voice too harsh to be called female, yet too shrill for a man :-" What's kept you on the road sae lang?—maun ither folk do your wark?"

He looked up; the spokeswoman was very tall, had a voluminous handkerchief rolled round her head, grizzled hair flowing in elf-locks from beneath it, a long red cloak, and a staff in her band, headed with a sort of spear-point—it was, in short, Meg Merrilies. Hazlewood had never seen this remarkable figure before; he drew up his reins in astonishment at her appearance, and made a full stop. "I think," continued she, "they that hae taen interest in the house of Ellangowan suld sleep nane this night; three men hae been seeking ye, and you are gaun hame to sleep in your bed—d'ye think if the lad-bairn fa's, the sister will do weel? na. na!"

"I don't understand you, good woman," said Hazlewood . "If you speak of Miss—I mean of any of the late Ellangowan family, tell me what I can do for them."

"Of the late Ellangowan family?" she answered with great vehemence; "of the late Ellangowan family! and when was there ever, or when will there ever be, a family of Ellangowan, but bearing the gallant name of the bauld Bertram?"

"But what do you mean, good woman?"

"I am nae good woman—a' the country kens I am bad eneugh, and baith they and I may be sorry eneugh that I am nae better. But I can do what good women canna, and daurna do. I can do what would freeze the blood o' them that is bred in biggit wa's [*Built-walls] for naething but to bind bairns' heads, and to hap them in the cradle. Hear me—the guard's drawn off at the Custom-house at Portanferry, and it's brought up to Hazlewood House by your father's orders, because he thinks his house is to be attacked this night by the smugglers;—there's naebody means to touch his house; he has gude blood and gentle blood—I say little o' him for himself, but there's naebody thinks him worth meddling wi'. Send the horsemen back to their post, cannily [*Cautiously] and quietly—see an they winna hae wark the night—ay will they—the guns will flash and the swords will glitter in the braw moon."

"Good God! what do you mean?" said Hazlewood; "your words and manner would persuade me you are mad, and yet there is a strange combination in what you say."

"I am not mad!" exclaimed the gipsy, "I have been imprisoned for mad—scourged for mad—banished for mad—but mad I am not. Hear ye, Charles Hazlewood of Hazlewood : d'ye bear malice against him that wounded you?"

"No, dame, God forbid; my arm is quite well, and I have always said the shot was discharged by accident. I should be glad to tell the young man so himself."

"Then do what I bid ye," answered Meg Merrilies, "and ye'll do him mair gude than ever he did you ill; for if he was left to his ill-wishers he would be a bloody corpse ere morn, or a banished man—but there's ane abune [*Above] a'.—Do as I bid you; send back the soldiers to Portanferry. There's nae mair fear o' Hazlewood House than there's o' Cruffelfell." And she vanished with her usual celerity of pace.

It would seem that the appearance of this female, and the mixture of frenzy and enthusiasm in her manner, seldom failed to produce the strongest impression upon those whom she addressed. Her words, though wild, were too plain and intelligible for actual madness, and yet too vehement and extravagant for sober-minded communication. She seemed acting under the influence of an imagination rather strongly excited than deranged; and it is wonderful how palpably the difference, in such cases, is impressed upon the mind of the auditor. This may account for the attention with which her strange and mysterious hints were heard and acted upon. It is certain, at least, that young Hazlewood was strongly impressed by her sudden appearance and imperative tone. He rode to Hazlewood at a brisk pace. It had been dark fort some time before he reached the house, and on his arrival there, he saw a confirmation of what the sibyl had hinted.

Thirty dragoon horses stood under a shed near the offices, with their bridles linked together. Three or four soldiers attended as a guard, while others stamped up and down with their long broadswords and heavy boots in front of the house. Hazlewood asked a non-commissioned officer from whence they came?

"From Portanferry."

"Had they left any guard there?"

"No; they had been drawn off by order of Sir Robert Hazlewood for defence of his house, against an attack—which was threatened by the smugglers."

Charles Hazlewood instantly went in quest of his father, and, having paid his respects to him upon his return, requested to know upon what account he had thought it necessary to send for a military escort. Sir Robert assured his son in reply, that from the information, intelligence, and tidings, which had been communicated to, and laid before him, he had the deepest reason to believe, credit, and be convinced, that a riotous assault would that night be attempted and perpetrated against Hazlewood House, by a set of smugglers, gipsies, and other desperadoes.

"And what, my dear sir," said his son, "should direct the fury of such persons against ours rather than any other house in the country?"

"I should rather think, suppose, and be of opinion, sir," answered Sir Robert, "with deference to your wisdom and experience, that on these occasions and times, the vengeance of such persons is directed or levelled against the most important and distinguished in point of rank, talent, birth, and situation, who have checked, interfered with, and discountenanced their unlawful and illegal and criminal actions or deeds."

Young Hazlewood, who knew his father's foible answered, that the cause of his surprise did not lie where Sir Robert apprehended, but that he only wondered they should think of attacking a house where there were so many servants, and 'where a signal to the neighbouring tenants could call in such strong assistance; and added that he doubted much whether the reputation of the family would not in some degree suffer from calling soldiers from their duty at the Custom-house, to protect them, as if they were not sufficiently strong to defend themselves upon any ordinary occasion. He even hinted, that in case their house's enemies should observe that this precaution had been taken unnecessarily, there would be no end of their sarcasms.

Sir Robert Hazlewood was rather puzzled at this intimation, for, like most dull men, he heartily hated and feared ridicule. He gathered himself up, and looked with a sort of pompous embarrassment, as if he wished to be thought to despise the opinion of the public, which in reality he dreaded.

"I really should have thought," he said, "that the injury which had already been aimed at my house in your person, being the next heir and representative of the Hazlewood family, failing me—I should have thought and believed, I say, that this would have justified me sufficiently in the eyes of the most respectable and the greater part of the people, for taking such precautions as are calculated to prevent and impede a repetition of outrage.—"

"Really, sir," said Charles, "I must remind you of what I have often said before, that I am positive the discharge of the piece was accidental."

"Sir, it was not accidental," said his father angrily but you will be wiser than your elders."

"Really, sir," replied Hazlewood, "in what so intimately concerns myself—"

"Sir, it does not concern you but in a very secondary degree— that is, it does not concern you, as a giddy young fellow, who takes pleasure in contradicting his father; but it concerns the country, sir; and the county, sir; and the public, sir; and the kingdom of Scotland, in so far as the interest of the Hazlewood family, sir, is committed, and interested, and put in peril, in, by, and through you, sir. And the fellow is in safe custody, and Mr. Glossin thinks—"

"Mr. Glossin, sir?"

"Yes, sir, the gentleman who has purchased Ellangowan—you know who I mean, I suppose?"

"Yes, sir," answered the young man, "but I should hardly have expected to hear you quote such authority. Why, this fellow—all the world knows him to be sordid, mean, tricking; and I suspect him to be worse. And you yourself, my dear sir, when did you call such a person a gentleman in your life before?"

"Why, Charles, I did not mean gentleman in the precise sense and meaning, and restricted and proper use, to which, no doubt, the phrase ought legitimately to be confined; but I meant to use it relatively, as marking something of that state to which he has elevated and raised himself—as designing, in short, a decent and wealthy and estimable sort of a person."

"Allow me to ask, sir," said Charles, "if it was by this man's orders that the guard was drawn from Portanferry?"

"Sir," replied the Baronet, "I do apprehend that Mr. Glossin would not presume to give orders, or even an opinion, unless asked, in a matter in which Hazlewood House and the house of Hazlewood—meaning by the one this mansion-house of my family, and by the other, typically, metaphorically, and parabolically, the family itself—I say then where the house of Hazlewood, or Hazlewood House, was so immediately concerned."

"I presume, however, sir," said the son, "this Glossin approved of the proposal?"

"Sir," replied his father, "I thought it decent and right and proper to consult him as the nearest magistrate, as soon as report of the intended outrage reached my ears; and although he declined, out of deference and respect, as became our relative situations, to concur in the order, yet he did entirely approve of my arrangement."

At this moment a horse's feet were heard coming very fast up the avenue. In a few minutes the door opened, and Mr. Mac-Morlan presented himself. "I am under great concern to intrude, Sir Robert, but—"

"Give me leave, Mr. Mac-Morlan," said Sir Robert, with a gracious flourish of welcome; "this is no intrusion, sir; for your situation as Sheriff-substitute calling upon you to attend to the peace of the county (and you, doubtless, feeling yourself particularly called upon to protect Hazlewood House), you have an acknowledged, and admitted, and undeniable right, sir, to enter the house of the first gentleman in Scotland, uninvited—always presuming you to be called there by the duty of your office."

"It is indeed the duty of my office," said Mac-Morlan, who waited with impatience an opportunity to speak, "that makes me an intruder."

"No intrusion!" reiterated the Baronet, gracefully waving his hand.

"But permit me to say, Sir Robert," said the Sheriff-substitute, "I do not come with the purpose of remaining here, but to recall these soldiers to Portanferry, and to assure you that I will answer for the safety of your house."

"To withdraw the guard from Hazlewood House!" exclaimed the proprietor in mingled displeasure and surprise; "and you will be answerable for it! And, pray, who are you, sir, that I should take your security, and caution, and pledge, official or personal, for the safety of Hazlewood House?—I think, sir, and believe, sir, and am of opinion, sir, that if any one of these family pictures were deranged, or destroyed, or injured, it would be difficult for me to make up the loss upon the guarantee which you so obligingly offer me."

"In that case I shall be sorry for it, Sir Robert," answered the downright Mac-Morlan; "but I presume I may escape the pain of feeling my conduct the cause of such irreparable loss, as I can assure you there will be no attempt upon Hazlewood House whatever, and I have received information which induces me to suspect that the rumour was put afloat merely in order to occasion the removal of the soldiers from Portanferry. And under this strong belief and conviction, I must exert my authority as sheriff and chief magistrate of police, to order the whole, or greater part of them, back again. I regret much, that by my accidental absence, a good deal of delay has already taken place, and we shall not now reach Portanferry until it is late."

As Mr. Mac-Morlan was the superior magistrate, and expressed himself peremptory in the purpose of acting as such, the Baronet, though highly offended, could only say, "Very well, sir, it is very well. Nay, sir, take them all with you—I am far from desiring any to be left here, sir. We, sir, can protect ourselves, sir. But you will have the goodness to observe, sir, that you are acting on your own proper risk, sir, and peril, sir, and responsibility, sir, if anything shall happen or befall to Hazlewood House, sir, or the inhabitants, sir, or to the furniture and paintings, sir."

"I am acting to the best of my judgment and information, Sir Robert," said Mac-Morlan, "and I must pray of you to believe so, and to pardon me accordingly. I beg you to observe it is no time for ceremony—it is already very late."

But Sir Robert, without deigning to listen to his apologies, immediately employed himself with much parade in arming and arraying his domestics. Charles Hazlewood longed to accompany the military, which were about to depart for Portanferry, and which were now drawn up and mounted by direction and under the guidance of Mr. Mac-Morlan, as the civil magistrate. But it would have given just pain and offence to his father to have left him at a moment when he conceived himself and his mansion-house in danger. Young Hazlewood therefore gazed from a window with suppressed regret and displeasure, until he heard the officer give the word of command—"From the right to the front, by files, m-a-r-ch. Leading file, to the right wheel—Trot."—The whole party of soldiers then getting into a sharp and uniform pace, were soon lost among the trees, and the noise of the hoofs died speedily away in the distance.

CHAPTER XLVIII.

W! coulters [*The fore-iron of a plough.] and wi' forehammers We garr'd [*Made] the bars bang merrily, Until we came to the inner prison where Willie O, Kinmont he did lie. Old Border Ballad.

We return to Portanferry, and to Bertram and his honest-hearted friend, whom we left most innocent inhabitants of a place built for the guilty. The slumbers of the farmer were as sound as it was possible.

But Bertram's first heavy sleep passed away long before midnight, nor could he again recover that state of oblivion. Added to the uncertain and uncomfortable state of his mind, his body felt feverish and oppressed. This was chiefly owing to the close and confined air of the small apartment in which they slept. After enduring for some time the broiling and suffocating feeling attendant upon such an atmosphere, he rose to endeavour to open the window of the apartment, and thus to procure a change of air. Alas! the first trial reminded him that he was in jail, and that the building being contrived for security, not comfort, the means of procuring fresh air were not left at the disposal of the wretched inhabitants.

Disappointed in this attempt, he stood by the unmanageable window for some time. Little Wasp, though oppressed with the fatigue of his journey on the preceding day, crept out of bed after his master, and stood by him rubbing his shaggy coat against his legs, and expressing, by a murmuring sound, the delight which he felt at being restored to him. Thus accompanied, and waiting until the feverish feeling which at present agitated his blood should subside, into a desire for warmth and slumber, Bertram remained for some time looking out upon the sea.

The tide was now nearly full, and dashed hoarse and near below the base of the building. Now and then a large wave reached even the barrier or bulwark which defended the foundation of the house, and was flung upon it with greater force and noise than those which only broke upon the sand. Far in the distance, under the indistinct light of a hazy and often overclouded moon, the ocean rolled its multitudinous complication of waves, crossing, bursting, and mingling with each other.

"A wild and dim spectacle," said Bertram to himself, "like those crossing tides of fate which have tossed me about the world from my infancy upwards. When will this uncertainty cease, and how soon shall I be permitted to look out for a tranquil home, where I may cultivate in quiet, and without dread and perplexity, those arts of peace from which my cares have been hitherto so forcibly diverted? The ear of Fancy, it is said, can discover the voice of sea-nymphs and tritons amid the bursting murmurs of the ocean; would that I could do so, and that some siren or Proteus would arise from these billows, to unriddle for me the strange maze of fate in which I am so deeply entangled!—Happy friend!" he said, looking at the bed where Dinmont had deposited his bulky person, "thy cares are confined to the narrow round of a healthy and thriving occupation! Thou canst lay them aside at pleasure, and enjoy the deep repose of body and mind which wholesome labour has prepared for thee!"

At this moment his rejections were broken by little Wasp, who, attempting to spring up against the window,—began to yelp and bark most furiously. The sound reached Dinmont's ears, but without dissipating the illusion which had transported him from this wretched apartment to the free air of his own green hills. "Hoy, Yarrow, man!—far yaud—far yaud!" he muttered between his teeth, imagining, doubtless, that he was calling to his sheep-dog, and hounding him in shepherds' phrase, against some intruders on the grazing. The continued barking of the terrier within was answered by the angry challenge of the mastiff in the courtyard, which had for a long time been silent, excepting only an occasional short and deep note, uttered when the moon shone suddenly from among the clouds. Now, his clamour was continued and furious, and seemed to he excited by some disturbance distinct from the barking of Wasp, which had first given him the alarm, and which, with much trouble, his master had contrived to still into an angry note of low growling.

At last Bertram, whose attention was now fully awakened, conceived that he saw a boat upon the sea, and heard in good earnest the sound of oars and of human voices, mingling with the dash of the billows. Some benighted fishermen, he thought, or perhaps some of the desperate traders from the Isle of Man. They are very hardy, however, to approach so near to the Custom-house, where there must be sentinels. It is a large boat, like a longboat, and full of people; perhaps it belongs to the revenue service.—Bertram was confirmed in this last opinion, by observing that the boat made for a little quay which ran into the sea behind the Custom-house, and 'jumping ashore one after another, the crew, to the number of twenty hands, glided secretly up a small lane which divided the Custom-house from the Bridewell, and disappeared from his sight, leaving only two persons to take care of the boat.

The dash of these men's oars at first, and latterly the suppressed sounds of their voices, had excited the wrath of the wakeful sentinel in the courtyard, who now exalted his deep voice into such a horrid and continuous din, that it awakened his brute master, as savage a ban-dog as himself. His cry from a window, of "How now, Tearum, what's the matter, sir?—down, d-n ye, down!" produced no abatement of Tearum's vociferation, which in part prevented his master from bearing the sounds of alarm which his ferocious vigilance was in the act of challenging. But the mate of the two-legged Cerberus was gifted with sharper ears than her husband. She also was now at the window; "B-t ye, gae down and let loose the dog," she said, "they're sporting the door of the Custom-house, and the auld sap at Hazlewood House has ordered off the guard. But ye hae nae mair heart, than a cat." And down the Amazon sallied to perform the task herself, while her helpmate, more jealous of insurrection within doors, than of storm from without, went from cell to cell to see that the inhabitants of each were carefully secured.

These latter sounds, with which we have made the reader acquainted, had their origin in front of the house, and were consequently imperfectly heard by Bertram, whose apartment, as we have already noticed, looked from the back part of the building upon the sea. He heard, however, a stir and tumult in the house, which did not seem to accord with the stern seclusion of a prison at the hour of midnight, and, connecting them with the arrival of an armed boat at that dead hour, could not but suppose that something extraordinary was about to take place. In this belief he shook Dinmont by the shoulder—"Eh!—Ay!—Oh!—Ailie, woman, it's no time to get up yet," growled the sleeping man of the mountains. More roughly shaken, however, he gathered himself up, shook his ears, and asked, "In the name of Providence, what's the matter?"

"That I can't tell you," replied Bertram; "but either the place is on fire, or some extraordinary thing is about to happen. Are you not sensible of a smell of fire? Do you not hear what a noise there is of clashing doors within the house, and of hoarse voices, murmurs, and distant shouts on the outside? Upon my word, I believe something very extraordinary has taken place—Get up, for the love of Heaven, and let us be on our guard."

Dinmont rose at the idea of danger, as intrepid and undismayed as any of his ancestors when the beaconlight was kindled. "Odd, Captain, this is a queer place! they winna let ye out in the day, and they winna let ye sleep in the night. Deil, but it wad break my heart in a fortnight. But, Lordsake, what a racket they're making now! Odd, I wish we had some light. Wasp-Wasp, whisht, hinny—whisht, my bonnie man, and let's hear what they're doing.—Deil's in ye, will ye whisht?"

They sought in vain among the embers the means of lighting their candle, and the noise without still continued. Dinmont in his turn had recourse to the window, "Lordsake, Captain! come here.—Odd, they hae broken the Custom-house!"

Bertram hastened to the window, and plainly saw a miscellaneous crowd of smugglers, and blackguards of different descriptions, some carrying lighted torches, others bearing packages and barrels down the lane to the boat that was lying at the quay, to which two or three other fisher-boats were now brought round. They were loading each of these in their turn, and one or two had already put off to seaward.

111

"This speaks for itself," said Bertram; "but I fear something worse has happened. Do you perceive a strong smell of smoke, or is it my fancy?"

"Fancy?" answered Dinmont, "there's a reek like a killogie. [*A lime-kiln.] Odd, if they burn the Custom-house, it will catch here, and we'll lunt [*Burn] like a tar-barrel a' thegither.—Eh! it wad be fearsome to be burnt alive for naething, like as if ane had been a warlock! [*witch]—Mac-Guffog, hear ye!"—roaring at the top of his voice; "an ye wad ever hae a haill bane in your skin, let's out, man! let's out!"

The fire began now to rise high, and thick clouds of smoke rolled past the window, at which Bertram and Dinmont were stationed. Sometimes, as the wind pleased, the dim shroud of vapour hid everything from their sight; sometimes a red glare illuminated both land and sea, and shone full on the stern and fierce figures, who, wild with ferocious activity, were engaged in loading the boats. The fire was at length triumphant, and spouted in jets of flame out at each window of the burning building, while huge flakes of flaming materials came driving on the wind against the adjoining prison, and rolling a dark canopy of smoke over all the neighbourhood. The shouts of a furious mob resounded far and wide; for the smugglers, in their triumph, were joined by all the rabble of the little town and . neighbourhood, now aroused, and in complete agitation, notwithstanding the lateness of the hour; some from interest in the free trade, and most from the general love of mischief and tumult, natural to a vulgar populace.

Bertram began to be seriously anxious for their fate. There was no stir in the house; it seemed as if the jailor had deserted his charge, and left the prison with its wretched inhabitants to the mercy of the conflagration which was spreading towards them. In the meantime a new and fierce attack was heard upon the outer gate of the Correction-house, which, battered with sledge-hammers and crows, was soon forced. The keeper, as great a coward as a bully, with his more ferocious wife, had fled; their servants readily surrendered the keys. The liberated prisoners, celebrating their deliverance with the wildest yells of joy, mingled among the mob which had given them freedom.

In the midst of the confusion that ensued, three or four of the principal smugglers hurried to the apartment of Bertram with lighted torches, and armed with cutlasses and pistols. —"Der deyvil," said the leader, "here's our mark!" and two of them seized on Bertram, but one whispered in his ear, "Make no resistance till you are in the street." The same individual found an instant to say to Dinmont—"Follow our friend, an help when you see the time come."

In the hurry of the moment, Dinmont obeyed and followed close. The two smugglers dragged Bertram along the passage, downstairs, through the courtyard, now illuminated by the glare of fire, and into the narrow street to which the gate opened, where, in the confusion, the gang were necessarily in some degree separated from each other. A rapid noise, as of a body of horse advancing, seemed to add to the disturbance. "Hagel and wetter, what is that?" said the leader; "keep together, kinder, look to the prisoner."—but in spite of his charge, the two who held Bertram were the last of the party.

The sounds and signs of violence were heard in front. The press became curiously agitated, while some endeavoured to defend themselves, others to escape; shots were fired, and the glittering broadswords of the dragoons began to appear, flashing above the beads of the rioters. "Now," said the warning whisper of the man who held Bertram's left arm, the same who had spoken before, "shake off that fellow, and follow me."

Bertram, exerting his strength suddenly and effectually, easily burst from the grasp of the man who held his collar on the right side. The fellow attempted to draw a pistol, but was prostrated by a blow of Dinmont's fist, which an ox could hardly have received without the same humiliation. "Follow me quick," said the friendly partisan, and dived through a very narrow and dirty lane which led from the main street.

No pursuit took place. The attention of the smugglers had been otherwise and very disagreeably engaged by the sudden appearance of Mac-Morlan and the party of horse. The loud manly voice of the provincial magistrate was heard proclaiming the Riot Act, and charging "all those unlawfully assembled to disperse at their own proper peril." This interruption would indeed have happened in time sufficient to have prevented the attempt, had not the magistrate received upon the road some false information, which led him to think that the smugglers were to land at the Bay of Ellangowan. Nearly two hours were lost in consequence of this false intelligence, which it may be no lack of charity to suppose that Glossin, so deeply interested in the issue of that night's daring attempt, had contrived to throw in Mac-Morlan's way, availing himself of the knowledge that the soldiers had left Hazlewood House, which would soon reach an ear so anxious as his.

In the meantime, Bertram followed his guide, and was in his turn followed by Dinmont. The shouts of the mob, the trampling of the horses, the dropping pistol-shots, sunk more and more faintly upon their ears; when at the end of the dark lane they found a post-chaise with four horses. "Are you here, in God's name?" said the guide to the postilion who drove the leaders.

"Ay, troth am I," answered Jack Jabos, "and I wish I were any gate else."

"Open the carriage, then—You, gentlemen, get into it—in a short time you'll be in a place of safety—and (to Bertram) remember your promise to the gipsy wife!"

Bertram, resolving to be passive in the hands of a person who had just rendered him such a distinguished piece of service, got into the chaise as directed. Dinmont followed; Wasp, who had kept close by them, sprung in at the same time, and the carriage drove off very fast. "Have a care a' me," said Dinmont, "but this is the queerest thing yet!—Odd, I trust they'll no coup [*Upset.] us—and then what's to come o' Dumple?—I would rather be on his back than in the Deuke's coach, God bless him."

Bertram observed, that they could not go at that rapid rate to any great distance without changing horses, and that they might insist upon remaining till daylight at the first inn they stopped at, or at least upon being made acquainted with the purpose and termination of their journey, and Mr. Dinmont might there give directions about his faithful horse, which would probably be safe at the stables where he had left him.—"Aweel, aweel, e'en sae be it for Dandie. —Odd, if we were ance out o' this trindling kist [*Rolling chest.] o' a thing, I am thinking they wad find it hard wark to gar us gang ony gate but where we liked oursells."

While he thus spoke, the carriage making a sudden turn, showed them, through the left window, the village at some distance, still widely beaconed by the fire, which, having reached a storehouse wherein spirits were deposited, now rose high into the air, a wavering column of brilliant light. They had not long time to admire this spectacle, for another turn of the road carried them into a close lane between plantations, through which the chaise proceeded in nearly total darkness, but with unabated speed.

CHAPTER XLIX.

The night drave on wi' sangs and clatter,
And aye the ale was growing better.
    Tam o' Shanter

We must now return to Woodbourne, which, it may be remembered, we left just after the Colonel had given some directions to his confidential servant. When he returned, his absence of mind, and an unusual expression of thought and anxiety upon his features, struck the ladies whom he joined in the drawing-room. Mannering was not, however, a man to be questioned, even by those whom he most loved, upon the cause of the mental agitation which these signs expressed. The hour of tea arrived, and the party were partaking of that refreshment in silence, when a carriage drove up to the door, and the bell announced the arrival of a visitor. "Surely," said Mannering, "it is too soon by some hours."

There was a short pause, when Barnes, opening the door of the saloon. announced Mr. Pleydell. In marched the lawyer, whose well-brushed black coat, and well-powdered wig, together with his point ruffles, brown silk stockings, highly varnished shoes, and gold buckles, exhibited the pains which the old gentleman had taken to prepare his person for the ladies' society. He was welcomed by Mannering with a hearty shake by the hand. "The very man I wished to see at this moment!"

"Yes," said the counsellor, "I told you I would take the first opportunity; so I have ventured to leave the Court for a week in session time—no common sacrifice—but I had a notion I could be useful, and I was to attend a proof here about the same time. But will you not introduce me to the young ladies?—Ah! there is one I should have known at once, from her family likeness! Miss Lucy Bertram, my love, I am most happy to see you."—and he folded her in his arms, and gave her a hearty kiss on each side of the face, to which Lucy submitted in blushing resignation.

"On n'arrete pas dans un si beau chemin," continued the gay old gentleman, and, as the Colonel presented him to Julia, took the same liberty with that fair lady's cheek. Julia laughed, coloured, and disengaged herself. "I beg a thousand pardons," said the lawyer, with a bow which was not at all professionally awkward; "age and old fashions give privileges, and I can hardly say whether I am most sorry just now at being too well entitled to claim them at all, or happy in having such an opportunity to exercise them so agreeably—"

"Upon my word, sir," said Miss Mannering, laughing, "If you make such flattering apologies, we shall begin to doubt whether we can admit you to shelter yourself under your alleged qualifications."

"I can assure you, Julia," said the Colonel, "you are perfectly right; my friend the counsellor is a dangerous person; the last time I had the pleasure of seeing him, he was closeted with a fair lady, who, had granted him a tete-a-tete at eight in the morning."

"Ay, but, Colonel," said the counsellor, "you should add, I was more indebted to my chocolate than my charms for so distinguished a favour, from a person of such propriety, of demeanour as Mrs. Rebecca."

"And that should remind me, Mr. Pleydell," said Julia, "to offer you tea—that is, supposing you have dined."

"Anything, Miss Mannering, from your hands," answered the gallant jurisconsult; "yes, I have dined-that is to say, as people dine at a Scotch inn."

"And that is indifferently enough," said the Colonel, with his hand upon the bell-handle "give me leave to order something."

"Why, to say truth," replied Mr. Pleydell, "I had rather not; I have been inquiring into that matter, for you must know I stopped an instant below to pull off my boot-hose, "a world too wide for my shrunk shanks,'" glancing down with some complacency upon limbs which looked very well for his time of life, "and I had some conversation with your Barnes, and a very intelligent person whom I presume to be the housekeeper; and it was settled among us—tota re perspecta—I beg Miss Mannering's pardon for my Latin—that the old lady should add to your light family-supper the more substantial refreshment of a brace of wild-ducks. I told her (always under deep submission) my poor thoughts about the sauce, which concurred exactly with her own; and, if you please, I would rather wait till they are ready before eating anything solid."

"And we will anticipate our usual hour of supper," said the Colonel.

"With all my heart," said Pleydell, "providing I do not lose the ladies' company a moment the sooner. I am of counsel with my old friend Burnet; [*See Note VIII. Lord Monboddo.] I love the caena, the supper of the ancients, the pleasant meal and social glass that wash out of one's mind the cobwebs that business or gloom have been spinning in our brains all day.' "

Mr. Pleydell's look and manner, and the quietness with which he made himself at home on the subject of his little Epicurean comforts, amused the ladies, but particularly Miss Mannering, who immediately gave the counsellor a great deal of flattering attention; and more pretty things were said on both sides during the service of the tea-table than we have leisure to repeat.

As soon as this was over, Mannering led the counsellor by the arm into a small study which opened from the saloon, and where, according to the custom of the family, there were always lights and a good fire in the evening.

"I see," said Mr. Pleydell, "you have got something to tell me about the Ellangowan business—Is it terrestrial or celestial? What says my military Albumazar? Have you calculated the course of futurity? have you consulted your Ephemerides, your Almochoden, your Almuten?"

"No, truly, counsellor," replied Mannering, "you are the only Ptolemy I intend to resort to upon the present occasion—a second Prospero, I have broken my staff, and drowned my book far beyond plummet depth. But I have great news notwithstanding. Meg Merrilies, our Egyptian sibyl, has appeared to the Dominie this very day, and, as I conjecture, has frightened the honest man not a little."

"Indeed?"

"Ay, and she has done me the honour to open a correspondence with me, supposing me to be as deep in astrological mysteries as when we first met. Here is her scroll, delivered to me by the Dominie."

Pleydell put on his spectacles. "A vile greasy scrawl, indeed—and the letters are uncial or semi-uncial, as somebody calls your large text hand, and in size and perpendicularity resemble the ribs of a roasted pig—I can hardly make it out."

"I will try," answered the lawyer. "' You are a good seeker, but a bad finder; you set yourself to prop a falling house, but had a gey guess it would rise again. Lend your hand to the wark that's near, as you lent your ee to the weird [*Destiny] that was far. Have a carriage This night by ten o'clock, at the end of the Crooked Dykes at Portanferry, and let it bring the folk to Woodbourne that shall ask them, if they be there IN GOD'S NAME.'-Stay, here follows some poetry- Dark shall be light, And wrong done to right, When Bertram's right and

113

Bertram's might Shall meet on Ellangowan's height.' A most mystic epistle truly, and closes in a vein of poetry worthy of the Cumaean sibyl—and what have you done?"

"Why," said Mannering, rather reluctantly, "I was loth to risk any opportunity of throwing light on this business. The woman is perhaps crazed, and these effusions may arise only from visions of her imagination;—but you were of opinion that she knew more of that strange story than she ever told. "

"And so," said Pleydell, "you sent a carriage to the place named?"

"You will laugh at me if I own I did," replied the Colonel.

"Who, I?" replied the advocate. "No, truly, I think it was the wisest thing you could do."

"Yes," answered Mannering, well pleased to have escaped the ridicule he apprehended; "you know the worst is paying the chaise-hire—I sent a post-chaise and four from Kippletringan, with instructions corresponding to the letter—the horses will have a long and cold station on the outposts to-night if our intelligence be false."

"Ay, but I think it will prove otherwise," said the lawyer. "This woman has played a part till she believes it; or, if she be a thorough-paced impostor, without a single grain of self-delusion to qualify her knavery, still she may think herself bound to act in character-this I know, that I could get nothing out of her by the common modes of interrogation, and the wisest thing we can do is to give her an opportunity of making the discovery her own way. And now have you more to say, or shall we go to the ladies?"

"Why, my mind is uncommonly agitated," answered the Colonel, "and—but I really have no more to say—only I shall count the minutes till the carriage returns; but you cannot be expected to be so anxious."

"Why, no—use is all in all," said the more experienced lawyer,—"I am much interested certainly, but I think I shall be able to survive the interval, if the ladies will afford us some music."

"And with the assistance of the wild-ducks, by and by?" suggested Mannering.

"True, Colonel; a lawyer's anxiety about the fate of the most interesting cause has seldom spoiled either his sleep or digestion. [*Note IX Lawyers' Sleepless Nights.] And yet I shall be very eager to hear the rattle of these wheels on their return, notwithstanding."

So saying, he rose and led the way into the next room, where Miss Mannering, at his request, took her seat at the harpsichord. Lucy Bertram, who sung her native melodies very sweetly, was accompanied by her friend upon the instrument, and Julia afterwards performed some of Scarlatti's sonatas with great brilliancy. The old lawyer, scraping a little upon the violoncello, and being a member of the gentlemen's concert in Edinburgh, was so greatly delighted with this mode of spending the evening, that I doubt if he once thought of the wild-ducks until Barnes informed the company that supper was ready.

"Tell Mrs. Allan to have something in readiness," said the Colonel—"I expect—that is, I hope—perhaps some company may be here to-night; and let the men sit up, and do not lock the upper gate on the lawn until I desire you."

"Lord, sir," said Julia, "whom can you possibly expect to-night?"

"Why, some persons, strangers to me, talked of calling in the evening on business," answered her father, not without embarrassment, for he would have little brooked a disappointment which might have thrown ridicule on his judgment; "it is quite uncertain."

"Well, we shall not pardon them for disturbing our party," said Julia, "unless they bring as much good-humour, and as susceptible hearts, as my friend and admirer, for so he has dubbed himself, Mr. Pleydell."

"Ah, Miss Julia," said Pleydell, offering his arm with an air of gallantry to conduct her into the eating-room, "the time has been—when I returned from Utrecht in the year i738—"

"Pray don't talk of it," answered the young lady,—"we like you much better as you are—Utrecht, in heaven's name!—I dare say you have spent all the intervening years in getting rid so completely of the effects of your Dutch education."

"Oh, forgive me, Miss Mannering," said the lawyer; "the Dutch are a much more accomplished people in point or gallantry than their volatile neighbours are willing to admit. They are constant as clock-work in their attentions."

"I should tire of that," said Julia.

"Imperturbable in their good temper," continued Pleydell.

"Worse and worse," said the young lady.

"And then," said the old beau garcon, "although for six times three hundred and sixty-five days, your swain has placed the capuchin round your neck, and the stove under your feet, and driven your little sledge upon the ice in winter, and your cabriole through the dust in summer, you may dismiss him at once, without reason or apology, upon the two thousand one hundred and ninetieth day, which, according to my hasty calculation, and without reckoning leap-years, will complete the cycle of the supposed adoration, and that without your amiable feelings having the slightest occasion to be alarmed for the consequences to those of Mynheer."

"Well," replied Julia, "that last is truly a Dutch recommendation, Mr. Pleydell—crystal—and hearts would lose all their merit in the world, if it were not: for their fragility."

"Why, upon that point of the argument, Miss Mannering, it is as difficult to find a heart that will break, as a glass that will not; and for that reason I would press the value of mine own—were it not that I see Mr. Sampson's eyes have been closed, and his hands clasped—for some time, attending the end of our conference to begin the grace.—And, to say the truth, the appearance of the wild-ducks is very appetising." So saying, the worthy counsellor sat himself to table, and laid aside his gallantry for awhile, to do honour to the good things placed before him. Nothing further is recorded of him for some time, excepting an observation that the ducks were roasted to a single turn, and that Mrs. Allan's sauce of claret, lemon, and cayenne, was beyond praise.

"I see," said Miss Mannering, "I have a formidable rival in Mr. Pleydell's favour, even on the very first night of his avowed admiration."

"Pardon me, my fair lady," answered the counsellor, "your avowed rigour alone has induced me to commit the solecism of eating a good supper in your presence; how shall I support your frowns without reinforcing my strength? Upon the same principle, and no other, I will ask permission to drink wine with you."

"This is the fashion of Utrecht also, I suppose, Mr. Pleydell?"

"Forgive me, madam," answered the counsellor; "the French themselves, the patterns of all that is gallant, term their tavern-keepers restaurateurs, alluding, doubtless, to the relief they afford the disconsolate lover, when bowed down to the earth by his mistress's severity.

My own case requires so much relief, that I must trouble you for that other wing, Mr. Sampson, without prejudice to my afterwards applying to Miss Bertram for a tart;—be pleased to tear the wing, sir, instead of cutting it off—Mr. Barnes will assist you, Mr. Sampson,—thank you, sir—and, Mr. Barnes, a glass of ale, if you please."

While the old gentleman, pleased with Miss Mannering's liveliness and attention, rattled away for her amusement and his own, the impatience of Colonel Mannering began to exceed all bounds. He declined sitting down at table, under pretence that he never ate supper; and traversed the parlour, in which they were, with hasty and impatient steps, now throwing tip the window to gaze upon the dark lawn, now listening for the remote sound of the carriage advancing up the avenue. At length, in a feeling of uncontrollable impatience, he left the room, took his hat and cloak, and pursued his walk up the avenue, as if his so doing would hasten the approach of those whom he desired to see. "I really wish," said Miss Bertram, "Colonel Mannering would not venture out after nightfall. You must have heard, Mr. Pleydell, what a cruel fright we had."

"Oh, with the smugglers?" replied the advocate—"they are old friends of mine. I was the means of bringing some of them to justice a long time since, when Sheriff of this county."

"And then the alarm we had immediately afterwards," added Miss
Bertram, from the vengeance of one of these wretches."

"When young Hazlewood was hurt—I heard of that too."

"Imagine, my dear Mr. Pleydell," continued Lucy, "how much Miss Mannering and I were alarmed, when a ruffian, equally dreadful for his great strength, and the sternness of his features, rushed out upon us!"

"You must know, Mr. Pleydell," said Julia, unable to suppress her resentment at this undesigned aspersion of her admirer, "that young Hazlewood is so handsome in the eyes of the Young ladies of this country, that they think every person shocking who comes near him."

"Oho!" thought Pleydell, who was by profession an observer of tones and gestures, "there's something wrong here between my young friends.—Well, Miss Mannering, I have not seen young Hazlewood since he was a boy, so the ladies may be perfectly right; but I can assure you, in spite of your scorn, that if you want to see handsome men you must go to Holland; the prettiest fellow I ever saw was a Dutchman, in spite of his being called Vanbost, or Vanbuster, or some such barbarous name. He will not be quite so handsome now, to be sure."

It was now Julia's turn to look a little out of countenance at the chance hit of her learned admirer, but that instant the Colonel entered the room. "I can hear nothing of them yet," he said "still, however, we will not separate—Where is Dominie Sampson?"

"Here, honoured sir."

"What is that book you hold in your hand, Mr. Sampson?"

"It's even the learned De Lyra, sir—I would crave his honour Mr. Pleydell's judgment, always with his best leisure, to expound a disputed passage."

"I am not in the vein, Mr. Sampson," answered Pleydell; "here's metal more attractive—I do not despair to engage these two young ladies in a glee or a catch, wherein I, even I myself, will adventure myself for the bass part—Hang De Lyra, man; keep him for a fitter season."

The disappointed Dominie shut his ponderous tome, much marvelling in his mind how a person, possessed of the lawyer's erudition, could give his mind to these frivolous toys. But the counsellor, indifferent to the high character for learning which he was trifling away, filled himself a large glass of Burgundy, and after preluding a little with a voice somewhat the worse for wear, gave the ladies a courageous invitation to join in "We be three poor Mariners," and accomplished his own part therein with great eclat.

"Are you not withering your roses with sitting up so late, my young ladies?" said the Colonel.

"Not a bit, sir," answered Julia; "your friend, Mr. Pleydell, threatens to become a pupil of Mr. Sampson's to-morrow, so we must make the most of our conquest to-night."

This led to another musical trial of skill, and that to lively conversation. At length, when the solitary sound of one o'clock had long since resounded on the ebon ear of night, and the next signal of the advance of time was close approaching, Mannering, whose impatience had long subsided into disappointment and despair, looked at his watch, and said, "We must now give them up"—when at that instant—But what then befell will require a separate chapter.

CHAPTER L.

Justice. This does indeed confirm each circumstance The
gipsy told!—No orphan, nor without a friend art thou—
I am thy father, here's thy mother, there Thy uncle—This
thy first cousin, and these Are all thy near relations!
The Critic.

As Mannering replaced his watch, he heard a distant and hollow sound—"It is a carriage for certain—no, it is but the sound of the wind among the leafless trees. Do come to the window, Mr. Pleydell. "The counsellor, who, with his large silk handkerchief in his hand, was expatiating away to Julia upon some subject which he thought was interesting, obeyed, however, the summons, first, wrapping the handkerchief round his neck by way of precaution against the cold air. The sound of wheels became now very perceptible, and Pleydell, as if he had reserved all his curiosity till that moment, ran out to the hall. The Colonel rung for Barnes to desire that the persons who came in the carriage might be shown into a separate room, being altogether uncertain whom it might contain. It, stopped, however, at the door, before his purpose could he fully explained. A moment after, Mr. Pleydell called out, "Here's our Liddesdale friend, I protest, with a strapping young fellow of the same calibre. "His voice arrested Dinmont, who recognised him with equal surprise And pleasure. "Odd, if it's your honour, we'll a' be as right and tight as thack and rape can make us." [*When a farmer's crop is got safely into the barn-yard, it is said to be made fast with thack and rape—Anglic, straw and rope.]

But while the farmer stopped to make his bow, Bertram, dizzied with the sudden glare of light, and bewildered with the circumstances of his situation, almost unconsciously entered the open door of the parlour, and confronted the Colonel, who was just advancing towards it. The strong light of the apartment left no doubt of his identity, and he himself was as much confounded with the appearance of those to whom he so unexpectedly presented himself, as they were by the sight of so utterly unlooked-for an object. It must be remembered that each individual present had their own peculiar reasons for looking with terror upon what seemed at first sight a spectral apparition.

Mannering saw before him the man whom he supposed he had killed in India; Julia beheld her lover in a most peculiar and hazardous situation; and Lucy Bertram at once knew the person who had fired upon young Hazlewood. Bertram, who interpreted the fixed and motionless astonishment of the Colonel into displeasure at his intrusion, hastened to say that it was involuntary, since he had been hurried hither without even knowing whither he was to be transported.

"Mr. Brown, I believe!" said Colonel Mannering.

"Yes, sir," replied the young man modestly, but with firmness, "the same you knew in India; and who ventures to hope, that what you did then know of him is not such as should prevent his requesting you would favour him with your attestation to his character, as a gentleman and man of honour."

"Mr. Brown—I have been seldom—never—so much surprised—certainly, sir, in whatever passed between us, you have a right to command my favourable testimony."

At this critical moment entered the counsellor and Dinmont. The former beheld, to his astonishment, the Colonel but just recovering from his first surprise, Lucy Bertram ready to faint with terror, and Miss Mannering in an agony of doubt and apprehension, which she in vain endeavoured to disguise or suppress. "What is the meaning of all this?" said he; "has this young fellow brought the Gorgon's head in his hand?-let me look at him.—By Heaven!" he muttered to himself, "the very image of old Ellangowan!—Yes, the same manly form and handsome features, but with a world of more intelligence in the face—Yes!—the witch has kept her word." Then instantly passing to Lucy, "Look at that man, Miss Bertram, my dear; have you never seen any one like him?"

Lucy had only ventured one glance at this object of terror, by which, however, from his remarkable height and appearance, she at once recognised the supposed assassin of young Hazlewood; a conviction which excluded, of course, the more favourable association of ideas which might have occurred on a closer view.—"Don't ask me about him, sir," said she, turning away her eyes; "send him away, for Heaven's sake! we shall all be murdered!"

"Murdered! where's the poker?" said the advocate in some alarm; "but nonsense! we are three men besides the servants, and there is honest Liddesdale worth half a dozen to boot—we have the major vis upon our side—however, here, my friend Dandie—Davie—what do they call You?—keep between that fellow and us for the protection of the ladies."

"Lord! Mr. Pleydell," said the astonished farmer, "that's Captain Brown; d'ye no ken the Captain?"

"Nay, if he's a friend of yours, we may be safe enough," answered Pleydell; "but keep near him."

All this passed with such rapidity, that it was over before the Dominie had recovered himself from a fit of absence, shut the book which he had been studying in a corner, and advancing to obtain a sight of the strangers, exclaimed at once, upon beholding Bertram, "If the grave can give up the dead, that is my dear and honoured master!"

"We're right after all, by Heaven! I was sure I was right," said the lawyer; "he is the very image of his father.—Come, Colonel, what do you think of, that you do not bid your guest welcome? I think—I believe—I trust we're right—never saw such a likeness!—But patience—Dominie, say not a word.—Sit down, young gentleman."

"I beg pardon, sir; if I am, as I understand, in Colonel Mannering's house, I should wish first to know if my accidental appearance here gives offence, or if I am welcome?"

Mannering instantly made an effort. "Welcome? most certainly, especially if you can point out how I can serve you. I believe I may have some wrongs to repair towards you—I have often suspected so; but your sudden and unexpected appearance, connected with painful recollections, prevented my saying at first, as I now say, that whatever has procured me the honour of this visit, it is an acceptable one."

Bertram bowed with an air of distant, yet civil acknowledgment, to the grave courtesy of Mannering.

"Julia, my love, you had better retire. Mr. Brown, you will excuse my daughter; there are circumstances which I perceive rush upon her recollection."

Miss Mannering rose and retired accordingly; yet, as—she passed Bertram, could not suppress the words, "Infatuated! a second time!" but so pronounced as to be heard by him alone. Miss Bertram accompanied her friend, much surprised, but without venturing second glance at the object of her terror. Some mistake she saw there was, and was unwilling to increase it by denouncing the stranger as an assassin. He was known, she saw, to the Colonel, and received as a gentleman; certainly he either was not the person she suspected, or Hazlewood was right in supposing the shot accidental.

The remaining part of the company would have formed no bad group for a skilful painter. Each was too much embarrassed with his own sensations to observe those of the others. Bertram most unexpectedly found himself in the house of one, whom he was alternately disposed to dislike as his personal enemy, and to respect as the father of Julia; Mannering was struggling between his high sense of courtesy and hospitality, his joy at finding himself relieved from the guilt of having shed life in a private quarrel, and the former feelings of dislike and prejudice, which revived in his haughty mind at the sight of the object against whom he had entertained them; Sampson, supporting his shaking limbs by leaning on the back of a chair, fixed his eyes upon Bertram, with a staring expression of nervous anxiety which convulsed his whole visage; Dinmont, enveloped in his loose shaggy greatcoat, and resembling a huge bear erect upon his hinder legs, stared on the whole scene with great round eyes that witnessed his amazement.

The counsellor alone was in his element, shrewd, prompt, and active; he already calculated the prospect of brilliant success in a strange, eventful, and mysterious lawsuit, and no young monarch, flushed with hopes, and at the head of a gallant army, could experience more glee when taking the field on his first campaign. He bustled about with great energy, and took the arrangement of the whole explanation upon himself.

"Come, come, gentlemen, sit down; this is all in my province: you must let me arrange it for you. Sit down, my dear Colonel, and let me manage; sit down, Mr. Brown, aut quocunque alio nomine vocaris—Dominie, take your seat—draw in your chair, honest Liddesdale."

"I dinna ken, Mr. Pleydell," said Dinmont, looking at his dreadnought-coat, then at the handsome furniture of the room, "I had maybe better gang some gate else, [*Somewhere else.] and leave ye till your cracks—I'm no just that weel put on."

The Colonel, who by this time recognised Dandie, immediately went up and bid him heartily welcome; assuring him, that from what he had seen of him in Edinburgh, he was sure his rough coat and thick—soled boots would honour a royal drawing-room.

"Na, na, Colonel, we're just plain up-the-country folk; but nae doubt I would fain hear o' ony pleasure that was gaun to happen the Captain, and I'm sure a' will gae right if Mr. Pleydell will take his bit job in hand."

"You're right, Dandie—spoke like a Hieland oracle [*It may not be unnecessary to tell southern readers, that the mountainous country in the south-western borders of Scotland, is called Hieland, though totally different from the much more mountainous and more extensive districts of the north, usually accented Hielands.]—and now be silent. —Well, you are all seated at last; take a glass of wine till I begin my catechism methodically. And now," turning to Bertram, "my dear boy, do you know who or what you are?"

In spite of his perplexity, the catechumen could not help laughing at this commencement, and answered, "Indeed, sir, I formerly thought I did; but I own late circumstances have made me somewhat uncertain."

"Then tell us what you formerly thought yourself."

"Why, I was in the habit of thinking and calling myself Vanbeest Brown, who served as a cadet or volunteer under Colonel Mannering, when he commanded the—regiment, in which capacity I was not unknown to him."

"There," said the Colonel, "I can assure Mr. Brown of his identity; and add, what his modesty may have forgotten, that he was distinguished as a young man of talent and spirit."

"So much the better, my dear sir," said Mr. Pleydell; "but that is to general character—Mr. Brown must tell us where he was born."

"In Scotland, I believe, but the place uncertain."

"Where educated?"

"In Holland, certainly."

"Do you remember nothing of your early life before you left
Scotland?"

"Very imperfectly; yet I have a strong idea, perhaps more deeply impressed upon me by subsequent hard usage, that I was during my childhood the object of much solicitude and affection. I have an indistinct remembrance of a good-looking man whom I used to call papa, and of a lady who was infirm in health, and who, I think, must have been my mother but it is an imperfect and confused recollection. I remember too a tall thin kind tempered man in black, who used to teach me my letters and walk out with me;—and I think the very last time—"

Here the Dominie could contain no longer. While every succeeding word served to prove that the child of his benefactor stood before him, he had struggled with the utmost difficulty to suppress his emotions; but, when the juvenile recollections of Bertram turned towards his tutor and his precepts, he was compelled to give way to his feelings. He rose hastily from his chair, and with clasped bands, trembling limbs, and streaming eyes, called out aloud, "Harry Bertram!—look at me—was I not the man?"

"Yes!" said Bertram, starting from his seat as if a sudden light had burst in upon his mind,—"Yes—that was my name!—and that is the voice and the figure of my kind old master!"

The Dominie threw himself into his arms, pressed him a thousand times to his bosom in convulsions of transport, which shook his whole frame, sobbed hysterically, and, at length, in the emphatic language of Scripture, lifted up his voice and wept aloud. Colonel Mannering had recourse to his handkerchief; Pleydell made wry faces, and wiped the glasses of his spectacles; and honest Dinmont, after two loud blubbering explosions, exclaimed, "Deil's in the man! he's garr'd me do that I haena done since my auld mither died."

"Come, come," said the counsellor at last, "silence in the court.—We have a clever party to contend with; we must lose no time in gathering our information—for anything I know, there may be something to be done before daybreak."

"I will order a horse to be saddled, if you please," said the
Colonel.

"No, no, time enough—time enough—but come, Dominie, I have allowed you a competent space to express your feelings. I must circumduce the term—you must let me proceed in my examination."

The Dominie was habitually obedient to any one who chose to impose commands upon him; he sunk back into his chair, spread his checked handkerchief over his face, to serve, as I suppose, for the Grecian painter's veil, and, from the action of his folded hands, appeared for a time engaged in the act of mental thanksgiving. He then raised his eyes over the screen, as if to be assured that the pleasing apparition had not melted into air—then again sunk them to resume his internal act of devotion, until he felt himself compelled to give attention to the counsellor, from the interest which his questions excited.

"And now," said Mr. Pleydell, after several minute inquiries concerning his recollection of early events—"And now, Mr. Bertram, for I think we ought in future to call you by your own proper name, will you have the goodness to let us know every particular which you can recollect concerning the mode of your leaving Scotland?"

"Indeed, sir, to say the truth, though the terrible outlines of that day are strongly impressed upon my memory, yet somehow the very terror which fixed them there has in a great measure confounded and confused the details. I recollect, however, that I was walking somewhere or other—in a wood, I think—"

"Oh yes, it was in Warroch Wood, my dear," said the Dominie.

"Hush, Mr. Sampson," said the lawyer.

"Yes, it was in a wood," continued Bertram, as long past and confused ideas arranged themselves in his reviving recollection "and some one was with me—this worthy and affectionate gentleman, I think."

"Oh, ay, ay, Harry, Lord bless thee—it was even I myself."

"Be silent, Dominie, and don't interrupt the evidence," said
Pleydell.—"and so, sir?" to Bertram.

"And so, sir," continued Bertram, "like one of the changes of a dream, I thought I was on horseback before my guide."

"No, no," exclaimed Sampson, "never did I put my own limbs, not to say thine, into such peril.

"On my word this is intolerable!—Look ye, Dominie, if you speak another word till I give you leave, I will read three sentences out of the Black Acts, whisk my cane round my head three times, undo all the magic of this night's work, and conjure Harry Bertram back again into Vanbeest Brown."

"Honoured and worthy sir," groaned out the Dominie, "I humbly crave pardon—it was verbum volens."

"Well, nolens volens, you must hold your tongue," said Pleydell.

"Pray, be silent, Mr. Sampson," said the Colonel; "it is—of great consequence to your recovered friend, that you permit Mr. Pleydell to proceed in his inquiries."

"I am mute," said the rebuked Dominie.

"On a sudden," continued Bertram, "two or three men sprung out upon us, and we were pulled from horseback. I have little recollection of anything else, but that I tried to escape in the midst of a desperate scuffle, and fell into the arms of a very tall woman who started from the bushes, and protected me for some time—the rest is all confusion and dread—a dim recollection of a sea-beach, and a cave, and of some strong potion which lulled me to sleep for a length of time. In short, it is all a blank in my memory, until I recollect myself first an ill-used and half-starved cabin-boy aboard a sloop, and then a school-boy—in Holland under the protection of an old merchant, who had taken some fancy for me."

"And what account," said Mr. Pleydell, "did your guardian give of your parentage?"

"A very brief one," answered Bertram, "and a charge to inquire no further. I was given to understand, that my father was concerned in the smuggling trade carried on on the eastern coast of Scotland, and was killed in a skirmish with the revenue officers; that his correspondents in Holland had a vessel on the coast at the time, part of the crew of which were engaged in the affair, and that they brought me off after it was over, from a motive of compassion, as I was left destitute by my father's death. As I grew older there was much of this story seemed inconsistent with my own recollections, but what could I do? I had no means of ascertaining my doubts, nor a single friend with whom I could communicate or canvass them. The rest of my story is known to Colonel Mannering: I went out to India to be a clerk in a Dutch house; their affairs fell into confusion—I betook myself to the military profession, and, I trust, as yet I have not disgraced it."

"Thou art a fine young fellow, I'll be bound for thee," said Pleydell, "and since you have wanted a father so long, I wish from my heart I could claim the paternity myself. But this affair of young Hazlewood—"

"Was merely accidental," said Bertram. "I was travelling in
Scotland for pleasure, and after a week's residence with my friend,
Mr. Dinmont, with whom I had the good fortune to form an accidental
acquaintance—"

"It was my gude fortune that," said Dinmont "odd, my brains wad hae been knockit out by twa blackguards, if it hadna been for his four quarters."

"Shortly after we parted at the town of—, I lost my baggage by thieves, and it was while residing at Kippletringan I accidentally met the young gentleman. As I was approaching to pay my respects to Miss Mannering, whom I had known in India, Mr. Hazlewood, conceiving my appearance none of the most respectable, commanded me rather haughtily to stand back, and so gave occasion to the fray in which I had the misfortune to be the accidental means of wounding him.—And now, sir, that I have answered all your questions-"

"No, no, not quite all," said Pleydell, winking sagaciously; "there are some interrogatories which I shall delay till to-morrow, for it is time, I believe, to close the sederunt for this night, or rather morning."

"Well, then, sir," said the young man, "to vary the phrase, since I have answered all the questions which you have chosen to ask to-night, will you be so good as to tell me who you are that take such interest in my affairs, and whom you take me to be, since my arrival has occasioned such commotion?"

"Why, sir, for myself," replied the counsellor, "I am Paulus Pleydell, an advocate at the Scottish bar; and for you, it is not easy to say distinctly who you are at present; but I trust in a short time to hail you by the title of Henry Bertram, Esq., representative of one of the oldest families in Scotland, and heir of tailzie and provision to the estate of Ellangowan—Ay," continued be, shutting his eyes and speaking to himself, "we must pass over his father, and serve him heir to his grandfather Lewis, the entailer—the only wise man of his family that I ever heard of."

They had now risen to retire to their apartments for the night, when Colonel Mannering walked up to Bertram, as he stood astonished at the counsellor's words. "I give you joy," he said, "of the prospects which fate has opened before you. I was an early friend of your father, and chanced to be in the house of Ellangowan as unexpectedly as you are now in mine, upon the very night in which you were born. I little knew this circumstance when—but I trust unkindness will be forgotten between us. Believe me, your appearance here, as Mr. Brown, alive and well, has relieved me from most painful sensations; and your right to the name of an old friend renders your presence, as Mr. Bertram, doubly welcome."

"And my parents?" said Bertram.

"Are both no more—and the family property has been sold, but I trust may be recovered. Whatever is wanted to make your right effectual, I shall be most happy to supply."

"Nay, you may leave all that to me," said the counsellor;" 'tis my vocation. Hal. I shall make money of it."

"I'm sure it's no for the like o' me," observed Dinmont, "to speak to you gentlefolks; but if siller would help on the Captain's plea, and they say nae plea gangs an weel without it—"

"Except on Saturday night," said Pleydell.

"Ay, but when your honour wadna take your fee Ye wadna hae the cause neither, sae I'll ne'er fash you on a Saturday at e'en again—but I was saying, there's some siller in the spleuchan [*A spleuchan is a tobacco pouch, occasionally used as a purse.] that's like the Captain's ain, for we've aye counted it such, baith Ailie and me."

"No, no, Liddesdale—no occasion, no occasion whatever—keep thy cash to stock thy farm."

"To stack my farm? Mr. Pleydell, your honour kens mony things, but ye dinna ken the farm o' Charlies-hope—it's sae weel stockit already, that we sell maybe sax hundred pounds off it ilka year, flesh and fell thegither—na, na."

"Can't you take another then?"

"I dinna ken—the Deuke's no that fond o' led farms, and he canna bide to put away the auld tenantry; and then I wadna like, mysel, to gang about whistling and raising the rent on my neighbours." [*Whistling, among the tenantry of a large estate, is, when an individual gives such information to the proprietor, or his managers, as to occasion the rent of his neighbour's farms being raised, which, for obvious reasons, is held a very unpopular practice.]

"What, not upon thy neighbour at Dawston—Devilstone—how d'ye call the place?"

"What, on Jock o' Dawston? hout na—he's a camsteary [*Obstinate and unruly.] chield, and fasheous [*Troublesome] about marches, and we've had some bits o' splores thegither; but deil o' me if I wad wrang Jock o' Dawston neither."

"Thou'rt an honest fellow," said the lawyer; "get thee to bed. Thou wilt sleep sounder, I warrant thee, than many a man that throws off an embroidered coat, and puts on a laced nightcap.—Colonel, I see you are busy with our Enfant trouve. But Barnes must give me a summons of wakening at seven to-morrow morning, for my servant's a sleepy-headed fellow; and I dare say my clerk, Driver, has had Clarence's fate, and is drowned by this time in a butt of your ale; for Mrs. Allan promised to make him comfortable, and she'll soon discover what he expects from that engagement. Good-night, Colonel—good-night, Dominie Sampson—good-night, Dinmont the downright—good-night, last of all, to the new-found representative of the Bertrams, and the Mac-Dingawaies, the Knarths, the Arths, the Godfreys, the Dennises, and the Rolands, and, last and dearest title, heir of tailzie and provision of the lands and barony of Ellangowan, under the settlement of Lewis Bertram, Esq., whose representative you are."

And so-saying, the old gentleman took his candle and left the room; and the company dispersed, after the Dominie had once more hugged and embraced his "little Harry Bertram," as he continued to call the young soldier of six feet high.

CHAPTER LI.

—My imagination Carries no favour in it but Bertram's; I
am undone; there is no living, none, If Bertram be away.—
    All's well that Ends Well.

At the hour which he had appointed the preceding evening, the indefatigable lawyer was seated by a good fire, and a pair of wax candles, with a velvet cap on his head, and a quilted silk night-gown on his person, busy arranging his memoranda of proofs and indications concerning the murder of Frank Kennedy. An express had also been despatched to Mr. Mac-Morlan, requesting his attendance at Woodbourne as soon as possible, on business of importance. Dinmont, fatigued with the events of the evening before, and finding the accommodations of Woodbourne much preferable to those of Mac-Guffog, was in no hurry to rise. The impatience of Bertram might have put him earlier in motion, but Colonel Mannering had intimated an intention to visit him in his apartment in the morning, and he did not choose to leave it. Before this interview he had dressed himself, Barnes having, by his master's orders, supplied him with every accommodation of linen, etc., and now anxiously waited the promised visit of his landlord.

In a short time a gentle tap announced the Colonel, with whom Bertram held a long and satisfactory conversation. Each, however, concealed from the other one circumstance. Mannering could not bring himself to acknowledge the astrological prediction; and Bertram was, from motives which may be easily conceived, silent respecting his love for Julia. In other respects, their intercourse was frank and grateful to both, and had latterly, upon the Colonel's part, even an approach to cordiality. Bertram carefully measured his own conduct by that of his host, and seemed rather to receive his offered kindness with gratitude and pleasure, than to press for it with solicitation.

Miss Bertram was in the breakfast-parlour when Sampson shuffled in, his face all radiant with smiles, a circumstance so uncommon, that Lucy's first idea was, that somebody had been bantering him with an imposition, which had thrown him into this ecstasy. Having sat for some time, rolling his eyes and gaping with his mouth like the great wooden head at Merlin's exhibition, he at length began— "And what do you think of him, Miss Lucy?"

"Think of whom, Mr. Sampson?" asked the young lady.

"Of Har—no—of him that you know about?" again demanded the
Dominie.

"That I know about?" replied Lucy, totally at a loss to comprehend his meaning.

"Yes, the stranger, you know, that came last evening in the post vehicle—he who shot young Hazlewood—ha, ha, ho!" burst forth the Dominie, with a laugh that sounded like neighing.

"Indeed, Mr. Sampson," said his pupil, "you have chosen a strange subject for mirth—I think nothing about the man, only I hope the outrage was accidental, and that we need not fear a repetition of it."

"Accidental! ho, ho, ha!" again whinnied Sampson.

"Really, Mr. Sampson," said Lucy, somewhat piqued," you are unusually gay this morning."

"Yes, of a surety I am I ha, ha, ho! face-ti-ous—ho, ho, ha!"

"So unusually facetious, my dear sir," pursued the young lady, "that I would wish rather to know the meaning of your mirth, than to be amused with its effects only."

"You shall know it, Miss Lucy," replied poor Abel Do you remember your brother?"

"Good God! how can you ask me?—no one knows better than you, he was lost the very day I was born."

"Very true, very true," answered the Dominie, saddening at the recollection; "I was strangely oblivious—ay, ay—too true. But you remember your worthy father?"

"How should you doubt it, Mr. Sampson? it is not so many weeks since—"

"True, true—ay, too true," replied the Dominie, his Houyhnhnm laugh sinking into a hysterical giggle,—"I will be facetious no more under these remembrances—but look at that young man!"

Bertram at this instant entered the room. "Yes, look at him well—he is your father's living image; and as God has deprived you of your dear parents—O my children, love one another!"

"It is indeed my father's face and form," said Lucy, turning very pale; Bertram ran to support her—the Dominie to fetch water to throw upon her face (which in his haste he took from the boiling tea-urn)—when fortunately her colour returning rapidly, saved her from the application of this ill-judged remedy. "I conjure you yet to tell me, Mr. Sampson," she said, in an interrupted, solemn voice, is this my brother?"

"It is—it is!—Miss Lucy, it is little Harry Bertram, as sure as
God's sun is in that heaven!"

"And this is my sister?" said Bertram, giving way to all that family affection, which had so long slumbered in his bosom for want of an object to expand itself upon.

119

"It is!—it is Miss Lucy Bertram," ejaculated Sampson, "whom by my poor aid you will find perfect in the tongues of France, and Italy, and even of Spain—in reading and writing her vernacular tongue, and in arithmetic and bookkeeping by double and single entry—I say nothing of her talents of shaping, and hemming, and governing a household, which, to give every one their due, she acquired not from me, but from the housekeeper—nor do I take merit for her performance upon stringed instruments, whereunto the instructions of an honourable young lady of virtue and modesty, and very facetious withal—Miss Julia Mannering—hath not meanly contributed—Suum cuique tribuilo."

"You, then," said Bertram to his sister, "are all that remains to me!—Last night, but more fully this morning, Colonel Mannering gave me an account of our family misfortunes, though without saying I should find my sister here."

"That," said Lucy, "he left to this gentleman to tell you, one of the kindest and most faithful of friends, who soothed my father's long sickness, witnessed his dying moments, and amid the heaviest clouds of fortune would not desert his orphan."

"God bless him for it!" said Bertram, shaking the Dominie's hand;" he deserves the love with which I have always regarded even that dim and imperfect shadow of his memory which my childhood retained."

"And God bless you both, my dear children," said Sampson; "if it had not been for your sake, I would have been contented (had Heaven's pleasure so been) to lay my head upon the turf beside my patron."

"But, I trust," said Bertram, "I am encouraged to hope we shall all see better days. All our wrongs shall be redressed, since Heaven has sent me means and friends to assert my right."

"Friends indeed!" echoed the Dominie, "and sent, as you truly say, by Him, to whom I early taught you to look up as the source of all that is good. There is the great Colonel Mannering from the Eastern Indies, a man of war from his birth up-wards, but who is not the less a man of great erudition, considering his imperfect opportunities; and there is, moreover, the great advocate Mr. Pleydell, who is also a man of great erudition, but who descendeth to trifles unbeseeming thereof; and there is Mr. Andrew Dinmont, whom I do not understand to have possession of much erudition, but who, like the patriarchs of old, is cunning in that which belongeth to flocks and herds—Lastly, there is even I myself, whose opportunities of collecting erudition, as they have been greater than those of the aforesaid valuable persons, have not, if it becomes me to speak, been pretermitted by me, in so far as my poor faculties have enabled me to profit by them. Of a surety, little Harry, we must speedily resume our studies. I will begin from the foundation—yes, I will reform your education upward from the true knowledge of English grammar, even to that of the Hebrew or Chaldaic tongue."

The reader may observe, that, upon this occasion, Sampson was infinitely more profuse of words than he had hitherto exhibited himself. The reason was, that in recovering his pupil his mind went instantly back to their original connection, and he had in his confusion of ideas, the strongest desire in the world to resume spelling lessons and half-text with young Bertram. This was the more ridiculous, as towards Lucy he assumed no snob powers of tuition. But she had grown up under his eye, and had been gradually emancipated from his government by increase in years and knowledge, and a latent sense of his own inferior tact in manners, whereas his first ideas went to take up Harry pretty nearly where he had left him. From the same feelings of reviving authority, he indulged himself in what was to him a profusion of language; and as people seldom speak more than usual without exposing themselves, he gave those whom he addressed plainly to understand, that while he deferred implicitly to the opinions and commands, if they chose to impose them, of almost every one whom he met with, it was under an internal conviction, that in the article of Erudition, as he usually pronounced the word, he was infinitely superior to them all put together. At present, however, this intimation fell upon heedless cars, for the brother and sister were too deeply engaged in asking and receiving intelligence concerning their former fortunes to attend much to the worthy Dominie.

When Colonel Mannering left Bertram, he went to Julia's dressing-room, and dismissed her attendant. "My dear sir," she said as he entered, "you have forgot our vigils last night, and have hardly allowed me time to comb my hair, although you must be sensible how it stood on end at the various wonders which took place."

"It is with the inside of your head that I have some business at present, Julia; I will return the outside to the care of your Mrs. Mincing in a few minutes."

"Lord, papa," replied Miss Mannering, "think how entangled all my ideas are, and you to propose to comb them out in a few minutes! If Mrs. Mincing were to do so in her department, she would tear half the hair out of my head."

"Well then, tell me," said the Colonel, "where the entanglement lies, which I will try to extricate with due gentleness!"

"Oh, everywhere," said the young lady—"the whole is a wild dream."

"Well then, I will try to unriddle it." He gave a brief sketch of the fate and prospects of Bertram, to which Julia listened with an interest which she in vain endeavoured to disguise—"Well," concluded her father, "are your ideas on the subject more luminous?"

"More confused than ever, my dear sir," said Julia. "Here is this young man come from India, after he had been supposed dead, like Aboulfouaris the great voyager to his sister Canzade and his provident brother Hour. I am wrong id the story, I believe—Canzade was his wife—but Lucy may represent the one, and the Dominie the other. And then this lively crack-brained Scotch lawyer appears like a pantomime at the end of a tragedy.—And then how delightful it will be if Lucy gets back her fortune!"

"Now I think," said the Colonel, "that the most mysterious part of the business is, that Miss Julia Mannering, who must have known her father's anxiety about the fate of this young man Brown, or Bertram, as we must now call him, should have met him when Hazlewood's accident took place, and never once mentioned to her father a word of the matter, but suffered the search to proceed against this young gentleman as a suspicious character and assassin."

Julia, much of whose courage had been hastily assumed to meet the interview with her father, was now unable to rally herself; she hung down her head in silence, after in vain attempting to utter a denial that she recollected Brown when she met him.

"No answer—well, Julia," continued her father, gravely but kindly, "allow me to ask you, Is this the only time you have seen Brown since his return from India?—still no answer. I must then naturally suppose that it is not the first time—Still no reply. Julia Mannering, will you have the kindness to answer me? Was it this young man who came under your window and conversed with you during your residence at Mervyn Hall? Julia—I command I entreat you to be candid."

Miss Mannering raised her head. "I have been, sir—I believe I am still very foolish—and it is perhaps more hard upon me that I must meet this gentleman, who has been, though not the cause entirely, yet the accomplice of my folly, in your presence."—Here she made a full stop.

"I am to understand, then," said Mannering, "that this was the author of the serenade at Mervyn Hall?"

There was something in this allusive change of epithet, that gave Julia a little more courage—"He was indeed, sir; and if I am very wrong, as I have often thought, I have some apology."

"And what is that?" answered the Colonel, speaking quick, and with something of harshness.

"I will not venture to name it, sir—but"—She opened a small cabinet, and put some letters into his hands; "I will give you these, that you may see how this intimacy began, and by whom it was encouraged."

Mannering took the packet to the window—his pride forbade a more distant retreat—he glanced at some passages of the letters with an unsteady eye and an agitated mind—his stoicism, however, came in time to his aid; that philosophy, which, rooted in pride, yet frequently bears the fruits of virtue. He returned towards his daughter with as firm an air as his feelings permitted him to assume.

"There is great apology for you, Julia, as far as I can judge from a glance at these letters—you have obeyed at least one parent. Let us adopt a Scotch proverb the Dominie quoted the other day—'Let bygones be bygones, and fair play for the future.'—I will never upbraid you with your past want of confidence—do you judge of my future intentions by my actions, of which hitherto you have surely had no reason to complain. Keep these letters—they were never intended for my eye, and I would not willingly read more of them than I have done, at your desire and for your exculpation. And now, are we friends? Or rather, do you understand me?"

"O my dear, generous father," said Julia, throwing herself into his arms, "why have I ever for an instant misunderstood you?"

"No more of that, Julia," said the Colonel; "we have both been to blame. He that is too proud to vindicate the affection and confidence which he conceives should be given without solicitation, must meet much, and perhaps deserved disappointment. It is enough that one dearest and most regretted member of my family has gone to the grave without knowing me; let me not lose the confidence of a child, who ought to love me if she really loves herself."

"Oh! no danger—no fear!" answered Julia; "let me but have your approbation and my own, and there is no role you can prescribe so severe that I will not follow."

"Well, my love," kissing her forehead, "I trust we shall not call upon you for anything too heroic. With respect to this young gentleman's addresses, I expect in the first place that all clandestine correspondence—which no young woman can entertain for a moment without lessening herself in her own eyes, and in those of her lover—I request, I say, that clandestine correspondence of every kind may be given up, and that you will refer Mr. Bertram to me for the reason. You will naturally wish to know what is to be the issue of such a reference. In the first place, I desire to observe this young gentleman's character more closely than circumstances, and perhaps my own prejudices, have permitted formerly—I should also be glad to see his birth established. Not that I am anxious about his getting the estate of Ellangowan, though such a subject is held in absolute indifference nowhere except in a novel; but certainly Henry Bertram, Heir of Ellangowan, whether possessed of the property of his ancestors or not, is a very different person from Vanbeest Brown, the son of nobody at all. His fathers, Mr. Pleydell tells me, are distinguished in history as following the banners of their native princes, while our own fought at Cressy and Poictiers. In short, I neither give nor withhold my approbation, but I expect you will redeem past errors; and as you can now unfortunately only have recourse to one parent, that you will show the duty of a child, by reposing that confidence in me, which I will say my inclination to make you happy renders a filial debt upon your part."

The first part of this speech affected Julia a good deal; the comparative merit of the ancestors of the Bertrams and Mannerings excited a secret smile, but the conclusion was such as to soften a heart peculiarly open to the feelings of generosity. "No, my dear sir," she said, extending her hand, "receive my faith, that from this moment you shall be the first person consulted respecting what shall pass in future between Brown—I mean Bertram, and me; and that no engagement shall be undertaken by me, excepting what you shall immediately know and approve of. May I ask—if Mr. Bertram is to continue a guest at Woodbourne?"

"Certainly," said the Colonel, "while his affairs render it advisable."

"Then, sir, you must be sensible, considering what is already past, that he will expect some reason for my withdrawing—I believe I must say the encouragement, which he may think I have given."

"I expect, Julia," answered Mannering, "that he will respect my roof, and entertain some sense perhaps of the services I am desirous to render him, and so will not insist upon any course of conduct of which I might have reason to complain; and I expect of you, that you will make him sensible of what is due to both."

"Then, sir, I understand you, and you shall be implicitly obeyed."

"Thank you, my love; my anxiety (kissing her) is on your account.—Now wipe these witnesses from your eyes, and so to breakfast."

CHAPTER LII.

And, Sheriff, I will engage my word to you, That I will by
to-morrow dinner time, Send him to answer thee, or any man,
For anything he shall he charged withal.

Henry IV. Part I

When the several by-plays, as they may be termed, had taken place among the individuals of the Woodbourne family, as we have intimated in the preceding chapter, the breakfast party at length assembled, Dandie excepted, who had consulted his taste in viands, and perhaps in society, by partaking of a cup of tea with Mrs. Allan, just laced with two teaspoonfuls of Cogniac, and reinforced with various slices from a huge round of beef. He had a kind of feeling that he could eat twice as much, and speak twice as much, with this good dame and Barnes, as with the grand folk in the parlour. Indeed, the meal of this less distinguished party was much more mirthful than that in the higher circle, where there was an obvious air of constraint on the greater part of the assistants. Julia dared not raise her voice in asking Bertram if he chose another cup of tea. Bertram felt embarrassed while eating his toast-and-butter under the eye of Mannering. Lucy, while she indulged to the uttermost her affection for her recovered brother, began to think of the quarrel betwixt him and Hazlewood. The Colonel felt the painful anxiety natural to a proud mind, when it deems its slightest action subject for a moment to the watchful construction of others. The lawyer, while sedulously buttering his roll, had an aspect of unwonted gravity, arising, perhaps, from the severity of his morning studies. As for the Dominie, his state of mind was ecstatic!—He looked at Bertram—he looked at Lucy—he whimpered—he sniggled—he grinned—he committed all manner of solecisms in point of form—poured the whole cream (no unlucky mistake) upon the plate of porridge, which was his own usual breakfast—threw the slops of what he called his "crowning dish of tea" into the sugar-dish instead of the slop-basin, and concluded with spilling the scalding liquor upon old Plato, the Colonel's favourite spaniel, who received the libation with a howl that did little honour to his philosophy.

The Colonel's equanimity was rather shaken by this last blunder. "Upon my word, my good friend, Mr. Sampson, you forget the difference between Plato and Zenocrates."

"The former was chief of the Academics, the latter of the Stoics," said the Dominie, with some scorn of the supposition.

"Yes, my dear sir, but it was Zenocrates, not Plato, who denied that pain was an evil."

"I should have thought," said Pleydell, "that very respectable quadruped, which is just now limping out of the room upon three of his four legs, was rather of the Cynic school."

"Very well hit off—But here comes an answer from Mac-Morlan."

It was unfavourable. Mrs. Mac-Morlan sent her respectful compliments, and her husband had been, and was, detained, by some alarming disturbances which had taken place the preceding night at Portanferry, and the necessary investigation which they had occasioned.

"What's to be done now, counsellor?" said the Colonel to Pleydell.

"Why, I wish we could have seen Mac-Morlan," said the counsellor, "who is a sensible fellow himself, and would besides have acted under my advice. But there is little harm. Our friend here must be made sui juris—he is at present an escaped prisoner; the law has an awkward claim upon him; he must be placed rectus in curia, that is the first object. For which purpose, Colonel, I will accompany you in your carriage down to Hazlewood House. The distance is not great; we will offer our bail; and I am confident I can easily show Mr.—I beg his pardon—Sir Robert Hazlewood, the necessity of receiving it."

"With all my heart," said the Colonel and, ringing the bell, gave the necessary orders. "And what is next to be done?"

"We must get hold of Mac-Morlan, and look out for more proof."

"Proof!" said the Colonel, "the thing is as clear as daylight; here are Mr. Sampson and Miss Bertram, and you yourself, at once recognise the young gentleman as his father's image; and he himself recollects all the very peculiar circumstances preceding his leaving this country—What else is necessary to conviction?"

"To moral conviction nothing more, perhaps," said the experienced lawyer, "but for legal proof a great deal. Mr. Bertram's recollections are his own recollections merely, and therefore are not evidence in his own favour; Miss Bertram, the learned Mr. Sampson, and I, can only say, what every one who knew the late Ellangowan will readily agree in, that this gentleman is his very picture—But that will not make him Ellangowan's son, and give him the estate."

"And what will do so?" said the Colonel.

"Why, we must have a distinct probation. There are these gipsies,—but then, alas! they are almost infamous in the eye of law—scarce capable of bearing evidence, and Meg Merrilies utterly so, by the various accounts which she formerly gave of the matter, and her impudent denial of all knowledge of the fact when I myself examined her respecting it."

"What must be done then?" asked Mannering.

"We must try," answered the legal sage, "what proof can be got at in Holland, among the persons by whom our young friend was educated.—But then the fear of being called in question for the murder of the gauger may make them silent; or if they speak, they are either foreigners, or outlawed smugglers. In short, I see doubts."

"Under favour, most learned and honoured sir," said the Dominie, "I trust HE, who hath restored little Harry Bertram to his friends, will not leave His own work imperfect."

"I trust so too, Mr. Sampson," said Pleydell; "but we must use the means; and I am afraid we shall have more difficulty in procuring them than I at first thought.—But a faint heart never won a fair lady—and, by the way (apart to Miss Mannering, while Bertram was engaged with his sister), there's a vindication of Holland for you! what smart fellows do you think Leyden and Utrecht must send forth, when such a very genteel and handsome young man comes from the paltry schools of Middleburgh?"

"Of a verity," said the Dominie, jealous of the reputation of the Dutch seminary,—"of a verity, Mr. Pleydell, but I make it known to you that I myself laid the foundation of his education."

"True, my dear Dominie," answered the advocate, "that accounts for his proficiency in the graces, without question—but here comes your carriage, Colonel. Adieu, young folks: Miss Julia, keep your heart till I come back again—let there be nothing done to prejudice my right, whilst I am non volens agere."

Their reception at Hazlewood House was more cold and formal than usual; for in general the Baronet expressed great respect for Colonel Mannering, and Mr. Pleydell, besides being a man of good family and of high general estimation, was Sir Robert's old friend. But now he seemed dry and embarrassed in his manner. "He would willingly," he said, "receive bail, notwithstanding that the offence had been directly perpetrated, committed, and done, against young Hazlewood of Hazlewood; but the young man had given himself a fictitious description, and was altogether that sort of person, who should not be liberated, discharged, or let loose upon society; and therefore—"

"I hope, Sir Robert Hazlewood," said the Colonel, you do not mean to doubt my word, when I assure you that he served under me as a cadet in India?"

"By no means or account whatsoever. But you call him a cadet; now he says, avers, and upholds, that he was a captain, or held a troop in your regiment."

"He was promoted since I gave up the command."

"But you must have heard of it?"

"No. I returned on account of family circumstances from India, and have not since been solicitous to hear particular news from the regiment; the name of Brown, too, is so common, that I might have seen his promotion in the Gazette without noticing it. But a day or two will bring letters from his commanding officer."

"But I am told and informed, Mr. Pleydell," answered Sir Robert, still hesitating, "that he does not mean to abide by this name of Brown, but is to set up a claim to the estate of Ellangowan, under the name of Bertram."

"Ay, who says that?" said the counsellor.

"Or," demanded the soldier, "whoever says so, does that give a right to keep him in prison?"

"Hush, Colonel," said the lawyer; "I am sure you would not, any more than I, countenance him, if he prove an impostor. —And, among friends, who informed you of this, Sir Robert?"

"Why, a person, Mr. Pleydell," answered the Baronet, "who is peculiarly interested in investigating, sifting, and clearing out this business to the bottom—you will excuse my being more particular."

"Oh, certainly," replied Pleydell—"well, and he says—"

"He says that it is whispered about among tinkers, gipsies, and other idle persons, that there is such a plan as I mentioned to you, and that this young man, who is a bastard or natural son of the late Ellangowan, is pitched upon as the impostor, from his strong family likeness."

"And was there such a natural son, Sir Robert?" demanded the counsellor.

"Oh, certainly, to my own positive knowledge. Ellangowan had him placed as cabin-boy or powder-monkey on board an armed sloop or yacht belonging to the revenue, through the interest of the late Commissioner Bertram, a kinsman of his own."

"Well, Sir Robert," said the lawyer, taking the word out of the mouth of the impatient soldier—"you have told me news, I shall investigate them, and it I find them true, certainly Colonel Mannering and I will not countenance this young man. In the meanwhile, as we are all willing to make him forthcoming, to answer all complaints against him, I do assure you, you will act most illegally, and incur heavy responsibility, if you refuse our bail."

"Why, Mr. Pleydell," said Sir Robert, who knew the high authority of the counsellor's opinion, "as you must know best, and as you promise to give up this young man—"

"If he proves an impostor," replied the lawyer, with some emphasis.

"Ay, certainly—under that condition I will take your bail; though I must say, an obliging, well-disposed, and civil neighbour of mine, who was himself bred to the law, gave me a hint or caution this morning against doing so. It was from him I learned that this youth was liberated and had come abroad, or rather had broken prison.—But where shall we find one to draw the bail-bond?"

"Here," said the counsellor, applying himself to the bell, "send up my clerk, Mr. Driver—it will not do my character harm if I dictate the needful myself." It was written accordingly and signed, and, the justice having subscribed a regular warrant for Bertram alias Brown's discharge, the visitors took their leave.

Each threw himself into his own corner of the post-chariot, and said nothing for some time. The Colonel first broke silence : "So you intend to give up this poor young fellow at the first brush?"

"Who, I?" replied the counsellor "I will not give up one hair of his head, though I should follow them to the court of last resort in his behalf—but what signified mooting points and showing one's hand to that old ass? Much better he should report to his prompter, Glossin, that we are indifferent or lukewarm in the matter. Besides, I wished to have a peep at the enemies' game."

"Indeed!" said the soldier. "Then I see there are stratagems in law as well as war. Well, and how do you like their line of battle?"

"Ingenious!" said Mr. Pleydell, "but I think desperate—they are finessing too much; a common fault on such occasions."

During this discourse the carriage rolled rapidly towards Woodbourne without anything occurring worthy of the reader's notice, excepting their meeting with young Hazlewood, to whom the Colonel told the extraordinary history of Bertram's reappearance, which he heard with high delight, and then rode on before to pay Miss Bertram his compliments on an event so happy and so unexpected.

We return to the party at Woodbourne. After the departure of Mannering, the conversation related chiefly to the fortunes of the Ellangowan family, their domains, and their former power. "It was, then, under the towers of my fathers," said Bertram, "that I landed some days since, in circumstances much resembling those of a vagabond? Its mouldering turrets and darksome arches even then awakened thoughts of the deepest interest, and recollections which I was unable to decipher. I will now visit them again with other feelings, and, I trust, other and better hopes."

"Do not go there now," said his sister. "The house of our ancestors is at present the habitation of a wretch as insidious as dangerous, whose arts and villainy accomplished the ruin and broke the heart of our unhappy father."

"You increase my anxiety," replied her brother, "to confront this miscreant, even in the den he has constructed for himself—I think I have seen him."

"But you must consider," said Julia, "that you are now left under Lucy's guard and mine, and are responsible to us for all your motions—consider I have not been a lawyer's mistress twelve hours for nothing, and I assure you it would be madness to attempt to go to Ellangowan just now.—The utmost to which I can consent is, that we shall walk in a body to the head of the Woodbourne avenue, and from that perhaps we may indulge you with our company as far as a rising ground in the common, whence your eyes may be blessed with a distant prospect of those gloomy towers, which struck so strongly your sympathetic imagination."

The party was speedily agreed upon; and the ladies, having taken their cloaks, followed the route proposed, under the escort of Captain Bertram. It was a pleasant winter morning, and the cool breeze served only to freshen, not to chill, the fair walkers. A secret though unacknowledged bond of kindness combined the two ladies, and Bertram, now hearing the interesting accounts of his own family, now communicating his adventures in Europe and in India, repaid the pleasure which he received. Lucy felt proud of her brother, as well from the bold and manly turn of his sentiments, as from the dangers he had encountered, and the spirit with which he had surmounted them. And Julia, while she pondered on her father's words, could not help entertaining hopes, that the independent spirit which had seemed to her father presumption in the humble and plebeian Brown, would have the grace of courage, noble bearing, and high blood, in the far-descended heir of Ellangowan.

They reached at length the little eminence or knoll upon the highest part of the common, called Gibbie's-knowe—a spot repeatedly mentioned in this history, as being on the skirts of the Ellangowan estate. It commanded a fair variety of hill and dale, bordered with natural woods, whose naked boughs at this season relieved the general colour of the landscape with a dark purple hue; while in other places the prospect was more formally intersected by lines of plantation, where the Scotch firs displayed their variety of dusky green. At the distance of two or three miles lay the bay of Ellangowan, its waves rippling under the influence of the western breeze. The towers of the ruined castle, seen high over every object in the neighbourhood, received—a brighter colouring from the wintry sun.

"There," said Lucy Bertram, pointing them out in the distance, "there is the seat of our ancestors. God knows, my dear brother, I do not covet in your behalf the extensive power which the lords of these ruins are said to have possessed so long, and sometimes to have used so ill. But, oh that I might see you in possession of such relics of their fortune as should give you an honourable independence, and enable you to stretch your hand for the protection of the old and destitute dependants of our family, whom our poor father's death—"

"True, my dearest Lucy," answered the young heir of Ellangowan; "and I trust, with the assistance of Heaven, which has so far guided us, and with that of these good friends, whom their own generous hearts have interested in my behalf, such a consummation of my hard adventures is now not unlikely.—But as a soldier, I must look with some interest upon that worm-eaten hold of ragged stone; and if this undermining scoundrel, who is now in possession, dare to displace a pebble of it—"

He was here interrupted by Dinmont, who came hastily after them up the road, unseen till he was near the party :—"Captain, Captain! ye're wanted—Ye're wanted by her ye ken o'."

And immediately Meg Merrilies, as if emerging out of the earth, ascended from the hollow way, and stood before them. "I sought ye at the house," she said, "and found but him (pointing to Dinmont), but ye are right, and I was wrang. It is here we should meet, on this very spot, where my eyes last saw your father. Remember your promise, and follow me."

CHAPTER LIII.

To hail the king in seemly sort The ladie was full fain;
But King Arthur, all sore amazed, No answer made again.
'What wight art thou," the ladie said "That will not speak to me?
Sir, I may chance to ease thy pain, Though I be foul to see."
The Marriage of Sir Gawaine.

The fairy bride of Sir Gawaine, while under the influence of the spell of her wicked stepmother, was more decrepit probably, and what is commonly called more ugly, than Meg Merrilies; but I doubt if she possessed that wild sublimity which an excited imagination communicated to features, marked and expressive in their own peculiar character, and to the gestures of a form, which, her sex considered, might be termed gigantic. Accordingly, the Knights of the Round Table did not recoil with more terror from the apparition of the loathly lady placed between "an oak and a green holly," than Lucy Bertram and Julia Mannering did from the appearance of this Galwegian sibyl upon the common of Ellangowan.

"For God's sake," said Julia, pulling out her purse, give that dreadful woman something, and bid her go away."

"I cannot," said Bertram "I must not offend her."

"What keeps you here?" said Meg, exalting the harsh and rough tones of her hollow voice; "why do you not follow?—Must your hour call you twice?—Do you remember your oath? —were it at kirk or market, wedding or burial,"—and she held high her skinny forefinger in a menacing attitude.

Bertram turned round to his terrified companions. "Excuse me for a moment; I am engaged by a promise to follow this woman."

"Good heavens! engaged to a madwoman?" said Julia.—

"Or to a gipsy, who has her band in the wood ready to murder you!" said Lucy.

"That was not spoken like a bairn of Ellangowan," said Meg, frowning upon Miss Bertram. "It is the ill-doers are ill-dreaders."

"In short, I must go," said Bertram, "it is absolutely necessary. wait for me five minutes on this spot."

"Five minutes?" said the gipsy; "five hours may not bring you here again."

"Do you hear that? said Julia for Heaven's sake do not go!"

"I must, I must—Mr. Dinmont will protect you back to the house."

"No," said Meg, "he must come with you; it is for that he is here. He maun take part wi' hand and heart; and weel his part it is, for redding his quarrel might have cost you dear,"

"Troth, Luckie, it's very true," said the steady farmer; "and ere I turn back frae the Captain's side, I'll show that I haena forgotten't."

"Oh yes!" exclaimed both the ladies at once, "let Mr. Dinmont go with you, if go you must, on this strange summons."

"Indeed I must," answered Bertram, "but you see I am safely guarded—Adieu for a short time; go home as fast as you can."

He pressed his sister's hand, and took a yet more affectionate farewell of Julia with his eyes. Almost stupefied with surprise and fear, the young ladies watched with anxious looks the course of Bertram, his companion, and their extraordinary guide. Her tall figure moved across the wintry heath with steps so swift, so long, and so steady, that she appeared rather to glide than to walk. Bertram and Dinmont, both tall men, apparently scarce equalled her in height, owing to her longer dress and high head-gear. She proceeded straight across the common, without turning aside to the winding path, by which passengers avoided the inequalities and little rills that traversed it in different directions. Thus the diminishing figures often disappeared from the eye, as they dived into such broken ground, and again ascended to sight when they were past the hollow. There was something frightful and unearthly, as it were, in the rapid and undeviating course which she pursued, undeterred by any of the impediments which usually incline a traveller from the direct path. Her way was as straight, and nearly as swift, as that of a bird through the air. At length they reached those thickets of natural wood which extended from the skirts of the common towards the glades and brook of Derncleugh, and were there lost to the view.

"This is very extraordinary," said Lucy after a pause, and turning round to her companion—"What can he have to do with that old hag?"

"It is very frightful," answered Julia, "and almost reminds me of the tales of sorceresses, witches,' and evil genii, which I have heard in India. They believe there in a fascination of the eye, by which those who possess it control the will and dictate the motions of their victims. What can your brother have in common with that fearful woman, that he should leave us, obviously against his will, to attend to her commands?"

"At least," said Lucy, "we may hold him safe from harm; for she would never have summoned that faithful creature Dinmont, of whose strength, courage, and steadiness Henry said so much, to attend upon an expedition where she projected evil to the person of his friend. And now let us go back to the house till the Colonel returns—perhaps Bertram may be back first; at any rate, the Colonel will judge what is to be done."

Leaning then upon each other's arm, but yet occasionally stumbling, between fear and the disorder of their nerves, they at length reached the head of the avenue, when they heard the tread of a horse behind. They started, for their ears were awake to every sound, and beheld to their great pleasure young Hazlewood. "The Colonel will be here immediately," he said; "I galloped on before to pay my respects to Miss

Bertram, with the sincerest congratulations upon the joyful event which has taken place in her family. I long to be introduced to Captain Bertram, and to thank him for the well. deserved lesson he gave to my rashness and indiscretion."

"He has left us just now," said Lucy, "and in a manner that has frightened us very much."

Just at that moment the Colonel's carriage drove up, and, on observing the ladies, stopped, while Mannering and his learned counsel alighted and joined them. They instantly communicated the new cause of alarm.

"Meg Merrilies again!" said the Colonel; she certainly is a most mysterious and unaccountable personage; but I think she must have something to impart to Bertram, to which she does not mean we should be privy."

"The devil take the bedlamite old woman," said the counsellor; "will she not let things take their course, prout de lege, but must always be putting in her oar in her own way?—Then, I fear from the direction they took they are going upon the Ellangowan estate—that rascal Glossin has shown us what ruffians he has at his disposal. I wish honest Liddesdale may be guard sufficient."

"If you please," said Hazlewood, "Ishould be most happy to ride in the direction which they have taken. I am so well known in the country, that I scarce think any outrage will be offered in my presence, and I shall keep at such a cautious distance as not to appear to watch Meg, or interrupt any communication which she may make."

"Upon my word," said Pleydell (aside), "to be a sprig, whom I remember with a whey face and a satchel not so very many years ago, I think young Hazlewood grows a fine fellow. I am more afraid of a new attempt at legal oppression than at open violence, and from that this young man's presence would deter both Glossin and his understrappers.—Hie away, then, my boy—peer out—peer out—you'll find them somewhere about Derncleugh, or very probably in Warroch Wood."

Hazlewood turned his horse. "Come back to us to dinner, Hazlewood," cried the Colonel. He bowed, spurred his horse, and galloped off.

We now return to Bertram and Dinmont, who continued to follow their mysterious guide through the woods and dingles, between the open common and the ruined hamlet of Derncleugh. As she led the way, she never looked back upon her followers, unless to chide them for loitering, though the sweat, in spite of the season, poured from their brows. At other times she spoke to herself in such broken expressions as these—"It is to rebuild the auld house—it is to lay the corner-stone—and did I not warn him?—I tell'd him I was born to do it, if my father's head had been the stepping-stane, let alane his. I was doomed—still I kept my purpose in the cage and in the stocks;—I was banished—I kept it in an unco land;—I was scourged—I was branded—My resolution lay deeper than scourge or red iron could reach-and now the hour is come."

"Captain," said Dinmont, in a half whisper, "I wish she binna uncanny! [*Mad] her words dinna seem to come in God's name, or like other folk's. Odd, they threep [*Declare] in our country that there are sic things."

"Don't be afraid, my friend," whispered Bertram in return.

"Fear'd! fient a haet [*Not a whit.] care I," said the dauntless farmer, "be she witch or deevil; it's a' ane to Dandie Dinmont."

"Haud your peace, gudeman," said Meg, looking sternly over her shoulder; "is this a time or place for you to speak, think ye?"

"But, my good friend," said Bertram, "as I have no doubt in your good faith, or kindness, which I have experienced; you should in return have some confidence in me—I wish to know where you are leading us."

"There's but ae answer to that, Henry Bertram," said the sibyl.—"Iswore my tongue should never tell, but I never said my finger should never show. Go on and meet your fortune, or turn back and lose it—that's a' I hae to say."

"Go on then," answered Bertram "I will ask no more questions."

They descended into the glen about the same place where Meg had formerly parted from Bertram., She paused an instant beneath the tall rock where he had witnessed the burial of a dead body, and stamped upon the ground, which, notwithstanding all the care that had been taken, showed vestiges of having been recently moved. "Here rests ane," she said, "he'll maybe hae neibors sune."

She then moved up the brook until she came to the ruined hamlet, where, pausing with a look of peculiar and softened interest before one of the gables which was still standing, she said in a tone less abrupt, though as solemn as before, "Do you see that blackit and broken end of a shealing? [*Hut]—there my kettle boiled for forty years—there I bore twelve buirdly sons and daughters—where are they now?—where are the leaves that were on that auld ash-tree at Martinmas!—the west wind has made it bare—and I'm stripped too.—Do you see that saugh-tree?—it's but a blackened rotten stump now—I've sat under it mony a bonnie summer afternoon, when it hung its gay garlands ower the poppling water.—I've sat there, and," elevating her voice, "I've held you on my knee, Henry Bertram, and sung ye sangs of the auld barons and their bloody wars—it will ne'er be green again, and Meg Merrilies will never sing sangs mair, be they blithe or sad. But ye'll no forget her, and ye'll gar big up [*Cause to be built up.] the auld wa's for her sake?—and let somebody live there that's, ower gude to fear them of another warld—For if ever the dead came back amang the living. I'll be seen in this glen mony a night after these crazed banes are in the mould."

The mixture of insanity and wild pathos with which she spoke these last words, with her right arm, bare and extended, her left bent and shrouded beneath the dark red drapery of her mantle, might have been a study worthy of our Siddons herself. "And now," she said, resuming at once the short, stern, and hasty tone which was most ordinary to her—"let us to the wark—let us to the wark."

She then led the way to the promontory on which the Kaim of Derncleugh was situated, produced a large key from her pocket, and unlocked the door. The interior of this place was in better order than formerly. "Ihave made things decent," she said; "I may be streekit, [*Stretched out] here or night.—There will be few, few at Meg's lykewake, [*Watching over a corpse by night.] for mony of our folk will blame what I hae done, and am to do!"

She then pointed to a table, upon which was some cold meat, arranged with more attention to neatness than could have been expected from Meg's habits. "Eat," she said, "eat; ye'll need it this night yet."

Bertram, in complaisance, ate a morsel or two and Dinmont, whose appetite was unabated either by wonder, apprehension, or the meal of the morning, made his usual figure as a trencherman. She then offered each a single glass of spirits, which Bertram drank diluted, and his companion plain.

"Will ye taste naething yourself, Luckie?" said Dinmont.

"I shall not need it," replied their mysterious hostess. "And now," she said, "ye maun hae arms—ye maunna gang on dry-handed—but use them not rashly—take captive, but save life—let the law hae its ain—he maun speak ere he die."

125

"Who is to be taken?—who is to speak?" said Bertram in astonishment, receiving a pair of pistols which she offered him, and which, upon examining, he found loaded and locked.

"The flints are gude," she said, "and the powder dry—I ken this wark weel."

Then, without answering his questions, she armed Dinmont also with a large pistol, and desired them to choose sticks for themselves out of a parcel of very suspicious-looking bludgeons, which she brought from a corner. Bertram took a stout sapling, and Dandie selected a club which might have served Hercules himself. They then left the hut together, and, in doing so, Bertram took an opportunity to whisper to Dinmont, "There's something inexplicable in all this—But we need not use these arms unless we see necessity and lawful occasion—take care to do as you see me do."

Dinmont gave a sagacious nod; and they continued to follow, over wet and over dry, through bog and through fallow, the footsteps of their conductress. She guided them to the wood of Warroch by the same track which the late Ellangowan had used when riding to Derncleugh in quest of his child, on the miserable evening of Kennedy's murder.

When Meg Merrilies had attained these groves, through which the wintry sea-wind was now whistling hoarse and shrill, she seemed to pause a moment as if to recollect the way. "We maun go the precise track," she said, and continued to go forward, but rather in a zigzag and involved course than according to her former steady and direct line of motion. At length she guided them through the mazes of the wood to a little open glade of about a quarter of an acre, surrounded by trees and bushes, which made a wild and irregular boundary. Even in winter it was a sheltered and snugly sequestered spot; but when arrayed in the verdure of spring, the earth sending forth all its wild flowers, the shrubs spreading their waste of blossom around it, and the weeping birches, which towered over the underwood, drooping their long and leafy fibres to intercept the sun, it must have seemed a place for a youthful poet to study his earliest sonnet, or a pair of lovers to exchange their first mutual avowal of affection. Apparently it now awakened very different recollections. Bertram's brow, when he had looked round the spot, became gloomy and embarrassed. Meg, after uttering to herself, "This is the very spot!" looked at him with a ghastly side-glance,—"D'ye mind it?"

"Yes answered Bertram, "imperfectly I do."

"Ay!" pursued his guide, "on this very spot the man fell from his horse—I was behind that bourtree-bush at the very moment. Sair, sair he strove, and sair he cried for mercy—but he was in the hands of them that never kenn'd the word!—Now will I show you the further track—the last time ye travelled it was in these arms."

She led them accordingly by a long and winding passage almost overgrown with brushwood, until, without any very perceptible descent, they suddenly found themselves by the seaside. Meg then walked very fast on between the surf and the rocks, until she came to a remarkable fragment of rock detached from the rest. "Here," she said in a low and scarcely audible whisper, "here the corpse was found."

"And the cave," said Bertram, in the some tone, is close beside it—are you guiding us there?"

"Yes," said the gipsy in a decided tone. "Bend up both your hearts—follow me as I creep in—I have placed the firewood so as to screen you. Bide behind it for a gliff [*Little] till I say, The hour and the man are baith come; then rin in on him, take his arms, and bind him till the blood burst frae his finger nails."

"I will, by my soul," said Henry—"if he is the man I suppose—Jansen?"

"Ay, Jansen, Hatteraick, and twenty mair names are his."

"Dinmont, you must stand by me now," said Bertram, "for this fellow is a devil."

"Ye needna doubt that," said the stout yeoman—"but I wish I could mind a bit prayer or I creep after the witch into that hole that she's opening—It wad be a sair thing to leave the blessed sun, and the free air, and gang and, be killed, like a tod that's run to earth, in a dungeon like that. But, my sooth, they will be hard-bitten terriers will worry Dandie; so, as I said, deil hae me if I baulk you." This was uttered in the lowest tone of voice possible. The entrance was now open. Meg crept in upon her hands and knees, Bertram followed and Dinmont, after giving a rueful glance toward the daylight, whose blessings he was abandoning, brought up the rear.

CHAPTER LIV.

—Die, prophet! in thy speech; For this, among the rest,
was I ordained.

Henry VI. Part III.

The progress of the Borderer, who, as we have said,—was the last of the party, was fearfully arrested by a hand, which caught hold of his leg as he dragged his long limbs after him in silence and perturbation through the low and narrow entrance of the subterranean passage. The steel heart of the bold yeoman had well-nigh given way, and he suppressed with difficulty a shout, which, in the defenceless posture and situation which they then occupied, might have cost all their lives. He contented himself, however, with extricating his foot from the grasp of the unexpected follower. Be still," said a voice behind him, releasing him I am a friend—Charles Hazlewood."

These words were uttered in a very low voice, but they produced sound enough to startle Meg Merrilies, who led the van, and who, having already gained the place where the cavern expanded, had risen upon her feet. She began, as if to confound any listening ear, to growl, to mutter, and to sing aloud, and at the same time to make a bustle among some brushwood which was now heaped in the cave.

"Here—beldam—Deyvil's kind," growled the harsh voice of Dirk Hatteraick from the inside of his den, what makest thou there?"

"Laying the roughies [*Withered boughs.] to keep the cauld wind frae a—you, ye desperate do-nae-good—Ye're e'en ower weel off, and wots na; it will be otherwise soon."

"Have you brought me the brandy, and any news of my people?" said Dirk Hatteraick.

"Here's the flask for ye. Your people-dispersed—broken— gone—or cut to ribbands by the red-coats."

"Der Deyvil!—this coast is fatal to me."

"Ye may hae mair reason to say sae."

While this dialogue went forward, Bertram and Dinmont had both gained the interior of the cave, and assumed an erect position. The only light which illuminated its rugged and sable precincts was a quantity of wood burnt to charcoal in an iron grate, such as they use in spearing salmon by night. On these red embers Hatteraick from time to time threw a handful of twigs or splintered wood; but these, even when they blazed up, afforded a light much disproportioned to the extent of the cavern; and, as its principal inhabitant lay upon the side of the grate most remote from the entrance, it was not easy for him to discover distinctly objects which lay in that direction. The intruders, therefore, whose number was now augmented unexpectedly to three, stood behind the loosely-piled branches with little risk of discovery. Dinmont had the sense' to keep back Hazlewood with one hand till he whispered to Bertram, "A friend—young Hazlewood."

It was no time for following up the introduction, and they all stood as still as the rocks around them, obscured behind the pile of brushwood, which had been probably placed there to break the cold wind from the sea, without totally intercepting the supply of air. The branches. were laid so loosely above each otter, that, looking through them towards the light of the fire-grate, they could easily discover what passed in its vicinity, although a much stronger degree of illumination than it afforded, would not have enabled the persons placed near the bottom of the cave to have descried them in the position which they occupied.

The scene, independent of the peculiar moral interest and personal danger which attended it, had, from the effect of the light and shade on the uncommon objects which it exhibited, an appearance emphatically dismal. The light in the fire-grate was the dark-red glare of charcoal in a state of ignition, relieved from time to time by a transient flame of a more vivid or duskier light, as the fuel with which Dirk Hatteraick fed his fire was better or worse fitted for his purpose. Now a dark cloud of stifling smoke rose up to the roof of the cavern, and then lighted into a reluctant and sullen blaze, which flashed wavering up the pillar of smoke, and was suddenly rendered brighter and more lively by some drier fuel, or perhaps some splintered fir-timber, which at once converted the smoke into flame. By such fitful irradiation, they could see, more or less distinctly, the form of Hatteraick, whose savage and rugged cast of features, now rendered yet more ferocious by the circumstances of his situation, and the deep gloom of his mind, assorted well with the rugged and broken vault, which rose in a rude arch over and around him. The form of Meg Merrilies, which stalked about him, sometimes in the light, sometimes partially obscured in the smoke or darkness, contrasted strongly with the sitting figure of Hatteraick as he bent over the flame, and from his stationary posture was constantly visible to the spectator, while that of the female flitted around, appearing or disappearing like a spectre.

Bertram felt his blood boil at the sight of Hatteraick. He remembered him well under the name of Jansen, which the smuggler had adopted after the death of Kennedy; and he remembered also, that this Jansen, and his mate Brown, the same who was shot at Woodbourne, had been the brutal tyrants of his infancy. Bertram knew further, from piercing his own imperfect recollections with the narratives of Mannering and Pleydell, that this man was the prime agent in the act of violence which tore him from his family and country, and had exposed him to so many distresses and dangers. A thousand exasperating reflections rose within his bosom; and he could hardly refrain from rushing upon Hatteraick and blowing his brains out.

At the same time this would have been no safe adventure. The flame, as it rose and fell, while it displayed the strong, muscular, and broad-chested frame of the ruffian, glanced also upon two brace of pistols in his belt, and upon the hilt of his cutlass: it was not to be doubted that his desperation was commensurate with his personal strength and means of resistance. Both, indeed, were inadequate to encounter the combined power of two such men as Bertram himself and his friend Dinmont, without reckoning their unexpected assistant Hazlewood, who was unarmed, and of a lighter make; but Bertram felt, on a moment's reflection, that there would be neither sense nor valour in anticipating the hangman's office, and he considered the importance of making Hatteraick prisoner alive. He therefore repressed his indignation, and awaited that should pass between the ruffian and his gipsy guide.

"And how are ye now?" said the harsh and discordant tones of his female attendant "Said I not it would come upon you—ay, and in this very cave, where ye harboured after the deed."

"Wetter and sturm, ye hag!" replied Hatteraick, "keep your deyvil's matins till they're wanted. Have you seen Glossin?"

"No," replied Meg Merrilies. "you've missed your blow, ye blood-spiller! and ye have nothing to expect from the tempter."

"Hagel!" exclaimed the ruffian, "if I had him but by the throat!-and what am I to do then?"

"Do?" answered the gipsy; "die like a man, or be hanged like a dog!"

"Hanged, ye hag of Satan!-the hemp's not sown that shall hang me."

"It's sown, and it's grown, and it's heckled, and it's twisted. Did I not tell ye, when ye wad take away the boy Harry Bertram, in spite of my prayers,—did I not say he would come back when he had dree'd his weird in foreign land till his twenty-first year?—Did I not say the auld fire would burn down to a spark, but wad kindle again?"

"Well, mother, you did say so," said Hatteraick in a tone that had something of despair in its accents; "and, donner and blitzen! I believe you spoke the truth—that younker of Ellangowan has been a rock ahead to me all my life! and now, with Glossin's cursed contrivance, my crew have been cut off, my boats destroyed, and I dare say the lugger's taken—there were not men enough left on board to work her, far less to fight her—a dredge-boat might have taken her. And what will the owners say?—Hagel and sturm! I shall never dare go back again to Flushing."

"You'll never need," said the gipsy.

"What are you doing there," said her companion, "and what makes you say that?"

During this dialogue, Meg was heaping some flax loosely together. Before answer to this question, she dropped a firebrand upon the flax, which had been previously steeped in some spirituous liquor, for it instantly caught fire, and rose in a vivid pyramid of the most brilliant light up to the very top of the vault. As it ascended, Meg answered the ruffian's question in a firm and steady voice:-"Because the Hour's come, and the Man."

At the appointed signal, Bertram and Dinmont sprung over the brushwood, and rushed upon Hatteraick. Hazlewood, unacquainted with their plan of assault, was a moment later. The ruffian, who instantly saw he was betrayed, turned his first vengeance on Meg Merrilies, at whom he discharged a pistol. She fell, with a piercing and dreadful cry, between the shriek of pain and the sound of laughter, when at its highest and most suffocating height.

"I kenn'd it would be this way," she said.

Bertram, in his haste, slipped his foot upon the uneven rock which floored the cave; a fortunate stumble, for Hatteraick's second bullet whistled over him with so true and steady an aim, that had he been standing upright, it must have lodged in his brain. Ere the smuggler could draw another pistol, Dinmont closed with him, and endeavoured by main force to pinion down his arms. Such, however, was the wretch's personal strength, joined to the efforts of his despair, that, in spite of the gigantic force with which the Borderer grappled him, he dragged Dinmont through the blazing flax, and had almost succeeded in drawing a third pistol, which might have proved fatal to the honest farmer, had not Bertram, as well as Hazlewood, come to his assistance, when, by main force, and no ordinary exertion of it, they threw Hatteraick on the ground, disarmed him, and bound him. This scuffle, though it takes up some time in the narrative, passed in less than a single minute. When he was fairly mastered, after one or two desperate and almost convulsionary struggles, the ruffian lay perfectly still and silent. "He's gaun to die game ony how," said Dinmont; "weel, I like him na the waur for that."

This observation honest Dandie made while he was shaking the blazing flax from his rough coat and shaggy black hair, some of which had been singed in the scuffle. "He is quiet now," said Bertram; "stay by him, and do not permit him to stir till I see whether the poor woman be alive or dead." With Hazlewood's assistance he raised Meg Merrilies.

"I kenn'd it would be this way," she muttered, and it's e'en this way that it should be."

"The ball had penetrated the breast below the throat. It did not bleed much externally; but Bertrarn, accustomed to see gun-shot. wounds, thought it the more alarming. "Good God! what shall we do for this poor woman?" said he to Hazlewood, the circumstances superseding the necessity of previous explanation or introduction to each other.

"My horse stands tied above in the wood," said Hazlewood. "I have been watching you these two hours—I will ride off for some assistants that may be trusted. Meanwhile, you had better defend the mouth of the cavern against every one till I return." He hastened away. Bertram, after binding Meg Merrilies's wound as well as he could, took station near the mouth of the cave with a cocked pistol in his hand; Dinmont continued to watch Hatteraick, keeping a grasp, like that of Hercules, on his breast. There was a dead silence in the cavern, only interrupted by the low and suppressed moaning of the wounded female, and by the hard breathing of the prisoner.

CHAPTER LV.

For though, seduced and led astray, Thou'st travell'd far
and wander'd long, Thy God hath seen thee all the way, And
all the turns that led thee wrong.

The Hall of Justice.

After the space of about three-quarters of an hour, which the uncertainty and danger of their situation made seem almost thrice as long, the voice of young Hazlewood was heard without. "Here I am," he cried, "with a sufficient party."

"Come in then," answered Bertram, not a little pleased to find his guard relieved. Hazlewood then entered, followed by two or three countrymen, one of whom acted as a peace-officer. They lifted Hatteraick up, and carried him in their arms as far as the entrance of the vault was high enough to permit them; then laid him on his back, and dragged him along as well as they could, for no persuasion would induce him to assist the transportation by any exertion of his own. He lay as silent and inactive in their hands as a dead corpse, incapable of opposing, but in no way aiding, their operations. When he was dragged into daylight, and placed erect upon his feet among three or four assistants, who had remained without the cave, he seemed stupefied and dazzled by the sudden change from the darkness of his cavern. While others were superintending the removal of Meg Merrilies, those who remained with Hatteraick attempted to make him sit down upon a fragment of rock which lay close upon the high-water mark. A strong shuddering convulsed his iron frame for an instant, as he resisted their purpose. "Not there—Hagel!—you would not make me sit There?"

These were the only words he spoke; but their import, and the deep tone of horror in which they were uttered, served to show what was passing in his mind.

When Meg Merrilies had also been removed from the cavern, with all the care for her safety that circumstances admitted, they consulted where she should be carried. Hazlewood had sent for a surgeon, and proposed that she should be lifted in the meantime to the nearest cottage. But the patient exclaimed with great earnestness, "Na, na, na! To the Kaim o' Derncleugh—the Kaim o' Derncleugh—the spirit will not free itself o' the flesh but there."

"You must indulge her, I believe," said Bertram "her troubled imagination will otherwise aggravate the fever of the wound."

They bore her accordingly to the vault. On the way her mind seemed to run more upon the scene which had just passed, than on her own approaching death. "There were three of them set upon him—I brought the twasome—but wha was the third?—It would be himself, returned to work his airs vengeance!" '

It was evident that the unexpected appearance of Hazlewood, whose person the outrage of Hatteraick left her no time to recognise, had produced a strong effect on her imagination. She often recurred to it. Hazlewood accounted for his unexpected arrival to Bertram, by saying, that he had kept them in view for some time by the direction of Mannering; that, observing them disappear into the cave, he had crept after them, meaning to announce himself and his errand, when his hand in the darkness encountering the leg of Dinmont, had nearly produced a catastrophe, which, indeed, nothing but the presence of mind and fortitude of the bold yeoman could have averted.

When the gipsy arrived at the hut, she produced the key; and when they entered, and were about to deposit her upon the bed, she said, in an anxious tone, "Na, na! not that way, the feet to the east;" and appeared gratified when they reversed her posture accordingly, and placed her in that appropriate to dead body.

"Is there no clergyman near," said Bertram, "to assist this unhappy woman's devotions?"

A gentleman, the minister of the parish, who had been Charles Hazlewood's tutor, had, with many others, caught the alarm, that the murderer of Kennedy was taken on the spot where the deed had been done so many years before, and that a woman was mortally wounded. From curiosity, or rather from the feeling that his duty called him to scenes of distress, this gentleman had come to the Kaim of Derncleugh, and now presented himself. The surgeon arrived at the same time, and was about to probe the wound; but Meg resisted the assistance of either. "It's no what man can do, that will heal my body, or save my spirit. Let me speak what I have to say, and then ye may work your will; I'se be nae hinderance.—But where's Henry Bertram?"—the assistants, to whom this same had been long a stranger, gazed upon each other.—"Yes!" she said, in a stronger and harsher tone, "Isaid Henry Bertram of Ellangowan. Stand from the light and let me see him."

All eyes—were turned towards Bertram, who approached the wretched couch. The wounded woman took hold of his hand. "Look at him," she said, "all that ever saw his father or his grandfather, and bear witness if he is not their living image?" A murmur went through the crowd—the resemblance was too striking to be denied. "And now hear me—and let that man," pointing to Hatteraick, who was seated with his keepers on a sea-chest at some distance-" let him deny what I say, if he can. That is Henry Bertram, son to Godfrey Bertram, umquhile of Ellangowan; that young man is the very lad-bairn that Dirk Hatteraick carried off from Warroch Wood the day that he murdered the gauger. I was there like a wandering spirit—for I longed to see that wood or we left the country. I saved the bairn's life, and sair, sair I prigged [*Begged] and prayed they would leave him wi' me—But they bore him away, and he's been lang ower the sea, and now he's come for his ain, and what should withstand him?—I swore to keep the secret till he was ane-an'-twenty—I kenn'd he believed to dree his weird [*Fulfil his destiny] till that day cam—I keepit that oath which I took to them—but I made another vow to mysell, that if I lived to see the day of his return, I would set him in his father's seat, if every step was on a dead man. I have keepit that oath too, I will be ae step mysell—He (pointing to Hatteraick) will soon be another, and there will be ane mair yet."

The clergyman, now interposing, remarked it was a pity this deposition was not regularly taken and written down, and the surgeon urged the necessity of examining the wound, previously to exhausting her by questions. When she saw them remove Hatteraick, in order to clear the room and leave the surgeon to his operations, she called out aloud, raising herself at the same time upon the couch, "Dirk Hatteraick, You and I will never meet again until we are before the judgment-seat-Will ye own to what I have said, or will you dare deny it?" He turned his hardened brow upon her, with a look of dumb and inflexible defiance. "Dirk Hatteraick, dare ye deny, with my blood upon your hands, one word of what my dying breath is uttering?"—He looked at her with the same expression of hardihood and dogged stubbornness, and moved his lips, but uttered no sound. "Then fareweel!" she said, "and God forgive you! Your hand has sealed my evidence.—When I was in life, I was the mad randy gipsy, that had been scourged, and banished, and branded—that had begged from door to door, and been hounded like a stray tike [*Dog.] from parish to parish—wha would hae minded her tale?—But now I am a dying woman, and my words will not fall to the ground, any more than the earth will cover my blood!"

She here paused, and all left the hut except the surgeon and two or three women. After a very short examination, he shook his head, and resigned his post by the dying woman's side to the clergyman.

A chaise returning empty to Kippletringan had been stopped on the high-road by a constable, who foresaw it would be necessary to convey Hatteraick to jail. The driver, understanding what was going on at Derncleugh, left his horses to the care of a black-guard boy, confiding, it is to be supposed, rather in the years and discretion of the cattle, than in those of their keeper, and set off full speed to see, as he expressed himself, "whaten a sort o' fun was gaun on." He arrived just as the group of tenants and peasants, whose numbers increased every moment, satiated with gazing upon the rugged features of Hatteraick, had turned their attention towards Bertram. Almost all of them, especially the aged men who had seen Ellangowan in his better days, felt and acknowledged the justice of Meg Merrilies's appeal. But the Scotch are a cautious people; they remembered there was another in possession of the estate, and they as yet only expressed their feelings in low whispers to each other. Our friend Jock Jabos, the postilion, forced his way into the middle of the circle; but no sooner cast his eyes upon Bertram, than he started back in amazement, with a solemn exclamation, "As sure as there's breath in man, it's auld Ellangowan arisen from the dead!"

This public declaration of an unprejudiced witness was just the spark wanted to give fire to the popular feeling, which burst forth in three distinct shouts:—"Bertram forever!"—"Long life to the heir of Ellangowan!"—"God send him his ain, and to live among us as his forebears did of yore!"

"I hae been seventy years an the land," said one person.

"I and mine hae been seventy and seventy to that said another; "I have a right to ken the glance of a Bertram."

"I and mine hae been three hundred years here," said another old man, "and I sall sell my last cow, but I'll see the young laird placed in his right."

The women, ever delighted with the marvellous, and not less so when a handsome young man is the subject of the tale, added their shrill acclamations to the general all-hail. "Blessings on him—he's the very picture o' his father!—the Bertrams were aye the wale o' the country-side!"

"Eh! that his puir mother, that died in grief and in doubt about him, had but—lived to see this day!" exclaimed some female voices.

"But we'll help him to his ain, kimmers," cried others; "and before Glossin sall keep the Place of Ellangowan, we'll howk him out o't wi' our nails!"

Others crowded around Dinmont, who was nothing loth to tell what he knew of his friend, and to boast the honour which he had in contributing to the discovery. As he was known to several of the principal farmers present, his testimony afforded an additional motive to the general enthusiasm. In short, it was one of those moments of intense feeling, when the frost of the Scottish people melts like a snow-wreath, and the dissolving torrent carries dam and dyke before it.

The sudden shouts interrupted the devotions of the clergyman; and Meg, who was in one of those dozing fits of stupefaction that precede the close of existence, suddenly started-" Dinna ye bear?-dinna ye hear?—he's owned!-he's owned!—I lived but for this. I am a sinful woman; but if my curse brought it down, my blessing has taen it off! And now I wad hae liked to hae said mair. But it canna be. Stay"—she continued, stretching her head towards the gleam of light that shot through the narrow slit which served for a window, "Is he not there?—stand out o' the light, and let me look upon him ance mair. But the darkness is in my ain een," she said, sinking back, after an earnest gaze upon vacuity—"it's a' ended now,

Pass breath,
Come death."

And, sinking back upon her couch of' straw, she expired without a groan. The clergyman and the surgeon carefully noted down all that she had said, now deeply regretting they had not examined her more minutely, but both remaining morally convinced of the truth of her disclosure.

Hazlewood was the first to compliment Bertram upon the near prospect of his being restored to his name and rank in society. The people around, who now learned from Jabos that Bertram was the person who had wounded him, were struck with his generosity, and added his name to Bertram's in their exulting acclamations.

Some, however, demanded of the postilion how he had not recognised Bertram when he saw him some time before at Kippletringan? to which he gave the very natural answer,—"Hout, what was I thinking about Ellangowan then?—It was the cry that was rising e'en now that the young laird was found, that put tire on finding out the likeness—There was nae missing it ance ane was set to look for't."

The obduracy of Hatteraick, during the latter part of this scene, was in some slight degree shaken. He was observed to twinkle with his eyelids—to attempt to raise his bound hands for the purpose of pulling his hat over his brow—to look angrily and impatiently to the road,

129

as if anxious for the vehicle which was to remove him from the spot. At length Mr. Hazlewood, apprehensive that the popular ferment might take a direction towards the prisoner, directed he should be taken to the post-chaise, and so removed to the town of Kippletringan to be at Mr. MacMorlan's disposal; at the same time he sent an express to warn that gentleman of what had happened. "And now," he said to Bertram, "Ishould be happy if you would accompany me to Hazlewood House; but as that. might not be so agreeable just now as I trust it will be in a day or two, you must allow me to return with you to Woodbourne. But you are on foot."—"Or if the young laird would take my horse!"—"Or mine"—"Or mine," said half a dozen voices—"Or mine; he can trot ten mile an hour without whip or spur, and he's the young—. laird's frae this moment, if he likes to take him for a herezeld, [*This hard word is placed in the mouth of one of the aged tenants. In the old feudal tenures, the herezeld constituted the best horse or other animal in the vassal's lands, became the right of the superior. The only remnant of this custom is what is called the sasine, or a fee of certain estimated value, paid to the sheriff of the county, who gives possession to the vassals Of the Crown.] as they ca'd it lang syne."—Bertram readily accepted the horse as a loan, and poured forth his thanks to the assembled crowd for their good wishes, which they repaid with shouts and vows of attachment.

While the happy owner was directing one lad to "gae doun for the new saddle"; another, "just to rin the beast ower wi' a dry wisp o' strae"; a third, "to hie doun and borrow Dan Dunkieson's plated stirrups," and expressing his regret, "that there was nae time to gie the nag a feed, that the young laird might ken his mettle," Bertram, taking the clergyman by the arm, walked into the vault, and shut the door immediately after them. He gazed in silence for some minutes upon the body of Meg Merrilies, as it lay before him, with the features sharpened by death, yet still retaining the stern and energetic character, which had maintained in life her superiority as the wild chieftainess of the lawless people amongst whom she was born. The young soldier dried the tears which involuntarily rose on viewing this wreck of one, who might be said to have died a victim to her fidelity to his person and family. He then took the clergyman's hand, and asked solemnly, if she appeared able to give that attention to his devotions which befitted a departing person.

"My dear sir," said the good minister, "I trust this poor woman had remaining sense to feel and join in the import of my prayers. But let us humbly hope we are judged of by our opportunities of religious and moral instruction. In some degree she might be considered as an uninstructed heathen, even in the bosom of a Christian country; and let us remember, that the errors and vices of an ignorant life were balanced by instances of disinterested attachment, amounting almost to heroism. To Him, who can alone weigh our crimes and errors against our efforts towards virtue, we consign her with awe, but not without hope."

"May I request," said Bertram, "that you will see every decent solemnity attended to in behalf of this poor woman? I have some property belonging to her in my hands-at all events I will be answerable for the expense—you will hear of me at Woodbourne."

Dinmont, who had been furnished with a horse by one of his acquaintance, now loudly called out that all was ready for their return; and Bertram and Hazlewood, after a strict exhortation to the crowd, which was now increased to several hundreds, to preserve good order in their rejoicing, as the least ungoverned zeal might be turned to the disadvantage of the young Laird, as they termed him, took their leave amid the shouts of the multitude.

As they rode past the ruined cottages at Derncleugh, Dinmont said, "I'm sure when ye come to your ain, Captain, ye'll no forget to big [*Build] a bit cot-house there? Deil be in me but I wad dot mysell, an it werena in better hands.—I wadna like to live in't though, after what she said. Odd, I wad put in auld Elspeth, the bedral's [*Beadle's] widow—the like o' them's used wi' graves and ghaists, and thae things."

A short but brisk ride brought them to Woodbourne. The news of their exploit had already flown far and wide, and the whole inhabitants of the vicinity met them on the lawn with shouts of congratulation. "That you have seen, me alive," said Bertram to Lucy, who first ran up to him, though Julia's eyes even anticipated hers, "you must thank these kind friends."

With a blush expressing at once pleasure, gratitude, and bashfulness, Lucy curtsied to Hazlewood, but to Dinmont she frankly extended her hand. The honest farmer, in the extravagance of his joy, carried his freedom farther than the hint warranted, for he imprinted his thanks on the lady's lips, and was instantly shocked at the rudeness of his own conduct. "Lord-sake, madam, I ask your pardon," he. said; "I forgot but ye had been a bairn o' my ain—the Captain's sae hamely, he gars ane forget himsell."

Old Pleydell now advanced. "Nay, if fees like these are going—" he said.

"Stop, stop, Mr. Pleydell," said Julia, "you had your fees beforehand—remember last night."

"Why, I do confess a retainer," said the barrister; but if I don't deserve double fees from both Miss Bertram and you when I conclude my examination of Dirk Hatteraick tomorrow—Gad, I will so supple him!—You shall see, Colonel, and you, my saucy misses, though you may not see, shall hear."

"Ay, that's if we choose to listen, counsellor," replied Julia.

"And you think," said Pleydell, "it's two to one you won't choose that?—But you have curiosity that teaches you the use of your ears now and then."

"I declare, counsellor," answered the lively damsel, "that such saucy bachelors, as you would teach us the use of our fingers now and then."

"Reserve them for the harpsichord, my love," said the counsellor.
"Better for all parties."

While this idle chat ran on, Colonel Mannering introduced to
Bertram a plain good-looking man, in a gray coat and waistcoat,
buckskin breeches, and boots. "This, my dear sir, is Mr.
Mac-Morlan."

"To whom," said Bertram, embracing him cordially, "my sister was indebted for a home, when deserted by all her natural friends and relations."

The Dominie then pressed forward, grinned, chuckled, made a diabolical sound in attempting to whistle, and finally, unable to stifle his emotions, ran away to empty the feelings of his heart at his eyes.

We shall not attempt to describe the expansion of heart and glee of this happy evening.

—How like a hateful ape, Detected grinning 'midst his
pilfer'd hoard, A cunning man appears, whose secret frauds

Are open'd to the day! Count
Basil.

There was a great movement at Woodbourne early on the following morning, to attend the examination at Kippletringan. Mr. Pleydell, from the investigation which he had formerly bestowed on the dark affair of Kennedy's death, as well as from the general deference due to his professional abilities, was requested by Mr. Mac-Morlan and Sir Robert Hazlewood, and another justice of peace who attended, to take the situation of chairman, and the lead in the examination. Colonel Mannering was invited to sit down with them. The examination, being previous to trial, was private in other respects.

The counsellor resumed and re-interrogated former evidence. He then examined the clergyman and surgeon respecting the dying declaration of Meg Merrilies. They stated, that she distinctly, positively, and repeatedly, declared herself an eye-witness of Kennedy's "death by the hands of Hatteraick" and two or three of his crew; that her presence was accidental; that she believed their resentment at meeting him, when they mere in the act of losing their vessel through 'the means of his information, led to the commission of the crime; that she said there was one witness of the murder, but who refused to participate in it, still alive,—her nephew, Gabrie Faa; and she had hinted at another person, who was an accessory after not before, the fact; but her strength there failed her. They did not forget to mention her declaration, that she had saved the child, and that he was torn from her by the smugglers, for the purpose of carrying him to Holland.—All these particulars were carefully reduced to writing.

Dirk Hatteraick was then brought in, heavily ironed; for he had been strictly secured and guarded, owing to his former escape. He was asked his name; he made no answer—His profession; he was silent :—Several other questions were put, to none of which he returned any reply. Pleydell wiped the glasses of his spectacles, and considered the prisoner very attentively. "A very truculent-looking fellow," he whispered to Mannering; "but, as Dogberry says, I'll go cunningly to work with him.—Here, call in Soles—Soles the shoemaker.—Soles, do you remember measuring some footsteps imprinted on the mud at the wood of Warroch, on—November 17—, by my orders?" Soles remembered the circumstance perfectly. "Look at that paper—is that your note of the measurement?"—Soles verified the memorandum— "Now, there stands a pair of shoes on that table; measure them, and see if they correspond with any of the marks you have noted there." The shoemaker obeyed, and declared, "that they answered exactly to the largest of the footprints."

"We shall prove," said the counsellor, aside to Mannering, "that these shoes, which were found in the ruins of Derncleugh, belonged to Brown, the fellow whom you shot on the lawn at Woodbourne.—Now, Soles, measure that prisoner's feet very accurately."

Mannering observed Hatteraick strictly, and could notice a visible tremor. "Do these measurements correspond with any of the foot-prints?"

The man looked at the note, then at his foot-rule and measure—then verified his former measurement by a second. "They correspond," he said, "within a hair-breadth, to a foot-mark broader and shorter than the former."

Hatteraick's genius here deserted him—"Der deyvil!" he broke out, "how could there be a foot-mark on the ground, when it was a frost as hard as the heart of a Memel log?"

"In the evening, I grant you, Captain Hatteraick," said Pleydell, "but not in the forenoon—will you favour me with information where you were upon the day you remember so exactly?"

Hatteraick saw his blunder, and again screwed up his hard features for obstinate silence—"Put down his observation, however," said Pleydell to the clerk.

At this moment the door opened, and, much to the surprise of most present, Mr. Gilbert Glossin made his appearance. That worthy gentleman had, by dint of watching and eavesdropping, ascertained that he was not mentioned by name in Meg Merrilies's dying declaration, a circumstance, certainly not owing to any favourable disposition towards him, but to the delay of taking her regular examination, and to the rapid approach of death. He therefore supposed himself safe from all evidence but such as might arise from Hatteraick's confession; to prevent which he resolved to push a bold face, and join his brethren of the bench during his examination.—"I shall be able," he thought, "to make the rascal sensible his safety lies in keeping his own counsel and mine; and my presence, besides, will be a proof of confidence and innocence. If I must lose the estate, I must—but I trust better things."

He entered with a profound salutation to Sir Robert Hazlewood. Sir Robert, who had rather begun to suspect that his plebeian neighbour had made a cat's-paw of him, inclined his head stiffly, took snuff, and looked another way.

"Mr. Corsand," said Glossin to the other yoke-fellow of justice, "your most humble servant."

"Your humble servant, Mr. Glossin," answered Mr. Corsand dryly, composing his countenance regis ad exemplar, that is to say, after the fashion of the Baronet.

"Mac-Morlan, my worthy friend," continued Glossin, how d'ye do—always on your duty—?"

"Umph," said honest Mac-Morlan, with little respect either to the compliment or salutation. "Colonel Mannering (a low bow slightly returned) and Mr. Pleydell (another low bow), I dared not have hoped for your assistance to poor country gentlemen at this period of the session."

Pleydell took snuff, and eyed him with a glance equally shrewd and sarcastic—"I'll teach him," he said aside to Mannering, "the value of the old admonition, No accesseris in consilium antequam voceris."

"But perhaps I intrude, gentlemen?" said Glossin, who could not fail to observe the coldness of his reception.—"Is this an open meeting?"

"For my part," said Mr. Pleydell, "so far from considering your attendance as an intrusion, Mr. Glossin, I was never so pleased in my life to meet with you; especially as I think we should, at any rate, have had occasion to request the favour of your company in the course of the day."

"Well, then, gentlemen," said Glossin, drawing his chair to the table, and beginning to bustle about among the papers, "where are we?—how far have we got? where are the declarations?"

"Clerk, give me all these papers," said Mr. Pleydell;—"I have an odd way of arranging my documents, Mr. Glossin, another person touching them puts me out-but I shall have occasion for your assistance by and by."

Glossin, thus reduced to inactivity, stole one glance at Dirk Hatteraick, but could read nothing in his dark scowl save malignity and hatred to all around. "But, gentlemen," said Glossin, "is it right to keep his poor man so heavily ironed, when he is taken up merely for examination?"

This was hoisting a kind of friendly signal to the prisoner. "He has escaped once before," said Mac-Morlan dryly, and Glossin was silenced.

Bertram was now introduced, and, to Glossin's confusion, was greeted in the most friendly manner by all present, even by Sir Robert Hazlewood himself. He told his recollections of, his infancy with that candour and caution of expression which afforded the best warrant for his good faith. "This seems to be rather a civil, than a criminal question", said Glossin rising; "and as you cannot be ignorant, gentlemen, of the effect which this young person's pretended parentage may have on my patrimonial interest, I would rather beg leave to retire."

"No, my good sir," said Mr. Pleydell. "we can by no means spare you. But why do you call this young man's claims pretended?—I don't mean to fish for your defences against them, if you have any, but—"

"Mr. Pleydell," replied Glossin, "I am always disposed to act aboveboard, and I think I can explain the matter at once.—This young fellow, whom I take to be a natural son of the late Ellangowan, has gone about the country for some weeks under different names, caballing with a wretched old madwoman, who, I understand, was shot in a late scuffle, and with other tinkers, gipsies, and persons of that description, and a great brute farmer from Liddesdale, stirring up the tenants against their landlords, which, as Sir Robert Hazlewood of Hazlewood knows—"

"Not to interrupt you, Mr. Glossin," said Pleydell, "I ask who you say this young man is?"

"Why, I say," replied Glossin, "and I believe that gentleman (looking at Hatteraick) knows, that the young man is the natural son of the late Ellangowan, by a girl called Janet Lightoheel, who was afterwards married to Hewit the shipwright, that lived in the neighbourhood of Annan. His name is Godfrey Bertram Hewit, by which name he was entered on board the Royal Caroline excise yacht."

"Ay said Pleydell, that is a very likely story—but, not to pause upon some difference of eyes, complexion, and so forth—be pleased to step forward, sir."—A young seafaring man came forward.—"Here," proceeded the counsellor, "is the real Simon Pure—here's Godfrey Bertram Hewit, arrived last night from Antigua via Liverpool, mate of a West Indian, and in a fair way of doing well in the world, although he came somewhat irregularly into it."

While some conversation passed between the other justices and this young man, Pleydell lifted from among the papers on the table Hatteraick's old pocket-book. A peculiar glance of the smuggler's eye induced the shrewd lawyer to think there was something here of interest. He therefore continued the examination of the papers, laying the book on the table, but instantly perceived that the prisoner's interest in the research had cooled.—"It must be in the book still, whatever it is," thought Pleydell; and again applied himself to the packet-book, until he discovered, on a narrow scrutiny, a slit between the pasteboard and leather, out of which he drew three small slips of paper. Pleydell now, turning to Glossin, requested the favour that he would tell them if he had assisted at the search for the body of Kennedy, and the child of his patron, on the day when they disappeared.

"I did not—that is—I did," answered the conscience-struck
Glossin.

"It is remarkable though," said the advocate, that, connected as you were with the Ellangowan family, I don't recollect your being examined, or even appearing before me, while that investigation was proceeding?"

"I was called to London," answered Glossin, "on most important business, the morning after that sad affair."

"Clerk," said Pleydell, "minute down that reply.—I presume the business, Mr. Glossin, was to negotiate these three bills, drawn by you on Messrs. Vanbeest and Vanbruggen, and accepted by one Dirk Hatteraick in their name on the very day of the murder. I congratulate you on their being regularly retired, as I perceive they have been. I think the chances were against it." Glossin's countenance fell. "This piece of real evidence," continued Mr. Pleydell, "makes good the account given of your conduct on this occasion by a man called Gabriel Faa, whom we have now in custody, and who witnessed the whole transaction between you and that worthy prisoner—Have you any explanation to give?"

"Mr. Pleydell," said Glossin, with great composure, presume, if you were my counsel, you would not advise me to answer upon the spur of the moment to a charge which the basest of mankind seem ready to establish by perjury."

"My advice," said the counsellor, "would be regulated by my opinion of your innocence or guilt. In your case, I believe you take the wisest course; but you are aware you must stand committed?"

"Committed? for what, sir replied Glossin. "Upon a charge of murder?"

"No; only as art and part of kidnapping the child."

"That is a bailable offence."

"Pardon me," said Pleydell, "it is plagium, and plagium is felony."

"Forgive me, Mr. Pleydell; there is only one case upon record, Torrence and Waldie. They were, you remember, resurrection-women, who had promised to procure a child's body for some young surgeons. Being upon honour to their employers, rather than disappoint the evening lecture of the students, they stole a live child, murdered it, and sold the body for three shillings and sixpence. They were hanged, but for the murder, not for the plagium. [*This is, in its circumstances and issue, actually a case tried and reported] Your civil law has carried you a little too far."

"Well, sir; but, in the meantime, Mr. Mac-Morlan must commit you to the county jail, in case this young man repeats the same story.—Officers, remove Mr. Glossin and Hatteraick, and guard them in different apartments."

Gabriel, the gipsy, was then introduced, and gave a distinct account of his deserting from Captain Pritchard's vessel and joining the smugglers in the action, detailed how Dirk Hatteraick set fire to his ship when he found her disabled, and under cover of the smoke escaped with his crew, and as much goods as they could save, into the cavern, where they proposed to lie till nightfall. Hatteraick himself, his mate Vanbeest Brown, and three others, of whom the declarant was 'one, went into the adjacent woods to communicate with some of their friends in the neighbourhood. They fell in with Kennedy unexpectedly, and Hatteraick and Brown, aware that he was the occasion of their disasters, resolved to murder him. He stated, that he had seen them lay violent hands on the officer, and drag him through the woods, but had not partaken in the assault, nor witnessed its termination. That he returned to the cavern, by a different route, where he again met Hatteraick and his accomplices; and the captain was in the act of giving an account how he and Brown had pushed a huge crag over, as Kennedy lay groaning on the beach, when Glossin suddenly appeared among them. To the whole transaction by which Hatteraick purchased his secrecy he was witness. Respecting young Bertram. he could give a distinct account till he went to India, after which he had lost sight of him until he unexpectedly met with him in Liddesdale. Gabriel Faa further stated, that he instantly sent notice to his aunt, Meg Merrilies, as well as to Hatteraick, who he knew was then upon the coast; but that he had incurred his aunt's displeasure upon the latter account. He concluded, that his aunt had immediately declared that she would do all that lay in her power to help young Ellangowan to his right, even if it should be by informing against Dirk Hatteraick; and that many of her people assisted her besides himself, from a belief that she was gifted with supernatural inspirations. With the same purpose, he understood, his aunt had given to Bertram the treasure of the tribe, of which she had the custody. Three or four gipsies, by the express command of Meg Merrilies, mingled in the crowd when the Custom-house was attacked, for the purpose of liberating Bertram, which he had himself effected. He said, that in obeying Meg's dictates they did not pretend to estimate their propriety or rationality, the respect in which she was held by her tribe precluding all such subjects of speculation. Upon further interrogation, the witness added, that his aunt had always said that Harry Bertram carried that round his neck which would ascertain his birth. It was a spell, she said that an Oxford scholar had made for him, and she possessed the smugglers with an opinion, that to deprive him of it would occasion the loss of the vessel.

Bertram here produced a small velvet bag, which he said he had worn round his neck from his earliest infancy, and which he had preserved, first from superstitious reverence, and, latterly, from the hope that it might serve one day to aid in the discovery of his birth. The bag, being opened, was found to contain a blue silk case, front which was drawn a scheme of nativity. Upon inspecting this paper, Colonel Mannering instantly admitted it was his own composition; and afforded the strongest and most satisfactory evidence, that the possessor of it must necessarily be the young heir of Ellangowan, by avowing his having first appeared in that country in the character of an astrologer.

"And now," said Pleydell, "make out warrants of commitment for Hatteraick and Glossin until liberated in due course of law. Yet," he said, "I am sorry for Glossin."

"Now, I think," said Mannering, "he's incomparably the least deserving of pity of the two. The other's a bold fellow, though as hard as flint."

"Very natural, Colonel," said the advocate, "that you should be interested in the ruffian, and I in the knave—that's all professional taste—but I can tell you Glossin would have been a pretty lawyer, had he not had such a turn for the roguish part of the profession."

"Scandal would say," observed Mannering, "he might not be the worse lawyer for that."

"Scandal would tell a lie, then," replied Pleydell, "'as she usually does. Law's like laudanum; it's much more easy to use it as a quack does, than to learn to apply it like a physician."

CHAPTER LVII.

Unfit to live or die—O marble heart!
After him, fellows, drag him to the block.

Measure for Measure

The jail at the county town of the shire of—was one of those old-fashioned dungeons which disgraced Scotland until of late years. When the prisoners and their guard arrived there, Hatteraick, whose violence and strength were well known, was secured in what was called the condemned ward. This was a large apartment near the top of the prison. A round bar of iron, about the thickness of a man's arm above the elbow, crossed the apartment horizontally at the height of about six inches from the floor; and its extremities were strongly built into the wall at either end. Hatteraick's ankles were secured within shackles, which were connected by a chain at the distance of about four feet, with a large iron ring, which travelled upon the bar we have described. Thus a prisoner might shuffle along the length of the bar from one side of the room to another, but could not retreat farther from it in any other direction than the brief length of the chain admitted. [*This mode of securing prisoners was universally practised in Scotland after condemnation. When a man received sentence of death, he was put upon the Gad, as it was called, that is, secured to the bar of iron in the manner mentioned in the text. The practice subsisted in Edinburgh till the old jail was taken down some years since, and perhaps may be still in use.] When his feet had been thus secured, the keeper removed his handcuffs, and left his person at liberty in other respects. A pallet-bed was placed close to the bar of iron, so that the shackled prisoner might lie down at pleasure, still fastened to the iron bar in the manner described.

Hatteraick had not been long in this place of confinement before Glossin arrived at the same prison-house. In respect to his comparative rank and education, he was not ironed, but placed in a decent apartment, under the inspection of MacGuffog, who, since the destruction of the Bridewell of Portanferry by the mob, had acted here as an under-turnkey. When Glossin was enclosed within this room, and had solitude and leisure to calculate all the chances against him and in his favour, he could not prevail upon himself to consider the game as desperate.

"The estate is lost," he said, "that must go; and, between Pleydell and Mac-Morlan, they'll cut down my claim on it to a trifle. My character—but if I get off with life and liberty, I'll win money yet, and varnish that over again. I knew not the gauger's job until the rascal had done the deed, and though I had some advantage by the contraband, that is no felony. But the kidnapping of the boy-there they touch me closer. Let me see.—This Bertram was a child at the time-his evidence must be imperfect—the other fellow is a deserter, a gipsy, and an outlaw—Meg Merrilies, d-n her, is dead. These infernal bills! Hatteraick brought them with him, I suppose, to have the means of threatening me, or extorting money from me. I must endeavour to see the rascal;—must get him to stand steady; must persuade him to put some other colour upon the business."

His mind teeming with schemes of future deceit to cover former villainy, he spent the time in arranging and combining them until the hour of supper. Mac-Guffog attended as turnkey on this occasion. He. was, as we know, the old and special acquaintance of the prisoner who was now under his charge. After giving the turnkey a glass of brandy, and sounding him with one or two cajoling speeches, Glossin made it his request that he would help him, to an interview with Dirk Hatteraick. "Impossible! utterly impossible! it's contrary to the express orders of Mr. Mac-Morlan, and the captain" (as the head jailor of a county jail is called in Scotland)" would never forgie me."

"But why should he know of it?" said Glossin, slipping a couple of guineas into Mac-Guffog's hand.

The turnkey weighed the gold, and looked sharp at Glossin. "Ay, ay, Mr. Glossin, ye ken the ways o' this place.—Lookee, at lock-up hour, I'll return and bring ye upstairs to him—But ye must stay a' night in his cell, for I am under necessity to carry the keys to the captain for the night, and I cannot let you out again until morning—then I'll visit the wards half an hour earlier than usual, and ye may get out, and be snug in your ain berth when the captain gangs his rounds."

When the hour of ten had pealed from the neighbouring steeple, Mac-Guffog came prepared with a small dark lantern. He said softly to Glossin, "Slip your shoes off, and follow me." When Glossin was out of the door, Mac-Guffog, as if in the execution of his ordinary duty, and speaking to a prisoner within, called aloud, "Good-night to you, sir," and locked the door, clattering the bolts with much ostentatious noise. He then guided Glossin up a steep and narrow stair, at the top of which was the door of the condemned ward; he unbarred and unlocked it, and, giving Glossin the lantern, made a sign to him to enter, and locked the door behind him with the same affected accuracy.

In the large dark cell into which he was thus introduced, Glossin's feeble light for some time enabled him to discover nothing. At length he could dimly distinguish the pallet-bed stretched on the floor beside the great iron bar which traversed the room, and on that pallet reposed the figure of a man. Glossin approached him. "Dirk Hatteraick!"

"Donner and hagel! it is his voice," said the prisoner, sitting up, and clashing his fetters as he rose; "then my dream is true!—Begone, and leave me to myself—it will be your best."

"What! my good friend," said Glossin, "will you allow the prospect of a few weeks' confinement to depress your spirit?"

"Yes," answered the ruffian sullenly—"when I am only to be released by a halter!—Let me alone—go about your business, and turn the lamp from my face!"

"Psha! my dear Dirk, don't be afraid," said Glossin—"I have a glorious plan to make all right."

"To the bottomless pit with your plans!" replied his accomplice. "You have planned me out of ship, cargo, and life; and I dreamt this moment that Meg Merrilies dragged you here by the hair, and gave me the long clasped knife she used to wear—you don't know what she said. Sturm wetter! it will be your wisdom not to tempt me!"

"But, Hatteraick, my good friend, do but rise and speak to me," said Glossin.

"I will not!" answered the savage doggedly—"you have caused all the mischief; you would not let Meg keep the boy; she would have returned him after he had forgot all."

"Why, Hatteraick, you are turned driveller!"

"Wetter! will you deny that all that cursed attempt at Portanferry, which lost both sloop and crew, was your device for your own job?"

"But the goods, you know—"

"Curse the goods!" said the smuggler,—"we could have got plenty more; but, der deyvil! to lose the ship and the fine follows, and my own life, for a cursed coward villain, that always works his own mischief with other people's hands! Speak to me no more—I'm dangerous."

"But, Dirk—but, Hatteraick, hear me only a few words."

"Hagel! nein."

"Only one sentence."

"Tausand curses—nein!"

"At least get up for an obstinate Dutch brute!" said Glossin, losing his temper, and pushing Hatteraick with his foot.

"Donner and blitzen!" said Hatteraick, springing up and grappling with him; "you will have it then?"

Glossin struggled and resisted; but, owing to his surprise at the fury of the assault, so ineffectually, that he fell: under Hatteraick, the back part of his neck coming full upon the iron bar with stunning violence. The death-grapple continued. The room immediately below the condemned ward, being that of Glossin, was, of course, empty; but the inmates of the second apartment beneath felt the shock of Glossin's heavy fall, and heard a noise as of struggling and of groans. But all sounds of horror were too congenial to this place to excite much curiosity or interest.

In the morning, faithful to his promise, Mac-Guffog came—"Mr. Glossin," said be, in, a whispering voice.

"Call louder," answered Dirk Hatteraick.

"Mr. Glossin, for God's sake come away!"

"He'll hardly do that without help," said Hatteraick.

"What are you chattering there for, Mac-Guffog?" called out the captain from below.

"Come away, for God's sake. Mr. Glossin!" repeated the. turnkey.

At this moment the jailor made his appearance with a light. Great was his surprise, and even horror, to observe Glossin's body lying doubled across the iron bar, in a posture that excluded all idea of his being alive. Hatteraick was quietly stretched upon his pallet within a yard of his victim. On lifting Glossin, it was found he had been dead for some hours. His body bore uncommon marks of violence. The spine where it joins the skull had received severe injury by his first fall. There were distinct marks of strangulation about the throat, which corresponded with the blackened state of his face. The head was turned backward over the shoulder, as if the neck had been wrung round with desperate violence. So that it would seem that his inveterate antagonist had fixed a fatal gripe upon the wretch's throat, and never quitted it while life lasted. The lantern, crushed and broken to pieces, lay beneath the body.

Mac-Morlan was in the town, and came instantly to examine the corpse. "What brought Glossin here?" he said to Hatteraick.

"The devil!" answered the ruffian.

"And what did you do to him?"

"Sent him to hell before me!" replied the miscreant.

"Wretch," said Mac-Morlan, "you have crowned a life spent without a single virtue, with the murder of your own miserable accomplice!"

"Virtue?" exclaimed the prisoner; "donner! I was always faithful to my shipowners—always accounted for cargo to the last stiver. Hark ye! let me have pen and ink, and I'll write an account of the whole to our house; and leave me alone a couple of hours, will ye—and let them take away that piece of carrion, donner wetter!"

Mac-Morlan deemed it the best way to humour the savage; he was furnished with writing materials and left alone. When they again opened the door, it was found that this determined villain had anticipated justice. He had adjusted a cord taken from the truckle-bed, and attached it to a bone, the relic of his yesterday's dinner, which he had contrived to drive into a crevice between two stones in the wall at a height as great as he could reach, standing upon the bar. Having fastened the noose, he had the resolution to drop his body as if to fall on his knees, and to retain that posture until resolution was no longer necessary. The letter he had written to his owners, though chiefly upon the business of their trade, contained many allusions to the younker of Ellangowan, as he called him, and afforded absolute confirmation of all Meg Merrilies and her nephew had told.

To dismiss the catastrophe of these two wretched men, I shall only add, that Mac-Guffog was turned out of office, notwithstanding his declaration (which he offered to attest by oath), that he had locked Glossin safely in his own room upon the night preceding his being found dead in Dirk Hatteraick's cell. His story, however, found faith with the worthy Mr. Skreigh, and other lovers of, the marvellous, who still hold that the Enemy of Mankind brought these two wretches together upon that night, by supernatural interference, that they might fill up the cup of their guilt and receive its meed, by murder and suicide.

CHAPTER LVIII.

To sum the whole-the close of all.

DEAN SWIFT.

As Glossin died without heirs, and without payment of the price, the estate of Ellangowan was again thrown upon the hands of Mr. Godfrey Bertram's creditors, the right of most of whom was however defensible, in case Henry Bertram should establish his character of heir of entail. This young gentleman put his affairs into the hands of Mr. Pleydell and Mr. Mac-Morlan, with one single proviso, that though he himself should be obliged again to go to India, every debt, justly and honourably due by his father, should be made good to the claimant. Mannering, who heard this declaration, grasped him kindly by the hand, and from that moment might be dated a thorough understanding between them.

The hoards of Miss Margaret Bertram, and the liberal assistance of the Colonel, easily enabled the heir to make provision for payment of the just creditors of his father, while the ingenuity and research of his law friends detected, especially in the accounts of Glossin, so many overcharges as greatly diminished the total amount. In these circumstances the creditors did not hesitate to recognise Bertram's right, and to surrender to him the house and property of his ancestors. All the party repaired from Woodbourne to take possession, amid the shouts of the tenantry and the neighbourhood; and so eager was Colonel Mannering to superintend certain improvements which he had recommended to Bertram, that he removed with his family from Woodbourne to Ellangowan, although at present containing much less and much inferior accommodation.

The poor Dominie's brain was almost turned with joy on returning to his old habitation. He posted upstairs, taking three steps at once, to a little shabby attic, his cell and dormitory in former days, and which the possession of his much superior apartment at Woodbourne had never banished from his memory. Here one sad thought suddenly struck the honest man—the books!—no three rooms in Ellangowan were capable to contain them. While this qualifying reflection was passing through his mind, he was suddenly summoned by Mannering to assist in calculating some proportions relating to a large and splendid house, which was to be built on the site of the New Place of Ellangowan, in a style corresponding to the magnificence of the ruins in its vicinity. Among the various rooms in the plan, the Dominie observed, that one of the largest . vas entitled THE LIBRARY; and close beside was a snug well-proportioned chamber, entitled, MR. SAMPSON'S APARTMENT.—"Prodigious, prodigious, pro-di-gi-ous!" shouted the enraptured Dominie.

Mr. Pleydell had left the party for some time; but he returned, according to promise, during the Christmas recess of the courts. He drove up to Ellangowan when all the family were abroad but the Colonel, who was busy with plans of buildings and pleasure-grounds, in which he was well skilled, and took great delight.

"Ah ha!" said the counsellor, "so here you are! Where are the ladies? where is the fair Julia?"

"Walking out with young Haziewood, Bertram, and Captain Delaserre, a friend of his, who is with us just now. They are gone to plan out a cottage at Derncleugh. Well, have you carried through your law business?"

"With a wet finger," answered the lawyer; "got our youngster's special service retoured into Chancery. We had him served heir before the macers."

"Macers? who are they?"

"Why, it is a kind of judicial Saturnalia. You must know, that one of the requisites to be a macer, or officer in attendance upon our supreme court, is, that they shall be men of no knowledge."

"Very well!"

"Now, our Scottish legislature, for the joke's sake I suppose, have constituted those men of no knowledge into a peculiar court for trying questions of relationship and descent, such as this business of Bertram, which often involve the most nice and complicated questions of evidence."

"The devil they have? I should think that rather inconvenient," said Mannering.

"Oh, we have a practical remedy for the theoretical absurdity. One or two of the judges act upon such occasions as prompters and assessors to their own doorkeepers. But you know what Cujacius says, 'Multa sunt in moribus dissentanea, multa sine ratione.' [*The singular inconsistency hinted at is now, in a great degree, removed] However, this Saturnalian court has done our business; and a glorious batch of claret we had afterwards at Walker's. Mac-Morlan will stare when he sees the bill."

"Never fear," said the Colonel, "we'll face the shock, and entertain the county at my friend Mrs. Mac-Candlish's to boot."

"And choose Jock Jabos for your master of horse?" replied the lawyer.

"Perhaps I may."

"And where is Dandie, the redoubted Lord of Liddesdale?" demanded the advocate.

"Returned to his mountains; but he has promised Julia to make a descent in summer, with the good wife, as he calls her, and I don't know how many children."

"Oh, the curly-headed varlets! I must come to play at Blind Harry and Hy Spy with them.—But what is all this?" added Pleydell, taking up the plans;—"tower in the centre to be an imitation of the Eagle Tower at Caernarvon—corps de logis—the devil!—wings—wings? why, the house will take the estate of Ellangowan on its back, and fly away with it!"

"Why then, we must ballast it with a few bags of Sicca rupees," replied the Colonel.

"Aha! sits the wind there? Then I suppose the young dog carries off my mistress Julia?"

"Even so, counsellor."

"These rascals, the post-nati, get the better of us of the old school at every turn," said Mr. Pleydell. "But she must convey and make over her interest in me to Lucy."

"To tell you the truth, I am afraid your flank will be turned there too," replied the Colonel.

"Indeed?"

"Here has been Sir Robert Hazlewood," said Mannering, "upon a visit to Bertram, thinking, and deeming, and opining—"

"O Lord I pray spare me the worthy Baronet's triads!"

"Well, sir," continued Mannering to make short, he conceived that as the property of Singleside lay like a wedge between two farms of his, and was four or five miles separated from Ellangowan, something like a sale, or exchange, or arrangement might take place. to the mutual convenience of both parties."

"Well, and Bertram—"

"Why, Bertram replied, that he considered the original settlement of Mrs. Margaret Bertram as the arrangement most proper in the circumstances of the family, and that therefore the estate of Singleside was the property of his sister."

"The rascal!" said Pleydell, wiping his spectacles, "he'll steal my heart as well as my mistress—Et puis?"

"And then, Sir Robert retired after many gracious speeches; but last week he again took the field in force, with his coach and six horses, his laced scarlet waistcoat, and best bob-wig—all very grand, as the good-boy books say."

"Ay! and what was his overture?" Why, he talked with great form of an attachment on the part of Charles Hazlewood to Miss Bertram."

"Ay, ay; he respected the little god Cupid when he saw him perched on the Dun of Singleside. And is poor Lucy to keep house with that old fool and his wife, who is just the knight himself in petticoats?"

"No—we parried that. Singleside House is to be repaired for the young people, and to be called hereafter Mount Hazlewood."

"And do you yourself, Colonel, propose to continue at Woodbourne?"

"Only till we carry these plans into effect. See, here's the plan of my Bungalow, with all convenience for being separate and sulky when I please."

"And, being situated, as I see, next door to the old castle, you may repair Donagild's tower for the nocturnal contemplation of the celestial bodies? Bravo, Colonel!"

"No, no, my dear counsellor! here ends THE ASTROLOGER."

NOTES

Note, 1.—MUMPS'S HA'.

IT is fitting to explain to the reader the locality described in this chapter. There is, or rather I should say there was, a little inn, called Mumps's Hall, that is, being interpreted, Beggar's Hotel, near to Gilsland, which had not then attained its present fame as a Spa. It was a hedge alehouse, where the Bolder farmers of either country often stopped to refresh themselves and their nags, in their way to and from the fairs and trysts in Cumberland, and especially those who came from or went to Scotland, through a barren and lonely district, without either road or pathway, emphatically called the Waste of Bewcastle. At the period when the adventures described in the novel are supposed to have taken place, there were many instances of attacks by freebooters on those who travelled through this wild, district, and Mumps's Ha' had a bad reputation for harbouring the banditti who committed such depredations.

An old and sturdy yeoman belonging to the Scottish side, by surname an Armstrong or Elliot, but known by his soubriquet of Fighting Charlie of Liddesdale, and still remembered for the courage he displayed in the frequent frays which took place on the Border fifty or sixty years since, had the following adventure in the Waste, which suggested the idea of the scene in the text .

Charlie had been at Stagshaw-bank fair, had sold his sheep or cattle, or whatever he had brought to market, and was on his return to Liddesdale. There were then no country banks where cash could be deposited, and bills received instead, which greatly encouraged robbery in that wild country, as the objects of plunder were usually fraught with gold. The robbers had spies in the fair, by means of whom they generally knew whose purse was best stocked, and who took a lonely and desolate road homeward,—those, in short, who were best worth robbing, and likely to be most easily robbed.

All this Charlie knew full well; but he had a pair of excellent pistols, and a dauntless heart. He stopped at Mumps's Ha', notwithstanding the evil character of the place. His horse was accommodated where it might have the necessary rest and feed of corn; and Charlie himself, a dashing fellow, grew gracious with the landlady, a buxom quean, who used all the influence in her power to induce him to stop all night. The landlord was from home, she said, and it was ill passing the Waste, as twilight must needs descend on him before he gained the Scottish side, which was reckoned the safest. But Fighting Charlie, though he suffered himself to be detained later than was prudent, did not account Mumps's Ha' a safe place to quarter in during the night. He tore himself away, therefore, from Meg's good fare and kind words, and mounted his nag, having first examined his pistols, and tried by the ramrod whether the charge remained in them.

He proceeded a mile or two, at a round trot, When, as the Waste stretched black before him apprehensions began to awaken in his mind, partly arising out of Meg's unusual kindness, which he could not help thinking had rather a suspicious appearance. He, therefore, resolved to reload his pistols, lest the powder had become damp; but what was his surprise, when he drew the charge, to find neither powder nor ball, while each barrel had been carefully filled with bore, up to the space which the loading had occupied! and, the priming of the weapons being left untouched, nothing but actually drawing and examining the charge could have discovered the inefficiency of his arms till the fatal minute arrived when their services were required. Charlie bestowed a hearty Liddesdale curse on his landlady, and reloaded—his pistols with care and accuracy, having now no doubt that he was to be waylaid and assaulted. He was not far engaged in the Waste, which was then, and is now, traversed only by such routes as are described in the text, when two or three fellows, disguised and variously armed, started from a moss-hag, while, by a glance behind him for, marching, as the Spaniard says, with his beard on his shoulder, he reconnoitred in every direction, Charlie instantly saw retreat was impossible, as other two stout men appeared behind him at some distance. The Borderer lost not a moment in taking his resolution, and boldly trotted against his enemies in front, who called loudly on him to stand and deliver; Charlie spurred on, and presented his pistol. "D-n your pistol," cried the foremost robber; whom Charlie to his dying day protested he believed to have been the landlord of Mumps's Ha'. "D-n your pistol—care not a curse for it."—"Ay, lad," said the deep voice of Fighting Charlie, "but the tow's out now." He had no occasion to utter another word; the rogues, surprised at finding a man of redoubted courage well armed, instead of being defenceless, took to the moss in every direction, and he passed on his way without further molestation.

The author has heard this story told by persons who received it from Fighting Charlie himself; he has also heard that Mumps's Ha' was afterwards the scene of some other atrocious villainy, for which the people of the house suffered. But these are all tales of at least half a century old, and the Waste has been for many years as safe as any place in the kingdom.

Note II.—DANDIE DINMONT.

The author may here remark, that the character of Dandie Dinmont was drawn from no individual. A dozen, at least, of stout Liddesdale yeomen with whom he has been acquainted, and whose hospitality he has shared in his rambles through that wild country, at a time when it was totally inaccessible save in the manner described in the text, might lay claim to be the prototype of the rough, but faithful. hospitable, and generous farmer. But one circumstance occasioned the name to be fixed upon a most respectable individual of this class, now no more. Mr. James Davidson of Hindlee, a tenant of Lord Douglas, besides the points of blunt honesty, personal strength, and hardihood, designed to he expressed in the character of Dandie Dinmont, had the humour of naming a celebrated race of terriers which he, possessed, by the generic names of Mustard and Pepper (according as their colour was yellow, or grayish-black), without any other individual distinction, except as according to the nomenclature in the text. Mr. Davidson resided at Hindlee, a wild farm, on the very edge of the Teviotdale mountains, and bordering close an Liddesdale, where the rivers and brooks divide as they take their course to the Eastern and Western seas. His passion for the chase, in all its forms, but especially for fox-hunting, as followed in the fashion described in the next chapter, in conducting which he was skilful beyond most men in the South Highlands, was the distinguishing point in his character.

When the tale on which these comments are written became rather popular, the name of Dandie Dinmont was generally given to him, which Mr. Davidson received with great good humour, only saying, while he distinguished the author by the name applied to him in the country, where his own is so common—"that the Sheriff had not written about him mair than about other folk, but only about his dogs." An English lady of high rank and fashion being desirous to possess a brace of the celebrated Mustard and Pepper terriers, expressed her wishes in a letter, which was literally addressed to Dandie Dinmont, under which very general direction it reached Mr. Davidson, who was justly proud of the application, and failed not to comply with a request which did him and his favourite attend ants so much honour.

"I trust I shall not he considered as offending the memory of a kind and worthy man, if I mention a little trait of character which occurred in Mr. Davidson's last illness. I use the words of the excellent clergyman who attended him, who gave the account to a reverend gentleman of the same persuasion :—

"I read to Mr. Davidson the very suitable and interesting truths you addressed to him. He listened to them with great seriousness, and has uniformly displayed a deep concern about his soul's salvation. He died on the first Sabbath of the year (1820); an apoplectic stroke deprived him in an instant of all sensation, but happily his brother was at his bed-side, for he had detained him from the meeting-house that day to be near him, although he felt himself not much worse than usual.—So you have got the last little Mustard that the hand of Dandie Dinmont bestowed.

"His ruling passion was strong even on the eve of death. Mr. Baillie's fox-bounds had started a fox opposite to his window a few weeks ago, and as soon as he heard the sound of the dogs, his eyes glistened; he insisted on getting out of bed, and with much difficulty got to the window, and there enjoyed the fun, as he called it. When I came down to ask for him, he said, 'he had seen Reynard, but had not seen his death. If it had been the will of Providence,' he added, 'I would have liked to have been after him; but I am glad that I got to the window, and am thankful for what I saw, for it has done me a great deal of good.' Notwithstanding these eccentricities (adds the sensible and liberal clergyman), I sincerely hope and believe he has gone to a better world, and better company and enjoyments."

If some part of this little narrative may excite a smile, it is one which is consistent with the most perfect respect for the simple-minded invalid, and his kind and judicious religious instructor, who, we hope, will not he displeased with our giving we trust, a correct edition of an anecdote which has been pretty generally circulated. The race of Pepper and Mustard are in the highest estimation at this day, not only for vermin-killing, but for intelligence and fidelity. Those who, like the author, possess a brace of them, consider them as very desirable companions.

Note III.—Lum Cleeks.

The cleek here intimated is the iron book, or hooks, depending from the chimney of a Scottish cottage, on which the pot is suspended when boiling. The same appendage is often called the crook. The salmon is usually dried by hanging it up, after being split and rubbed with salt, in the smoke of the turf fire above the cleeks, where it is said to reist, that preparation being so termed. The salmon thus preserved is eaten as a delicacy, under the name of kipper, a luxury to which Dr. Redgill has given his sanction as an ingredient of the Scottish breakfast.—See the excellent novel entitled Marriage.

Note IV.—CLAN SURNAMES.

The distinction of individuals by nicknames when they possess no property, is still common on the Border, and indeed necessary, from the number of persons having the same name. In the small village of Lustruther, in Roxburghshire, there dwelt, in the memory of man, four inhabitants, called Andrew, or Dandie Oliver. They were distinguished as Dandie Eassil-gate, Dandie Wassil-gate, Dandie Thumbie, and Dandie Dumbie. The two first had their names from living eastward and westward in the street of the village; the third for something peculiar in the conformation of his thumb; the fourth from his taciturn habits.

It is told as a well-known jest, that a beggar woman, repulsed from door to door as she solicited quarters through a village of Annandale, asked, in her despair, if there were no Christians in the place. To which the hearers, concluding that she inquired for some persons so surnamed, answered, "Na, na, there are nae Christians here; we are a' Johnston and Jardines."

Note V.—GIPSY SUPERSTITIONS.

The mysterious rites in which Meg Merrilies is described as engaging, belong to her character as a queen of her race. All know that gipsies in every country claim acquaintance with the gift of fortune-telling; but, as is often the case, they are liable to the superstitions of which they avail themselves in others. The correspondent of Blackwood, quoted in the: Introduction to this tale, gives us some information on the subject of their credulity.

"I have ever understood," he says, speaking of the Yetholm gipsies, "that they are extremely superstitious—carefully noticing the formation of the clouds, the flight of particular birds, and the soughing of the winds, before attempting any enterprise. They have been known for several successive days to turn back with their loaded carts, asses, and children, on meeting with persons whom they considered of unlucky aspect; nor do they ever proceed on their summer peregrinations without some propitious omen of their fortunate return.

"They also burn the clothes of their dead, not so much from any apprehension of infection being communicated by them, as the conviction that the very circumstance of wearing them would shorten the days of their living. They likewise carefully watch the corpse by night and day till the time of interment, and conceive that 'the deil tinkles at the lykewake' of those who felt in their dead-thraw the agonies and terrors of remorse."

These notions are not peculiar to the gipsies; but having been once generally entertained among the Scottish common people, are now only found among those who are the most rude in their habits, and most devoid of instruction. The popular idea, that the protracted struggle between life and death is painfully prolonged by keeping the door of the apartment shut, was received as certain by the superstitious eld of Scotland. But neither was it to be thrown wide open. To leave the door ajar, was the plan adopted by the old crones who understood the mysteries of deathbeds and lykewakes, In that case, there was room for the imprisoned spirit to escape; and yet an obstacle, we have been assured, was offered to the entrance of any frightful form which might otherwise intrude itself. The threshold of a habitation was in some sort a sacred limit, and the subject of much superstition. A bride, even to this day, is always lifted over it, a rule derived apparently from the Romans.

Note VI.—TAPPIT HEN.

The Tappit Hen contained three quarts of claret—

Weel she loed a Hawick gill, And leugh to see a Tappit Hen.

I have seen one of these formidable stoups at Provost Haswell's, at Jedburgh, in the days of yore. It was a pewter measure, the claret being in ancient days served from the tap, and had the figure of a hen upon the lid. In later times, the name was given to a glass bottle of the same dimensions. These are rare apparitions among the degenerate topers of modern days.

Note VII.—CONVIVIAL HABITS OF THE SCOTTISH BAR.

The account given by Mr. Pleydell, of his sitting down in the midst of a revel to draw an appeal case, was taken from a story told me by an aged gentleman, of the elder President Dundas of Arniston (father of the younger President, and of Lord Melville). It had been thought very desirable, while that distinguished lawyer was King's counsel, that his assistance should be obtained in drawing an appeal case, which, as occasion for such writings then rarely occurred, was held to be matter of great nicety. The solicitor employed for the appellant, attended by my informant acting as his clerk, went to the Lord Advocate's chambers in the Fishmarket Close, as I think. It was Saturday at noon, the Court was just dismissed, the Lord Advocate had changed his dress and booted himself, and his servant and horses were at the foot of the close to carry him to Arniston. It was scarcely possible to get him to listen to a word respecting business. The wily agent, however, on pretence of asking one or two questions, which would not detain him half an hour, drew his Lordship, who was no less an eminent bon vivant than a lawyer of unequalled talent, to take a whet at a celebrated tavern, when the learned counsel became gradually 'Involved in a spirited discussion of the law points of the case. At length it occurred to him, that he might as well ride to Arniston in the cool of the evening. The horses were directed to he put in the stable, but not to be unsaddled. Dinner was ordered, the law was laid aside for a time, and the bottle circulated very freely. At nine o'clock at night, after he bad been honouring Bacchus for so many hours, the Lord Advocate ordered his horses to be unsaddled,—paper, pen, and ink were brought—he began to dictate the appeal case—and continued at his task till four o'clock the next morning. By next day's post, the solicitor sent the case to London, a chef-d'oeuvre of its kind; and in which, my informant assured me, it was not necessary on revisal to correct five words. I am not, therefore, conscious of having overstepped accuracy in describing the manner in which Scottish lawyers of the old time occasionally united the worship of Bacchus with that of Themis. My informant was Alexander Keith, Esq., grandfather to my friend, the present Sir Alexander Keith of Ravelstone, and apprentice at the time to the writer who conducted the cause.

Note VIII.—LORD MONBODDO,

The Burnet, whose taste for the evening meal of the ancients is quoted by Mr. Pleydell, was the celebrated metaphysician and excellent man, Lord Monboddo, whose coenae will not be soon forgotten by those who have shared his classic hospitality. As a Scottish judge, he took the designation of his family estate. His philosophy, as is well known, was of a fanciful and somewhat fantastic character; but his learning was deep, and he was possessed of a singular power of eloquence, which reminded the hearer of the os rotundum of the Grove ,or Academe. Enthusiastically partial to classical habits, his entertainments were always given in the evening, when there was a circulation of excellent Bordeaux, in flasks garlanded with roses, which were also strewed on the table after the manner of Horace. The, best society, whether in respect of rank or literary distinction, was always to be found in St. John's Street, Canongate. The conversation of the excellent old man, his high, gentleman-like, chivalrous spirit, the learning and wit with which he defended his fanciful paradoxes, the kind and liberal spirit of his hospitality, must render these noctes coenaeque dear to all who, like the author (though then young), had the honour of sitting at his board.

Note IX.—LAWYERS' SLEEPLESS NIGHTS.

It is probably true, as observed by Counsellor Pleydell, that a lawyer's anxiety about his case, supposing him to have been some time in practice, will seldom disturb his rest or digestion. Clients will, however, sometimes fondly entertain a different opinion. I was told by an excellent judge, now no more, of a country gentleman, who, addressing his leading counsel, my informer, then an advocate in great practice, on the morning of the day on which the case was to be pleaded, said, with singular bonhomie, "Weel, my lord (the counsel was Lord Advocate), "the awful day is come at last. I have nae been able to sleep a wink for thinking of it—nor, I dare say your Lordship either."

ADDITIONAL NOTE
GALWEGIAN LOCALITIES AND PERSONAGES WHICH HAVE BEEN SUPPOSED TO BE ALLUDED TO IN THE NOVEL.

An old English proverb says, that more know Torn Fool than Tom Fool knows; and the influence of the adage seems to extend to works composed under the influence of an idle or foolish planet. Many corresponding circumstances are detected by readers, of which the author did not suspect the existence. He must, however, regard it as a great compliment, that in detailing incidents purely imaginary, he has been so fortunate in approximating reality, as to remind his readers of actual occurrences. It is therefore with pleasure he notices some pieces of local history and tradition, which have been supposed to coincide with the fictitious persons. incidents, and scenery of Guy Mannering.

The prototype of Dirk Hatteraick is considered as having been a Dutch skipper called Yawkins. This man was well known on the coast of Galloway and Dumfriesshire, as sole proprietor and master of a Buckkar, or smuggling lugger, called the Black Prince. Being distinguished by his nautical skill and intrepidity, his vessel was frequently freighted, and his own services employed, by French, Dutch, Manx, and Scottish smuggling companies.

A person well known by the name of Buckkar-tea, from having been a noted smuggler of that article, and also by that of Bogle-Bush, the place of his residence, assured my kind informant, Mr. Train, that he had frequently seen upwards of two hundred Lingtow-men assemble at one time, and go off into the interior of the country, fully laden with contraband goods.

In those halcyon days of the free trade, the fixed price for carrying a box of tea, or bale of tobacco, from the coast of Galloway to Edinburgh, was fifteen shillings, and a man with horses carried four such packages. The trade was entirely destroyed by Mr. Pitt's celebrated commutation law, which, by reducing the duties upon excisable articles, enabled lawful dealer to compete with the smuggler. The statute was called in Galloway and Dumfriesshire, by those who had thriven upon the contraband trade, "the burning and starving act."

Sure of such active assistance on shore, Yawkins demeaned himself so boldly, that his mere name was a terror to the officers of the revenue. He availed himself of the fears which presence inspired on one particular night, when, happening to be ashore with a considerable quantity of goods in his sole custody, a strong party of excisemen came down on him. Far from shunning the attack, Yawkins sprung forward, shouting, "Come on, my lads; Yawkins is before you." The revenue officers were intimidated, and relinquished their prize, though defended only by the courage and address of a single man. On his proper element, Yawkins was equally successful. one occasion, he was landing his cargo at the Manxman's lake, near Kirkcudbright, when two revenue cutters (the Pigmy and the Dwarf) hove in sight at once on different tacks, the coming round by the Isles of Fleet, the other between the point of Rueberry and the Muckle Ron. The dauntless free-trader instantly weighed anchor, and bore down right between the luggers, so close that he tossed his hat on the deck of the one and his wig on that of the other, hoisted a cask to his maintop, to show his occupation, and bore away under an extraordinary pressure of canvas, without receiving injury. To account for these and other hair-breadth escapes, popular superstition alleged that Yawkins insured his celebrated Buckkar by compounding with the devil for one-tenth of his crew every voyage. How they arranged the separation of the stock and tithes, is left to our conjecture. The Buckkar was perhaps called the Black Prince in honour of the formidable insurer.

The Black Prince used to discharge her cargo at Luce, Balcarry, and elsewhere on the coast; but her owner's favourite landing-places were at the entrance to the Dee and the Cree, near the old Castle of Rueberry, about six miles below Kirkcudbriglit. There is a cave of large dimensions in the vicinity of Rueberry, which, from its being frequently used by Yawkins, and his supposed connection with the smugglers on the shore, is now called Dirk Hatteraick's cave. Strangers who visit this place, the scenery of which is highly romantic, are also shown, under the name of the Gauger's Loup, a tremendous precipice, being the same, it is asserted, from which Kennedy was precipitated.

Meg Merrilies is in Galloway considered as having had her origin in the traditions concerning the celebrated Flora Marshal, one of the royal consorts of Willie Marshal, more commonly called the Caird of Barullion, King of the Gipsies of the Western Lowlands. That potentate was himself deserving of notice, from the following peculiarities. He was born in the parish of Kirkmichael, about the year 1671; and as he died at Kirkcudbright, 23rd November, 1792, he must then have been in the one hundred and twentieth year of his age. It cannot he said that this unusually long lease of existence was noted by any peculiar excellence of conduct or habits of life. Willie had been pressed or enlisted in the army seven times; and had deserted as often; besides three times running away from the naval service. He had been seventeen times lawfully married; and besides such a reason ably large share of matrimonial comforts, was, after his hundredth year, the avowed father of four children, by less legitimate affections. He subsisted in his extreme old age by a pension from the present Earl of Selkirk's grandfather. Will Marshal is buried in Kirkcudbright Church, where his monument is still shown, decorated with a scutcheon, suitably blazoned with two tups' horns and two cutty spoons.

In his youth he occasionally took an evening walk on the highway, with the purpose of assisting travellers by relieving them of the weight of their purses. On one occasion, the Caird of Barullion robbed the Laird of Bargally, at a place between Carsphairn and Dalmellington. His purpose was not achieved without a severe struggle, in which the Gipsy lost his bonnet, and was obliged to escape, leaving it on the road. A respectable farmer happened to be the next passenger, and seeing the bonnet, alighted, took it up, and rather imprudently put it on his own head. At this instant, Bargally came up with some assistants, and recognising the bonnet, charged the farmer of Bantoberick with having robbed him, and took him into custody. There being some likeness between the parties, Bargally persisted in his charge, and though the respectability of the farmer's character was proved or admitted, his trial before the Circuit Court came on accordingly. The fatal bonnet lay on the table of the court; Bargally swore that it was the identical article worn by the man who robbed him; and he and others likewise deponed that they had found the accused on the spot where the crime was committed, with the bonnet on his head. The case looked gloomily for the prisoner, and the opinion of the judge seemed unfavourable. But there was a person in the court who knew well both who did, and who did not, commit, the crime. This was the Caird of Barullion, who, thrusting. himself up to the bar, near the place where Bargally was standing, suddenly seized on the bonnet, put it on his head, and looking the Laird full in the face, asked him, with a voice which attracted the attention of the Court and crowded audience—"Look at me, sir, and tell me, by the oath you have sworn—Am not I the man who robbed you between Carsphairn and Dalmellington?" Bargally replied, in great astonishment, "By Heaven I you are the very man."—"You, see what sort of memory this gentleman has," said the volunteer pleader: "he swears to the bonnet, whatever features are under it. If you yourself, my Lord, will put it on your head, he will be willing to swear that your Lordship was the party who robbed him between Carsphairn and Dalmellington." The tenant of Bantoberick was unanimously acquitted, and thus Willie Marshal ingeniously contrived to save an innocent man from danger, without incurring any himself, since Bargally's evidence must have seemed to every one too fluctuating to be relied upon.

While the King of the Gipsies was thus laudably occupied, his royal consort, Flora, contrived, it is said, to steal the hood front the Judge's gown; for which offence, combined with her presumptive guilt as a gipsy, she was banished to New England, whence she never returned.

Now, I cannot grant that the idea of Meg Merrilies was, in the first concoction of the character, derived from Flora Marshal, seeing I have already said she was identified with Jean Gordon, and as I have not the Laird of Bargally's apology for charging the same fact on two several individuals. Yet I am quite content that Meg should he considered as a representative of her sect and class in general—Flora, as well as others.

The other instances in which my Gallovidian readers have obliged me, by assigning to

139

> Airy nothing
> A local habitation and a name,

shall also be sanctioned so far as the Author may be entitled to do so. I think the facetious Joe Miller records a case pretty much in point; where the keeper of a Museum, while showing, as he said, the very sword with which Balaam was about to kill his ass, was interrupted by one of the visitors, who reminded him that Balaam was not possessed of a sword, but only wished for one. "True, sir," replied the ready-witted Cicerone; "but this is the very sword he wished for." The Author, in application of this story, has only to add, that though ignorant of the coincidence between the fictions of the tale and some real circumstances, he is contented to believe he must unconsciously have thought or dreamed of the last, while engaged in the composition of Guy Mannering.

Printed in Great Britain
by Amazon.co.uk, Ltd.,
Marston Gate.

Guy Mannering

by Sir Walter Scott